The Empire's New Clothes

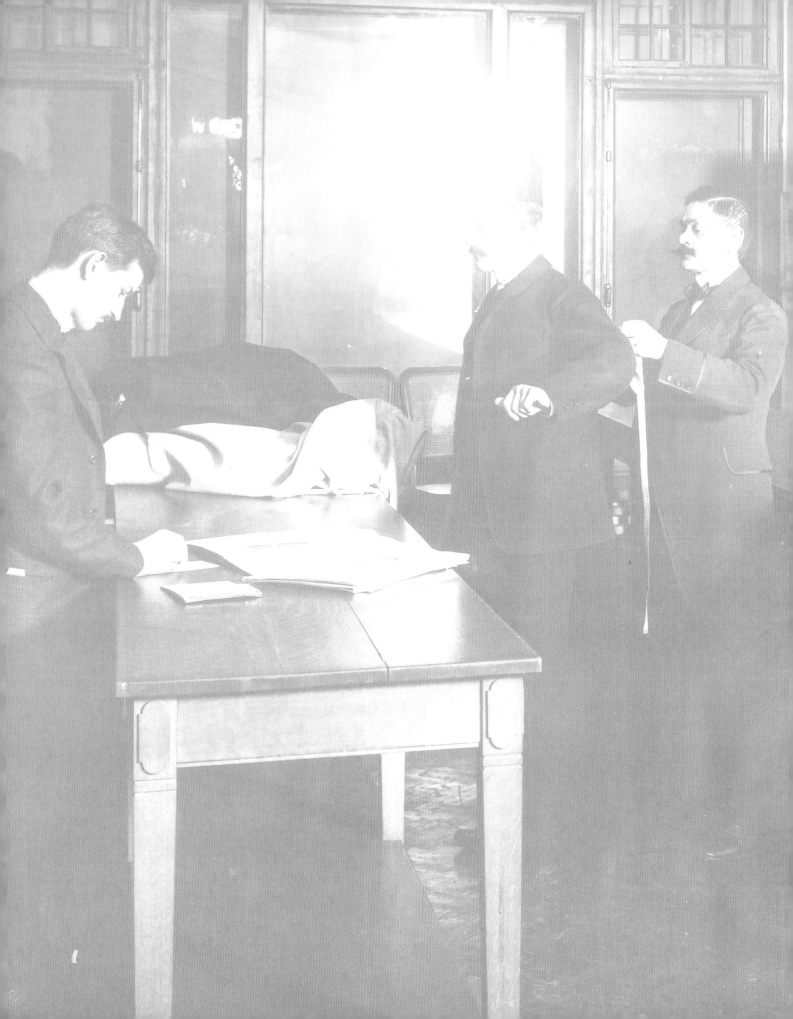

# CHRISTINE RUANE

# The Empire's New Clothes

A HISTORY OF THE RUSSIAN

FASHION INDUSTRY,

1700–1917

YALE UNIVERSITY PRESS

NEW HAVEN & LONDON

Designed by Gillian Malpass

Printed in China

**Library of Congress Cataloging-in-publication Data**
Ruane, Christine.
The empire's new clothes / Christine Ruane.
p. cm.
Includes bibliographical references and index.
ISBN 978-0-300-14155-9 (cl : alk. paper)
1. Clothing and dress—Russia—History. 2. Clothing trade—Russia—History.
3. Russia—History—1613–1917. I. Title.
GT1043.R83 2009
391.00947—dc22

2008049744

A catalogue record for this book is available from the British Library

*Page i*   A young couple from Riazan' trying to look fashionable for the camera but not quite succeeding,
late nineteenth century. Private collection.

*Pages ii–iii*   A tailor measuring a client for a new suit in 1908.
Central State Archive of Documentary Films, Photographs, and Sound Recordings of St. Petersburg.

*This page and facing*   Schoolchildren in 1899. Private collection.

*Note on illustrations*   Illustrations in the book that are not given dates in the captions are assumed to be from
the end of the nineteenth century or the early years of the twentieth century

To Brad,

and in memory of
all the Ruanes, Murrays, Heans, and Corcorans
who toiled in the fashion industry
in the United States and Ireland

While others might accessorize their outfits with purses or watches,
this young sportsman brought his bicycle for his photograph, early twentieth century.
Private collection.

# Contents

A studio portrait of an elegantly dressed Petersburg woman, December 1905.
Private collection.

# Acknowledgments

HISTORY BOOKS BEGIN IN ARCHIVES and libraries, and it has been my great pleasure to work in a number of excellent institutions. I spent many productive hours in the Russian State Historical Archive, the Russian Public Library, the State Archive of the Russian Federation and the Moscow City Archive. In particular, I want to thank the librarians at the Russian National Library. They allowed me to enter the stacks of that amazing institution free of charge to read as many fashion magazines and mail-order catalogues as I wanted. At a time when other libraries were charging a small fortune just to order one magazine, the Leninka's generosity made this book possible as these materials were indispensable to my understanding of the Russian fashion industry. I also want to thank Tatiana Strizhenova for a memorable day at the Museum of the City of Moscow and Galina Ulianova, Raisa Kirsanova, and Olga Vainshtein for their continued support over the years. Natasha, Zhenya, Zina, Lena, and Sergei have been the best of friends for a long time, and I want to extend my deepest thanks for their hospitality and practical help in negotiating daily life in Russia.

In the United States, I had the opportunity to make multiple trips to some of the major repositories of Russian history materials – the Library of Congress, Harvard University Libraries, and the library at University of Illinois, Urbana-Champaign. My heartfelt thanks to these dedicated professionals, and especially Helen Sullivan, the head of the Slavic Reference Service at the University of Illinois, who was an enthusiastic supporter of this project from its inception. I also want to acknowledge the assistance of the librarians and the Interlibrary Loan staff at the University of Tulsa.

Several institutions provided financial support for this project. The Russian Research Center at Harvard University awarded a fellowship as I began my work. Away from classroom responsibilities, I was able to utilize Harvard's vast treasure trove of written and visual materials as well as engage with a remarkable group of scholars. I also want to acknowledge grants from the International Research and Exchanges Board, the University of Texas at Austin, and the University of Tulsa.

Earlier versions of some chapters in this book have been published elsewhere and appear here with permission: "Clothes Shopping in Imperial Russia: The Development of a Consumer Culture," in *Journal of Social History* 28, 4 (Summer 1995); "The 1906 Moscow Garment Workers' Strike," in Donald Filtzer, Wendy Goldman, Gijs Kessler, and Simon Pirani, eds., *A Dream Deferred: New Studies in Russian and Soviet Labor History* (Bern: Peter Lang, 2008); and "Spreading the Word: The Development of a Russian Fashion Press," in Regina Lee Blaszczyk, ed., *Producing Fashion: Commerce, Culture, and Consumers* (Philadelphia: University of Pennsylvania Press, 2008), 21–41. Every effort was made to contact the copyright holders for the illustrations.

This book has benefited enormously from the careful ministrations of Gillian Malpass, my editor at Yale University Press, and her wonderful staff in London. Gillian did a superb job of matching illustration and text. I also want to thank the anonymous readers who provided valuable suggestions for improving the text, but I alone bear responsibility for the arguments presented in this book. I have used the Library of Congress transliteration system for Russian words except for the names of monarchs and prominent individuals, such as Leo Tolstoy. All dates are according to the Julian calendar.

There are a number of individuals who have helped me during this book's gestation. I have had the privilege and pleasure of participating the Midwest Russian Historians' Workshop. I want to thank all the members of this terrific organization for their intellectual rigor and friendship over the years. I am grateful to Linda Acton-Smith, Vicki Baker, Rosario Cabello, and Rebecca Deaton for helping me keep body and soul together while I was working on this project. My colleagues at the University of Tulsa provided me with a safe haven when there was no other to be found. A special thanks to Christine Worobec, James Ronda, Francis Ruane, and James Ruane Hinshaw who read earlier versions of the manuscript. They all provided incisive commentary on the text. The late Nancy Grant, Amy Nelson and Tom Ewing, Mary Lee Townsend, the late Reggie Zelnik, Bill Rosenberg, Dan Orlovsky, my parents, Francis and Jeanne Ruane, and my son, James Ruane Hinshaw, have all provided support when I needed it most. This book is dedicated my husband, Joseph Bradley. Brad and I have discussed the finer points of Russian history over innumerable meals and cups of coffee. But, most especially, his love and encouragement have supported me throughout our years together.

At the very end of this project, a trip to Ireland rekindled my interest in learning more about my antecedents. This genealogical research has yielded a family tree filled with men and women who participated in the fashion industry in Ireland and the United States. In uncovering the history of the Russian fashion industry, I have indirectly discovered a large part of my own family's history. Since it was their hard work and sacrifice that have allowed me the luxury of an academic life, this book represents a loving acknowledgment of my debt to them.

# *Introduction*

THIS IS THE STORY of the Russian revolution in dress. While foreigners and some Russians had worn European clothing in seventeenth-century Muscovy,[1] on 4 January 1700 Tsar Peter the Great (1672–1725) commanded his male courtiers to wear a Hungarian caftan instead of the Muscovite one. Not content with this, a year later the tsar issued a much more sweeping decree:

> . . . all residents of the city of Moscow including those serfs who come to the city to trade, but excluding the clergy and agricultural laborers, must wear German dress. Outerwear must consist of French or Saxon coats, and underneath men must wear camisoles [sleeved vests], breeches, boots, shoes, and German hats. And they must ride in German saddles. Women of all ranks – women of the clergy, wives of officers, musketeers, and soldiers – and their children must wear German dress, hats, skirts, and shoes. From this day forward no one will be allowed to wear Russian dress, Caucasian caftans, sheepskin coats, pants, or boots, nor will anyone be permitted to ride in Russian saddles. Finally, artisans will not be allowed to make or trade [in these goods].

Those who entered the city gates in Russian dress were to be fined while those who produced or sold Russian clothing faced unspecified forms of "dreadful punishment."[2] While virtually every book written about Peter the Great mentions his sartorial revolution, there has been no attempt to understand how his decrees were implemented. What began as a dress code for courtiers quickly became the uniform for public life throughout the empire.

Peter the Great's dress decrees were part of a comprehensive set of social, economic, political, and cultural reforms whose purpose was to make the Russian Empire an equal partner in the European family of nations.[3] To achieve that goal, Peter believed that Russia must become more like western Europe. Through the forceful exercise of his autocratic power, the tsar laid the foundation for a new state. He created a modern military and a more efficient government bureaucracy. He reinvigorated Russian life by creating new opportunities for social and economic advancement based on merit. Finally, Peter launched a revolution in appearances and manners. Courtiers, aristocrats, and city residents had to wear "German dress," and conduct themselves according to western European customs.[4]

Peter's westernization policies created a fissure in Russian life.[5] From the beginning, there were those Russians who quickly gave up indigenous dress and adopted a European lifestyle and outlook. Others believed that to abandon their traditional way of life was to give up those qualities that made them Russian. More than a century later, in the 1840s, two groups of intellectuals within Russia gave public voice to these opposing views. The westernizers argued that Peter's reforms marked the beginning of state-sponsored efforts to make Russia a bastion of European civilization. If Russia still lagged behind western Europe in the nineteenth century, it was because the Russian government had adopted only those European ideas that furthered its own autocratic power. For the westernizers, Peter's reforms had not gone far enough – they wanted even more change. Their opponents, the Slavophiles, believed that the tsar had introduced foreign, alien elements into his native land that destroyed the organic wholeness and sense of community that had characterized pre-Petrine life.[6] Both sides offered compelling interpretations of the Russian past to support their position, but neither side emerged as the victor in this controversy. Long after the debates between the original westernizers and Slavophiles had ceased, their fundamental disagreements over Russia's place in the world continued to influence intellectual life and public policy. How did Russia define itself? Was Russia a European nation or was it somehow a part of the cultural world of the East? The precise nature of Russia's relationship to the West preoccupied both the Russian government and the educated public. At stake was Russian identity itself, both as a polity and as a people, and dress came to symbolize that search to define identity.

This study takes a fresh look at the impact of westernization upon Russian life by analyzing the changes initiated by Peter's dress reforms. At first glance, examining the introduction of European fashions may seem like an odd way to discuss so weighty a question. After all, fashion concerns itself with personal adornment, not high politics. Yet, dress offers a unique perspective from which to observe complex social forces at work. Humans have decorated their bodies for thousands of years. While the purpose of some garments is simply protection against the elements, the desire for personal adornment is more complex. Humans use their clothing to fashion an identity for themselves. Clothes can give clues to a person's geographic location, membership in a particular community, social rank, economic circumstances, gender, ideological beliefs, and aesthetic preferences. Clothes can reveal an individual's conscious and unconscious desires. But people also use clothing to conceal their identities. They dress in a particular style so as to confuse others as to their true identity. Individuals use their bodies like an artist's blank canvas upon which they compose deeply personal and ambiguous messages.[7]

At the same time, clothing serves as a visual metaphor for abstract intellectual forces. In Russia, as elsewhere, clothing acted as a vital but complex marker of ethnic, social, political, and gender identities. Because Russians wore those messages upon their bodies, group dynamics and identity politics entered into the mainstream of everyday life, making these abstract issues impossible to ignore. The philosophical debates between the Slavophiles and westernizers were conducted in a few salons and journals. Nevertheless, when one of the leading Slavophiles, Konstantin Aksakov, decided to wear Russian dress in polite society, he made his dissenting views apparent to everyone with whom he came into contact, including illiterate peasants and workers. Aksakov's sartorial preferences made him the object of ridicule, but at the same time they served as a visual reminder of his philosophical differences with the government and other intellectuals. In a society with strict censorship such as Russia's, the ability to express differing political and intellectual perspectives through dress was an important tool. After 1700 Russians could and did wear their clothing to express their political, social, and cultural allegiances. Thus, the acceptance of westernization by Russians can be measured in large part by their adoption or rejection of European dress.

Before discussing the role of clothing in Russian identity politics, a few terms need to be defined. Unfortunately, words like "dress", "clothing", "fashion", and "costume" have multiple, overlapping meanings. While recognizing these ambiguities, I will use these terms in the following ways in this study. "Dress" and "clothing" are the collective nouns used to describe garments worn by individuals in their daily lives. Both terms are dynamic concepts. A person's clothing reflects his or her financial resources, aesthetic tastes, and whims. The only time individuals wear identical clothing is when they are required to wear a uniform to work, school, or other event. Uniforms are created to eliminate an individual's ability to change his or her appearance at will. Their purpose is to identify and

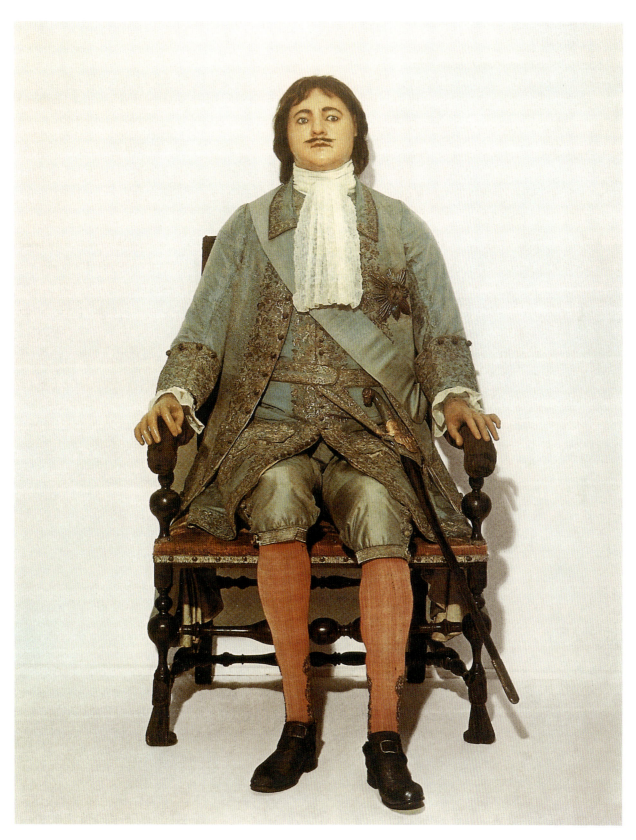

I  Bartolomeo Rastrelli's wax effigy of Peter the Great wearing early eighteenth-century European men's court dress. The State Hermitage Museum, St. Petersburg.

create groups who share common experiences and attitudes.

The concept of fashion transforms both clothing and identity. Fashion is the continual and rapid change in clothing styles. In a very real sense, fashion amplifies the dynamic nature of clothing by codifying change. At the same time, fashion categorizes people into groups. Self-appointed arbiters of fashion declare what is in fashion and what is not. Others choose to flaunt fashion's dictates. These individuals create their own fashionable outfits in defiance of current styles or reject fashion altogether. But because fashion at its core represents change for the sake of change, it embraces both the fashionable and the unfashionable simultaneously. Those who reject fashion are still responding to it, making escape from fashion impossible.

Costume represents the opposite of fashion, clothing, dress, and uniforms. Although costume originates as clothing, it becomes those garments that are to be preserved without any further changes or adaptations. Costume loses its adaptability and becomes frozen in time. The static nature of costume means that most individuals wear costume for special occasions when they are consciously trying to invoke the past or a particular ritual. For daily wear, most of us prefer to wear garments that reflect the dynamic nature of our lives. As our financial resources, moods, and tastes change, we want to wear clothing or fashions that express our evolving sense of self. As we shall see, these different ways of understanding clothes played an important role in Russian developments.

## FASHION AND ETHNICITY

When Peter the Great introduced western fashions into Russia in 1700, the role of clothing in western European society had long ago undergone a profound change: It had become fashion. Most costume historians agree that fashion began in fourteenth-century Europe. Prior to this time, pictorial and anthropological evidence suggests that changes in modes of dress happened very slowly. The fourteenth century marks a qualitative change as courtiers changed their style of dress more frequently just for the sake of having a new look. Much of this clothing was made from textiles shipped from China along the Silk Road, making the garments very expensive. Obviously, only the wealthy elite could regularly afford to order a new set of clothes, but many gave their discarded clothes to the poorer classes who then wore slightly out-of-date fashions. As the concept of fashion spread across Europe, new designs could be created more easily. In the sixteenth century, design books were published to illustrate the newest hairstyles, clothes, and footwear. Trade routes multiplied and spread, allowing Europeans to import silks and other fabrics more easily. By the time of Peter the Great's decree, the idea of continual changes in clothing styles had become an accepted practice in western Europe. Although Paris was the capital of the fashion industry, European *haute couture* attempted to transcend national borders and take on an international or transnational character. The chief purpose of fashion was to create a cosmopolitan identity.[8]

Yet, fashion was itself an amalgam of different cultural aesthetics. Initially, it consisted of design elements borrowed from those ethnic groups that populated the western half of the European continent. The incessant need to create new fashions encouraged designers to look outside their own culture for more exotic garments that would help them create a new look for their clients. For example, the British conquest of India produced a number of innovations. Turbans, cashmere shawls, calico prints, and pajamas all became part of the European design vocabulary. In 1814 English tailors popularized a new style of men's trousers called "Cossacks" following the visit of Tsar Alexander I (1777–1825) to London. Thus, fashion consisted of both western and eastern design elements incorporated into a brand-new and ever-changing look. Paradoxically, fashion asserted the supremacy of a modern, western culture, but it did so only through constant interaction with the national cultures it was trying to colonize.[9]

Consequently, Peter the Great's dress reforms introduced not only a different style of dress but a different approach to clothing. In the early eighteenth century, Russia was a land rich in religious and cultural diversity. Clothing played a central role in distinguishing one group from another, differentiating Tatars,

2   A rust-colored *robe à la française* from the middle of the eighteenth century. The State Hermitage Museum, St. Petersburg.

3   Tsar Nicholas II dressed in the seventeenth-century clothing of Tsar Aleksei Mikhailovich, Peter the Great's father. *Al'bom kostiumirovovannogo bala v Zimnem Dvortse v fevrale 1903 g.*, 1. Library of Congress Collections.

4 Tsaritsa Alexandra Fedorovna, Nicholas II's wife, wearing the seventeenth-century clothing of the Tsaritsa Maria Il'inichna Miloslavskaia, Aleksei Mikhailovich's first wife. *Al'bom kostiumirovovannogo bala v Zimnem Dvortse v fevrale 1903 g.*, II. Library of Congress Collections.

Finns, Balts, and Poles from the Orthodox Slavs. But even among the Orthodox Slavs there were tribal and cultural differences. Men and women from Tver' did not dress the same as their counterparts in Riazan' or Vologda. Clothing helped to maintain ethnic and tribal differences while at the same time providing a rich sartorial landscape. Fashion changed all that. Instead of maintaining cultural and tribal differences, fashion sought to break down those barriers and replace them with new views of the self, permitting residents of Tver', Riazan', and Vologda to dress the same as their counterparts in western Europe. The universal, cosmopolitan ideals of the Enlightenment asserted themselves over the particularism of the Muscovite era.[10]

The attempt to eliminate ethnic diversity was troubling many Russians by the end of the eighteenth century. Influenced by romantic nationalism, they tried to preserve the uniqueness of their cultural heritage in the face of cosmopolitan westernization, and dress was crucial to their nationalist sensibility. Nationalists created a single category of "Russian dress" which included garments worn by the various peoples who had lived in the Russian heartland. The dress of the Waldai, Cheremis, Muscovites, and many others was now labeled as "Russian". Tribal differences were interpreted as demonstrating the wonderful variety and resourcefulness of Russian cultural life. At the same time, cultural nationalists also appropriated the dress of non-Slavic peoples. Tatar, Caucasian, and Central Asian clothing was categorized as Russian. Thus, "Russian dress" served to identify Russians as an ethnic group and a colonial power.

Because Russian dress was supposed to preserve the uniqueness of Russian culture from westernization, any change in design became anathema. By the mid-nineteenth century, Russian ethnographers traveled to all parts of the empire to gather and preserve those clothes discarded by ordinary Russians who wanted to wear European fashions. The ethnographers believed that Russians had worn these garments since time immemorial and somehow projected the essence of the Russian spirit. This clothing, removed from the dynamic culture that had created it, began a new life as costume and historical artifact, silently decaying in museum displays. But, in their desperate attempts to preserve the world they were losing, these ethnographers overlooked that Russian dress had never remained static, but had changed, however slowly, in response to new economic and cultural impulses.[11] Once ethnic dress had been redefined as costume, however, Russians were no longer interested in wearing it. Costume was fine for masquerades and special occasions, but most Russians wanted clothing that reflected their ever-changing needs and whims. As the pace of life quickened in late Imperial Russia, they wanted clothing that would allow them to create a modern Russian identity, not to be seen as relics of the past. At the turn of the twentieth century, fashion infused with Russian design elements provided the means to create such an identity.

## FASHION AND SOCIAL STATUS

Clothing has served not only to distinguish one ethnic group from another but also to delineate social groups. In the early modern period, Europe as well as Russia was a society of estates – the nobility, the clergy, townspeople, and peasants. Individuals were lifelong members of the social group into which they were born. Status was based upon land ownership and service to a lord, noble, prince, or monarch. The elites jealously guarded their status in a variety of ways. Intermarriage allowed noble lands to remain within elite families, and royal service was restricted to those with the proper pedigree. European aristocrats also spent large sums of money on elaborate dress, food, and estates. Political rulers participated in displays of power combining ornate dress and ritual. Many rulers enacted sumptuary laws that codified who could wear what clothing. The introduction of fashion in the fourteenth century had proved invaluable in enhancing the position of the elite. The constant changes in fashionable dress helped them to maintain their social position because few townspeople and no peasants could afford to keep up with the latest styles. At the same time, fashion helped to foster social solidarity among the elite. Uniformity of appearance suggested uniformity of beliefs and goals. Everyone in Europe knew that individuals who wore the latest fashions were part of

the ruling elite. Thus, fashion allowed individuals to be part of a larger group.

Paradoxically, fashion also encouraged individualism. Because fashion placed such an emphasis on innovation and change, those who created their own style were seen as trendsetters and quickly gained a kind of celebrity or notoriety. By publicizing what was new, these innovators or rebels encouraged others to follow their lead. In this way fashion helped to break down old social categories and create new ones in their place. Perhaps the most important example of this has become known as the "great masculine renunciation" of fashionable dress. According to David Kuchta, in the late 1600s a group of English aristocrats who were unhappy with both the policies and the excessive displays of luxury at court adopted a plainer form of dress. These men abandoned the lace collars, colorful fabrics, elaborate wigs, and high-heeled shoes in favor of simple dark clothing. Following their lead, the English bourgeoisie in the eighteenth century borrowed this

5 A group photograph of peasant boys and young women wearing Russian dress. The boys are wearing unembroidered, unbleached linen shirts worn over their trousers. The young women are wearing clothing worn for special occasions. Library of Congress Collections.

style of dress in their attack upon royal power and aristocratic privilege.[12] This austere dress, the precursor to the suit and tie, became the uniform for middle-class men throughout Europe and America. Rejecting sumptuous dress as a reflection of aristocratic waste and idleness, European middle-class men wore clothing that reflected the values to which they aspired – thrift, utility, and modesty. Thus, fashion simultaneously fostered conformity and nonconformity. It is precisely this slipperiness, this ability to be both at once, that gives fashion such power as a marker of social identities.

Fashion played this complex and contradictory role in Russian society. Peter the Great commanded that all

those who served the tsar – courtiers, bureaucrats, military officers, provincial nobility, and urban dwellers of whatever rank – wear western clothing at work and at home. The only two groups excluded from Peter's dress reforms were the clergy, who had their own distinctive style of dress, and the peasantry, who were allowed to wear traditional clothing so long as they remained in the countryside. As a result, Peter's dress reforms not only introduced a western/Russian split among the population but also an urban/rural divide. In fact, Russians often referred to European fashions as "city clothes" (*obshchegorodskaia odezhda*).

By the end of the eighteenth century, the Russian social landscape had changed dramatically. At the very top were the elite who lived in elegant European palaces and townhouses, dressed themselves in the latest fashions, and spoke French. According to one historian,

> He [the Russian nobleman] had spent his whole life pondering "European ways," enlightened society;

*La Petite Marchande d'Oeufs d'Octha*.

6   A peasant woman's holiday outfit from Tambov, mid-nineteenth century. The outfit includes a long-sleeved linen chemise, a jumper, and pinafore. The bright colors are typical of Russian peasant dress. State Historical Museum, Moscow. *Kostium v Rossii xv–nachalo xx veka*, 85.

7 (*right*)   A late eighteenth-century French engraving showing a Russian peasant girl selling eggs. She is wearing a chemise underneath a jumper called a sarafan. Private collection.

he had tried to be at home among foreigners and merely became a foreigner at home. In Europe he was regarded as a Tatar in European dress, while in his own eyes he seemed a Frenchman who had been born in Russia.[13]

Beneath the Frenchified aristocracy were those who tried with varying degrees of success to imitate the elegant manners and dress of the elite, while the vast majority of Russians – the peasants – continued to wear native dress and live according to ancestral ways. These two Russias stared at each other from across what appeared to be a vast divide.

Yet the same western culture that had created this breach in Russian society also contained within it the possibility of bridging that gulf, and fashion's role was central to this process. By the nineteenth century,

8  A photograph of young men in Ukrainian ethnic dress. Ukrainians were just one of many ethnic groups that lived within the Russian Empire. Library of Congress Collections.

Russians began to use fashion as a form of political and social protest. Fashion gave nonconformists in an autocratic state a means to express their discontent either by creating a new fad in dress or by rejecting fashion altogether in favor of ethnic dress. At the same time, the Russian system of estates (*sosloviia*) was giving way to a class society. Industrialization, bureaucratization, and education disrupted the old way of life, bringing about profound and troubling changes to Russia. The old social categories proved inadequate to contain the dynamic society that was emerging.

Fashion allowed new social groups such as the bourgeoisie and the working class to create a class identity for themselves while it allowed older groups such as the nobility and the peasantry to update their image. By the beginning of the twentieth century, Russia's sartorial landscape had become much more complicated, reflecting the growing complexity of Russian society itself.

## FASHION AND GENDER

The third category in which fashion has played a central role is gender. One historian has pointed out that there are five fundamental forms of clothing worn by both sexes, and yet, despite the similar design and function of these garments, humans have tended to see clothing as a way of separating themselves along gender lines.[14] Consequently, clothing worn by both sexes has changed dramatically over the years, creating a wondrous variety of styles. But just as fashion appeared to distinguish the sexes, it also created the possibility of transgressing those boundaries. To give one example, in the 1840s some European artists and intellectuals began wearing "Turkish trousers" (a pair of billowy pants worn in the Ottoman Empire) at a time when most elegant men were wearing rather tight-fitting trousers. But beyond issues of personal comfort, donning Turkish pants allowed European men to express their disaffection. They shocked polite society by choosing to dress as Turks, and thereby identifying themselves with the East. These young men gained a certain celebrity for their ethnic cross-dressing. Their defiance of cultural norms enhanced their manhood.

The same was not the case for women. In the 1850s the American women's rights advocate Amelia Bloomer popularized Turkish pants for women. Bloomer believed that if women were going to be accepted as men's equals, they needed to give up their cumbersome outfits. She encouraged women to wear Turkish trousers underneath short, full skirts. Women dressed in men's clothing both fascinated and frightened Europeans, and polite society ridiculed the idea of women wearing "bloomers." Because clothing supposedly symbolized the inner qualities of each sex,

females wearing men's pants proved very threatening. Women were portrayed as unnatural for attempting to transgress their gender by wearing the wrong clothing.[15] This one example demonstrates how a single piece of clothing was interpreted very differently depending upon the gender of the wearer, but fashion also demonstrated how easy it was to transgress those gender boundaries that seemed to be "natural" and "immutable."

Peter the Great's dress decrees coupled with his other edicts helped to introduce a new gender order into Russia. The long, flowing Muscovite robes gave way to clothing that revealed the body. Men wore tight-fitting breeches; women wore décolleté gowns. Instead of traditional head coverings, both sexes wore wigs. Clothed in their new outfits, men and women of the elite began to socialize together on a regular basis. European balls, theater, and assemblies became popular forms of entertainment among the aristocracy. The tsar encouraged the Russian elite to behave like their western European counterparts, and the new clothes caused Russians to see each other from a fresh perspective. From these encounters, a new gender order began to take shape.

Russians of both sexes were quick to realize the transgressive potential of European fashions. During the nineteenth and early twentieth centuries, Russian women used fashion in complex and interesting ways to call attention to their inequality and to demand greater freedom. But men, too, used fashion as a form of protest. Many noblemen preferred the understated uniform of the bourgeoisie to the more opulent aristocratic dress that was increasingly seen as effeminate, while others, like Leo Tolstoy, rejected fashion altogether and wore Russian dress. At the end of the nineteenth century, working-class and peasant men began to wear European fashions in an effort to challenge the old order but also in an attempt to redefine masculinity. Thus, both sexes and all classes manipulated fashion to redefine their role in society.

★　★　★

9 (*facing page*)　A scarlet silk gown reflecting the fashions of the 1810s. The State Hermitage Museum, St. Petersburg.

Peter the Great's dress decree was directed not only at identity politics but also at economic considerations. The last sentence of the decree essentially outlawed the production and sale of those articles of clothing that most Russians wore. This created a huge problem for Peter's subjects: how were they supposed to obtain the proper clothing now that native dress was banned from public life? The few foreign tailors in Moscow who could make European garments could hardly keep up with the demand for fashionable dress that Peter's code engendered. The solution to this dilemma was to create a Russian fashion industry. From the early eighteenth century Russian entrepreneurs set out to do just that, using the fashion industry in western Europe as their model.

The fashion industry's role in the development of capitalism has been overlooked until very recently.[16] The reasons for this are not hard to find. Much of the literature on capitalist development links it with industrialization. Industrialization, in turn, is associated with the creation of large mechanized factories. Although the early factories produced textiles, very few scholars have tried to determine what happened to the fabric once it left the factory. Instead, they have tended to focus their studies on how factory production and mechanization transformed heavy industry. The rise of the new capitalist factory resulted in the mass production of iron, steel, concrete, and glass, the building blocks of modern life. There is little room in this picture for the small sewing sweatshop. Unlike the factory-made automobiles, railroad cars, and bicycles, the goods produced in the sweatshops were often discarded. Perhaps even more crucially, the literature on the role of industrialization in capitalist development contains an important assumption. Scholars have assumed that the availability of the new industrial goods created the demand for them. This view privileges the role of production, making consumption a byproduct of industrialization. Consequently, the history of mechanization and the factory system has dominated discussions of European capitalist development.

Recent scholarship has challenged these assumptions. A group of historians who study early modern Europe have begun to rethink the industrialization paradigm. They have argued that an "industrious revolution" preceded the Industrial Revolution. Ordinary Europeans observing the lifestyle of the elite dreamt of possessing luxury goods, which ranged from small items such as ribbons, mirrors, and combs to more expensive items such as clothing, china, and furniture. None of these objects was essential for the maintenance of life. Nevertheless, they provided beauty and color, and allowed their owners to raise their social standing as possessors of luxury items. These historians emphasize the role of consumption as central to the origins of capitalism and industrialization.[17] Other scholars have stressed the key role that small artisanal workshops played in the Industrial Revolution; they persisted in Europe long after mechanization and the development of the factory system. Some industries such as the garment trades could not be mechanized in the same way as the textile or steel industries. Yet, to leave these artisanal industries out of the history of capitalism is to omit an important part of the story.[18]

This challenge to the older industrialization paradigm has led to a heated debate among scholars about the origins of capitalism and the relationship between consumption and production.[19] Whatever the outcome of this debate, one thing is clear. The history of capitalism is much richer and more complex than a narrow focus on industrial production will allow. Capitalism consists of a variety of productive forces and labor relations. It also engenders new attitudes and practices in the distribution and consumption of merchandise. Capitalist entrepreneurs created special forms of publicity and retailing to sell the growing numbers of goods produced in factories and workshops. Capitalism then can be seen as a cultural system as well as an economic one, and like any other cultural artifact it is shaped by forces within each country.

The standard view of Russian industrialization and capitalism differs in a number of important ways from the western European paradigm. Russia is usually described as economically backward. While the beginnings of Russian industrialization can be found in the eighteenth century, serfdom retarded capitalist economic development until the emancipation of the serfs in 1861. After the emancipation of the serfs, the government initiated a rapid industrialization program. By putting in place economic programs that favored heavy industry, it became the first and best customer of the Russian military–industrial complex. The Russian peasantry and working class paid a huge price for rapid industrialization, for it was they who produced the goods in unsafe, poorly managed factories. Because the government played such a critical role in economic life, the Russian bourgeoisie is portrayed as either "missing" or underdeveloped in contrast to their counterparts in western Europe.[20] And yet, as dissimilar as this picture is from the history of western European capitalism, this view of Russian economic history also privileges production over consumption, factories over small workshops.[21]

A history of the Russian fashion industry provides a much-needed corrective to this interpretation by bringing a neglected consumer industry into the discussion of economic developments. In the case of fashion, there can be no debate about which came first, production or consumption, supply or demand. Peter the Great's decree had the effect of making European fashions the uniform for the nobility, the military, and all townspeople, creating a demand for these goods virtually overnight. Even though the Russian government initiated dress reform, elite Russians quickly grew comfortable in their new clothes. The court and aristocracy became known for their lavish expenditures on luxury goods of all kinds, including clothing.[22] Just a generation after Peter's decree, his later successors, Elizabeth I (1709–1762) and Catherine II (the Great; 1729–1796), issued their own sumptuary edicts proscribing excessive displays of sartorial finery at court.[23] As the *beau monde* adopted European fashion as its own, those who aspired to become part of polite society

10   Examples of clothing of Russian manufacture at the beginning of the nineteenth century. The man's olive green suit consists of woolen fabric and a stripped silk vest. The woman's gown is made from a wool/silk blend with decorative trim at the hem and neckline; her shawl is of foreign manufacture. The woman's outfit shows how fashion-conscious Russians often combined domestic and imported articles, depending on their budgets. State Historical Museum, Moscow.

quickly began to wear western-inspired clothing as well. Eventually even workers and peasants purchased fashionable clothing.

The demand for European fashions heralded the introduction of European designs and manufacturing into Russia. This was a two-stage process. Beginning in the eighteenth century, foreign tailors and dressmakers came to Russia and set up small workshops and boutiques. They trained Russians in the principles of European design. In the middle of the nineteenth century, ready-to-wear manufacture transformed the Russian garment trades just as it had in western Europe. Clothing production became centered in sweatshops where garment workers did not labor over a single garment but developed specializations. A group of workers began the process by cutting hundreds of pieces of cloth that were then sent out to pants makers, raincoat makers, shirt sewers, buttonholers, and finishers. The end product – a skirt, blouse, or suit – would have passed through the hands of several workers before it was finally finished. Customers could buy these pre-assembled copies of fashionable clothing in department stores or specialized clothing stores. Moreover, these customers knew what to buy from reading about the latest styles in fashion magazines or advice columns.

These production and business practices became central not only to the creation of a fashion industry but also to the development of capitalism in Russia. This book seeks to broaden our understanding of capitalism by showing how one industry that remained wedded to artisanal forms of production helped to introduce changes in retailing and publicity, thereby transforming Russian economic life. Furthermore, gender, class, and ethnicity gave shape to these capitalist practices. In order to understand the full role that fashion played in Russia, it is essential to combine concerns about its role in identity politics with economic developments. The result is a richer analysis of the social, economic, and political forces that were transforming Russia by the beginning of the twentieth century.

★　★　★

## SOURCES

The sources for a study of the Russian fashion industry present complex challenges to the historian. To begin with, it proved impossible to gather precise data about this industry in the imperial period. The statistics that exist woefully underestimate the amount of clothing that was actually being produced. Many tailors refused to register their businesses with municipal authorities to avoid paying taxes. Extra-legal sweatshops and women sewing at home evaded government inspectors. The number of garment workers and the amount of clothing they manufactured remain elusive. Furthermore, most of the business records for the shops, clothing manufacturers, and the fashion press have not survived. The few scraps of paper that do remain sometimes provide a brief glimpse into the life of a particular enterprise, but are not enough to write a sustained history of any one organization. These problems exist in varying degrees in other national histories of fashion as well, and may help to explain why the fashion industry is usually left out of most economic histories in the West. The data to write a traditional economic history are either missing or problematic.

Nevertheless, the Russian fashion industry has left behind a rich source base from which to reconstruct its history. I have made use of trade-union materials and the memoir literature preserved in the State Archive of the Russian Federation to reconstruct garment workers' lives. Russian literature and mail-order catalogues have been invaluable in recreating the world of shopping. A careful reading of fashion magazines reveals not only what Russians were supposed to wear but also what they thought about their new clothes. The fashion press also reveals the growing sophistication of the Russian media and capitalist entrepreneurs as they helped to create an expanding market for fashion. These sources, coupled with a judicious use of government statistics, economic, labor, and costume histories, provide a window onto the complex forces that shaped the Russian revolution in dress.

Peter the Great's sartorial revolution, unlike many of Russia's other revolutions, was an unqualified success. By the beginning of the twentieth century, members of polite society wore only European fashions. Workers and peasants also abandoned handmade traditional clothing and tried to purchase western ready-to-wear clothes whenever their meager budgets allowed. When the Bolsheviks came to power in 1917, they introduced their own version of Soviet chic, which was itself an offshoot of European design. As a result, traditional Russian clothing became costume that was either preserved in museums or worn only for special occasions or in performance. And while the dress revolution did not take place overnight, there was no turning back. Russia's sartorial landscape had changed forever.

11  A young woman of the 1870s. This picture gives an example of Russian haute couture with the gown's lace collar and beading at the sleeves and on the skirt. Private Collection.

# 1

# *The Emperor's New Clothes: The Creation of a Fashion Industry*

Like so many other of his edicts, Peter the Great's dress decree was an impetuous act. While Peter and his family could rely on Kremlin tailors to make their clothing, other Russians were not so fortunate. To create an entirely new industry was not an easy task, but the indomitable Peter set about doing just that. Most scholars agree that mercantilism shaped the tsar's economic philosophy by allowing for government intervention in economic life through the regulation of trade, territorial expansion, and other measures.[1] To encourage Russians to purchase their clothes at home rather than abroad, the tsar began by providing economic incentives for the creation of a domestic textile industry and by recruiting European artisans to set up shop in Russia so that they could train Russian workers in the fine art of western tailoring and dressmaking.

Yet the history of the Russian fashion industry is not wholly the story of an autocratic government forcing its will upon a reluctant people. In the beginning, Peter used his power to coerce his courtiers to don wigs and waistcoats, but, after his death in 1725 and by the middle of the eighteenth century, the elite had grown comfortable in their new clothes and no longer appeared in Russian dress at public gatherings unless commanded to do so. Russian and foreign entrepreneurs responded to government initiatives with enthusiasm, particularly after it became clear that there was money to be made. The history of the fashion industry elucidates the development of a complex relationship between government, business, and consumer interests, providing a fascinating case history of capitalist development in Russia.

## THE CREATION OF A MARKET FOR EUROPEAN DRESS

At first glance, the introduction of uniforms might seem an odd place to begin the story of the Russian fashion industry. The very idea of the uniform is to eliminate the constant fluctuations in styles which are an intrinsic part of fashion. In particular, uniforms express the power of governments to eliminate individual choice in clothing in favor of a collective identity. By donning uniforms, individuals give up the right to act freely, and subordinate themselves to a greater authority.[2] And yet, the introduction of uniforms played an essential role in Peter's reform of the Russian government. In 1722 the tsar introduced the Table of Ranks, which restructured the governmental bureaucracy with the intention of bringing rational, European bureaucracy to Russia. Now state service rather than birth determined an individual's position in the civil,

counterparts. The new uniforms eliminated ethnic differences, allowing Russian servitors to blend in with other Europeans. With his dress decrees and a new system of state service, Peter had announced the arrival of Russia as a member of the European community. In order that Russian officials should no longer be perceived as backward and semi-Asiatic, their uniforms were vital in creating a new self-image for officialdom both at home and abroad.

These state uniforms remained a distinctive feature of the Russian sartorial landscape until the fall of the Romanov dynasty in 1917, a visual sign of each servitor's loyalty and obedience to the autocracy. Because uniforms had this direct and explicit link to political authority, improper care of uniforms could have serious consequences for their wearers. In 1842 Nicholas I (1796–1855) went to visit his sister, Grand Duchess

13 A news agent selling newspapers on the street in his uniform. Library of Congress Collections.

12 The head of the Mikhailovskii Artillery Academy in St. Petersburg in uniform. Private collection.

military, and court administrations. To mark this new beginning, European-style uniforms were introduced for each branch of state service.[3] These new uniforms had two purposes. First, they helped to indicate one's position in the Table of Ranks to both government officials and those outside the government.[4] Second, they also announced to the rest of the world that Russian functionaries were equal to their European

Maria Pavlovna. One of her servants met the tsar's carriage wearing a dirty uniform. When he returned home, Nicholas immediately called in his aide, Prince Nikolai Dolgorukov. The angry tsar demanded that the retainer be fired, and that new regulations governing the care of servants' government uniforms be issued immediately. His orders were carried out the next day.[5] Each servitor, no matter how lowly or inconsequential, was a symbol of imperial might and glory. Any violation of the dress code could affect job security and advancement in government service.

Having established a uniform for state servitors, Peter the Great's goal of introducing European modes and manners into court circles proved more challenging and relied less on imperial edicts than on royal example. The first step was to ensure that all members of the royal family and Peter's immediate entourage dressed in European clothes not only when performing

14 A family portrait taken in 1860. The two young sons are wearing their school uniforms. Central State Archive of Documentary Films, Photographs, and Sound Recordings of St. Petersburg.

public functions but at home as well. The tsar abandoned traditional Muscovite dress completely. For state occasions, he wore clothes befitting his role as monarch, but at other times he dressed as a European gentleman. His wife and daughters also ordered gowns that reflected early eighteenth-century fashion trends. More importantly, pictorial representations of the tsar and his family showed them in European finery, thereby helping to publicize the new look. To create the appropriate public space to wear European fashion, Peter built a new capital city, St. Petersburg. Called the "Venice of the North," the new city with its lovely

15  Teachers at a secondary school in St. Petersburg. As state servitors, the men were required to wear a uniform. The priests pictured are wearing their clerical robes. Since women were barred from the civil service, they did not wear uniforms. Nevertheless, they were required to wear dark, high-collared woolen dresses to work. Library of Congress Collections.

architecture and public spaces was to rival all other European capitals. In its new palaces, the tsar introduced European forms of entertainment. While men and women had socialized separately in Muscovy, Peter invited Russians of both sexes to join him in playing European card games and dancing.[6] Between 1700 and 1725, the tsar had introduced European clothing, architecture, and sociability into Russia, a true cultural revolution.

However, the tsar's invitation to join his new court was not received with universal acceptance. Many considered the new European fashions "indecent" (*neprilichnyi*), a violation of Russian notions of beauty and taste.[7] Some aristocrats, especially those of the older generation who lived in the more remote areas of the empire, refused outright to change their clothing or behavior. Others did so only for public occasions, but continued to wear Muscovite dress in the privacy of their own homes. Nevertheless, a core group of ambitious aristocrats eagerly adopted European dress, seeing it as a way to gain access to the court and express their support for Peter's other reforms. These individuals imported clothes from Paris and London. They built European-inspired townhouses in St. Petersburg and grand palaces on their country estates. They learned new forms of etiquette and deportment. If at first they felt awkward in their new clothes and surroundings, the desire to enhance their social status proved greater than their discomfort. However, the importation of these luxury goods was very expensive, and many aristocrats found themselves in debt as they tried to create European cultural oases in the Russian countryside. If dress reform was going to succeed, Russians were going to have to find cheaper ways to manufacture fashionable European clothes.[8]

Eighteenth-century European clothing required fabrics that were either not available in Russia or very expensive to import. Thousands of yards of rich brocades, velvets, silks, and wools were needed just to clothe the imperial courtiers and royal family. Consequently, the demand for these new fabrics spurred the development of a Russian textile industry. In order to understand Russian textiles in this period, a word is needed about European trends.

The industrialization of textile production in Europe is an oft-told tale of scientific and technological breakthroughs that transformed European society. All aspects of textile production were mechanized and eventually performed in a factory setting. These profound changes in manufacturing became known as the Industrial Revolution. Recently, scholars have begun to emphasize other factors that played an equally vital role in industrial development.[9] One such factor was fashion's role in dictating which fabrics people wanted to wear. Prior to the eighteenth century, most Europeans clothed themselves in linen, wool, furs, and silk. Linen was used to make clothes that were worn closest to the skin because it was easy to clean and durable. It was also light enough for summer wear. Outer garments were made from wool, fur, and silk. In most European countries, only the elites wore silk as it was expensive to produce. All this changed with the introduction of cotton cloth. In the second half of the seventeenth century, British colonial merchants introduced Indian chintzes and calicos to the British market, and suddenly cotton cloth became fashionable. The English saw these new fabrics as unusual and exotic, but just as important, cotton cloth was more versatile than linen. Raw cotton could be woven into the lightest of summer fabrics, but it could also be worn in winter, particularly if it was blended with wool or linen. Cotton was also easy to clean like linen, and was cheaper to produce. Over the course of the next two centuries, cotton replaced linen as the most commonly used fabric, not just in Great Britain but all over Europe.[10]

At the same time, wool cloth also became more popular and replaced fur or sheepskins as the chief fabric to be worn in cold weather. Wool was much easier to care for than fur and less expensive to produce because its production could be mechanized. Wool could also be manufactured at different weights, making it a versatile cloth for coats, suits, and cloaks. It could be worn when the first cool breezes of autumn blew, but also in the depths of winter. The versatility and ease of production of cotton and wool helped bring about the revolution in European tastes in fabrics and dress.[11]

Prior to 1700 Russians wore linen, wool, furs, and silk, although only the Muscovite elite could afford silk which was imported from Asia, Persia, and Italy.[12] After Peter the Great's dress decree, it was apparent that Russia would have to produce its own textiles or face eternal dependence upon European manufacturers and suppliers. Therefore, the tsar created a series of economic incentives to encourage Russian entrepreneurs to develop a native textile industry.

A history of Russian textiles is beyond the scope of the present book, but a brief overview of important developments in their manufacture is essential for a full understanding of its sister industry, Russian fashion. Peter the Great himself set the tone by only wearing garments made from Russian cloth.[13] Government orders of woolen cloth for army uniforms, silks for court dress, and linen sailcloth for the new Russian navy provided the initial impetus for noble and merchant entrepreneurs to begin textile production, first in peasant huts but later in factory settings. Financial incentives such as cash advances, fixed prices, and conscripted laborers were other measures employed by the government in the early 1700s to stimulate textile production.[14] As Russia's population grew steadily during the eighteenth and nineteenth centuries, consumer demand began to play a greater role in textile development than government orders. By the second half of the nineteenth century, the government's role consisted primarily of setting up protectionist tariffs for the textile industry while continuing to favor Russian firms when it placed its own orders for fabric. To give an example, in 1896 the Empress Alexandra Fedorovna and her mother-in-law both wore coronation gowns made from Russian silks.[15] These policies were similar to those enacted by other European governments in

the second half of the nineteenth century when protectionist tariffs and trade wars were a common feature
of European economic life.[16]

Although cotton, silk, linen, and wool production
developed differently from one another, they all shared
two important features. Russian manufacturers were
never able to compete successfully with European
manufacturers of high-quality fabrics. British cottons
and woolens, Irish linens, and French silks set the standards that all other nations tried to achieve. Wealthy
Russians who could afford the best preferred to buy
these imported fabrics. Despite government attempts to
encourage the use of Russian textiles among the elite,
a certain snob appeal favoring imported cloth persisted
throughout the imperial period. Furthermore, the
Russian textile trade remained dependent upon
imported raw materials, foreign technology, technicians,
and fashions. Particularly at the high end of the market,
the costs necessary to produce luxury textiles made it
difficult to manufacture large quantities of these goods
in Russia.

Nevertheless, Russian textile manufacturers were
extremely successful in producing medium and lower
quality textiles for the domestic market. Cotton manufacturers led the way in producing inexpensive but
fashionable fabrics. Russia developed into a leading
producer of cotton cloth by the beginning of the
twentieth century, fourth behind Great Britain,
Germany, and the United States.[17] The success of
Russian textile manufacturing was due to its ability to
respond quickly to changing tastes and fashions. For
example, in 1882 the Tsindel' cotton manufacturer
began making plaid cotton fabric (*shotlandka*). Plaids
had become extremely popular in the mid 1800s, and
Tsindel' was the first Russian firm to master the art of
printing plaid cloth. As a result, sale of the Russian-
made plaids soared.[18] Although Russian consumption
per capita grew at a slower rate than in western Europe,
nevertheless, it rose consistently throughout the nineteenth century, and much of that growth was due to
consumer demand for domestic cloth.[19] It was precisely

16 (*left*)  A suit made by Kremlin tailors for Emperor Peter II
in the 1730s. The State Hermitage Museum, St. Petersburg.

these large quantities of inexpensive cottons, woolens, silks, and to a lesser extent linens, that were essential for the development of a fashion industry in Russia.

## THE DEVELOPMENT OF EUROPEAN CUSTOM TAILORING AND DRESSMAKING

One of the hallmarks of eighteenth-century European dress was the fitted nature of the garments. In contrast to Russian clothing, European dress required a well-trained artisan to fit the fabric to the shape of the body, a time-consuming and challenging process that required many fittings. In the early eighteenth century Peter the Great's government began a campaign to lure European tailors to Russia. Once there they could set up their own shops and train Russian apprentices in the fine art of western tailoring. Those foreign tailors who decided to make the voyage to a new land signed special labor contracts which dictated how long they were to work in Russia and their obligation to teach Russian apprentices their specialized skills.[20]

European tailoring was more than a particular style of cutting and sewing – it was also a way of life that had evolved over centuries in the guilds. Tailors and dressmakers began as apprentices, matured into journeymen, and finally became masters. This process initiated the young into the craft by teaching them the appropriate skills and labor discipline. The similarity in training and work experiences as well as the creation of ritualized ceremonies created a sense of community among garment workers where everyone knew their place and each individual had a clear set of obligations as a member of the craft. The male and female artisans who emigrated to Russia brought this craft tradition with them along with the patterns and tools they needed to set up shop in their new homes. This European work culture shaped the development of tailoring and dressmaking in imperial Russia.

17 (*left*)  One of Russia's great fashion designers, Nadezhda Lamanova, created this gown for a female relative of a leading textile manufacturer just prior to the 1905 Revolution. Made from broadcloth and chiffon, the embroidery was done with satin and chiffon ribbon. State Historical Museum, Moscow.

18 A Petersburg fabric store located in the exclusive upper Nevskii Prospekt shopping district. *Ves' Peterburg na 1910 g.,* XXII. Harvard University Collections.

## APRENTICES [21]

The decision to apprentice a Russian child to a tailor or dressmaker was a complex one, involving a number of individuals. Until the abolition of serfdom in 1861, landlords regularly sent a few of their serfs to the cities to apprentice as garment workers. Upon the conclusion of their apprenticeship, the serfs either stayed in the city and worked as journeymen or they returned to their landlords where they sewed for the landlords' families. How landlords selected serfs to apprentice in the needle trades remains a mystery, but there is plenty of circumstantial evidence to suggest that not much thought went into the process. In Denis Fonvizin's eighteenth-century satire, "The Adolescent," Trishka serves as a literary example of a serf-tailor with no

knack for sewing.[22] In 1847 Vasilii Riazanov, a well-established Petersburg tailor, roundly criticized landlords for sending illiterate children with no artistic talents to learn the craft. These children usually made poor artisans.[23]

Among urban workers and peasants after 1861, parents made the decision to apprentice their adolescent children usually when they were between the ages of twelve and sixteen. A number of factors played a role. Frequently, parents chose to apprentice their children in the same craft that they themselves practiced. To give one example, Anna Fedorovna Platonova was born in 1896 to a tailor and his wife living in Moscow. At age eight, her parents enrolled her in a Moscow public school. At the end of each school day, she returned home to help in the family business, making men's apparel. Three years later she graduated from her primary school with honors. Her teacher thought so highly of her potential that she arranged for Anna to receive a scholarship so that she could continue her studies. Instead of pursuing further schooling, Anna's father apprenticed her to a tailor who made women's coats for the Petukhov clothing store in the heart of Moscow's fashionable shopping district. He chose this particular craft for his daughter both because he was a tailor and because garment workers who sewed women's coats made higher wages than many other needleworkers.[24] In other situations, children tried to influence what occupation their parents chose for them. In 1881, nine-year-old A. G. Iusim joined his father at a tobacco factory in Proskurov, Podol'sk province. For six years the child toiled next to his father, hating his job. Finally, when his younger brother was old enough to work in his place, Iusim begged his father to find him other work. His father agreed and apprenticed him to a village tailor.[25] In both of these

19 An apprentice sewing and a journeyman ironing. L. Nikulin and G. Ryklin, eds., *V staroi Moskve: Kak khoziainichali kuptsy i fabrikanty*, following p. 208.

cases, Platonova and Iusim had the talent necessary to become skilled tailors, but many parents chose to apprentice their children in the needle trades simply because there was an opening, not because their children showed any particular aptitude. These children, therefore, entered the trade out of obedience to their parents.

Once a position had been found for a child apprentice in a tailoring establishment, parents entered into a contractual arrangement with the master artisan. Both parties agreed to a specific length of time for the apprenticeship, ranging from two to six years; the average in the needle trades was four or five years. The master agreed to provide room and board for the apprentices, but parents frequently had to supply clothing. Once the contract had been concluded, parents left their offspring with the artisan and usually did not see them again until the end of the contract. The only apprentices who were able to see their parents at regular intervals were those who lived just a few blocks away, but they were few in number.

The central tenet of an apprentice's life was unquestioning obedience to the master. Apprentices fetched firewood, mopped the floors, stoked the fires in the stove, kept the irons hot, and ran errands for their masters. In small towns apprentices often had to bring the cows in from pasture.[26] Masters also used apprentices as babysitters for their children and for other domestic tasks. Although the chief purpose of an apprenticeship was to train future tailors and dressmakers, most apprentices did not begin their lessons until the last year of their contract. At that time, an adult worker would instruct an apprentice how to make the different parts of an outfit. Starting with fabric that had been discarded, they began by making sleeves, collars, and linings. A year was not sufficient time to master all aspects of the trade. As a result, apprentices usually finished their training with only a rudimentary understanding of the craft.[27]

Critics attacked this system of apprenticeship. They argued that apprentices were little more than servants performing menial tasks that no one else wanted to do. Because of their servile status, their living conditions were substandard. They were poorly fed and given little time to rest. Most apprentices slept in the workshops on the floor, on workbenches, or shared beds with other youths. At the same time, apprentices often fell under the influence of unsavory individuals. Adult workers exposed the youngsters to gambling, drinking, profanity, and sexual promiscuity. While running errands for their masters, apprentices became acquainted with the urban underworld of crime and prostitution. The masters were responsible for counteracting these negative influences by providing some form of general education or religious upbringing, but few did so. Some masters went even further and abused the power they wielded over their apprentices. Apprenticed to a Petersburg tailor in 1900, an eleven-year-old boy named Pirogov suffered numerous beatings from his master. The child ran away after a year, but his father forced him to go back to the same master where the beatings continued. Pirogov ran away again, but this time his father relented and found him a master who treated him better. In return Pirogov performed his duties well and displayed real talent as a tailor. As a reward for his hard work, the master took his apprentice with him to the theater. At the end of his four-year contract, Pirogov agreed to continue for another year.[28] This one young man had experienced the worst and the best of masters during his years of apprenticeship. Most masters fell somewhere between these two extremes.

Despite the barrage of criticism and calls for reform, this system of apprenticeship remained unchanged. The masters defended their treatment of the young trainees, arguing that they performed tasks that were essential to the success of any tailoring establishment. Since adult workers were busy sewing garments, this left the menial tasks to the apprentices. The masters claimed that there was not enough of a profit margin to provide better food or shelter, nor could they reduce their apprentices' exposure to vice and depravity. Despite all of the negative publicity, nothing was done to ameliorate conditions. The system of apprenticeship offered tailors an economical way to operate their business, and in exchange they were supposedly training a whole new generation of garment workers. Perhaps even more importantly, tailors argued that apprentices were a crucial component in the whole system of artisanal manufacture. This kind of specialized training,

no matter how undisciplined it seemed to outsiders, separated tailors from other kinds of workers. Apprenticeship served as a form of initiation into the craft and its particular way of life. This system had worked well for their fathers and grandfathers, and tailors saw no reason to change it.

## JOURNEYMEN

Upon completion of their apprenticeship, apprentices were either retained by their masters as adult workers or allowed to seek employment with another master. These young men and women entered into a new phase of their training and were now considered journeymen. The occasion was marked in the needle trades with a change in clothing. Instead of wearing home-spun garments including a short caftan tied in front and bast shoes, young men donned "city clothes" – trousers, shirts made from factory-produced cloth, and shoes. Peasant girls gave up their traditional clothing to wear the attire of young female workers in Europe. Having survived their initiation, tailors and dressmakers were allowed to don the clothes of their trade.[29]

Despite their change of appearance, journeymen's lives were little better than those of apprentices. Some received room and board from their employer, while others arranged for their own accommodation. Those who chose not to live at the workshop were paid more, but the additional income was usually not enough to pay the rent for a separate apartment, so most needle-workers rented a room or even a corner of a room.[30] For those who had no home except the workshop, they slept on workbenches, on filthy beds shared with other workers, or on the floor. In shops that employed male and female workers, owners did not attempt to provide separate sleeping arrangements. Furthermore, there were constant complaints about the food. Most journeymen subsisted on cabbage soup, bread, and tea. Although the law allowed for an hour's lunch break and a half-hour break for breakfast and tea, workers usually ate as quickly as they could in order to appease the owners who were constantly complaining about lost time.[31] In the bigger tailoring and dress shops, the public rooms where the owners met with customers

were clean and nicely decorated, but the workshops were overcrowded and dirty. A government inspector reported in 1897 that dressmaking establishments were always cleaner than men's tailoring shops, but workers in both complained.[32] At an exclusive women's dress shop in the Petersburg shopping arcade, Passazh, women workers ate their food in the basement with leaking pipes and garbage everywhere. Meanwhile, the workshop was in the attic. The low ceilings made the room stifling hot all year round and the owner forbade the women from opening the window because it would create a draft in the store.[33]

20 Ivan Bogdanov, *The Novice*, 1893. This painting depicts a drunken tailor scolding his young apprentice. The tailor has placed lithographs from the fashion press on his shop walls. *The Itinerants: Russian Realist Artists of the Late Nineteenth and Early Twentieth Centuries*, 5.

One Petersburg garment worker, S. Gruzdev, left behind a description of one of the city's most exclusive establishments, Kalina, located at 27 Bol'shaia Morskaia Street, in the heart of the city's fashionable shopping district. Leopold V. Kalina, an Austrian subject,

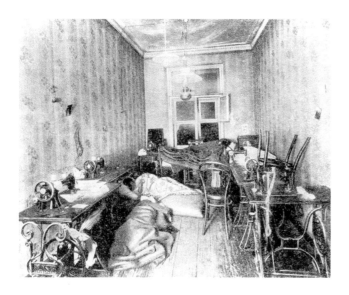

21 Garment workers sleeping on the workshop floor, 1890s. *Ocherki istorii Leningrada*, II: 209. Library of Congress Collections.

had come to Petersburg as a cutter for Ganri's, a firm patronized by the imperial family. Eventually, Kalina set up his own shop which had about twenty employees in 1905. Kalina's clients included the minister of finance, V. Kokovtsev, industrialists, brokers, and other members of Petersburg's financial elite. Kalina ran the shop himself but employed three cutters, a trimmings specialist, one salesclerk, and one individual who worked as a janitor and delivery boy. The workshop was on the second floor and consisted of three rooms and a kitchen. There were nine windows in the workshop facing the courtyard. During the evening hours two or three workers shared the light of one electric lamp. According to Gruzdev, there was no set lunch hour for workers, but they could either eat in the workshop kitchen or dine at some nearby cook shops and greasy spoons. Because of his firm's excellent reputation, Kalina hired only the best journeymen, who, in turn, lorded their position over other garment workers. Gruzdev claimed that when garment workers gathered on pay day at their favorite taverns, Zelenki and Strelka, the Kalina journeymen spoke only to each other.[34]

Despite these better than average working conditions, the Kalina journeymen shared the same problem with other garment workers – their dependency upon their employers. Masters were the sole authority in sewing workshops. Their orders were law. Even though journeymen were no longer apprentices, they had little freedom. The only option available to them was to quit and find another position. Furthermore, because journeymen had received so little training as apprentices, they depended upon the masters to provide them with on-the-job training during the early years of their employment. This required good working relations. As one female worker commented, "The owner is God for us before whom we tremble, as in a fever."[35]

Stories about the arbitrary behavior of employers toward their workers were legion, but a few examples will serve to illustrate the journeyman's difficult position. All garment workers complained about the crude language that owners used towards their employees. Gruzdev reported that Kalina would often be heard screaming at some unfortunate employee, "Oh, the devil take you, the work is spoiled again!" in his heavily accented Russian.[36] Another tailor arrived at his shop one day carrying a package. He flung a herring down on the workbench saying, "Here, fellows, I have brought you a salmon." One of the workers replied, "Uncle, that's not a salmon, it's a herring." The tailor became enraged and shrieked, "And you want to call my salmon a herring! Here's your passport and leave my workshop at once." The worker quickly responded, "Oh, I am mistaken. It's a young salmon. Please don't be angry, master." The apology appeased the tailor who allowed the worker to remain in his employ.[37] In one shop devoted to men's military uniforms in Petersburg, a group of journeymen, tired of their awful working conditions, asked for a meeting with their employer, Iakov Filippovich. The two sides met on a Sunday. The workers asked Filippovich for a shorter working day with a substantial break for lunch and supper, and better wages. He listened quietly to their demands. After the workers concluded, he went up to them and threw two gold five-ruble coins in their faces and sneered at them, "Here, this is for vodka, go drink and eat, and I will look over your demands and think about them." The workers returned on Monday having drunk ten rubles' worth of vodka and found the owner waiting for them. He agreed to shorten the workday by one hour but sought retribution by lowering wages. There was little else the workers could do but accept the new conditions.[38] In all of these examples, tailors exercised their authority in ways designed to highlight the power they held over their workers. Journeymen suffered this kind of humiliating behavior on a daily basis.

In addition to the tyranny of their employers, all adult workers suffered from the vagaries of the clothing trade. In the nineteenth century, there were two seasons when most individuals purchased new clothes. The Easter season began in March and ended in June, and the winter season continued from September until December. Once the seasons had passed, employers usually laid off almost all of their journeymen as there was not enough business to compensate them for their labor. This created a rather desperate existence for garment workers. During the season, they stitched day and night to complete the orders for new clothes. The working day usually began at 7 am and lasted until midnight or later. In the off season needleworkers were unemployed, hungry, and physically exhausted from their backbreaking work.[39] Unless they had saved money while they were working, they were forced to find other types of work to support themselves. The seasonal nature of the garment trades made it difficult to support a family except for those lucky few who kept their jobs in the off season.

The hiring and firing of workers was yet another way for employers to keep employees in line. Employers only retained the best and most compliant workers at the end of the season. One story illustrates how this system worked. Stepan Samoilovich Kitavin, a future leader of the tailors' union, worked at Ganri's. He was an accomplished journeyman, having sewed for Ganri for more than three years, but shortly after Easter he fell ill. At the same time, he found out that his parents were near death in their village far from Petersburg. It was imperative that he return home at once. Unfortunately for Kitavin, Ganri had a rule that no worker could leave the shop for any reason during the Easter season which ended on the feast of the Holy Trinity. Kitavin went to his employer and explained the situation. Ganri promised to pay his back wages when he returned to work. Kitavin left for his native village

and returned to Petersburg a few weeks later having recovered his health. When he showed up for work, Ganri said that he did not need him any longer and suggested that he come back during the winter season. When Kitavin tried to argue with him, Ganri shouted that he would never rehire him because of his insolence.[40] It was precisely this kind of treatment that so angered garment workers. In the early 1900s, a group of women summarized the feelings of all garment workers when they complained that "In the season we fade away from the never-ending work, and when the season ends, they chuck us out like squeezed-out lemons."[41]

The stress of the garment trades drove many male workers to drink. Receiving their wages at the end of work on Saturdays, they headed to the nearest taverns. Here they relaxed and socialized. Returning to the workshops on Monday completely hung-over, garment workers often paid apprentices to go out and buy more liquor which they could drink in the shop. In the 1920s, Grigorii M. Sokolinskii remembered that drunken workers sometimes asked, "What is it now, day or night?" Usually by Tuesday they had sobered up enough to work again. The phenomenon of "Blue Monday" was common across Europe and among virtually all occupations, not just tailoring. As a result, most owners tolerated the custom. Drinking was frequently the only pastime enjoyed by garment workers, and masters encouraged them to drink because it made for a more politically quiescent workforce.[42]

For a journeyman the only way out of these difficult circumstances was to become a master tailor or dressmaker, but to achieve that there was an important transitional stage. After considerable practice at sewing garments together, journeymen were taught the art of cutting by their masters. Before the development of proportional sizing systems, tailors had to learn how to take a piece of fabric and mold it to the contours of the human body. This took time and experimentation. Tailors and dressmakers would take a piece of paper, hold it up to a client's body, and make small notches to indicate certain measurements. They would then take the paper and place it on top of the fabric, tracing an outline on the fabric with chalk. These measurements did not require any mathematical or reading skills, but rather an eye for proportions. Tailors usually made patterns for most garment pieces which they could reuse, altering them to fit different clients. No two systems of measuring and cutting were alike, so it was essential for a journeyman to learn these "trade secrets" from a master, otherwise he would not have the necessary skills to become an independent artisan.[43] Journeymen who had mastered the art of measuring and cutting became known as cutters (*zakroishchiki*). Cutters were among the elite of the journeymen, and employers only selected the most talented for such positions. A good cutter saved his master significant amounts of money by learning how to cut fabric without any waste. Because of their importance to the business, cutters were usually male and the best paid of all garment workers. One source reports that they were paid two to three times what ordinary workers received. Foreigners and Russians who knew a foreign language were the best paid of all cutters.[44] Cutters were in short supply in Russia throughout the imperial period. And yet, despite their privileged position, they were still subject to the will and authority of their employers who could fire them for any mistake or act of insubordination.[45]

## MASTERS

The dream of every journeyman was to become a master tailor or dressmaker. All the misery that garment workers endured was part of the process of becoming a master. There were two ways to achieve this goal. The first was the official method as laid out in the 1721 guild legislation. Once a journeyman had acquired the requisite skills and years of service, he or she applied to the guild to sit an examination. If he successfully completed the test, the new master could set up a shop with a sign, hire journeymen and apprentices, and become a member of the guild. Historians agree that most tailors in Russia were not guild members primarily to avoid the taxes that members paid.[46] This led to a second, extra-legal process of becoming a master. When journeymen had saved up enough money to rent a room or ideally a few rooms, they simply left their employer and went into business for themselves.

Since there was little government regulation of artisans in imperial Russia, these individuals could work for years and not suffer any consequences because they were not licensed. In the second half of the nineteenth century when needlework courses and handbooks became very popular, it was common for women who had neither received any training as an apprentice nor worked as a journeywoman to set up a dress shop.[47] Since the quality of training was so poor anyway, it mattered little how individuals had acquired their skills, so long as they could serve the customers' needs.

There were several different types of tailoring and dressmaking establishments in Russia. The first consisted of a single tailor working alone or with his family. Most journeymen who became masters began this way. They rented a room or rooms which they converted into a workshop for meeting customers and sewing garments. It was relatively easy for tailors to equip their workshops. They needed few tools, just some pairs of scissors, a measuring tape, needles, and thread. Long rectangular tables were the only furniture in the workshops which the artisans used for cutting fabric and for sewing the garments. Male tailors sat upon the tables, cross-legged and barefoot, while dressmakers sat in chairs.

Having set up shop, the next important step for a master tailor was marriage. According to N. Matveevskii, writing about tailoring in the 1850s, artisans usually sought out partners who could bring financial resources to a marriage. In his 1857 book about tailoring, *Portnoi*, Matveevskii has his fictional journeyman, Vanya, meet an attractive domestic servant. They marry and, with her dowry, Vanya is able to rent larger quarters for his workshop. Tailors usually tried to rent two-room apartments so that one room could serve as a reception area for customers while artisans and their families lived in the other room. Rooms that had a window or door onto the street were the best. A tailor could hang a sign which could be visible from the street. Unlicensed tailors could not advertise so they usually chose rooms hidden from public view.[48]

If their business continued to grow, master tailors hired journeymen and apprentices to sew the garments. Hiring additional laborers did not necessarily mean that masters found larger quarters for their businesses.

Frequently the adult workers and apprentices lived in the workshop while the master continued to occupy the other room. The goal of masters was to separate public work spaces from their private lives.[49] Such a separation usually allowed them to join the ranks of polite society. The final step was for a master to set up shop in a retail-shopping district. This required considerable capital, especially for those who wanted to establish their businesses in the elite shopping districts. The owner of the I. I. Lidval' shop, a prominent tailoring establishment in Petersburg, constructed two gigantic stone buildings that cost more than six million rubles in the first decade of the twentieth century. The tailor Ganri arrived at his shop in an automobile.[50] Only a small number of artisans ever achieved this level of success.

At the very top of the trade of master artisans stood the designers. Instead of copying French or English patterns, these men and women created their own fashions. In Russia many of these designers were foreigners, but by the middle of the nineteenth century Russians began to compete with them. In the early years of the fashion industry in Russia, the designers were master artisans who without any kind of formal training simply had a special talent for creating new clothing designs. By the late nineteenth century, some designers had attended art schools or other specialized courses. The best-known imperial Russian designer,

23  A Petersburg tailor and his cutter measuring a client for a new suit in the Esders and Skhefal's store on the Moika Canal in 1908. Although the shop is clean, note the simplicity of the light fixtures and furniture. Central State Archive of Documentary Films, Photographs, and Sound Recordings of St. Petersburg.

Nadezhda Lamanova, attended the dressmaking classes of O. A. Suvorova in 1883. The following year Voit-kovich hired her as a designer for his shop in the exclusive Passazh shopping arcade in Petersburg. In 1885 the twenty-four-year-old Lamanova set up her own atelier. She was renowned for creating the perfect outfit for each of her customers. Like other great cou-turiers, she had never learned to draw. Instead she pinned the fabrics on her models, creating particular styles of dress. Her fashions were popular with the royal family, the aristocracy, and the intelligentsia.[51]

All masters faced the same challenges. They needed hard-working employees, sufficient capital to operate their business, a steady clientele, and an excellent reputation. While master tailors had the upper hand in dealing with their employees, they certainly did not when it came to their relationships with the customers. Tailors and dressmakers, like all entrepreneurs, were usually good at self-promotion, but they also needed a certain amount of tact and trust, particularly since they had to deal with flawed bodies and delicate egos. They came into intimate contact with the bodies of their

customers frequently in their dressing rooms and bed-chambers, which also required discretion. One poorly made garment or offhand comment could send a customer in search of a new tailor.

Money also complicated the relations between tailors and their clients. Most tailors extended some form of credit to their customers. Once the fabric and design of a garment had been chosen, a tailor purchased the necessary materials, sewed, and fitted the garment. Only after the last fitting did customers receive a bill for their garments, and since they already had possession of the clothes they were in no hurry to pay the craftsmen. Indeed, among the elite it was customary to pay tailors once every few months or even less frequently. Many members of Russian high society

24   The reception room in the exclusive Ganri tailoring shop in Petersburg. This elegant room has ornate furniture, chandeliers, and ceiling decorations as well as portraits of Nicholas II, Alexandra, and Alexander III on the walls. The shop counted members of the royal family as customers. Central State Archive of Documentary Films, Photographs, and Sound Recordings of St. Petersburg.

ran up a tab worth thousands of rubles with their tailors. In *Anna Karenina*, Leo Tolstoy's novel of aristocratic manners, the author lists the rules of behavior for men in the elite, one of which included ". . . that one must pay a card shark, but need not pay a tailor . . ."[52] And yet, few tailors could take measures against these delinquent clients.

25  A pair of elegantly dressed young men, circa 1900 in Petersburg. Men and women were both photographed with accessories, in this case a hat and cane. Private Collection.

Before the advent of magazine advertising, tailors and dressmakers were dependent upon word of mouth to bring in new customers. A bad word from a distinguished customer could cause other customers to flee, thereby permanently destroying a tailor's livelihood. Tailors believed that they had to put up with the cavalier behavior of their more prominent clients so that they could continually expand their business. If a dressmaker had too many non-paying clients, however, the business usually collapsed since there was no money to pay for rent, wages, or fabrics.

No one caught the complex relationship between master tailor and customer better than Nikolai Gogol in his short story "The Overcoat." Gogol's hero, Akakii Akakevich, is a poor government clerk. A lonely bachelor, Akakii is the butt of many office jokes for his peculiar ways and shabby clothes. One day, fed up with his old, patched overcoat which no longer protects him from the cold, Akakii pays a visit to his tailor. Akakii

cannot afford one of the well-known tailors whose shops line Petersburg's Nevskii Prospekt. Instead he heads to a run-down part of the city where his tailor lives with his wife on the fourth floor of a dark, filthy tenement. Gogol describes the one-eyed tailor in rather unflattering terms: "Initially he was named simply Grigorii and was a serf to some landlord. He began to call himself Petrovich after he received his freedom. At first he drank heavily only on major holidays, but then he included all church holidays and finally he drank on any day which was marked with a cross on the calendar."[53] Akakii arrives to find Petrovich sober and argumentative. He gives the one-eyed tailor his coat telling him that he wants him to repair it, but Petrovich refuses. Arguing that the coat is beyond repair, Petrovich tells the clerk that he will make him a new coat with a marten collar and silk lining for 150 rubles. After intensive negotiations spanning several months, Akakii agrees to let Petrovich make him a new coat for eighty rubles. Instead of a marten collar with a silk lining, Petrovich makes him an overcoat with a collar of cat fur and a broadcloth lining. The ever-wily Petrovich assures Akakii that cat fur looks like marten from a distance and the broadcloth was of the highest quality. With great ceremony, he helps the clerk put on the coat. Petrovich assures Akakii that he has received a great bargain: "Petrovich did not lose the opportunity to say that it was he alone who could make the coat so cheaply because he lived without a sign [meaning that he was unlicensed] on a small street and had known Akakii for a long time."[54] Akakii is so delighted with his new garment that he pays the tailor immediately and rushes off to work to show off his new coat. Petrovich follows Akakii to the office to admire his handiwork.[55]

Although Petrovich was an unlicensed tailor at the very bottom of the occupational hierarchy, his relations with Akakii Akakevich were typical. Tailors and dressmakers used their sewing expertise to try to convince their customers to spend more than they had intended by ordering new garments rather than continually repairing old ones. There were no fixed prices in custom tailoring because the price of the garment depended upon the fabric and decorative elements used. This meant that there was constant haggling over prices between artisans and their clients. While Gogol satirizes Petrovich's posturing and bombast at these moments, every artisan needed to develop a clear sense of when to stop and set a price, or otherwise the customer would leave the shop without placing an order. In his story, Gogol observes that all tailors scrutinize their clients' clothing carefully when they first enter a shop, but successful tailors scrutinized their characters as well. A seasoned tailor, Petrovich knows from his first encounter with the meek and mild Akakii that he will be able to convince him to order a new coat even if he walks away the first time. Repeat visits by a customer to a tailor or dressmaker for fittings allowed tailors to learn a good deal about their clients' characters. With just the right amounts of bluster and flattery, Petrovich lures Akakii into ordering a coat that he cannot afford. In the end, though, both sides are happy. Akakii has a new coat with a cat collar to keep him warm.[56] Petrovich has his money and a guarantee that his customer will return to him for his next clothing purchase. In real life, happy outcomes were vital if the business was going to survive.

Capricious customers made life difficult for master tailors and dressmakers, but there was another aspect of

26 A Petersburg couple, circa 1900. Both outfits suggest careful attention to fashion and grooming. This couple is so thoroughly Europeanized that nothing about their appearance identifies them as Russians. Private Collection.

the trade that also caused much concern. One main purpose of all artisanal crafts was to pass on the trade secrets from one generation to the next. Before literacy became widespread among the laboring classes, each master was supposed to share with his or her workers those ways of performing some skill that would enhance the finished product. In the garment trades, these secrets centered on the sizing of garments, but masters were loathe to share their secrets with their employees. Once garment workers acquired that information, they were no longer dependent upon their master. By prolonging their employees' period of dependency upon them, masters tried to eliminate potential business rivals. This was why the position of cutter was such an important and difficult one in the garment trades. Cutters worked closely with the masters and learned the art of measurement from them, but they frequently left their master to set up their own shop.[57] In an attempt to build up their business, some new shop owners actually publicized their previous work as cutters for rival firms.[58]

The competition to control trade secrets was most intense between Russian and foreign tailors. In the eighteenth century, foreigners had an advantage over Russian needleworkers because they were already well trained in making European fashions while Russian tailors were unfamiliar with the types of measurements necessary to make the clothes. As a result, foreign tailoring establishments acquired an immediate cache in Russia. If a Russian nobleman wanted a well-fitted outfit in the latest style, he went to a foreign tailor. Because foreign establishments were very successful, artisans continued to migrate to Russia throughout the eighteenth and nineteenth centuries. Most came to St. Petersburg and Moscow where they joined the foreigners' guilds which had been created in 1818.[59] In 1824 a survey of guild memberships revealed that one out of every four tailors in St. Petersburg was a member of the foreign tailors' guild.[60] In 1869, census officials reported that more than 37,000 garment workers plied their trade in the Russian capital. Of that number, approximately 4,500 were identified as foreigners, which meant that one out of every eight garment workers was a non-Russian.[61] While the number of foreigners began to decline in the late nineteenth century, they continued to dominate custom tailoring and dressmaking, much to the unhappiness of their Russian competitors. Some Russian artisans tried to take advantage of this preference for foreign artisans by giving their shops a foreign name, but sophisticated shoppers were not fooled.

Foreign tailors and dressmakers had an excellent reputation in Russia. They usually came to Russia with enough capital to set up shop in the fancy shopping districts of Russia's major cities. Their reception rooms were clean and tastefully furnished. The masters and their employees were well groomed, and treated their customers with politeness and respect. But most of all, they were known for the superiority of their clothes. With great care, foreign masters produced lovely gowns and suits that fitted properly and did not fall apart after a few wearings. This excellent service and quality came with a high price tag, however, as foreign artisans charged much higher prices than their Russian counterparts. Nevertheless, Russian high society paid these prices because they believed that the goods that they purchased were well made and in the style of the day.

Most of these foreign artisans came from western Europe – France, Germany, and Great Britain, while smaller numbers came from Scandinavia and central Europe.[62] In particular, German tailors became the focus of Russian tailors' envy and anger. If German tailors were clean, polite, skilled craftsmen, Russians were the opposite – unkempt drunkards who created cheap, unattractive garments. This prejudice against Russian tailors so angered one of them that he wrote a book defending his fellow craftsmen. According to Vasilii Riazanov, the chief problem with foreign tailors was:

> Their methods of workmanship give them an important advantage over the methods of the Russians. It is necessary to be fair to them. They invent a fashion. And then they create a variety of patterns quickly – they issue them monthly or sometimes within a week. But the main problem is that they do not share their method of learning with others. Many Russians learn their craft under the direction of a foreigner, live in his workshop with other journeymen and study for seven or eight years. They leave with good skills, accomplished journeymen, but without having learned how to cut a garment using a pattern like those which foreigners use. . . . They cannot devise a new fashion or cut a garment.[63]

After years of experimentation, Riazanov had created his own system of measuring and cutting, which he published in his 1847 pamphlet so that other Russians could compete with the foreigners for business.

Some foreign artisans tried to bridge the gap between themselves and their Russian counterparts. In 1849 Eduard Diederich, a member of the foreign tailors' guild, petitioned the Petersburg city government to establish an employment bureau for masters and journeymen which would be open to all garment workers. His goal was to foster a greater sense of com-

munity among artisans and raise skill levels by making it easier for masters to find qualified workers for their shops. The government turned down his request. In 1857 and 1867 he tried again, but each time municipal officials found a reason to dismiss his plan. By the mid-nineteenth century, the Russian government wanted to develop its own legislation governing artisanal manufacturing which did not include increasing the corporate power of the guilds in Russia.[64] For the most part, however, foreign artisans ignored the Russian complaints. Given their superior position within the trade, they could continue to withhold trade secrets and keep their Russian journeymen in the dark. Their segrega-

27  The tailor Lidke and his wife celebrating their silver wedding anniversary with family and friends. Lidke made suits for Nicholas II. For an occasion such as this, all participants came in their finest garments. Central State Archive of Documentary Films, Photographs, and Sound Recordings of St. Petersburg.

tion within their own foreign tailors' guild helped to ensure that this antagonism between Russian and foreign tailors persisted.

Rather than supporting measures aimed to break down these ethnic tensions, some government officials

28  A Petersburg couple, circa 1890s. Both the husband and wife evince grace and comfort in their elegant clothes. They are a model of respectability. Private Collection.

bringing in more profits. Their goods are of a much higher quality, so much so that the words, 'Russian and foreign work,' are used in society as a code, meaning bad and good work." Having observed foreign artisans for a while, Komarov concluded that the chief difference between foreign craftsmen and "hardworking" Russians was their level of education. Foreigners had some form of formal education, attended public lectures, organized private exhibitions, and published trade magazines to develop in themselves a sense of taste and refinement which carried over into their work. Komarov argued that it was essential to raise the educational and cultural level of Russian artisans, if they were going to compete successfully with foreign artisans. Although the proposal to establish Sunday schools was not acted upon, permission to publish a trade journal was. *Russian Artisan* (*Russkii remeslennik*) began publication in 1862. One of the magazine's chief target audiences were tailors, and it featured fashion plates and patterns in each of its issues.[65] Unfortunately, the low educational and cultural level of Russian workers persisted, and publication ceased in 1867. More serious measures were needed to help Russian artisans compete with the sophisticated and shrewd foreign artisans.

★　★　★

The early years of the fashion industry clearly demonstrate the mutually beneficial relationships that were developing between government officials, businessmen and women, and Russian consumers. For its part, the government laid the foundation for the new industry. It adopted European fashions for men and women as the dress code for the empire, and it helped provide the raw materials and labor for the industry by encouraging the manufacture of domestic textiles and the recruitment of foreign artisans to practice their trade in Russia. All of these measures were similar to those that governments in France, England, and the German states had implemented to foster the development of their own fashion industries. These policies would not have worked unless there were a significant number of entrepreneurs willing to take on the task of building an entire new industry, despite fluctuations in styles,

tried to improve the quality of work produced by Russian artisans. In 1858, N. K. Komarov, the head of the artisan administration in St. Petersburg, sent a petition to the city council requesting that it publish a magazine and establish Sunday schools for artisans. According to Komarov, "One of our most important industries – artisanal manufacturing – has been left at a completely unsatisfactory level or is to be found in the hands of foreigners. . . ." While describing Russian goods as poorly made, he argued that ". . . foreigners are the opposite of that. The trades concentrated in their hands are of a vast scale, requiring less work but insufficient capital investment, and fierce competition. While many of the contributions of these individuals to the creation of fashion in Russia are now lost to the historian, nevertheless, it was their unsung dedication that allowed the fashion industry to grow. Finally, consumers played a critical role. If urban Russians had continued to look at their clothing as simply a uniform, then their fashion industry would never have succeeded. But what began as government fiat before too long became the natural way for courtiers and urban residents to dress. While city clothes remained expensive, the purchase of one item or a whole outfit marked an individual as an active participant in Russia's modernization drive. Thus, in a very real way, the creation of the Russian fashion industry marked a sincere and sustained moment of cooperation between state and society.

While the success of the fashion industry was real, problems persisted. As we have seen, so long as foreign artisans continued to set up shop in Russia's big cities, it was difficult for the Russian fashion industry to become fully independent and self-sustaining. However, while guild and government officials were attempting to determine how to deal with this complex issue, a new threat to custom tailoring was emerging. By the nineteenth century, sewing was increasingly seen as a female skill. This gendering of sewing had a profound impact on the development of the fashion industry in Russia, as it did in Europe and the United States. It is to this story that we now turn.

# 2

# *The Gendering of Sewing in Russia*

IN 1893 THE MINISTRY OF FINANCE sent an exhibit of Russian manufactured goods to the World's Columbian Exposition in Chicago. These products could be found in two separate pavilions of the exhibition, the Manufacturing and Liberal Arts Building and Women's Building.[1] The first pavilion chronicled Russia's growing industrial might by displaying goods from most of its manufacturing sectors – textiles, metalworking, and chemicals, to name just a few. Each display included a brief history of the factory where the goods were made as well as statistics on the labor force, machinery, and raw materials needed for production.[2] In the women's pavilion, other countries had sent a large variety of goods made by women for display, but the Russian section included huge quantities of needlework and not much else.[3] With very few exceptions, Russian women's work was represented by all different kinds of needlework from simple items of clothing to elaborate embroidery and knitting. The catalogue omitted both industrial histories of needlework in the women's pavilion and statistics indicating how many women worked in the needle trades; there were just endless descriptions of the items on display.

The contrast between these two pavilions could not have been starker. In the manufacturing pavilion's display, women workers were included in the labor statistics but male nouns were used throughout the catalogue. As a result, male workers' experiences were universalized which had the effect of making invisible female workers' contributions to Russian industrialization. The Russian displays in the women's pavilion emphasized their labors in the home, convent, and schoolroom, not in a factory setting. The actual conditions of women's needlework were deemed too insignificant to describe for readers of the catalogue. While it chronicled the significant amounts of raw materials and machinery necessary for men to produce many of the factory goods displayed in the manufacturing pavilion, women needed only a few needles, thread, and fabric. Women's work, therefore, appeared at the World's Columbian Exposition to be pre-industrial, a throwback to earlier days and forms of manufacture, while industrial manufacturing represented the wave of the future.

Several levels of selective representation were present in the Russian sections of the World's Columbian Exposition, which reveals the paradoxical position that sewing held in Russian economic life. Even though both sexes worked in the needle trades, sewing had become coded as women's work. While the number of women involved in the needle trades in Russia was growing in the late nineteenth century, large numbers of men also made their living through sewing, but examples of male tailors'

29 (*facing page*)  Detail of a spencer, a woman's short jacket. Made in the 1820s, the garment shows the detailed handsewing required to make such a lovely garment. The State Hermitage Museum, St. Petersburg.

work had no place in either pavilion at the Chicago exposition. Furthermore, the Russian organizers delegitimated women workers involved in trades other than needlework by not displaying the goods they made, suggesting that such work was not worthy of publicity. As a result, the organizers chose to emphasize sewing as the quintessential work of women. Performed primarily at home, sewing could be part of a woman's housework. The needle trades saved women from having to enter the industrial sector and thereby preserved their role in the family. The Russian government wanted to display this romanticized, domestic role for women at the World's Columbian Exposition.

Sewing may appear to describe the simple act of working with needle and thread, but over the course of the eighteenth and nineteenth centuries it became much more than that, as the Chicago exposition so clearly demonstrates.[4] Anne Phillips and Barbara Taylor pointed out over twenty years ago, "Skill definitions are saturated with sexual bias. . . . Far from being an objective economic fact, skill is often an ideological category imposed on certain types of work by virtue of the sex and power of the workers who perform it."[5] The contested nature of sewing reflected the changing conditions in the needle trades as well as the continuing debates about women's role in Russian life. As such, the gendering of sewing played a critical role in the development of domesticity, the sexual division of labor in imperial Russia, and the fashion industry.

## RUSSIAN WOMEN'S EDUCATION AND VOCATIONAL TRAINING

The influx of western ideas into Russia in the eighteenth century brought a profound change in the lives of the nobility. One of the most important of these changes was a new role for aristocratic women. Russian noblewomen adopted western European forms of aristocratic sociability and dress. At the same time, this new visibility placed Russian noblewomen under the scrutiny of Russia's writers and publicists, who by the second half of the eighteenth century found much to criticize in the behavior of gentry women. In the satiric plays produced and performed in Russia, noblewomen were portrayed as lazy, illiterate, frivolous creatures who know nothing of life and spend hours primping and preening in order to dress in the latest Parisian styles. In Iakov Kniazhnin's play of 1790, *Eccentrics*, a mother describes her daughter in the following manner:

> . . . she is removed from all coarseness; and keeping herself aloof from everything, as our dignity requires, she knows neither how to sew nor to weave, leaving such occupations to common people; she dances like a peacock, sings like a nightingale, and knowing French like a Frenchwoman, she would like to forget her Russian; she retires at three o'clock, rises at twelve, and passes two hours at her toilet.[6]

This rather typical critique suggests that the obsession of noblewomen with European modes and mores had detached them from Russian life. Freed from any kind of labor by the expansion of serfdom during the eighteenth century, they could spend their entire day mimicking western European aristocrats.

In the Age of Enlightenment, this kind of female behavior and lack of education became intolerable, not just in Russia but all over Europe.[7] Aristocratic women's constant pursuit of pleasure allegedly interfered with their true goal in life that was now defined as wife, mother, and household manager. Writers representing diverse views such as the French Roman Catholic prelate François Fénelon and the philosopher Jean Jacques Rousseau argued that women must be educated to fulfill their "natural" roles in society.[8] This perceived need to educate women in a certain way has been linked with the development during the late eighteenth century of an ideology of domesticity in western Europe. According to this view, women's primary role was in the home. They were supposed to be models of Christian morality, pure and modest at all times. Their chief task was to provide a moral education for their children, a task for which they themselves needed a proper education. Women were also to be trained in the practical affairs of running a household. The only activity outside the home sanctioned for their participation was charity work. As a result, women's education focused on those subjects that were thought to enhance their moral purity and domestic role.[9]

In Russia, Catherine II (the Great) became the first important proponent of women's education. Influenced fourth year and which included "all women's handicrafts (*rukodeliia*) and work, i.e., sewing, weaving, knitting, cooking, washing, cleaning, and all other housekeeping services."[13] As one educational historian has pointed out, "It is clear from this [description] that in this section the girls were educated for a working life . . ."[14] These two sections of the Smol'nyi Institute represented the foundation upon which the education of Russian women was built.

This educational edifice was remarkable for its coherent philosophy of Russian women's domestic role. As one scholar has commented, women's education "would be vocational training to prepare mothers, wives, and housekeepers of the privileged classes."[15] This domestic agenda was further enhanced when the Empress Maria

31   After Giovanni Battista Lampi, *Empress Maria Fedorovna*, late eighteenth century. Oil on Canvas. 74 × 57 cm. The State Hermitage Museum, St. Petersburg.

30   Aleksei Antropov, *Catherine the Great*, before 1766. Oil on Canvas. 51 × 38 cm. The State Hermitage Museum, St. Petersburg.

in particular by Fénelon's writings on women's education,[10] she and her educational advisor, Ivan Betskoi, established in 1764 the Smol'nyi Institute for indigent aristocratic girls.[11] Her hope was to create a new breed of women, not slothful, ignorant fashion plates, but capable wives and mothers. The four-year curriculum devised to produce this new breed of women included religion, reading and writing, arithmetic, foreign languages, history, geography, dancing, drawing, knitting, and sewing.[12] The following year Catherine opened a separate section of Smol'nyi for daughters of the petty bourgeoisie (*meshchanstvo*). In addition to the abovementioned subjects, this section had a subject called housekeeping (*domostroitel'stvo*), which was taught in the

Fedorovna was placed in charge of women's education after Catherine's death in 1796.[16] Maria Fedorovna had been raised in a German princely family where she had been educated in the new ideal of domesticity before coming to Russia. She believed that women played a central role in the creation of family life through devotion to their duties as wives and mothers. Because she herself was involved in the arts, she advocated a strong arts program for women's education that included music, painting, and needlework. She also espoused the importance of charitable work for privileged women. Under Maria Fedorovna domesticity became the ideology that not only reigned at court but also governed women's education at large.[17]

What is clear from these first attempts to educate Russian women is that sewing was seen as fundamental to women's education. Under the rubric of sewing many different skills such as dressmaking, knitting, lace making, and embroidery could be taught, depending upon the perceived needs of the pupils. For example, Maria Fedorovna instructed school officials at the Smol'nyi Institute to train noble girls in all aspects of sewing, but to emphasize needlework such as embroidery and lace making. In the school for non-noble daughters, the emphasis was on clothing production.[18] Gentry families had serfs to make their clothes for them, and consequently they did not need to master the fine art of dressmaking, but non-noble girls were expected to make clothes for themselves and their family members. All girls who entered Russian schools were taught the basics of the needle trades, but the emphasis in the different schools varied based on the social profile of the student population.[19]

At the same time, sewing required certain traits that had become associated with femininity. A woman needed above all great patience to perform the exacting work necessary to knit or sew. Sitting quietly for hours intent upon her work, the female needleworker appears to the outside world as passive, modest, hardworking, and virtuous. Elena Rostopchina caught this connection between sewing and the virtuous woman in her poem "The Unfinished Sewing," written in 1839:

The hour when woman sews her modest seam
Brings silence, peace, and space for sweet reflection;
Far from the worldly crowd, she's sunk in contemplation;
Enjoys a rest from parties, carriage rides;
Her respite from the world, from visitors, from strife;
Then she may read her soul, may gaze upon herself.
Full work-table to hand, she sits at her round frame,
And stitches rapidly, absorbed in what she sews.[20]

Thus, sewing became a visible, outward expression of those moral qualities that defined women's femininity and domesticity, giving a tangible expression of feminine virtues. The seamstress was safe from the corruption and licentiousness of the public world of crowds and parties. In her home, her private sphere, she created peace and harmony through her work with needle and thread as well as providing clothing for her loved ones. As the new domestic ideology and its curriculum took hold in Russia, sewing and femininity became inseparable.[21]

In order to ensure that this vision of tranquility remained in the private sphere of home and family, the needle trades were in the process of being defined as a decorative craft, not as fine art. Beginning in the Renaissance and culminating in the eighteenth century, a division occurred between fine arts and decorative arts, between arts and crafts. In the Enlightenment mania to chronicle all human knowledge in a scientific manner, painting, sculpture, music, and literature were defined as "art," an activity mostly performed by men. "Crafts" defined the manual trades performed by men with simple tools and materials. As we have seen, practitioners acquired their skills through an apprenticeship to a master craftsman. "Female crafts," however, appeared to require little training, just a needle and some thread, and could be practiced as a hobby, while those who devoted their whole lives to learning the complex skills of their vocation could only practice "the decorative arts."[22]

The needle trades underwent a similar transformation in Russia. In the late eighteenth century, government officials chose the Russian term *rukodelie*, meaning handwork or handicrafts, instead of *shit'e*, the word for sewing, as the official title for the sewing courses in the schools. Originally *rukodelie* meant any kind of handwork performed by an artisan. During the first half of the eighteenth century, *rukodelie*, *khudozhestvo* and *remeslo* were used interchangeably to describe artisanal skills.[23] By the second half of the century, these words had lost some of their flexibility. *Khudozhestvo* was applied to the fine arts, especially after the creation of the Academy of Fine Arts (*Akademiia khudozhestv*) in Petersburg in 1757. *Remeslo* took on the meaning of manual trade, which now meant artisanal trades such as carpentry and smithing that required long years of apprenticeship to a master. Finally, *rukodelie* came to mean women's sewing and needlework.[24] In defining sewing as a separate category, women's needlework did not appear to threaten male prerogatives in either the fine arts or in the artisanal trades.

It is important to note that, according to the architects of the Russian school curriculum, sewing was supposed to occur in the privacy of the home and not in the workplace. Nevertheless, the skills that these young women were taught also served as vocational training for those who needed to work outside the home. Thus, government policy toward women's education found itself in a paradoxical position. While on the one hand the government wanted to educate women of all classes to be better wives and mothers, thereby keeping women in the domestic sphere, this same education provided vocational training for women to work outside of the home. Although these policies did not have dramatic consequences in the late eighteenth century because of the limited numbers of girls who received a public education, the inherent contradiction in these policies created problems later on.

The educational philosophy that declared sewing to be a major part of a young woman's education created a fundamental difference between men's and women's education. No single trade was required in any of the schools created for young men. Occasionally certain manual trades were taught as electives, but only when a special teacher could be hired to teach the trade and certainly not in those schools designed for boys from the privileged classes. Consequently, the vast majority of boys

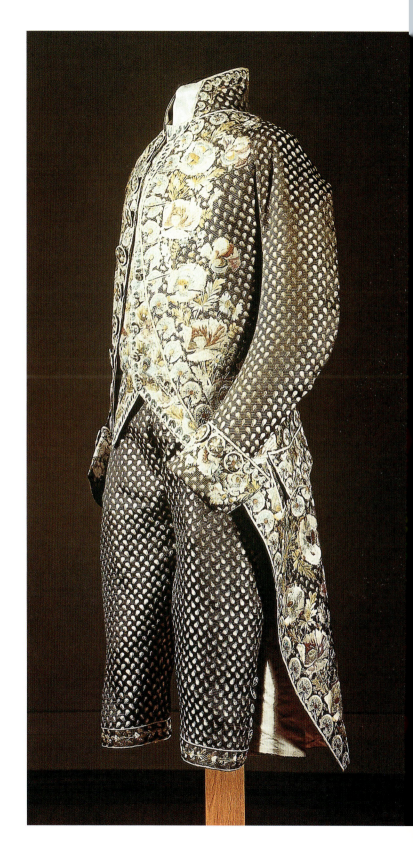

32   A suit belonging to Alexander I when he was a young man. The silk coat and vest are decorated with exquisite floral embroidery as was typical for men's court dress in the late eighteenth century. The State Hermitage Museum, St. Petersburg.

received their vocational training outside of the classroom. Young men who wished to learn a trade or craft apprenticed to an artisan who would teach them in a shop setting. Fathers taught their sons any other skills that were important for young boys to learn. This situation remained in effect until the creation of special trade schools for boys during the second half of the nineteenth century. There was no comparable craft to sewing as part of the curriculum in boys' schools.

Yet, despite these attempts to provide young women with training in household management, the girls' schools failed to win the support of Russian society. Parents criticized the aristocratic girls' institutes for not providing enough practical information about the running of households, while their daughters complained about the strict supervision and discipline that prevailed at the schools.[25] Perhaps Gogol summarized these views best when he described life on his imaginary gentry estate in his novel, *Dead Souls*:

Why, for instance, were the meals in the kitchen prepared so foolishly and haphazardly? Why was the pantry practically empty? Why was the housekeeper a thief? Why were all the servants so drunken and dirty? Why did all the household serfs spend most of their time sleeping and larking about? But all these things were too trivial and Mrs. Manilova was well brought up. And, as we all know, a good education is to be obtained in young ladies' boarding schools, and as we know, in young ladies' boarding schools, three subjects constitute the foundation of all happiness of family life: the French language, indispensable for family life, the pianoforte to provide agreeable moments for husbands, and finally, domestic science proper, such as the knitting of purses and other surprises.[26]

Once again, Russian noblewomen are portrayed as frivolous and silly creatures, but this time it is more explicitly because of their ineptitude as household managers.

As this quote also makes clear, serfs and other working women performed the real household work on noble

33   A nineteenth-century parade uniform for a member of the Emperor's entourage. The State Hermitage Museum, St. Petersburg.

34 A man's vest from the 1780s. Of Russian manufacture, the exquisite embroidery enlivens this white silk vest. State Historical Museum, Moscow.

estates as well as in the cities, but here, too, the efforts to educate non-elite women had also failed. With rare exceptions, female serfs did not receive a formal education of any kind. While Russian society may have accepted the idea that privileged women should be educated, the same cannot be said for the daughters of the lower urban orders. Government attempts to provide a public education for these young women petered out at the beginning of the nineteenth century with one important exception – charitable institutions.

## CHARITY AND YOUNG WOMEN'S EDUCATION

Russian charity began in earnest under Catherine the Great.[27] In order to emphasize the importance of public charity, most charities were placed under the aegis of the empress herself. After Catherine's death, Maria Fedorovna took charge of these organizations. Because she believed so sincerely in domesticity and in the role of women as the moral guardians of society, she encouraged other wealthy women to follow her example in participating in charitable relief work.[28]

The charitable institutions founded by Catherine the Great and Maria Fedorovna continued the educational program established for non-noble daughters at the Smol'nyi Institute. These organizations included public institutions for orphans and illegitimate children, such as foundling homes and private programs set up to help orphans and children of single parents. The foundling homes were established first, and Ivan Betskoi was their chief architect and administrator. Thus, the same individuals – Betskoi, Catherine the Great, and Maria Fedorovna – were involved in both women's education and charity work, which helps to explain why the same principles governed both institutions. Betskoi's plan was to take Russia's illegitimate children and make them into productive citizens.[29] In order to do this, the foundling homes were set up to provide these children with an elementary education and vocational training. Even when Maria Fedorovna modified Betskoi's scheme, those children who remained in the foundling homes continued to receive some education and vocational training.[30] What remained from Betskoi's original plan was the linking of education, vocational training, and charity. Maria Fedorovna further supported this view and made it a central tenet of Russian charitable institutions dealing with small children.

Charitable organizations of all different types were established in pre-reform Russia,[31] and of these the St. Petersburg Women's Patriotic Society was perhaps the most influential. In 1812 a group of Petersburg society women formed a charitable organization to help victims of the war with Napoleon and France. Initially they focused their efforts on assisting war orphans, which quickly developed into charitable efforts on behalf of all indigent

35  An eighteenth-century purse. State Historical Museum, Moscow.

children in St. Petersburg. Between 1813 and 1848, fifteen schools were established in every district "to provide general and vocational education for the population of the capital."[32] In addition to providing lessons in reading, writing, arithmetic, religion, history, and geography, the society trained the girls to work as seamstresses, dressmakers, knitters, and embroiderers. It began with only fifteen students, but by the 1850s between 450 and 500 girls attended classes each year.[33] The government was so pleased with the society's work that it became an imperial society and members of the royal family joined it.[34] Although the educational efforts of the Women's Patriotic Society were unusually successful, their program was similar to those offered by other charitable institutions.

What is striking about the efforts of Russian charities to educate indigent city girls is that the only vocational training that they offered was needlework, while programs for boys offered a variety of trades such as woodworking and metalworking. Although the schools for girls trained them in a variety of different needleworking skills, all of these trades involved the production and care of clothing, reflecting the domestic ideology that underlay the government's educational philosophy for non-elite women. Sewing was housework, an essential component in any woman's education, but especially for working women. Young girls needed sewing skills so that when they married, they could sew and mend clothing for their families. Russian orphanages, foundling homes, and shelters continued the government's gendered educational policy for non-elite children well before the development of public education in the 1860s and 1870s.

36    Examples of peasant women's needlework and clothing. The chemise, the sarafan, and the apron, made from homegrown flax and decorated with traditional Russian needlework, constituted the daily wardrobe of many peasant women. State Historical Museum, Moscow.

37  A fragment of a woman's skirt from the early nineteenth century. The embroidery represents the leaves and fruit of the mountain ash, a common tree found throughout the forests of Central Russia. State Historical Museum, Moscow.

There was another component in the agenda for women's vocational education within charitable institutions, one that had less to do with Christian acts of mercy and more with economic self-interest. During the first half of the nineteenth century, clothing styles were undergoing some important changes. Men's clothing was becoming more subdued in color and cut, and more uniform in appearance, while women's clothing was becoming more elaborate and the pace of change in fashions quickened. To help meet this growing consumer demand for fashionable women's clothing, Russian society women sponsored charity programs to train garment workers. Elite women could then either engage their protégées as seamstresses to work in their homes or as dressmakers to work in ateliers. In this way the interests of the government and the *beau monde* coincided very nicely. Russian society women could assist their government and perform their domestic and Christian duties by providing charitable assistance to the indigent, while these newly trained female garment workers could ful-

fill high society's desire for fashionable clothing. Since poor women were trained only as needleworkers and for no other trade, the Russian elite was assured of a plentiful supply of labor for some time to come. Once these seamstresses married, they could "supplement" the family income, when needed, through their home sewing. Thus, indigent girls' vocational education served to enhance their role in the home and in the workplace without doing violence to the domestic ideal that both the government and polite society espoused. While the numbers of young women who passed through these charitable institutions were not large, public attitudes toward women's work and toward garment workers in particular were taking shape.

Meanwhile, in 1844 this ideal of women's education received a further boost from the government. In that year women's schools were subdivided into separate categories, each with its own program. The purpose of this administrative reform was to provide young women with an education appropriate to their station in life. Wealthy, elite families could send their daughters to the institutes of the first category, where there was less emphasis on housekeeping and more on the social graces. Schools in the second category were for those children "who would return to families of limited means for survival and because of that they needed to spend more time learning the arts and needlework (*rukodelie*)."[35] Pupils in these schools included daughters of civil servants, professionals, and merchants. The third category included the public and private charitable institutions.[36] Girls from the laboring classes could attend the charity schools that trained them for a working life both in and out of the home. Despite the attempts of school officials to provide a caste education for young women, the philosophy that underlay these schools remained unchanged. Since all women were expected to become wives, mothers, and housewives, they must be trained in the domestic arts. And sewing, the quintessential domestic craft, remained a required subject in all girls' schools.

## SEWING AND THE "WOMAN QUESTION"

Between 1853 and 1856 Russia was engaged in the disastrous Crimean War against the Ottoman Empire, France, and Great Britain. Russia's army was no match for the new industrial might of England and France, and Russia's defeat precipitated a profound crisis in which members of the government, bureaucracy, and educated public began to speak openly about Russia's problems. The future of the peasantry, economic life, military preparedness, and the role of women in society were just some of the many issues raised in the days following the Crimean debacle. And while there was a sense of gloom about the general state of affairs, there was also a sense of guarded optimism that Russian society could transform itself into a more humane and productive nation.

It is no coincidence that the "woman question," as it was called, emerged just before the emancipation of the serfs in 1861. The noble way of life was based entirely upon serf labor. This was particularly true for noblewomen whose leisured existence depended upon legions of household servants, cooks, and nannies. Some of these gentry women, especially the young ones, felt a sense of guilt toward their serfs. They wanted to devote themselves to improving the lives of the peasants who had sacrificed so much for them. For other gentry women, the emancipation of the serfs appeared to bring an end to their leisured existence. If the serfs left their masters' service completely, it meant that there would be no income from agricultural products to help pay for the

38  An 1820s silk ball gown with gorgeous embroidery and beadwork. The State Hermitage Museum, St. Petersburg.

many expenses of a noble household, nor would there be anyone to work as servants in the urban townhouses and country estates of the elite. Thus, the emancipation of the serfs served as a direct threat to noblewomen's way of life.[37]

The discussion of the woman question began, not surprisingly, with another critique of elite women's education. Nikolai Pirogov, a doctor and educator, published an article called "Questions of Life" in 1856. Pirogov repeated the familiar criticism that young women were unprepared for their lives as wives and mothers. He argued that there was no more sacred duty than women's role as moral educators of their children, but they needed better education so that they could raise the new kinds of responsible citizens to govern a reformed Russia.[38] Pirogov's words, coming as they did from a private person and not a government official, stirred Russian society as no other words had. He called women to participate directly in Russia's rebirth through renewed devotion to their work as moral educators and as helpmates to their husbands. According to D. D. Semenov, a prominent educator, "This article revolutionized our views toward education. . . . It was read at court and in lowly apartments, it was read by high society ladies and modest housewives . . . Pirogov's ideal . . . made it necessary to ask ourselves what was the goal of our lives? What must we look for?"[39]

This rethinking of women's education did lead to reform, but one that was far less radical than many had hoped. Radicals like Nikolai Chernyshevskii, a writer, and Konstantin Ushinskii, a progressive educator, called for equal and identical education for both sexes. Conservatives simply wanted better training in the domestic arts, a position that was closer to Pirogov's own view of women being helpmates to men. In the late 1850s the government compromised and created two new types of women's schools: the Mariinskaia schools and the women's secondary schools (*gimnaziia*). Both schools provided better academic training than the old institutes, and graduates could receive teaching certificates at the end of their studies.[40]

Nevertheless, the government also affirmed its commitment to domesticity as the best way to train wives and mothers. The goal of the new schools was to train young women not just as teachers but also as wives and mothers. In other words, young gentry women were being trained to work both in and outside of the home just like women of the lower classes. The only difference in the two forms of education was that single women from the lower classes were supposed to work outside the home in those trades associated with the household, such as sewing, cooking, and laundering, while single women from the upper classes could teach. Upon marriage, women of all social classes were supposed to devote themselves to their husbands and children, and to the proper care of their home. As if to confirm this domestic agenda, sewing remained a required subject in all girls' schools.[41]

This combination of domesticity and academic training can be seen in the rhetoric of one school official's plea to the citizens of Kostroma to open a school for young women in 1856:

> You know that in a person's family life, good household management, Christian faith, peace, and happiness depend in large part upon the spiritual qualities of the housewife, on her intelligence and resourcefulness. The husband leaves for work every morning to earn a living and often returns home late in the evening. As a housewife, the woman spends her husband's wages with great economy. As a mother, she teaches her children the first moral rules of life. As a spouse, she thinks of what sweet words to greet her husband: Did his hard work tire him and cause wrinkles of unhappiness to furrow his brow? What a kind angel the family has in a woman! But you would agree that it is not possible to prepare her for this work without the proper education.[42]

Because many schools for young women were funded in part through private donations, a rationale for their existence that would appeal to a wide audience had to be offered. Government appeals such as this one demonstrate the importance of domesticity as the guiding philosophy, even in the new women's schools. Rather than being the retreat from domesticity that some had hoped for, the reform of women's education in the 1850s represented a renewal of the government's educational philosophy: Women needed to be trained as women.[43]

Public concern over women's education quickly evolved into a discussion of gentry women's desire to find meaningful work. If the Russian government believed that it had solved that problem by reaffirming women's domestic role with its educational policies, there were others in Russia who felt that other solutions must be found. And most of these other options involved women's participation in the paid labor force.

The person most responsible for bringing this issue to public attention was Maria Nikolaevna Vernadskaia, Russia's first female economist. Interestingly, she was not a product of the Russian educational system. Her father began her education at home, and her husband trained her in political economy. Together, she and her husband published *The Economic Index*, a journal that advocated *laissez-faire* economic policies for Russia.[44] In a series of articles published between 1858 and 1860, Vernadskaia tried to popularize her economic principles among educated women by writing about issues that would appeal to women readers. She offered these women a different role than that of dutiful wife and mother by advocating women's participation in the paid labor force as a direct path to emancipation and greater happiness. Paradoxically, sewing played a key role in her emancipation scheme.

According to Vernadskaia, Russian elite women frequently expressed frustration with their lives: "How often we hear women's complaints about their bitter fate. 'We are born for suffering! Men are forgiven everything, but for us the smallest mistake is made into a crime. Men are completely free, but we are slaves.'"[45] This slavery could best be seen in the mindless daily routine that most noblewomen endured. In words reminiscent of Gogol, Vernadskaia describes the life of upper-class women:

> First and foremost she must be well dressed, and in particular she must wear a corset morning, noon, and night (whether this is healthy or not is another question). Then she fulfills her daily requirements: playing the piano and singing, and afterwards the endless embroidering of useless collars. Why all this embroidery you ask? This is because women must always be at work, and sewing (*rukodelie*) is the most attractive of her duties . . .[46]

In this context, sewing represents the trivial nature of noblewomen's domestic lives. Embroidery is seen as merely a decorative craft rather than serving as mean-

39  This woman chose to add lace to her somber outfit. Central State Archive of Documentary Films, Photographs, and Sound Recordings in St. Petersburg.

ingful and productive labor, capturing the frustration elite women feel as their handiwork lies forgotten and useless, a symbol of the sterility of their leisured domestic life.

Part of the blame for this situation lay with upper-class women's socialization. According to Vernadskaia, men of all social classes grew up with the understanding that they must prepare themselves for a life of work. As a result, men developed habits conducive to work – they were dynamic, energetic, and chose careers for which they had some talent.[47] These images stood in stark contrast to the passivity and leisurely social gatherings that characterized most noblewomen's lives.

Vernadskaia takes this explanation a step further, however, and blames gentry women for their bitter plight: "Why is it that society women cannot work? The usual answer is that all careers are closed to women. They say that women cannot be anything but governesses and school monitors (*klassnye damy*). This accusation is not correct: the field of work, open to women, is very wide, but they do not wish to work upon it." She accuses gentry women of being ashamed to work for a living, finding wage labor a disgrace. She even tells the story of a woman who actually tried to hide her children's clothing business from others because of the social stigma attached to such work.[48] For Vernadskaia it is this social stigma that lies at the root of the problem.

Although Vernadskaia stresses that almost all fields of endeavor are open to women, she is the first to encourage educated women to seek employment as artisans. She argues that since physical strength was no longer a determining factor in many of the trades, women should be able to perform as well as men. Nevertheless, the trades that she identifies as suitable for educated women are not those performed by men but by non-noble women:

> Why should they not want to be artificial flower makers or dressmakers? Why do they run away from all such honest work that not only supplements income, but often even provides a decent living for lower-class women? But this is degrading work! Why is it? Why is it so shameful to make flowers, sew dresses, embroider, make lace caps, or look after children? Of course, it is more interesting to work in literature or fine arts, but what is one to do if one does not have the talent for working in such areas?[49]

This paragraph expresses Vernadskaia's complex economic vision for women. On the one hand, she appears to be arguing that talent, and not gender or social status, should be the sole factor in determining a person's occupation. Why become a painter if you cannot paint? However, even Vernadskaia appreciated the difficulty

women faced in choosing a career based solely on talent. Rather than leave her readers with this unobtainable utopian vision, she offers another possibility. In her writing she selects the needle trades and childcare, quintessential women's work, as her examples of honest work for noblewomen. In doing so, she is arguing that if respectable women chose to become needleworkers or childcare workers – tasks for which women had received some kind of training – this would raise the social prestige of this work in the eyes of society. Furthermore, Vernadskaia suggests that more men might be willing to marry seamstresses if more respectable women engaged in such work.[50] In other words, Vernadskaia is attempting to legitimate the work that women perform in the marketplace so that these trades would carry with them the same social status as literature or painting.

The difficulty with Vernadskaia's emancipatory scheme is that it reaffirms sewing as women's work. Rather than pursuing her view that all kinds of work were open to women, she retreats from the radical implications of that argument, which would have undermined the fundamental assumptions upon which gendered notions of work were based. Instead, she tries to make women's work more respectable by opening it up to women of all social classes. Thus, Vernadskaia's ideas end up supporting gendered notions of work rather than challenging them. Women should pursue those occupations for which they have talent, and for Vernadskaia that means especially the needle trades which women should perform not just to keep busy but also for wages. Additionally, while she is aware of the social dimension of the issues she raises, Vernadskaia does not try to critique the ideology of domesticity that underlay gendered notions of work.

Nikolai Chernyshevskii took up Vernadskaia's themes and gave them a new twist in his novel, *What Is to Be Done?* Published in 1863, Chernyshevskii's book created a sensation by introducing Russian society to a truly independent woman, Vera Pavlovna. While much of the novel's popularity with the reading public centered on Vera's complicated love life, her attempts to join the paid workforce also provided many Russian women with further thoughts on emancipation through work.

Part of the book's appeal was that Vera's childhood and adolescence were typical for girls of her social rank. At age twelve she was sent to boarding school and upon graduation she returned to her parents' house to prepare for marriage. However, when faced with an arranged marriage to a man she loathed, Vera broke free of society's constraints and contracted a fictitious (that is, unconsummated by mutual consent) marriage with her brother's tutor whereby they pledged to treat each other as equals. Once married, Vera set up a dress shop that was run cooperatively by all of the needleworkers. Her shop proved so successful that two others were established by the novel's end. Meanwhile, Vera Pavlovna decided that her work as a dressmaker was not satisfying enough, and so she embarked on a career as a medical doctor.

While Vera's activities after marriage establish her as a new woman, her sewing skills establish her as a real woman in the eyes of the reading public. At the very beginning of his story, Chernyshevskii tells us that Vera is an excellent seamstress – at age fourteen she sews the clothing for her entire family.[51] Where Vera learned her sewing skills remains a mystery, however. Her two years of sewing lessons at boarding school could not have provided her with the necessary instruction to make an entire wardrobe for her family. Moreover, her school lessons would not have included instructions in making men's clothes for her father and brother. By failing to indicate who her instructors were, Chernyshevskii's description suggests that Vera knows how to sew simply because she is a woman. Either she was born knowing how to sew or the process of learning to sew was so easy that no apprenticeship was necessary. Consequently, Chernyshevskii reaffirms women's work as a separate category. Men must spend years learning their job skills, but women are born with theirs.

While Vera was not a real person, Chernyshevskii's depiction is important because of the way in which sewing became a trope for domesticity and women's work in the novel. His choice of sewing for his utopian model reveals the complex ways in which sewing could represent both the positive and negative aspects of domesticity. As we have already seen, sewing was women's work most closely associated with female virtue and the domestic sphere. In setting up a dressmaking cooperative, Vera tries to take those virtues associated with women and family life, and apply them to the world of work. Vera's workers live and work together in harmony.

Complete cooperation governs the workshop and dormitory where the needlewomen and their families live, not the rough and tumble of unregulated, individualistic competition in the marketplace. Drawing upon the work of French utopian socialists like the comte de Saint-Simon, Chernyshevskii is proposing that the family values associated with the domestic realm – peace, harmony, and cooperation – usurp the masculine values of the marketplace in Russia's search for a better way of life.[52]

At the same time, Chernyshevskii's emphasis on these domestic virtues and their association with women serves to reinforce the importance of domesticity and the very notion of women's work. All he is doing is taking women's work and the values associated with it out of the home and into the male-dominated workplace. Vera maintains a fundamental connection with the domestic ideal and the virtues it represents through her work as a dressmaker. While this domestic ideal applied to the workplace is held up as a model for the future, none of the male characters ever participates in this new kind of work. It remains women's work, a separate category.

Thus, the proposals for women's emancipation through labor-force participation, which seemed quite radical in the 1850s and 1860s, are not quite as liberating as they first seemed. Vernadskaia and Chernyshevskii, each from their own particular vantage point, argue that elite women should end their status as men's slaves by finding meaningful work in the labor force. For both authors the needle trades best represented work well suited to women's supposed talents. The irony of this solution for women's emancipation is apparent. Noblewomen could now join the thousands of working-class women who were already employed in the needle trades in an attempt to make such work respectable. And yet, this discussion only reinforced the fundamental gendered notions of work that already existed, but now such notions had received the support of Russia's radical intelligentsia.

Chernyshevskii's choices were particularly important because his novel served as a guidebook for young women seeking greater freedom and happiness in Russian society. After the novel's publication, many young women who had either read it or knew about it fled their parental homes either on their own or as a result of fictitious marriages, and came to Russia's big cities in search of work. A number of them attempted to set up sewing cooperatives like Vera Pavlovna, usually with disastrous results.[53] The ease with which Vera set up her dress shop proved to be a poor model. Most of these young women were ill-prepared for the rigors of doing business in Russia. Furthermore, the needle trades were undergoing a profound transformation with the introduction of the sewing machine into Russia in the 1860s. Mechanization now challenged the needle trades.

## THE SEWING MACHINE

The sewing machine was one of the great inventions of the nineteenth century and became the first machine produced for the consumer market. It allowed large numbers of garments to be produced more rapidly and more uniformly, saving needleworkers from long, tedious hours of hand sewing. After many legal battles over patent rights among the machines' many American inventors,

40  A pre-revolutionary Singer sewing machine still in use. Private collection.

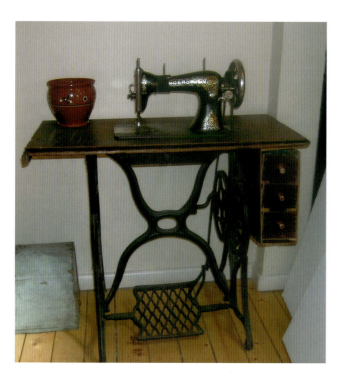

the first practical sewing machines for the home were introduced in the United States in 1851.[54]

Despite the obvious advantages that the sewing machine presented to home sewers and needleworkers, the manufacturers needed to develop marketing strategies to convince consumers that they should buy the machines. The I. M. Singer and Company first developed these marketing techniques in the United States. Singer introduced installment buying, monthly rental plans, and targeted respectable women for its advertisements. The company was famous for organizing special demonstrations to lure potential customers. At these demonstrations, women sales representatives operated the machines, proving beyond a doubt that women could own and operate a sewing machine. Singer also developed an extensive sales and repair network in the United States and Europe, so that if a machine broke down a company representative could quickly make the necessary repairs. As a result of these marketing strategies, the sewing machine became a symbol of middle-class respectability in the United States and Europe.[55]

The first sewing machines were imported into Russia shortly after they were introduced to the European markets. Because sewing machines were manufactured in the United States and England, Russians had to buy them from foreign agents of the American companies. In 1859 one of Singer's agents sold over three hundred machines in Russia.[56] In 1861 sewing machines were exhibited at the Russian Industrial Exhibition held in St. Petersburg. Demonstrations of the machines' capabilities delighted the crowds who attended the exhibition.[57] In 1863, the J. Block Company imported machines from all the major sewing-machine manufacturers and began selling them on the Russian market.[58] The company that experienced the greatest success in the Russian market was the Singer Sewing Machine Company.[59] The marketing strategies used by I. M. Singer so successfully in the United States were employed in Russia, although they were introduced more gradually. This incremental approach paid off. By 1914, Russia was the second-largest market for Singer sewing machines outside of the United States.[60]

Respectable women of the middle ranks were the first targets of the campaign to get Russian women to buy sewing machines. The problem that sewing-machine

manufacturers faced was that these women were not supposed to handle machinery. Nineteenth-century Europeans looked upon machinery as part of a man's world, but Singer executives decided that the sewing machine should be different. Although male tailors were the chief users of the first sewing machines, manufacturers had set their sights on creating a home market for their invention. Their task then was to link the sewing machine with the domestic world of women.

One example of this advertising campaign in Russia can be found in a catalogue published in 1868. It contained a translation of a German pamphlet written by Klara Walter, entitled "Notes From a Wonderful Composition, 'The Sewing Machine, Its Use and Meaning.'"

41   A crowd gathering in Petersburg to watch a live demonstration of a Singer sewing machine in the Zagorodnyi store. Central State Archive of Documentary Films, Photographs, and Sound Recordings of St. Petersburg.

Walter begins by establishing the primacy of women's domestic role: "The meaning of woman is to work and participate in domestic life. All other kinds of participation in the arts and literature, in industry and manual trades, are more or less always located outside her sphere . . ."[61] Having determined women's proper place in society, Walter then goes on to bemoan the failings of younger women who find domestic work tedious:

42   Made at the Joséphine Brousy shop in Moscow in the late 1870s, this gown combines machine-made lace with the exquisite hand-done embroidery on the skirt, train, and jacket. State Historical Museum, Moscow.

The slowness of the work causes young women to become bored and this cannot be allowed to exist in the age of steam engines and telegraphs in which the tempo of life is much faster for us than it was for our grandfathers. . . . The main fault lies in the very slowness and difficulty of sewing. This is why our daughters do not find pleasure in housework and why they would rather busy themselves with trifles, play the piano, and ruin their eyesight with childish embroidery rather than with useful housework like sewing their own clothes and other household items. This is why they generally do not have any love of housework which young men often look for in their future wives. It is rare now for a young person to know the pleasure that our grandmothers felt – the sewing

of their dowries that gave them such pride and honor.[62]

In this passage, Walter tries to make sense of the gap that she believes exists between mothers and daughters. The problem lies in the very nature of women's work. Why would young women born into the industrial age want to participate in preindustrial work? The pride and sense of accomplishment of handsewing is not enough for these modern young women. They want to be active participants in modern life just like their brothers.

The solution to this generational conflict lay in the purchase of a sewing machine. The sewing machine modernized domestic work by taking the tedium and long hours out of sewing, and at the same time it allowed women to become full partners in the modern industrial age. The advantages of the machine were enormous, according to Walter. Women with large families could prepare their daughters' dowries, housewives could use the machines for all sorts of household tasks, and widows could support themselves and their daughters through their needlework now performed on the machine. Walter rhapsodizes:

There is not any kind of sewing in which a single or married woman could not perform on a sewing machine. And if they must spend their last penny to purchase a machine, then they will gladly make such a sacrifice because the machine will bring in abundant profits and quickly pay for itself. A good sewer can earn two to three rubles a day by herself, but with the help of her mother, sisters, and friends more than twice that amount. Where can they find such profitable, and in addition, such pleasant work?[63]

Financial concerns are at the heart of this particular advertising campaign. According to Walter, the sewing machine provides a form of salvation for respectable Russian women. After the emancipation of the serfs, noblewomen were concerned about household expenses and their daughters' dowries. Widows constantly needed to provide some sort of income for themselves and their families. In a classic example of capitalistic reasoning, the purchase of a sewing machine could alleviate all of these financial anxieties. And better yet, this work could be performed in the privacy of a woman's home working with her female relatives, thereby preserving the primacy

of woman's domestic role. In these complex ways the sewing machine served to assist women with their household chores by saving them time and money, but at the same time women could give up their preindustrial mode of work and participate in the age of the machine. Thus, the sewing machine in Russia served as a symbol of domesticity, respectability, and modernity all at once.

Once the sewing machine came to represent modern domesticity, it very quickly became a powerful symbol in Russian cultural life. One example is the painting by D. E. Zhukov entitled *He Failed* (1878). Zhukov painted the moment after a young mother discovers that her son has failed his examinations. Everything in this painting suggests that the family is part of respectable society. The old woman standing in the doorway is the family servant. The room is well furnished with family portraits on the wall, a clock, and even a dog. Equally prominent in the painting is the sewing machine. Here the machine reinforces the domestic virtues of the young mother. Working as hard as she can by sewing at home, she saves all

43 D. E. Zhukov, *He Failed*. From *Zhivopisnoe obozrenie*, No. 35 (1878), 140. Library of Congress Collections.

her money to send her oldest son to an excellent school. The utter disappointment of his failure can clearly be seen in her face. Her sacrifices have been in vain. In this painting, the sewing machine helps to establish that this woman is a modern, hard-working, devoted mother who wants the best for her family. Her son's failure threatens her dreams for a better life.

## SEWING, PROSTITUTION, AND VOCATIONAL TRAINING

Writers, too, used sewing and the sewing machine as a symbol of the redemptive power of modern, domestic work for women. By the mid-nineteenth century, there was already a serious tradition in Russian literature that connected sewing and prostitution. In western European fiction and sociological literature, the seamstress was a stock figure of the woman who had fallen into prostitution.[64] In Russia, writers reversed this stereotype and frequently portrayed prostitutes as becoming seamstresses after they have been rescued from their life of ignominy.[65] Chernyshevskii included a rehabilitated prostitute as a seamstress in Vera Pavlovna's workshop in his novel *What Is to Be Done?*, as did Gogol and Dostoevsky in many of their masterpieces. Perhaps the best example comes from Anton Chekhov's short story, "An Attack of Nerves." The story, published in 1888, involves a student named Vasilyev who wants to "save" the prostitutes whom he meets one night in Moscow. Having considered the problem, Vasilyev concludes:

> "All these not very numerous attempts [to save prostitutes]," thought Vasilyev, "can be divided into three groups. Some, after buying the woman out of the brothel, took a room for her, bought her a sewing-machine, and she became a seamstress. And whether he wanted to or not, after having bought her out he made her his mistress. . . . Others, after buying her out, took a lodging apart for her, bought *the inevitable sewing-machine*, and tried teaching her to read, preaching at her, and giving her books. The woman stayed and sewed as long as it was interesting and a novelty to her, then getting bored, began receiving men on the sly. . . . Finally, those who were most ardent and self-sacrificing took a bold, resolute step: they married the woman. And when the insolent and spoiled, or stupid and crushed animal became a wife, the head of a household, and afterwards a mother, it turned her whole existence and attitude to life upside down, so that it was hard to recognize the fallen woman afterwards in the wife and the mother. Yes, marriage was the best and perhaps the only means."[66]

Nineteenth-century Russians like other Europeans believed that prostitutes had rejected domesticity when they became prostitutes. They referred to prostitutes as "public women," women who had rejected their role in the private sphere as dutiful wives and mothers. In turn, sewing functioned discursively as the leading occupation of rehabilitated prostitutes because public women returned to the private sphere of the small rooms and apartments their saviors rented for them in order to work as seamstresses. Although Chekhov's character, Vasilyev, appears to be arguing that marriage alone could truly reform these public women, nevertheless, the purchase of a sewing machine, the leasing of a room, and work as a seamstress clearly marked a step back into the private world of the home and toward a more proper domestic role for these women.

The return of public women to their proper place in society was a great concern for many educated Russians during the second half of the nineteenth century because the government's industrialization program begun in earnest after the Great Reforms of 1856–81 brought with it terrible social dislocation and poverty for thousands of ordinary Russians. Many peasants in search of work and a better life came to the cities but found instead irregular employment and inadequate housing. While some women turned to prostitution to try and earn enough money to survive, other women eked out a living doing whatever work they could find – domestic service, sewing, laundry – anything to provide life's necessities for themselves and their families. Although the numbers of women migrants were smaller than the large numbers of men migrants, particularly during the early years of industrialization, enough of these women were present in cities to cause educated Russians to view them as a social problem.[67] In order to alleviate the desperate conditions in which many lower-class women lived, government officials and members of educated society devised vocational training programs. Not surprisingly, the vocational training identified as essential to working women's survival centered on the needle trades, and the venue for this training was once again the schools.

## SEWING AND ELEMENTARY EDUCATION FOR GIRLS

Education played a key role in the government's plan to create a modern state. All Russian subjects were to receive an education designed for their station in life. For the children of the lower classes, this meant limited instruction in reading, writing, and arithmetic. In addition, these children were taught to serve God and

Country with deep devotion. This philosophy informed the Primary School Statute of 1864 and all subsequent legislation dealing with primary education.[68]

With the introduction of primary education in 1864, the statute's architects reaffirmed the importance of a domestic education for all girls who attended elementary schools. Although the curriculum in the girls' primary schools was virtually the same as in the boys' schools, the domestic agenda was achieved by making sewing a required subject for all female pupils. The sewing instructors in the primary schools were the regular classroom teachers, who in turn had learned how to sew while attending the women's high schools and institutes. Thus, by 1870 sewing was mandatory for all female students attending primary and secondary schools.

With the decision to make sewing a mandatory subject, the Russian government initiated a profound shift in power relations. The schools now took over a mother's control of her daughter's education. It was the government, and not other women, who would determine what constituted appropriate vocational and intellectual training for women. Yet, this same government denied women a voice in policy decisions that now defined domesticity and how it was to be taught in the schools. The educational transfer of power started by Catherine the Great was now complete.

For those young working women who failed to attend the newly established primary schools, a number of concerned Russians opened up private and public charitable institutions during the second half of the nineteenth century.[69] The purpose of these institutions was to provide poor women with the necessary sewing skills to support themselves and their families. Hundreds of sewing schools and workshops were established between 1860 and 1914 to train indigent girls and women to sew, knit, embroider, and make artificial flowers and hats.[70] Sometimes these schools and workshops also taught their pupils reading, writing, and arithmetic, but the primary emphasis was on vocational training. The history of one Moscow workshop was typical. When the Moscow municipal government set up poor-relief agencies, members of the city government decided that in addition to financial assistance they would provide work whenever possible. To accomplish this, they encouraged M. N. Ermolova, a lady-in-waiting at the court, to establish

a sewing workshop for indigent women. Initially, the women sewed at home, but eventually private teachers were hired to instruct their students in a new workshop. This workshop was deemed particularly useful because it taught "a woman, wanting to work at her place of residence, how to earn a living wage during hard times."[71] The purpose of these workshops was to train women needleworkers, who could earn additional income while taking care of their families at home. Thus, these charitable organizations attempted to protect the role of lower-class women in the home.

Although most of the sewing schools and workshops were intended for poor women, some were created to provide vocational training for respectable women. But here too, these schools shared the same philosophy as the other vocational schools, despite the difference in the students' social profile. One of the best-known schools was begun by the Society for the Dissemination of Practical Knowledge Among Educated Women. Founded in 1888 by members of Moscow's educated elite, the society's purpose was "to disseminate practical knowledge on household management both for supplying mothers with the possibility of improving their families' lives and for their own material well-being through work."[72] The society went on to establish a dressmaking school, a millinery school, a fine needlework school, a drawing and design school, a teacher training program, a culinary school for housewives, and other programs too numerous to list. The students came from all over central Russia to attend classes, and most students were daughters of the nobility, civil service, merchantry, and the petty bourgeoisie. By 1910 seven thousand students had attended the society's courses, the vast majority of students being enrolled in the needlework program.[73]

Members of the Russian educated elite, who were firmly convinced of the efficacy of domestic pursuits for women, established these private schools and workshops. Their goal was to educate both elite and non-elite women to become better mothers and household managers. By providing this alternative approach to vocational training, these schools were undermining not just the traditional relationship between mother and daughter but also the old artisanal system that had trained dressmakers and seamstresses. The participants received their training not from masters certified by the guilds but

44   The court dress worn by Grand Duchess Maria Fedorovna, wife of Alexander III in the 1860s. The gown is made of velvet, white satin, swan feathers, and silver thread embroidery. State Historical Museum, Moscow.

from teachers who were certified by the state. Furthermore, the purpose of the vocational training was not to prepare women to work in factories or workshops but rather to work alone in their own homes. These women were expected to perform housework, not regular wage labor. As one commentator put it rather succinctly, "Women work for the family and in the family!"[74]

★   ★   ★

The gendering of sewing had a profound impact on imperial Russia. Not only did it play a role in defining domesticity, it also marked the beginning of the deskilling of the garment trades. Skill acquisition, which formed the fundamental bond between master and apprentice, was broken. What used to be "skilled" work became "unskilled."[75] The result was a loss of status for the work performed and, inevitably, the lowering of wages. In the case of sewing, instead of private capital acquiring control of knowledge, the government attempted to control women's needlework through its agent, the schools. By insisting that all women must learn how to sew, government officials with the support of the educated public universalized sewing as a female skill, undermining the very concept of skill. Skill was supposed to be something that very few people possessed – it was scarcity that made it valuable. By mandating sewing as an essential part of every woman's education, government and society devalued the needle trades. There could be no prestige in a craft that all women knew how to do.

The implications of this profound change in the needle trades were deeply troubling for those women who needed to earn more than a few extra rubles from their sewing. First of all, it meant that society as a whole no longer valued women's needlework. Work performed in the home was categorized as unskilled. In fact, many did not even consider needlework to be work. Sewing was part of women's domestic duties – housework, not real work. Because there was such a vast pool of women needleworkers, employers no longer paid them as skilled artisans. Women needleworkers received wages comparable to other unskilled or semi-skilled forms of work. This decline in wages made it impossible for women to make a living wage in the needle trades. The decline in their wages also made it difficult for them to protest about these inequities. Employers could easily fire women who demanded better wages because there was a large pool of replacement workers desperate for work. Finally, the devaluation of the needle trades, which was the end result of the gendering of sewing, created, in turn, opportunities for manufacturers to develop a new form of clothing manufacture – ready-to-wear.

65

45　A Petersburg sewing workshop in 1905. Although the workshop has been cleaned up for the photograph, there is still thread lying on the stained floor. The sweatshop workers are wearing the simple blouses and dresses that Russian ready-to-wear firms produced in abundance. Central State Archive of Documentary Films, Photographs, and Sound Recordings of St. Petersburg.

# 3

# The Rise of Ready-to-Wear

EUROPEAN INDUSTRIALIZATION conjures up images of huge factories belching soot and other pollutants into the atmosphere. Inside these cavernous buildings overworked and undernourished laborers tend noisy, dangerous machines. These Dickensian landscapes have dominated our understanding of industrialization and its consequences for a long time, becoming the lens through which all industrialization is seen. And yet, artisanal production did not immediately give way to the factory system, but existed alongside it.[1] The old artisanal trades adapted to the new conditions, introduced new forms of mechanization and rationalization, and competed for customers as they had always done. No better example of this can be found than in the garment trades. Over the course of the nineteenth century, custom tailoring and dressmaking began to compete with a new branch of the clothing business, ready-to-wear. As the name suggests, ready-to-wear clothing was prefabricated. Customers could go into a shop and buy a garment "off the rack." To produce these garments in sufficient quantities, clothing manufacturers created a new system of production whose centerpiece was the sweatshop. In hot, overcrowded garrets all across Europe, garment workers created inexpensive copies of the latest fashions. While *haute couture* remained the preserve of high society and the *demi-mondaine*, ready-to-wear allowed the middle and lower classes to buy fashion goods. Fashionable dress became something to which everyone could aspire and this, in turn, allowed the fashion industry to expand its influence significantly.[2]

Ready-to-wear played a central role in Russia. By the middle of the nineteenth century European custom tailoring and dressmaking had become well established. It was precisely at this moment that the government introduced a series of reforms that expanded the market for fashion. Anyone who lived in urban areas and even peasant migrants needed "city clothes." Manufacturers quickly saw the benefits and potential profits of being able to meet this new demand. Once again, the government, foreign entrepreneurs, and Russian businessmen cooperated to harness the raw materials, labor, and technology to create a ready-to-wear industry whose goal was to dress every Russian subject in inexpensive copies of European clothing.

At the same time, government officials and the educated public renewed their discussion of women and work in the 1880s, focusing their concerns on plebeian women. The Russian industrialization drive was beginning to have a profound effect on working-class and peasant life. How were these women coping with the challenges they faced? What could the government or the educated public do to preserve plebeian family life? The results of these debates coupled with the introduction of ready-to-wear led to a crisis in the garment trades by 1900.

★ ★ ★

Sweating is the term used to describe a system of sub-contracting that developed in the traditional artisanal crafts during the nineteenth century. In the garment trades, manufacturers developed two different forms of sweating. The first involved subcontracting to individual workers while the second entailed hiring middlemen who then hired their own laborers to work together in small workshops that became known as sweatshops. While sweatshops appear to be similar to workshops in custom tailoring, there were significant differences. First of all, there was no attempt to teach sweatshop workers the art of tailoring. Manufacturers hired "sweaters," as the subcontracted laborers were known, because they already knew how to sew. They were needleworkers rather than tailors. Secondly, sweating remained unregulated every-where in Europe until the early twentieth century. Un-like tailors, middlemen did not hang out signs to advertise their presence. They looked instead to rent cheap lodgings for their workshops to keep overhead costs down. Most importantly, subcontractors introduced piece rates, paying sweaters for the quantity and not the quality of their work. Taken together, these changes pre-sented a formidable challenge to the artisanal traditions of custom tailoring and dressmaking.

In Russia two forms of subcontracting were practiced in the eighteenth and early nineteenth centuries. As the demand for western European clothing began to grow in Russia, many tailors and dressmakers found it difficult to complete their clients' orders in a timely fashion. The task of sewing just one outfit involved hours of backbreaking labor. In order to alleviate the pressure on their journey-men and apprentices, masters began to hire "finishers." Working from their homes, their job was to complete a garment by stitching hems and buttonholes, sewing buttons, and other such tasks.

For master tailors and dressmakers there were some clear advantages in hiring finishers. First, they worked at home and bought their own work supplies. Furthermore, because they had not served as apprentices or journey-men, their work was regarded by master craftsmen and women as "unskilled" labor. Finishers did many different kinds of sewing, but their work did not involve any detailed measurements, cutting, or fittings. As they were unskilled laborers, their masters felt justified in paying them meager piece rates. Since there were so many people desperate for employment and able to sew in the nineteenth century, there was a constant supply of indi-viduals willing to work for these low piece rates. Thus, this kind of subcontracting proved to be very profitable for master tailors and dressmakers.

Textile manufacturers and merchants also developed a system of subcontracting in the garment trades. In the early years of the nineteenth century, textile producers, hoping to expand the market for their goods, began to hire middlemen (*skupshchiki*). These middlemen created two different forms of subcontracting. The first involved hiring homeworkers (*odinochki*). Toiling in cramped apartments, often with the assistance of family members, these needleworkers would stitch together garments using pre-cut fabrics. When the order was completed, they would return the garments to the middleman for payment. It was essential to work as quickly as possible since employers paid homeworkers piece rates. The second system of subcontracting involved middlemen setting up small workshops and hiring additional work-ers. As with homeworkers, those who labored in the sub-contracting workshops sewed together pre-cut garments for which they received piece rates. It is impossible to determine how widespread these subcontracting opera-tions were in the first half of the nineteenth century, as the records have not survived. According to a number of unofficial accounts, subcontracting operations began in Petersburg and Moscow where foreign merchants set up stores in the exclusive shopping districts. Russian mer-chants soon imitated the subcontracting practices of their foreign competitors.[3]

By the middle of the nineteenth century, subcontract-ing had become an important but paradoxical feature of the garment trades. While it allowed tailors and dress-makers to keep up with consumer demand, it also began to erode those features that characterized custom tailor-ing. As in Europe, Russian tailors and dressmakers were unaware of the dangers that subcontracting posed for themselves and their livelihoods. In a business depending upon low overhead costs, any measures that achieved that goal appeared beneficial, but these innovations were helping to destroy the old artisanal system and laying the foundations for ready-to-wear.

Tailoring and dressmaking were exacting forms of labor. Measurements and fittings required a keen eye for human proportions as well as precision in the cutting and sewing of fabrics. Hunched over their sewing for hours on end, workers needed great care in stitching garments together. Sloppy sewing created gaps in the fabric or caused garments to pucker. Furthermore, as long as garment workers had no uniform system of sizing and relied upon hand sewing to produce clothing, there was no way to speed up the manufacturing process.

The goal of the ready-to-wear industry was to make garments in advance so that customers could purchase them without any further fittings or alterations. This was no easy task for it required the development of uniform sizing. While tailors and dressmakers had always relied upon a set of patterns as guides in measuring and cutting the fabric, they nevertheless stitched the garments to fit each individual. Ready-to-wear clothes were not created for individuals, however. Individuals had to fit themselves into prefabricated, sized garments. The new clothing sizes created and named categories of body types. Small, medium, and large were among the earliest labels, but eventually more precise sizing systems came into use.

Proportional sizing developed gradually in the nineteenth century. A few industrious tailors and dressmakers systematized their own set of calculations and began to market them for public consumption. These gifted individuals created specialized tools and instructions that allowed their fellow artisans to cut and sew garments more efficiently. In Russia, Madame Teodor's courses and books were very popular and provided this type of knowledge for dressmakers. Aleksandr Katun and Vasilii Riazanov wrote books publicizing their drafting systems.[4] Even more important for the dissemination of this knowledge was the decision of fashion magazines to publish simple patterns as a way to attract more subscribers.

These new drafting systems proved in the end to be disastrous for custom tailoring and dressmaking. They eliminated the need for years of apprenticeship since individuals could learn to make complicated garments simply by following the instructions provided with the new drafting systems.[5] The art and mystery of tailoring

46  A young worker in 1909. This photo shows the importance of proportional sizing for ready-to-wear garments. The coat does not hang evenly in the front and gives a rather lumpy appearance. Private collection.

was giving way to standardization as trade secrets became public knowledge. The process of deskilling, which had already started with the introduction of sewing into the school curriculum for girls, intensified. The distinction between unskilled needleworkers and skilled tailors and dressmakers began to blur.

At the same time that drafting systems were becoming more popular, the sewing machine had arrived in Russia in the 1860s, as we have seen. The sewing machine saved enormous amounts of time because it eliminated the basting and sewing of seams that were a fundamental feature of hand-sewn clothing. As one historian has calculated, "The shirt of a mid-Victorian gentleman had over 20,000 stitches. Sewing this shirt by hand, the sewer could average thirty-five stitches per minute; with a machine the worker could complete between 1,000 to 2,000 stitches per minute, or thirty times as many as a hand stitcher."[6] With the introduction of the sewing machine, garment workers could make many more clothes than had previously been possible. Although the machines were expensive to purchase, most tailors and dressmakers clearly saw the financial benefits of owning the machines and they bought them in record numbers. Eventually other machines such as buttonholers and electric fabric cutters eliminated other tedious tasks, and also helped to reduce the number of hours spent on each individual garment.

Although the sewing machine, drafting systems, and proportional measurements allowed garment workers to accelerate production, Russian clothing producers faced another serious problem. Most Russians preferred goods of foreign manufacture to domestic items. Foreign names and products had great cache in Russia throughout the nineteenth century. In the 1870s alone, Russia imported almost two million rubles' worth of ready-to-wear clothing from Europe.[7] The struggle to break the grip that European manufacturers exerted over the ready-to-wear market was beyond the power of Russian manufacturers alone. For that they needed help from the state.

## TARIFFS AND IMPORTED CLOTHING

Because Peter the Great had wanted to encourage Russians to wear European clothing, the tsar used tariff policy to facilitate his sartorial reforms. Initially, the government did not tax imported clothing. For much of the eighteenth century clothes made in Europe entered Russia duty free. The six tariff revisions enacted between 1724 and 1775 contained no duty for clothing, but they did levy duties on textiles of all kinds.[8] In 1782 new regulations took effect which drew government officials closer to taxing the clothes themselves. At this time, the amount of fabric in each article of men's and women's clothing[9] was now subject to a customs duty four times higher than the duty levied on textiles.[10] Finally, in 1796 the government enacted the first customs duties on imported clothing. Because European fashions were the undisputed mode of dress for the court, the military, and the bureaucracy, the government could now levy customs duties on imported garments knowing that this would not discourage Russians from wearing them, as might have happened earlier.

Tariff policy became two-pronged in the nineteenth century. In addition to providing government coffers with needed revenue, tariffs were also intended to protect Russian industrial development.[11] In the case of clothing, the need for protectionism caught on slowly. Following the Napoleonic Wars, Russia removed the duty on imported clothing. The decision was undoubtedly based upon Russians' inability to purchase foreign fashions as a result of the disruption in trade caused by the French Revolution and the resulting European conflagration. Indeed, for a while Russians believed that wearing French fashions was unpatriotic. With the Napoleonic invasion and the burning of Moscow in 1812, many noble families suffered serious loss of property that included furnishings and clothing. By eliminating the tariff on imported clothes, the Russian government allowed the elite a chance to recoup their losses in clothing without adding further expense. A few years later, however, the tariff was restored, and in 1822 a new tariff actually forbade the importation of new and used ordinary clothing and lingerie. Only fashionable clothing was permitted into Russia duty free.[12]

For almost thirty years the government pursued a protectionist trade policy to encourage domestic economic growth, but the result was that imported fashions became very expensive. French fashions went through a number of commercial agents before they reached Russia, and at each step the agents charged for their services. By the time the garments arrived in Russia, their price had doubled. One economist calculated that a French silk gown costing forty-three rubles in Paris would sell for ninety-eight rubles in Petersburg. Russian consumers faced a difficult problem: either they could pay the exorbitant prices for imported fashions or they could buy domestic copies. Because most members of Russian high society believed that Russian copies were inferior, they chose to purchase foreign goods despite the high cost.[13]

At mid-century, after much debate about the efficacy of protectionism, the Russian government revised the tariff regulations in 1850 and again in 1857 to reflect a belief in free-trade. These new regulations once again encouraged the import of all forms of men's and women's clothing from Europe. In 1854 Russia imported clothing valued at 86,189 rubles; in 1857 the figure had jumped to 220,342 rubles.[14]

By the second half of the nineteenth century, England, Germany, and France were looking for new markets for their own industrial goods. Fearing foreign competition, Russian textile manufacturers, industrialists from heavy industry, and some government officials called for protectionist tariffs again. Beginning with the tariff revision of 1882 until the end of the Romanov dynasty in 1917, the government pursued a protectionist policy. With each revision the duties were raised in order to promote industrial growth and revenue.[15]

In her magisterial history of tailoring in Russia, E. A. Oliunina attributes the growth of ready-to-wear in Russia to the raising of the tariff duties on imported clothing: "In June 1882 a duty on ready-to-wear clothing was enacted. The new customs duties were based upon the weight of the goods rather than their actual cost. In 1882 the duty on a *pood* of women's outerwear was eighty rubles, for men's wear fifty-two rubles [Seven men's suits constituted a *pood* on average]."[16] Furthermore, after 1882 the Russian government no longer accepted credit for tariff duties, but demanded that all customs must now be paid in gold. The two changes taken together made the customs duties significantly higher than they had been previously, and they had an immediate effect on imports. In 1882 before the tariff became law, fifty million rubles' worth of men's clothing entered Russia from Austria. By 1884 the figure had dropped to 300,000 rubles.[17]

With protectionist tariffs in place, the ready-to-wear industry developed quickly. Manufacturers created copies of European clothing which were cheaper than custom-made fashions. In order to understand more fully how the tariffs worked in conjunction with inexpensive textiles, the sewing machine, and Russian labor practices to create ready-to-wear in Russia, we shall look at the rise of the most successful of clothing manufacturers, the Austrian firm of M. and I. Mandl'.

★   ★   ★

## M. AND I. MANDL' COMPANY

The origins of the M. and I. Mandl' Company owe much to the convergence of Russia's political and economic policies during the second half of the nineteenth century, and reveal the extent to which clothing production plays a vital part in the history of any nation. In 1872 Austria, Germany, and Russia entered into a new alliance called the Three Emperors' League. The purpose of the league was to bring the three empires into closer cooperation and harmony. One direct result of these new relations was that Austrian exports of men's ready-to-wear clothing to Russia increased dramatically.[18] The Austrians had been looking for new markets for their manufactured goods, and Russia, which still did not produce significant amounts of ready-to-wear clothing, was a vast untapped market with great potential. Unfortunately for the Austrian clothing manufacturers, relations between the two empires deteriorated just a few years later when Russia went to war with Turkey. The Russo–Turkish War of 1877–78 and the Treaty of San Stefano translated into a shift in the balance of power in the Balkans away from the Ottoman Turks and toward the Russians. The Austrians and the British then forced the Russians at the Congress of Berlin to restore the delicate antebellum balance of power in the Balkans.[19] The Russian government retaliated against Austria for its role in the Balkans crises in a number of ways – one of which was to raise the import duties on Austrian goods. The 1882 protectionist tariff made it extremely difficult for Austrian clothing manufacturers to export their goods to Russia. The higher customs duties payable in gold at the border eliminated any profit that the manufacturers had made previously.

To circumvent the new tariff regulations, the Austrian firm of M. and I. Mandl' sent representatives to Moscow to explore the possibility of producing ready-to-wear clothing in Russia.[20] Mandl's agents wanted to reproduce in the Russian market their company's original success in Austria. They began by first setting up a wholesale men's clothing operation. They chose Moscow as the center of their business for a number of reasons. During the second half of the nineteenth century, the city was growing at a dramatic rate with large numbers of peasants migrating to the city in search of work and a better life. In addition to being a ready pool of labor, Moscow was the hub of Russia's railroad system which would allow the firm to send its products to the far reaches of the empire. Finally, Moscow was the center of the Russian textile trade. Many textile factories were located in the city or its environs. Thus, the city afforded the company ready access to the raw materials necessary for their business.

The Mandl' company needed more garment workers than Moscow could provide, so they created a system to take advantage of some very special Russian conditions. When the government emancipated the serfs in 1861, it did not allow them freedom of movement within the empire. Instead, the government decreed that peasants who wanted to leave their villages and move to the cities had to apply to village authorities for permission. The inability of Russian peasants to move around at will was compounded by the poor agricultural conditions that prevailed in much of Russia. Many peasant families simply could not support themselves in these poor areas and had long ago turned to handicraft manufacturing as a way to make ends meet. In 1883 Mandl' representatives journeyed to Beloomut, a small village on the Oka River in Riazan' province. The river regularly flooded each spring and made the land unsuitable for agricultural use. The village residents made their living by selling timber and making a number of handicraft items, but the Mandl' agents appeared to offer many residents a chance to improve their standard of living. Receiving a warm reception from the villagers, the company set up a sewing workshop that employed approximately sixty garment workers. The number of peasants who wanted to join grew so quickly that Mandl' abolished the workshop and set up a central distribution office instead. Henceforth, peasants came to the office to receive the materials and trimmings for their orders that they completed in their homes.[21] Because the rural workers were homeworkers or labored in rural sweatshops, Mandl' paid them less than its urban workforce. To give one example, in Moscow a garment worker earned seventy-five kopecks for sewing a boy's suit, while a peasant earned only twenty to thirty kopecks.[22] The wage differential allowed the company a greater profit margin. Mandl' reportedly made a 32 percent profit on a man's suit made in Beloomut.[23]

Beloomut was one of several such villages in the Moscow region that became part of the growing ready-to-wear clothing industry. Villagers in Zaraiskii, Egor'-evskii, and Ranenburgskii districts in Riazan' province worked as homeworkers and in subcontracting shops. In Moscow province, garment workers were located in Bronnitskii, Vereiskii, Zvenigorodskii, and Mozhaiskii districts, none of which had adequate soil to permit the peasants to make a living from agriculture. In 1911 more than 4,000 peasants in Moscow and Riazan' provinces worked for Moscow businessmen in the ready-to-wear clothing industry.[24] Thus, Mandl' set up an elaborate network of employees connecting city and countryside.

The success of its wholesale operation allowed Mandl' to expand. By 1900 the company had a number of retail outlets in Moscow, Petersburg, Kiev, and Tbilisi. All of the stores were located in the exclusive shopping districts in each of these cities. The stores expanded their clothing lines to include women's and children's ready-to-wear, and eventually established a mail-order business as well. An offshoot of the original business called the Mandl' and Raits Company made military uniforms.[25] Mandl' even had a dress shop in Moscow for women who wanted custom-made fashions. In 1897 the company produced 1,400,000 rubles' worth of clothing.[26]

The Mandl' company's wholesale and retail organization became a model that other manufacturers quickly emulated. Soon the firms of Rozentsvaig, Neishtadt, Petukhov and Brothers, and Ekselans (Excellence) began to compete with Mandl'. They too set up sweatshops in the cities and countryside to stitch reproductions of the latest fashions, and they established both wholesale and retail operations as Mandl' had done.[27] The results were readily apparent. In 1909 a government report calculated that ready-to-wear had become a sixty-million-ruble industry. The chief centers of production were Moscow and Petersburg, followed by Odessa, Warsaw, Kiev, Riga, Rostov-na-Donu, and Ekaterinoslav, but virtually all Russian provincial cities had outlets that also sold ready-to-wear. Those areas that did not have ready-to-wear operations of their own, such as the Russian Far North and Central Asia, exchanged raw materials for manufactured goods including ready-to-wear.[28] By the turn of the twentieth century, manufacturers of ready-to-wear clothing had established themselves as keen competitors in the production of European fashions for the Russian market.

47 The M. and I. Mandl' ready-to-wear store in St. Petersburg located in the heart of that city's exclusive shopping district. The store's workshops were located on the top floor of the building while the showrooms were located on the first and second floors. I. N. Bozherianov, *Nevskii Prospekt, 1703–1903*, xiii. Harvard University Collections.

The success of the ready-to-wear industry came at the expense of the men and women who sewed the clothes. The introduction of sweating broke down the artisanal structure of the garment trades. Although conditions in the artisanal workshops of the bespoke trade were not markedly different from those of the sweatshops, the artisanal work culture offered hope to its workers: if they worked hard enough at their craft they could become masters of their own shop. That was the workers' reward for all those hours of backbreaking labor for tailors and dressmakers. There was no such hope for those who toiled in sweatshops. Sweatshop workers could aspire to become subcontractors, but there were few opportunities beyond that. The rationalization that ready-to-wear brought to the industry – uniform sizing, drafting systems, and the sewing machine – undermined the notion of skill that was the hallmark of the bespoke trade.

\* \* \*

## WOMEN'S WORK AND
## THE NEEDLE TRADES

The declining prestige of the garment trades was occurring at the same time that government officials and the educated public turned their attention again to the role of women in the workforce. Having debated elite women's ability to participate in wage labor in the 1850s and 1860s, the focus in the second phase of this debate was plebeian women. In what capacity should these women participate in the workforce? Did their work threaten the family structure? How could working women combine their roles as wage laborers and household managers so that neither industry nor the family would suffer? It was these questions that energized the discussions about women and work in the 1880s. Because these polemics emphasized women's productive and reproductive roles, they became ensnared in the earlier debates about domesticity. And, since needlework had been enshrined as the quintessential female skill in Russian definitions of domesticity, this meant that it played a critical role in helping government officials and the educated public determine a role for plebeian women in the workforce which, in turn, led to the further deskilling of the garment trades.

## PEASANT WOMEN AND
## THE NEEDLE TRADES

The introduction of western fashions into the countryside alarmed many Russians. Initially, Peter the Great's dress decree had specifically excluded peasants from participating in his sartorial reforms. While residents of Russia's urban centers paraded around in French fashions, the peasants were to maintain their traditional ethnic dress so long as they were engaged in agricultural pursuits, creating a sharp visual marker between town and country. Even though noble landlords often dressed their servants in European uniforms or gave them outmoded fashions, the elite still clung to the notion that Russian peasants preferred wearing traditional ethnic dress. This visual demarcation of urban life from agricultural pursuits persisted until the emancipation of the serfs in 1861. That year marked an important shift, allowing

48    A young Petersburg family wearing city clothes. The young mother's skirt does not fit her well. The girl's left sleeve is shorter than her right one, while her skirt is uneven. Her brother's shirt is missing a button. Working-class families who had little money for fashionable outfits often wore clothes such as these. Private collection.

peasants to begin crafting a new identity for themselves. In 1873 a government commission reviewed the state of agriculture more than a decade after emancipation. Local officials, priests, and teachers in Russia's European provinces described conditions in their area. Most reported that peasants had begun wearing "city clothes," and many accused them of foppery (*shchegol'stvo*).[29] An official from Podol'sk province detailed the changes that had occurred:

> All clothes with the exception of undergarments are made from manufactured materials and cloth. Shoes are sewn to fit the foot more closely and in more

attractive styles. Homemade straw hats are worn only in hot weather; caps . . . are the usual headgear. In inclement weather a few use store-bought felt hats and in the winter sheepskin hats are made from local sheep costing one ruble fifty or more. Young men will wear ribbons in their straw hats. Ribbons are also used as neckties with turndown collars. Lately the use of vests has spread everywhere. Women wear calico skirts and aprons; only old women wear traditional dress. In general, women's clothing is factory-made rather than homemade. This dandyism is particularly noticeable near the cities and sugar factories. Peasants wear not only factory-made clothing, but they even buy linen. Practically every little trading outpost has a shop with these beautiful items.[30]

49  Two Russian peasants, late nineteenth century. Despite accusations of foppery, this is how many men dressed to work in the fields. There are patches at the elbows of the jacket of the man on the right and a gaping hole in the coat of the man on the left. Library of Congress Collections.

A Novgorod official summarized the horror of local officials best when he declared: "Luxury in dress is at scandalous proportions. It is not uncommon for a peasant to lay waste to his household and barn in order to buy his wife a 100-ruble dress and to clothe himself in city clothes."[31]

For those peasants who could not "lay waste" to their households and barns, other sources of income had to be

50 Workers' wedding dress. The man's suit is from the 1890s and is worn with a peasant shirt. The woman's dress was made in 1886 for a female textile worker. It was the plight of women workers such as the owner of this outfit that concerned many elite Russians. They assumed that these women, by marrying in "city clothes," rejected peasant patriarchal values in favor of modern, urban life. State Historical Museum, Moscow.

found in order to pay for their new wardrobes. In those areas outside the rich agricultural regions, peasant men migrated to the cities to look for work, leaving their women at home to tend the fields and care for the children in their absence. This outmigration intensified as the pace of Russia's industrialization drive quickened in the second half of the nineteenth century. More peasant men left in search of work and stayed away from their villages for longer periods of time. The outcome of this rural migration meant that women ran the farms alone for longer periods of time. Furthermore, ethnographers also noted that peasant women in the poorer agricultural areas had given up farming almost completely and worked at various crafts to support themselves and their families. By the early 1880s a growing number of peasant women were working at home, but now their work was intended for sale on the market, not for home consumption.[32]

There were many reports deploring peasant women's work for wages, but one of the most influential was written by M. K. Gorbunova for the Moscow *zemstvo* (local institution of self-government) published in 1882.[33] Gorbunova set out to write a history of women's crafts that were practiced in Moscow province at the time of her visit. By her count, peasant women participated in nineteen different crafts. Almost all of these involved the fashion industry – lacemaking, plaiting of straw hats, embroidery, and the making of trimmings. Of the three most commonly practiced crafts, two involved the fashion industry: knitting stockings and gloves, and unwinding cotton for textile manufacturers. In 1882 more than 37,000 peasant women worked in some kind of craft and more than 27,000 were involved in the garment trades.[34]

What troubled Gorbunova was how this work was changing the traditional patterns of peasant women's lives. She analyzed how the introduction of capitalist market mechanisms had had a profound impact upon women's work. First of all, the crafts found in Moscow province were those that matched current fashion trends. For instance, trim making, which had once been fashionable was dying out, but knitting was growing rapidly in response to the demand for stockings, gloves, and other items.[35] Thus, peasant women did not work at traditional Russian crafts as Gorbunova expected, but served the fickle fashion industry. Those women who worked at crafts that went out of fashion had either to learn how to make new items or face unemployment and poverty. Secondly, most peasant women did not work as independent artisans, but labored for middlemen and -women. Gorbunova was not alone in her condemnation of this deeply exploitative system. Peasant women's wages were not lucrative, and many middlemen and -women paid their workers in kind rather than in cash.

Yet, despite their low wages, peasant women's desire for manufactured goods, especially western fashions, continued to grow as a result of their greater exposure to urban goods and markets. Having calculated that peasant women earned on average between fifteen and thirty rubles per year for their work, Gorbunova observed that these women wanted to spend their wages on ready-to-wear clothing. Since they did not earn enough to purchase these items themselves, peasant women had to get their husbands to pay for the dresses. Furthermore, fathers were now supposed to supply their daughters with dowries replete with western clothing in order to make them attractive to potential spouses, because male outmigrants preferred women dressed in city clothes. In purchasing ready-to-wear clothing, peasant women gave up their traditional duty of making clothing for their families.[36] As if this was not bad enough, Gorbunova claimed that peasant women and girls did not even know how to sew, and had to pay to have their clothing patched.[37]

In Gorbunova's account, peasant women's loss of sewing skills, their desire to wear western fashions, and their participation in the capitalist market all served to symbolize peasant women's rejection of their traditional domestic role. Instead a new peasant woman was being created:

> Before us stands a free, young woman, not hampered by any kind of barriers; a young woman emancipated from her family and from everything that constitutes the conditions of the peasant woman's existence; a young woman who at any given moment can migrate from place to place, from boss to boss, and who at any moment can become unemployed without refuge, without a piece of bread.[38]

This new peasant woman was free, but at what terrible cost. Set adrift in society, she was free to leave her home

51   A worker buying a skirt for his daughter or wife in an open-air market in Moscow. The worker is wearing bast shoes, suggesting that he had recently arrived in the city. At the same time, he is also wearing the *furazhka*, the peaked cap that was worn by workers everywhere in Russia. Back home in the village, his daughter would add the skirt to her dowry in the hopes of marrying an urban worker. Joseph Bradley, *Muzhik and Muscovite: Urbanization in Late Imperial Russia*, 244.

52 A Cossack and two females, 1910. The man is wearing his Cossack uniform. The dress of his two female companions tells a different story. Both women are wearing garments that identify them as peasants – headscarves, long round skirts. Nevertheless, all of their garments are made from textiles produced in Russian factories rather than from homespun materials. The uniform sewing and the style of the blouses and skirts indicate that these were produced in ready-to-wear sweatshops rather than at home by the women themselves. It was precisely peasant women's abandonment of weaving and sewing in peasant huts in favor of just such ready-to-wear garments that had many educated Russians so upset. Private collection.

and family to face hunger, uncertainty, and danger wherever she roamed. In fact this new peasant woman strongly resembled those working women who struggled to survive in the cities without any help from their families or society. All these women had been emancipated from their class and domestic role, but their freedom endangered their very lives and, ultimately, the peasant way of life.

In order to save peasant women from this type of emancipation, some remedy needed to be found to preserve their role in the countryside. A group of noblewomen believed that they had found such a cure when they proposed the revival of women's *kustar* industries. The kustar art movement was a nationwide attempt to revive peasant arts and crafts that began in the 1870s and flourished until World War I. Its purpose was to save peasant arts that were beginning to die out as a result of changes in agriculture and western influences, and to provide peasants with the economic means to maintain their traditional way of life. According to Wendy Salmond, noblewomen who lived on their estates were keenly aware of the changes occurring in peasant life.[39] Seeking a more public role for themselves, as well as hoping to alleviate the immiseration of the peasantry, they chose the only socially acceptable avenue open to them – philanthropy. These noblewomen used their own money to hire artisans to train peasant women in small workshops in traditional peasant crafts. In fact, some of Russia's leading artists participated in these efforts to revive kustar industries and in the process transformed peasant art forms into modern art.[40]

Not surprisingly, the crafts selected for preservation were the needle trades – lacemaking, embroidery of all kinds, and knitting. While these crafts had been practiced since ancient times, some had never been produced for the market. For instance, peasant women had braided lace and sold it at markets since the twelfth century, but embroidery had been used only for home consumption and rarely produced for the market. Now both industries were reinvigorated, and their handiwork was exhibited at world's fairs such as the World's Columbian Exposition in Chicago in 1893. Eventually retail outlets opened in Russia's big cities and in some European capitals to sell peasant women's crafts to a growing market for these examples of traditional Russian art.

The primary advantage of needlework was that it could be produced at home. As Sofia Davydova, one of the leaders of the kustar revival explained:

Lacemaking, thanks to its exclusively domestic character, can be produced by each lacemaker, as they say, in front of the hearth. Moreover, lacemaking is so simple and easy, that it does not require any adapta-

53   A young family from Cherepovets, late nineteenth century. The husband is wearing a peasant shirt under his jacket and trousers tucked into his books. The jacket is rumpled, indicating a poorly made garment. The wife is wearing European fashion, a simple black ready-to-wear skirt with a striped blouse gathered in the front and at the waist. Her clothing suggests greater attention to style and is more expensive than her husband's. Although their son's clothing is plain, the couple are trying to demonstrate their financial success by including their son's toys in the picture. Private collection.

54   A young Petersburg shopkeeper and his wife, early 1900s. The photo shows how Russians combined Russian and European dress. The man is wearing a peasant shirt and trousers tucked into his boots in the Russian manner. His wife, however, is wearing European dress. The fact that the front panel of her skirt is slightly off center suggests that she purchased it at a store that sold ready-to-wear clothing. Central State Archive of Documentary Films, Photographs, and Sound Recordings of St. Petersburg.

tions in the rooms where the work is done, each woman works in her own way. Therefore the first available room, table, and bench are completely suitable for the preparation of the most delicate braiding. Under these conditions the only requirement is that everything must be clean. This condition usually prompts lacemakers to select the best room in the house, so that lace work always occurs in what they consider the cleanest room.[41]

Davydova's comments suggest the complex message directed at peasant women. Traditional peasant women's domestic role had entailed fieldwork, gardening, and care of farm animals. None of this work promoted a clean work environment, and many outside observers commented on the dirt and smoke that filled peasant huts.[42] In order to sell the lace, peasant women had to maintain clean working conditions so that consumers would want to buy their goods. But, at the same time, by making cleanliness a necessary condition for lacemaking, Davydova is also imposing respectable women's views of domesticity upon the peasants. Her image of peasant women sitting in front of the family fire tatting lace belies one of the motives of the revival of lacemaking and the other needle crafts, which was to impose a new view of women's domestic role. The purpose of this new domesticity was to keep peasant women on the farms and out of the factories. By providing them with clean, respectable work, the proponents of women's kustar industries hoped that peasant women's earnings would allow them to maintain what was viewed as their traditional way of life. Having observed the work of several of these kustar workshops, one commentator made this connection explicit:

> Thus, if the support and development of the kustar industries are essential for the male peasant population and the preservation of the link between the land and the maintenance of the land, then it is even more important *in this view* to maintain and develop among women peasants those crafts which do not distract them from the land and their homes and which favor the preservation and development of that branch of industry where agriculture and trades walk arm in arm, supporting each other.[43]

The emancipation of peasant women from their social and domestic role, clearly a danger to themselves and society, could be prevented by taking up needle and thread.

## FACTORY WOMEN AND THE LAW ON NIGHT WORK OF 1885

While some members of polite society attempted to remedy the plight of Russian peasant women, others turned their attention to the small but growing numbers of Russian factory women. More than a third of women in the industrial labor force in 1885 worked in textile factories, while another third labored in paper plants.[44] The addition of these women factory workers to the urban landscape by the early 1880s caused even more concern for government officials and the educated public already worried about the growing numbers of indigent seamstresses, servants, and prostitutes. Russia's economic

crisis could be seen in its most raw and painful form in the cities. And because the ideology of domesticity continued to insist that women's work should occur in the home and not in the public sphere, the presence of these poor working women was particularly troubling.

The proposed solution to society's concerns about women industrial workers was the 1885 law prohibiting night work for women and adolescents. According to Rose Glickman, a severe crisis in the textile industry caused the government to elicit the views of industrialists on how to remedy the situation. The 1885 law was the outcome of their discussions about women workers. And, like the discussions of the plight of peasant women, these deliberations were couched in the rhetoric of domesticity. While some industrialists argued that night work corrupted women both physically and morally, others insisted that it prevented women workers from spending their free time in taverns and other unsavory places, thereby saving women and their families from corruption. The Ministry of Finance sided with the former group and argued that night work endangered women and the proletarian family. Government views proved decisive in this matter for the law banned all night work for adolescents under the age of seventeen and women who worked in textile factories. Eventually the law was extended to include women working in all light industries.[45]

The law on night work was important for it was the only piece of labor legislation to deal specifically with women factory workers until 1913.[46] The concerns expressed in the discussions about the law reveal much about the government's and society's views of the impact of wage labor on working-class women. The central concern was for women's moral purity. When these women were freed from the home to enter into the factory, they were exposed to all of society's ills – poverty, hunger, unemployment, vice, and depravity. By putting at risk their moral purity, they were abandoning their domestic role and thereby endangering their femininity and their families. By returning proletarian women to their homes, if only for the night, this law sought to restore them to their proper role in the home and the family.

Thus, the solutions to the roles of both peasant and working-class women in the workforce were essentially the same. Government officials and educated society

tried to limit their opportunities to work outside the home by restricting their participation in the factories and by supporting occupational segregation in the peasant kustar industries. Furthermore, through these public discussions the state and society attempted to inscribe their own views of domesticity on both the peasantry and the working class. The promotion of values such as cleanliness and women's moral purity were not necessarily identical with peasant or proletarian views of the role of women. Nevertheless, government officials and the educated public hoped to contain plebeian women in the home, and in so doing eliminate many of the serious social consequences of Russia's industrialization program.

This is not to suggest that government and society were successful in their containment policy. On the contrary, the numbers of women who left the countryside in search of work continued to rise. Therefore, government and society made one more attempt to discuss publicly the problem of women and work. This occurred at a special women's vocational education section of the First Technical and Vocational Congress held in St. Petersburg during the Christmas vacation of 1889–90.

55  A group of women workers in their dormitory room at a textile factory in St. Petersburg, late nineteenth–early twentieth centuries. The fate of women such as these deeply concerned many Russians. Although two of the women are wearing headscarves, a sign of traditional female modesty in Russia, the others have abandoned any kind of traditional clothing and are wearing "city clothes." Central State Archive for Documentary Films, Photographs, and Sound Recordings in St. Petersburg.

## THE FIRST TECHNICAL AND VOCATIONAL CONGRESS AND SEWING

The first Congress of Russian Participants in Technical and Vocational Education was an important event. Representatives of government, industry, and educated society gathered together to hold public meetings on a topic of mutual concern. The Ministry of Finance sponsored the Congress to promote vocational education in Russia and to continue its battle with the Ministry of Education over control of the country's technical schools. Over 1,000 teachers, administrators, government officials, and even a few industrialists attended the meetings to discuss all aspects of technical education. The Congress was so successful that two more were held in 1895 and 1903.[47]

In order to create a place for the discussion of women's vocational education, the organizers had approved a separate section of the Congress, isolating women's issues from those that affected men's vocational education. In fact, the reports prepared for the women's vocational section only discussed the needle trades to the exclusion of all other work performed by women. The president of the women's section, Ia. T. Mikhailovskii, explained the reason for this decision:

> . . . in Russia the need to widen the sphere of women's vocational work has only recently been realized. . . . The results of this, as is well known, are schools to prepare women for specialties other than sewing. Such schools include commercial courses, graphic arts, printing, lithography, cooking, and many others. Unfortunately, only information about sewing was sent to the congress and more precisely only those schools who sent works displayed at the congress' exhibition hall. To be sure, women's sewing schools as they are considered at these meetings must be given greater priority and play the most visible role, both because we already have a large number of schools and also because women rarely compete with men in sewing. At the same time, as women must battle with men for access to other professions, from time immemorial the sphere of women's sewing has belonged to them and will continue to belong to them; and it remains for them to defend their sphere and to find the way to improve their handicrafts.[48]

This rather convoluted explanation provides an understanding of how the Congress organizers viewed sewing and women's work in 1889. According to Mikhailovskii, women's work and vocational training must remain separate from men's. Although women had begun to fight for recognition in occupations considered to be men's work, the Congress was unwilling to discuss these efforts, nor were they willing to try to improve vocational education so that more women could work in these areas. Instead, sewing occupied the center of the discussions of women's work because women already stitched in large numbers from "time immemorial." Mikhailovskii uses tradition and the existence of large

numbers of needlewomen to justify limiting the discussion of women's vocational training. So rather than assist women in expanding their economic opportunities through employment in other kinds of work, the Congress organizers insisted upon the segregation of work into men's and women's work.

Even more important is Mikhailovskii's concern about competition between men and women workers. While he argues that the sexes did not compete in the needle trades, that simply was not true. Men and women had always competed, and that competition was increasing in 1889 as a result of the growing demand for city clothes. Thus, Mikhailovskii's assertion that sewing is women's work alone belies the real competition that was taking place. But, because the organizers refused to acknowledge this competition, no discussion was necessary. At the very beginning of the Congress, sewing was established as the sole area of women's work, but the very real problems associated with that work could not be discussed because they did not exist. To emphasize the differences between men's and women's work even further, the Congress decreed that only men's work could be categorized as *ruchnoi trud* (literally, hand work). Sewing remained *rukodelie*, thereby reaffirming the gendering of labor discourse begun under Catherine the Great.[49]

Despite Mikhailovskii's claim that women were responsible for improving the needle trades, men were very much in evidence at the meetings. Of the fifty-five people who attended the sessions, thirty-four were men. Most, but not all, were local government officials involved with vocational training. The individuals charged with the actual running of the various sessions were all male, and ten of the fifteen presenters were male. One of the men in attendance actually highlighted the incongruity of these male interlopers into this female world. After a paper on how to make dress patterns, he observed that "Of course, I don't know how to make patterns, but . . ."[50] Nevertheless, he and the other men felt themselves to be experts not because they knew how to sew, but because they were in charge of those institutions that controlled access to those skills.

Yet, the women participants at the First Technical Congress presented a serious challenge to male expertise in the needle trades. Not only did they know how to sew, most of them had spent their lives teaching other women these same skills. To give a few examples, one presenter was Ekaterina Ianzhul, one of the founders of the Moscow Society for the Dissemination of Practical Knowledge for Educated Women. In addition to her duties as an instructor at the Moscow Society's sewing school, Ianzhul had undertaken a comparative study of sewing in European and American primary schools, which she published in 1890.[51] Another equally prominent participant was Sofia Davydova. Russia's leading expert on lacemaking, Davydova wrote extensively on the craft. In addition, she had founded schools in Petersburg and in the countryside to preserve the art of lacemaking. As we have already seen, she was a prominent activist in the revival of the kustar art industries. Her presence at the Congress served to bring together the debates about peasant and working-class women.[52]

These prominent participants and the others who attended the meetings had devoted their whole lives to the needle trades. They had made careers for themselves as experts in this most domestic of women's work. Furthermore, they had created a public space for themselves through their work in the private sphere, thereby blurring the boundaries between them. As a consequence, they challenged the linking of sewing and domesticity that had developed earlier in the century. Sewing was supposed to teach women the importance of family obligations, to inculcate in them passivity, meekness, and a willingness to work quietly at home. Yet, here were a group of women advocating the importance of sewing for women in a public forum and daring to challenge the authority of the male experts.

Furthermore, through their writings and work in the schools, these prominent women attempted to re-establish sewing as a craft with specialized knowledge that could only be acquired through vocational training. It is important to stress, however, that these women were not trying to restore dressmaking and the other needle trades as traditional artisanal crafts. They did not seek to re-establish the authority of the master craftswomen, but rather they were using these debates to claim a place for themselves in the new professional class that was developing in Russia. They insisted that the best vocational training for needlewomen occurred in the schools, not in the shops. Davydova, Ianzhul, and others came to the Congress to share their ideas on how to improve training in the needle trades, training that they hoped to control as professional women.

The central challenge facing the Congress was that after more than a century of concerted activity in establishing sewing as a vital component of women's education, there already existed a multiplicity of schools that taught young women how to sew. Yet, as everyone agreed, these different programs had failed to train women adequately in the needle trades. The goal of the participants was to propose a streamlined and systematic vocational training to be used in all schools; and it was here in their attempt to devise a single standard for sewing instruction that the ambiguities and contradictory nature of the discourse on sewing emerged. How could all young women be given the same instruction when some sewed only for themselves and their families while others stitched as wage laborers? It was this dilemma that divided those professionals interested in creating a uniform standard.

Not surprisingly, the struggle between the male and female experts emerged when Davydova gave her report to the assembly. As the most accomplished of all the women panelists, her opinions carried the greatest weight and presented the greatest challenge to the male experts. Her report dealt with the need to establish short-term sewing courses. Having reviewed the existing courses, Davydova concluded that they did not adequately prepare women dressmakers for their work. To remedy this situation, she proposed that two different kinds of courses be set up: one to prepare women artisans and the other to prepare women to teach sewing in the primary and secondary schools.[53]

In proposing this division of sewing into two different types of vocational training, Davydova was highlighting the contradictory nature of the discourse on sewing in Russia. While the official ideology held that all women sewed at home as part of their domestic role and only occasionally to supplement their husbands' wages, Davydova's proposal tacitly acknowledged that some women worked to support their families as wage earners, either in workshops or as homeworkers. By exposing the reality of what was meant by "home sewing," Davydova threatened to destroy the ideology that had carefully linked sewing and domesticity.

In the discussion that followed Davydova's remarks, two opposing positions formed. Davydova's opponents claimed that the purpose of women's vocational education was to prepare them to be better housewives.

According to I.V. Mikhailov, ". . . a sewing course should be created, and maybe a home economics course as well, these are essential for every married woman."[54] The sewing course should include instruction in sewing, embroidery, and knitting as the foundation of a healthy domestic economy. Davydova and her supporters believed that the purpose of women's vocational education was to provide them with greater training and specialization. As the sewing teacher Anna Alekseeva explained, "The purpose of the vocational school is to prepare women for the possibility of earning a living (*zarabatyvat' kusok khleba*). If she does not have any specialized training in a particular craft, but knows a little about all of them, what can she do after leaving school?"[55]

The chief difficulty in this debate was that neither side was able to uncouple the link between domesticity and sewing. Both sides agreed that all women, no matter what their social rank, should know how to sew. Furthermore, they believed that women should sew for home consumption. This is why the courses for training teachers were necessary: so that they could train girls in domestic management and domesticity. The major difference between the two sides was that those who supported specialization in the needle trades wanted to provide working women with the chance to make better wages through more skilled work. And while this difference was a great enough challenge to the existing economic system to cause concern, it did not fundamentally alter the link between domesticity and sewing. Even in Davydova's proposals, sewing remained women's work.

Neither side was able to convince the other of the efficacy of its proposals. Rather than allow the session to end in discord, Mikhailovskii suggested a resolution that essentially maintained the vocational training that was already in place.[56] The measure passed, although the vote was not unanimous.[57] Thus, the idea of training women to work outside the home as the equals of male workers proved too radical for the Congress delegates. The resolution reasserted the primacy of sewing as a crucial component of a young woman's domestic education.

If the participants thought that this resolution would end the discussion of women's vocational education, they were wrong. In his report to the Congress, Vladimir S. Sudylkovskii, director of the Demidov Home for Working Women, declared that:

> . . . the artisanal professionalism of women, in whose name are now opened what we call women's vocational schools, center mainly, if not exclusively, around the needle, the embroidery hoop, and knitting needles. . . . These tiny tools, as they say, were created exclusively for women. . . . The needle, the hoop, and knitting needles have always formed and will continue to form not only the most important requirement of domestic and family life, but also in some conditions and certain rare circumstances serve as supplementary help more suited to women's nature than any other artisanal tool.[58]

Despite Ekaterina Ianzhul's plea that the Congress acknowledge once and for all a distinction between women's vocational training and general education, no such resolution was forthcoming.[59] The women's vocational section of the First Technical Congress concluded on 6 January 1890 without having resolved this fundamental issue.

★　★　★

The First Technical Congress provides a critical moment in the gendering of sewing as the nineteenth century drew to a close. Supporters of women's vocational education in the form of training in the domestic arts regarded sewing as an excellent way to teach plebeian women how to be domestic and feminine. Because the plight of both working-class and peasant women had been discussed earlier in the decade, the congress provided a moment to reaffirm domesticity as the cure for their problems. For working-class women, that meant keeping them at home and out of the workplace as much as possible. Peasant women should remain in their villages where they could perform their traditional agricultural and familial roles. At the same time, teaching elite women to sew meant that they could then serve as sewing instructors in the schools for working-class and peasant girls.[60] In this way, all Russian girls would have received the necessary instruction in domesticity by the time they had reached adulthood.

Those who proposed greater specialization in the needle trades did so for complex reasons. Women such as

Davydova and Ianzhul were well acquainted with the lives of working-class and peasant women. They knew that these women did not sew for enjoyment or to supplement their husbands' wages. They worked out of necessity as single parents or to support their families when their husbands were unemployed. They also knew that except for a handful of master craftswomen, most needleworkers did not even receive a living wage because their work was seen as unskilled. These women professionals contested the domestic agenda of the official vocational training of women because they believed that women workers deserved greater opportunities than they had to demonstrate their skills as needleworkers which would lead, in turn, to better wages.

At the same time, however, these women professionals believed that their hard-won expertise entitled them to have a greater say over the nature of women's vocational training and control over skill acquisition. If sewing really was women's work, as everyone claimed, then women should be allowed to regulate their craft. Women professionals were asking that men simply acknowledge the full implications of their notion of sewing as women's work. Despite these attempts to reconsider the purpose of women's vocational training, the women professionals lost the argument. Their claims of professional competence proved too threatening to the male status quo.

Both groups remained caught up in the domestic ideology within which the gendering of sewing played such a dynamic role. After more than twenty years of demands by educated women for a greater role in the public sphere, coupled with the increasing numbers of women wage laborers, many government officials and members of the educated public felt it necessary to re-emphasize women's role in the private sphere. The First Russian Technical and Vocational Education Congress became an essential public forum in which to proclaim women's role in the family and in the home, to contain working women, in particular, within the confines of the home. Housework, whether it was performed in the peasant hut, proletarian apartment, or luxurious townhouse, remained unpaid and unrecognized as real work, and, as such, did not pose a threat to men's work.

At the same time, the women who tried to challenge the notion of sewing as unspecialized housework were caught up in the paradoxes of their own position. While they put forward arguments, which emphasized the degree of skill and competence necessary to become an accomplished needleworker, they continued to insist that sewing was the quintessential work of women. It was this part of their argument that undermined their attempts to challenge the linking of sewing and domesticity. If sewing was somehow the perfect work for women, then it must be linked to the attributes of their gender. Furthermore, when Davydova and Ianzhul tried to emphasize that women had sewn since time immemorial, it further substantiated the idea that sewing and domesticity were indissolubly linked. Although the gendering of sewing was contested at the First Technical and Vocational Congress, the women's arguments in favor of uncoupling sewing and domesticity did not succeed because these women could not break out of their own ideological framework. They wanted to improve women's work, not challenge the occupational sex segregation that underlay it.

Male workers suffered as well from the gendering of sewing. Having seen their work devalued as unskilled and labeled as women's work, male garment workers felt their craft and their livelihood threatened. Adding insult to injury, the popularity of ready-to-wear clothing further eroded the Russian consumer's desire to purchase expensive custom-made garments. The reliance of clothing manufacturers on sweating and outwork meant that male artisans found it more difficult to command wages commensurate with their training and skill. Economic survival in the bespoke industry was precarious enough, but the introduction of piece rates made it impossible for male workers alone to provide for their families.

This refusal to acknowledge the miserable conditions and poverty of needleworkers made Russia somewhat exceptional. In the late nineteenth and early twentieth centuries private individuals and government investigations exposed the horrors of sweating in the United States, England, and France.[61] In all three cases, the public outcry over sweating led to the creation of a minimum wage. But in Russia there was no government investigation into sweating.[62] Instead, angry garment workers sought other means to help them improve their working lives.

*Newest Fashions for October 1830.* *Costumes of All Nations N.º 59.*
*Morning, Evening, & Ball Dresses.* *Neapolitan.*

56  A fashion plate showing morning and evening dress as well as a Neapolitan costume, October 1830. Private collection.

# 4

## The Fashion Press in Imperial Russia

CLOTHING PRODUCTION WAS ONLY one part of the development of a European fashion industry in Russia. Another challenge was to create a market for fashion. The sartorial demands of government service did not necessarily create a demand for European *haute couture* outside government circles. Russia might produce ball gowns and business suits, but if no one wanted to wear them, all that effort would be in vain. In order for Peter the Great's dress revolution to succeed, individual Russians of all social ranks had to abandon their traditional garments for western clothing. This became the goal of the fashion industry.

By the time of Peter's dress reform, Europeans had already developed a number of mechanisms to sell the concept of fashion as well as the clothing itself. Fashion is about the art of visual display, so the best way to present new styles was to see them on real people. The play of light and movement upon the garments enhanced their allure as well as spectators' desire to dress *à la mode*. Public gatherings such as dances, theater, and opera became opportunities to see and be seen in the latest fashions. A second related form of presentation was the creation of window displays in the shops that sold fashion goods. These elaborate and luxurious exhibits lured customers into the shops in the hope that they might be able to afford an outfit like the one in the window.

Fashion enthusiasts quickly realized the problems of relying solely on the physical display of goods to sell fashion. Shop windows and human models could influence only a limited number of well-to-do people who had the money and leisure to shop and attend public cultural events. In order to make fashion popular outside the elite, a fashion press was essential to publicize new fashions through illustration and detailed description. By the beginning of the twentieth century, inexpensive fashion magazines became a very popular form of entertainment for all social classes, promoting new ideas of beauty, taste, production, and consumption. Even those who could not afford to buy the fashions participated vicariously in this new world of consumption simply by flipping through the pages of a magazine.

Industry specialists, like their counterparts in western Europe, saw the fashion press as critical for the success of their industry. During the first period in the development of a fashion press (1830–1870), men and women publishers created magazines that would appeal to the elite by reporting the fashion news in both Paris and Petersburg. The success of these first magazines then encouraged publishers to expand the market to include the provincial nobility who wanted to mimic the dress and mores of high society in Petersburg. The second period (1870–1917) marked the rise of the modern fashion magazine. Publishers extended the market beyond the elite to include individuals from the middle and sometimes even the lower strata of Russian society. Most magazines in this period dropped any coverage of Russian fashion news per se and reported only on what was *à la mode* in Paris. By eliminating coverage of Russian fashions, publishers helped to include Russian women in the world of high fashion, making them feel that they were on an equal footing with women in western Europe.[1]

## THE ORIGINS OF THE FASHION PRESS IN EUROPE AND RUSSIA

The development of a fashion press in Russia was intimately connected with the fashion press in western Europe. Prior to the mid-eighteenth century, it was very difficult for those individuals who lived away from court to dress fashionably. There simply was no reliable means to find out what the latest styles were without actually seeing the clothes. To overcome this problem, tailors and dressmakers clothed miniature dolls in replicas of the new styles and sent these little mannequins to their customers. Unfortunately, the dolls could not possibly satisfy the demand for information about fashion that existed even in the eighteenth century. Moreover, it was expensive to clothe and ship the dolls. It took months for customers to receive their mannequins, by which time the clothing was no longer in fashion. So another method needed to be found to publicize *la mode*.[2]

The solution to this problem proved to be the creation of the fashion plate. Commercial artists had developed two different types by the eighteenth century. The first were colored costume plates, which were very popular in Europe in the seventeenth and eighteenth centuries. These drawings recorded the national dress of various regions in Europe.[3] As beautiful as these plates were, their objective was to record traditional forms of dress, not the latest fashions. Nevertheless, the costume plates provided the inspiration for the creation of the second type of fashion plate whose sole purpose was to record current clothing styles. Fashion plates proved to be a great innovation. While many hours of intensive labor were required to make just one mannequin doll, large numbers of fashion plates could be printed in the same amount of time. Postage rates for plates were lower than for parcels, and the delivery time was quicker. Thus, news about the latest fashions could be disseminated rapidly and efficiently through the use of fashion plates.

Because fashion plates were dated material, publishers needed to find a mechanism for distributing them as quickly as possible. They soon realized that fashion was well suited for regular inclusion in the periodical press. By the end of the eighteenth century, fashion plates appeared in two different venues in the western European media. First, literary magazines and newspapers frequently included one or two fashion plates with a detailed description of the clothing as a regular feature. The plates were seen as part of their coverage of important cultural events. Second, fashion plates became the centerpiece of a new kind of periodical, the fashion magazine. The first such magazine, *The Gallant Messenger* (*Le Mercure gallant*), published only a few engravings, but over the course of the eighteenth century magazines devoted to dress increasingly included fashion plates along with detailed descriptions of the outfits.[4]

Publishers did not take very long to figure out that the inclusion of fashion plates helped in the sale of periodicals. Fashion, like war and politics, was news. During the eighteenth century, much of western Europe was undergoing a series of profound political, economic, and social changes. The aristocracy was losing its power to the new middle classes. The changing modes of dress simultaneously mirrored these events and helped to facilitate them.[5] Upper- and middle-class men adopted the dark suit at the same time as women's clothing became more elaborate and required more thought and time in order to dress according to the ever-changing fashions.

As already observed in chapter 2, gender roles were changing in eighteenth-century Europe. Influenced by Rousseau and others, Enlightenment thinkers argued that, while men should focus on business and civic affairs, women's natural role was in the home. Part of their household duties included the acquisition and maintenance of the family wardrobe. This domestic ideology proclaimed fashion as a woman's prerogative even though men continued to spend long hours at their tailors in order to purchase custom-made suits. Only with the advent of men's ready-to-wear clothing in the 1850s and 1860s were men able to reduce their involvement in the acquisition of their wardrobe. Ready-to-wear even allowed women for the first time to purchase clothing for their male relatives. But well before the introduction of ready-to-wear, publicists had proclaimed that fashion was women's responsibility.[6]

This gendering of fashion marked a decisive moment in the development of the fashion magazine. From its very inception, it became the quintessential women's periodical. Tailors' trade journals and etiquette manuals became the sole printed sources of information and advice about men's dress.[7] Presumably men did not need the print media to advise them since they observed the latest fashions in men's wear during the course of their daily activities. Women, on the other hand, were supposed to be confined to the home and therefore needed both visual representations of the latest fashions as well as guidance from fashion experts in the art of dress. Besides descriptions of the latest fashions, these magazines also included columns on cooking and housekeeping, sewing of all kinds, beauty, and light literary works considered suitable for ladies. By the middle of the nineteenth century, many fashion magazines regularly included paper patterns of featured outfits as well as patterns for embroidery, cross-stitch, and other decorative arts. By offering practical advice and services unavailable to the readers of other magazines, the fashion magazine established for itself an expanding, dynamic market of female readers eager to subscribe.

Russian publishers faced some serious challenges in their attempts to establish a domestic fashion press. The reading public was quite small in the eighteenth and early nineteenth centuries. Although no precise figures exist, one scholar has calculated that in the 1790s when the population of central Russia was about 28 million, publishers sold approximately 30,000 calendars per year, the most popular publication during that period. In fact, during the eighteenth century, the most popular published works included religious tracts of all kinds, almanacs, and calendars, followed by stories and novels.[8] Despite these inauspicious circumstances, the very first Russian fashion magazine appeared in 1791, *The Shop of New English, French, and German Fashions* (*Magazin angliiskikh, frantsuzskikh, i nemetskikh novykh mod*). Published in Moscow, it reported on foreign and Russian trends, and included two fashion plates.[9] Failing to find immediate success, it ceased publication after only three issues. Literate Russians preferred other kinds of reading material, and the market was simply too small to sustain a

periodical for women only. At this point in time, domestic ventures could not compete with foreign, and especially French, fashion magazines.

Nevertheless, some important changes began to reshape the Russian reading public in the first decades of the nineteenth century. After Napoleon's unsuccessful invasion of Russia in 1812, Russian Francophilia began to subside. The government and the reading public, under the spell of romantic nationalism, began to work toward the creation of a national literature written in Russian on Russian themes. Part of this new emphasis included the publication of periodicals called "thick" journals whose purpose was to discuss the serious political, social, and cultural issues of the day. These journals helped to create a wider market for printed material by making it easier for individuals outside of Moscow and Petersburg to read about and participate in Russian intellectual life.

There was one particularly important feature to this new Russian literature. Under the powerful influence of early nineteenth-century Romanticism, Russians like other Europeans defined literary genius as a male quality. According to this view, it was men's prerogative to write about the moral and philosophical issues of the day while women's literary output was to be confined to domestic matters. The impact of this domestic ideology had two outcomes. Women writers, discouraged from writing on "serious" topics, excelled at society tales. In these stories, women dominated the social scene which, in turn, gave them an important role in determining what constituted good taste.[10] While the cult of male genius helped reinforce women's domain as domestic, it also allowed women to serve as chroniclers of that domain. This, in turn, encouraged sophisticated and shrewd entrepreneurs to contemplate the creation of a Russian fashion magazine that would privilege women's interests and role as social arbiters.

## THE FASHION PRESS IN RUSSIA, 1830–1870

Creating a new kind of magazine was not an easy affair in Russia. In addition to finding the financial resources and fashions to produce such a periodical, publishers also needed government approval. Russia, like many other

57  A fashion plate from *Petit Courrier des Dames*, April 1837. It was French fashion plates that were essential to have in a Russian fashion magazine. Private collection.

European countries at that time, had strict censorship regulations that governed all publications including fashion magazines.[11] In order to gain government approval, publishers had to petition the Central Censorship Administration, explaining the need for a new journal, and submit a program of what was to be included in the periodical as well as how much it would cost. Once the censors had approved the format and price, neither of these could be altered unless the publisher petitioned the authorities again, outlining any changes. Furthermore, all text and illustrations for each and every issue of a magazine needed government approval before they could be

printed. The censorship regulations gave the Russian government considerable power over the fashion press, a power that it would use fitfully to control this segment of the Russian media.[12]

The first individual to petition successfully for government approval for a new fashion magazine was M. A. Bestuzhev-Riumin, successful publisher of the magazine, *Northern Mercury* (*Severnyi merkurii*). In 1830 he requested permission to publish a new periodical for elite women called *Garland: A Journal of Literature, Music, Fashion, and Theater* (*Girlanda: Zhurnal slovesnosti, muzyki, mod i teatrov*), whose purpose was to provide its readers with "delightful and significant stories from Russian literature, and in addition to reporting the latest news from the world of music, fashion, and the theater."[13] The petition was approved in the same year, and *Garland* became one of the most successful of the early fashion magazines. A few years later in 1835, the noblewoman Maria Koshelovskaia proposed publishing *Paris Fashion Herald* (*Vestnik parizhskikh mod*). She stated that, in consultation with one of the best French dressmakers working in Moscow, her journal would reproduce fashion plates from the leading French magazines. With the text in both French and Russian, Koshelovskaia, like Bestuzhev-Riumin, intended her publication for the elite market.[14]

A year later in 1836, one of the most important and dynamic leaders of the new fashion press, Elizaveta Frantsovna Safonova, began publishing her first magazine, *Magazine of the Latest Needlework* (*Zhurnal noveishago shit'ia*), in Moscow. Little is known about Safonova except that she was the wife and later widow of a minor government official with three children to support. While economic necessity may have driven her into publishing, it was her skills as a businesswoman that made her such a success. Shortly after she started her Moscow magazine, she moved to St. Petersburg where in 1838 she petitioned the Central Censorship Administration to allow her to change the name of her magazine to *St. Petersburg Journal of Sewing and Embroidery* (*Sanktpeterburgskii zhurnal raznogo roda shit'ia i vyshivaniia*).[15] Having gained government approval, Safonova petitioned again in 1838, this time asking permission to start a periodical called *High Society Pages* (*Listki dlia svetskikh liudei*). This time government authorities told her she could publish the plates but no stories as she had originally requested. By 1840 Safonova was the publisher of two successful fashion magazines.[16]

Despite the initial success of these first fashion magazines, the Central Censorship Administration did not always look with favor upon these types of publications. In 1841 a German woman asked to publish a fashion magazine in French, but the censorship committee refused, arguing that there were already several fashion magazines and Russia did not need another one.[17] In 1852 Safonova proposed publishing her third magazine which she wanted to call *Seamstress* (*Shveia*). This magazine was intended for dressmakers and seamstresses of all kinds, not just the elite of the craft. Safonova wanted to publish it three times a month instead of once a month, as was typical of other fashion magazines, and reduce the price, thereby making it more affordable for dressmakers. Ever mindful of marketing opportunities, Safonova proposed to publish her magazine in both Russian and Swedish (because there were no such periodicals in Finland where Swedish was the language of the upper classes). The Central Censorship Administration turned down her petition, stating that in 1841 the Ministry of Education had prohibited anyone from publishing more than two periodicals at one time without special permission. Furthermore, the censors argued that there was another journal published in Swedish, but since even that did not have enough readers, they saw no reason to authorize yet another pubication that was doomed to fail.[18]

These examples show that although Russian publishers were striving to create a multifaceted fashion press by the mid-nineteenth century, government officials sometimes thwarted their efforts. Unwilling to allow market forces free reign, government censors rather than readers determined the number and content of the magazines. Consequently, attempts to expand the market beyond elite circles had to be done with caution. In the early nineteenth century the elite wanted to maintain its monopoly over fashion by restricting access to fashion news. The fate of Safonova's magazine for ordinary dressmakers and seamstresses illustrates this tendency. The government and high society agreed that dress was to remain a clear marker of social rank.[19] This made the production of fashion magazines a capricious and difficult enterprise as publishers tried to outwit the ever-suspicious censors in their efforts to expand their audience.

By mid-century there were enough fashion magazines that they began to compete with each other for readers. Safonova's publishing enterprises illustrate how this competition developed. The two magazines that she published during the 1840s had two distinct programs. The *St. Petersburg Journal* provided patterns and practical advice for needleworkers; embroidery, cross-stitch, and lacemaking were the subjects of this magazine. Here the intended audience was primarily elite women and industrious women of the middle ranks who spent many hours creating beautiful pieces of needlework with which to decorate their homes and their person. *High Society Pages* disseminated French fashion plates. By separating these two functions into different magazines, Safonova cleverly expanded her potential readership. While the two markets almost certainly overlapped, nevertheless, women interested in needlework and fashion needed to subscribe to both magazines.

Another strategy Safonova adopted was to change the names of her magazines to distinguish them from those of her competitors. In 1846 she received permission to change the title of *High Society Pages* to *Journal of Paris Fashions* (*Zhurnal parizhskikh mod*), a title that she felt was more accurate. However, this title confused buyers and sellers alike, since there was a journal published in Moscow also called *Paris Fashions* (*Parizhskie mody*). In 1850 she asked that her journal be renamed *Fashion: A Magazine for High Society* (*Moda: Zhurnal dlia svetskikh liudei*).[20] This pattern of renaming periodicals was also common in western Europe. With each reincarnation, the periodicals' publishers tried to stay one step ahead of the competition.

In 1851, Safonova took a step that she probably regretted for the rest of her life. In that year, she asked for government approval to transfer ownership of her newly renamed journal, *Fashion*, to her daughter, Sofia Lund, but her daughter for unspecified reasons quickly relinquished the magazine to Olympiada Grigorevna Riumina in 1852. Riumina was the wife of Riumin, a staff officer and inspector of the Konstantin School for Cadets in St. Petersburg. As the wife of such a highly placed military officer, she had excellent connections in the capital, particularly among artists and storeowners.[21] This made her an ideal candidate to publish a magazine dedicated to high society. But, in addition, this change in publishers had removed *Fashion* from Safonova's control, and very quickly the publishers became rivals.

For two years, Riumina followed the publishing program that Safonova had developed for the magazine, but in 1854 Riumina turned over her publishing and editing duties to her husband. Unlike his wife, Riumin wanted to transform the magazine from a fashion magazine into a literary publication that would report on the Petersburg cultural and social scene more broadly. His mistake was that he proceeded with his plans to transform the magazine without first obtaining permission from the Central Censorship Administration, which led to a confrontation between government officials and the publishers.

The first salvo came when Riumin published a book on needlework, the first in a series. According to their respective publishing programs, only Safonova's journal *Vase* could produce sewing patterns. Safonova immediately demanded that the Central Censorship Administration look into the matter because, as the former publisher of *Fashion*, she knew full well that Riumin's needlework handbook exceeded his authority. In her petition, Safonova emphasized her obedience to the censors' wishes, but she also used gendered language to place herself in an unassailable position. She wrote that, in all of her years in business, she had only once violated her publication program when she placed an article about dancing in *Vase*. Other than this minor mistake, she had done nothing to undermine the trust that the censors had placed in her. Furthermore, Riumin's incursion into her area of the fashion market – sewing and embroidery – threatened her very livelihood, as his sewing handbook was clearly intended to lure away her subscribers. She also emphasized in her petition that she was a "poor" widow with a young son in the Russian Army, and her publishing business was her only means of support. Thus, Safonova cleverly used gendered language to present herself as on the verge of destitution, thereby masking her considerable skills as a shrewd businesswoman with over twenty years of experience in publishing.

Riumin foolishly went over the heads of the Central Censorship Administration and wrote a letter directly to the Minister of Education – whose job it was to oversee Russian censorship – in which he laid out his plans for a newly revised periodical. However, Riumin's actions demonstrate that he did not understand the publishing business and its relationship to the government. As an officer and an administrator of a cadet school, Riumin tried to use his social and professional connections to present his side of the story. He clearly thought that he could outmaneuver both Safonova and the government censor, Nikolai Elagin, whose job it was to oversee the fashion press, but instead Riumin underestimated the power of both to manipulate bureaucratic procedures in their favor.

When Elagin discovered what Riumin had done, he wrote a scathing report to the Minister of Education outlining the publisher's violations of government protocols. Elagin informed his superior that Riumin had not asked for permission to publish a series of sewing handbooks, a clear violation of the censorship laws. Secondly, Elagin had refused Riumin's request to publish an article on the Italian Renaissance artist, Benvenuto Cellini, but once again, Riumin went ahead and published it anyway. Elagin firmly believed that Cellini's checkered personal life was not appropriate material for a woman's fashion magazine, and he restated his firm belief that a fashion magazine should not be allowed to publish anything but descriptions of the clothing. Elagin urged his superiors to support the "poor" widow Safonova.

The outcome of this bureaucratic battle was as complex as the situation itself. Riumin ultimately failed to gain support for his position. In 1855, he petitioned the Central Censorship Administration to change the name and program of his magazine. The censors turned down his request, and he gave control of the magazine back to his wife. At the same time, however, his superiors removed Elagin as the censor responsible for the fashion press, allowing Safonova and Riumina to petition in 1856 for a change in their respective publication programs. Henceforth, *Vase* could add literary and fashion commentary, and *Fashion* could include articles about art, literature, and sewing.

The Central Censorship Administration's decision to abandon Elagin's narrow definition of the fashion magazine came at a critical moment in Russian history. This raising of the "woman question," discussed in chapter 2, allowed publishers like Safonova and Riumina to take advantage of the more liberal censorship regulations and create magazines that they hoped would cater to all aspects of women's lives while at the same time expanding the market for their publications beyond the aristocracy to include women of the middle ranks. The government's call to all subjects to participate in Russia's revitalization meant that the fashion market would of necessity expand as more and more Russians needed advice on what to wear. The fashion press was only too happy to oblige.

Reflecting these changes, in June 1861, Sofia Grigorevna Mei, the author of several short stories and translator of French literature, petitioned the censorship authorities to start a new journal called *Fashion Store* (*Modnyi magazin*). Mei wanted to include Paris and Petersburg fashions with plates, articles about housekeeping, and *feuilletons* in her magazine.[22] In her statement of intent to the Central Censorship Administration, she declared:

> In enlightened countries women have long understood the importance of useful work. Every educated Englishwoman already sews her own clothing and gives her fiancé a handmade shirt for a wedding gift, but we still waste time embroidering screens and pillows and other such things whose finishings use up so much money that would be so easy to manage without. Is it not time that we return to more practical pursuits and remember that "time is money"?[23]

Echoing Maria Vernadskaia's views of the emancipatory power of work for elite women (see chapter 2), Mei's sentiments reflected the changing attitudes toward women's work which were part of the spirit of the 1850s and 1860s. Not only was she advocating more productive labor for women in the home, but also her own right to make money as the publisher of a fashion magazine. Mei's bold statement of independence, which certainly must have startled the Central Censorship Administration, won her permission to publish her magazine. *Fashion Store* quickly gained a niche for itself in the market, and Mei presided over it during the 1860s and 1870s, retiring as publisher in 1883.[24] In that year she arranged with government authorities to hand over her magazine to Herman Goppe, a German who transformed the journal as part of his new publishing empire.[25] As we will see, the

fashion magazines published after 1870 differed in important ways from their predecessors.

If *Garland*, *Vase*, *Fashion*, *Fashion Store*, and the other fashion magazines that appeared during these years marked a distinct period in the history of the Russian fashion press, what were the common bonds that linked them? In order to answer that question, it is necessary to examine more fully the purpose of the magazines, and, in particular, the marketing strategies that publishers used to entice readers to buy their magazines.

## EARLY MARKETING STRATEGIES

The chief task for publishers and editors in the first half of the nineteenth century was to wean the reading public from relying on foreign periodicals for their fashion news. This proved to be a tricky problem because the fashions that everyone wanted to copy were French, and so it made sense that Russians should seek out that information from French magazines. The task then was to create a periodical that would report the fashion news in both countries. As dependent as Russian publishers were on foreign magazines for fashion plates and news, they hoped to devise a distinctly Russian fashion magazine which could not be confused with the European, and especially French, competition.[26] The strategy, which all the magazines quickly adopted, was to report on fashion in both Paris and Petersburg. Each issue contained information about the important cultural events in both capitals, who attended, and what they wore. For a number of years Olympiada Riumina, the publisher of *Fashion*, wrote a column on Paris fashions, while a Baroness von B-l-r reported on fashion in the Russian capital. Sofia Mei wrote columns about both Paris and Petersburg for her magazine, *Fashion Store*.

By reporting on the fashions in both capital cities, publishers and their editorial staffs accomplished two interrelated goals. The Paris features announced the current fashions while the stories about Petersburg demonstrated the superior taste of Russian women who transformed French fashions into something suitable for themselves. A benefit of this dual coverage was to establish the magazines as arbiters of good taste and judgment. The editorial staffs saw themselves as mediators between

Paris and Petersburg, with the ability to interpret what Parisian fashions were appropriate for their Russian clientele. As one columnist put it rather succinctly: "To order an expensive dress was not hard – it only required money, but to select one that was becoming and harmonize it with the rest of the outfit was no trifling matter."[27] To demonstrate their expertise, journalists believed it was their duty to report fashion mistakes that they had observed in order to keep Russian women from violating the laws of fashion. In 1852, for example, *Fashion* reported a most shocking innovation in women's fashions, the introduction of bloomers. The columnist declared that "the new invention of the transatlantic Mistress Bloomer could be seen everywhere where fashion reigns."[28] Two issues later, the same columnist reported a sighting on Nevskii Prospekt of two young women from wealthy families promenading in bloomers. The journalist described their outfits in detail, noting that they presented "an original, but slightly strange picture." The advice was to refrain from wearing such ridiculous costume.[29] It was precisely through advice such as this that fashion writers created a clientele for themselves and their magazines. The need to provide timely information on the latest styles and excesses became the *raison d'être* for the Russian fashion press.

Creating a rationale for a fashion press was not the same as creating a market for one. Indeed, given the lack of circulation figures for any magazine during this period, it is difficult to tell how many Russians were actually reading domestically produced fashion magazines. Circulation figures for some magazines are available only in the 1860s. For instance, in 1864, the Central Censorship Administration reported print runs for *Vase* of between 1,500 and 2,000 copies per year, and 4,500 for *Fashion Store*.[30] These figures can give only a rough idea of the magazine sales since many other periodicals also contained fashion news. Moreover, some women borrowed copies of the magazines from friends and neighbors, thereby learning about fashion without actually having to buy copies of the magazines. Thus, the market for the fashion media was greater than the print runs of the fashion magazines alone can suggest.

Although the precise size of the fashion market remains elusive, it is clear that Russian publishers were continually devising strategies to increase their sales. Pro-

ПРИВИЛЕГИРОВАННАЯ ВЪ РОССИИ
**ПРАЧЕШНАЯ МАШИНА,**
ДЛЯ СТИРКИ БѢЛЬЯ,
*изобрѣтенная Б. Муромъ въ Нью-Іоркѣ.*

58 An advertisement for an early washing machine. *Fashion* (15 December 1856), back page. Russian State Library Collections.

ducing a fashion magazine was a costly undertaking. The Parisian fashion plates were expensive to import, but no legitimate fashion magazine could afford to leave them out. The plates were invaluable in the creation of new garments because subscribers could take them to their dressmaker to serve as a model for the kind of outfit they wanted. During the early years of fashion journalism, the chief source of publishing income was through subscriptions. This placed publishers in a particularly difficult situation: How could they raise enough revenue to import the expensive plates and cover publication costs, but not raise the subscription prices too high, scaring readers away? This problem became even more acute when publishers sought to expand their market beyond the elite.

The solution was advertising. Initially, the advertisements were rather small: just a few lines announcing the type of merchandise, name, and address of the store. The ads quickly grew in size, offering more information about the items displayed in them. In 1858 *Fashion* introduced a further innovation by carrying a full-page advertisement on the last page of each issue entitled "The Best Petersburg Stores." The ad contained recommendations in a variety of categories: fabrics, dresses, flowers, cosmetics, shoes, and lingerie. Most of the stores mentioned were regular advertisers in the magazine or frequently mentioned in the fashion columns.[31] Advice about cosmetics ran in the same issue with an advertise-

59 An advertisement for stores, shops, and artisans in St. Petersburg. The ad contains a mix of French and Russian names. Most of the establishments would have been mentioned in various articles in the magazine, demonstrating how retailing and publishing worked in tandem from the earliest days of the fashion press. *Messenger of Fashion* (1 January 1856), back page. Russian State Library Collections.

ment for a new cosmetics store in the capital. A needlework column appeared simultaneously as the magazine offered books on the subject. The advice columns drew women subscribers not only to the magazines but also to the merchandise in the advertised shops, thereby

60  A fashion plate featuring a gown, sleeves, bonnets, and underblouse, February 1862. Private collection.

developing a mutually beneficial system of rewards for subscribers, advertisers, and publishers.

While advertising revenues did help to pay for some of the publication costs, the price of the magazines remained high. To offset this, publishers offered a number of services to their readers. In 1857 *Fashion* provided complete patterns of the outfits it featured in each issue.[32] In addition, *Vase* and *Fashion* both sent out a selection of books and patterns on embroidery, knitting, and other handicrafts, and these supplements were usually included in the cost of a yearly subscription.[33] To judge from the number of services and supplements offered, these various marketing strategies were popular with the Russian reading public. Before long the magazines began to

include, for those who lived outside of Petersburg, the instructions on how to obtain these services. In 1856, *Fashion* duly noted that six copies of the magazine were mailed to Omsk.[34] The fashion magazines provided the provincial gentry with valuable information about the cultural scene in the capital, allowing them to feel themselves a part of the social whirl, if only vicariously. Certainly it is safe to conclude that by the 1850s interest in western fashions was no longer confined to Petersburg and Moscow. Using the fashion magazines as a guide, the provincial elites recreated on their estates the cultural milieu of the metropolitan elite.

The growing popularity of the Russian fashion press was due primarily to the business instincts of its male and female publishers. Although very little is known about any of these remarkable individuals, they came from different backgrounds. As we have noted, Bestuzhev-Riumin was already a successful publisher (of *Northern Mercury*) before he started *Garland*; Safonova was the wife, then widow, of a civil servant; Mei was a successful short-story writer and translator of French literature; and the Riumins were well-placed members of Petersburg high society. The one common thread that linked them is they all lived in the Russian capital. During the first half of the nineteenth century, Petersburg was the point of entry for Parisian *haute couture* into Russia. This made residence there essential for anyone interested in reporting on fashion. By observing high society up close, writers for the magazines could report with greater accuracy the latest trends and styles. A Petersburg address also allowed publishers to deal more quickly with the slow and cumbersome bureaucracy of the Central Censorship Administration.

Perhaps the most remarkable feature of these publishing developments was the role of women in the establishment of a Russian fashion press. It was Safonova, Riumina, and Mei whose marketing strategies, fashion sense, and business acumen succeeded in creating profitable fashion magazines during the first half of the nineteenth century. Their motivations for undertaking their publishing ventures were as varied as the women themselves. Safonova made clear in her various government petitions that she was the sole breadwinner for her family after her husband's death. Riumina and Mei were both married and, with their husbands' support, undoubtedly sought to improve their financial and social status through publishing.[35] For ambitious, educated women who lived in St. Petersburg, the fashion press offered a rare opportunity to have a meaningful professional life.

At a time when Russian women had virtually no opportunities for a career, their few successes in fashion journalism were all that more remarkable. After all, Safonova began her publishing house in the 1830s well before anyone had raised "the woman question" in Russia. What undoubtedly made her success possible was the very nature of the fashion magazine itself. Its purpose was to provide women with practical advice and support for their roles as wife, mother, and household manager. Because the fashion magazine was aimed at women only, who better to run such a venture than women themselves? The irony was that at the same time that these women publishers were touting the importance of women's domestic role, they were creating a counter role for women outside the home. Ultimately this professional model for women contradicted the domestic agenda publicized in the fashion magazines. By the 1850s when the woman question emerged in Russia, those educated women interested in working outside the home like Sofia Mei could look to the fashion press as a career open to women for whom "time is money."[36]

By 1870 a distinctly Russian fashion magazine had taken shape. Produced primarily by women for women, the magazines included detailed descriptions of the activities and dress of high society in both Paris and Petersburg, information that could not be found in any other printed source. More importantly, by making Russian fashions "news," the magazines integrated Russia into the world of European high fashion. An example from *Fashion* best illustrates this integration. The Crimean War of 1853–1856 made France and Russia enemies. As a result, many Russian women felt that it was unpatriotic to continue to buy French fashions during the war. In order to demonstrate their patriotism, some elite women had taken to wearing Russian dress to balls and soirées. Society women appeared in long Russian jumpers called sarafans and traditional Russian headdresses to dance the polonaise and the waltz. This state of affairs shocked many Russians. Wearing traditional Russian clothing to European-style social gatherings presented a clash of cultures that could not be permitted to continue even in the name of patriotism.

In July 1856 an article appeared in *Fashion* entitled "Russian and General European Costume." According to the author of this anonymous article, "Native dress reflects the nature and education of its people, both in the past and in the present." The reporter went on to criticize the misplaced patriotism of Russian women. This journalist compared these women to children who dress in ridiculous costumes to fight their imaginary enemies. If Russian women insisted upon wearing traditional dress, then they needed to return to their Muscovite ancestors' style of living. To support these claims the author quoted from Nikolai Grech, a well-known Russian conservative, who complained, "Jumping around during a polka or waltzing in the style of dress of the Empress Natal'ia Kirilovna [Peter the Great's mother who lived during the seventeenth century] is absurd and funny." Grech begged the women of Russia to dress "like all the other well-bred women and girls in Europe. Wear sarafans and ribbons only when they suit you and to please your husbands. But do not think that patriotism consists of this: a beautiful hat interferes with healthy thoughts and a French corset stifles a Russian heart."[37] Echoing Grech, the journalist argued that the very idea that patriotism could find expression in clothing was absurd. The expert's advice was "that the dress of women from educated society should be tasteful, conforming to the habits and customs of the modern (*sovremmenoi*) epoch."[38]

*Fashion*'s columnist offered an interesting solution to this sartorial conundrum. Rather than simply saying that with the conclusion of the Crimean War Russian women could again wear French fashions without guilt, the author advanced a more far-reaching proposal. The fashion critic began by arguing that Muscovite and European cultures were separate entities; elements of one could not be used with the other. This was why wearing Russian traditional dress to dance the waltz was so offensive. If Russians insisted upon wearing national costume, then it was necessary for them to adopt the entire lifestyle of their Muscovite ancestors, according to the author.[39] They must abandon their European palaces, furnishings, and food, and return to a seventeenth-century style of living.

Returning to the old Muscovite ways was not something that most members of Russian high society wanted to do. They considered their cosmopolitan European lifestyle a vast improvement over the dark, overcrowded palaces of their Muscovite ancestors. Elite women, especially, had a lot to lose if this approach were adopted for it would mean returning to a very different way of life. Moreover, the very separateness of Muscovite culture meant that Russians could never become members of the European community. This position was anathema both to members of the Russian government and elite society. Nor did the editorial staff of fashion magazines favor the adoption of Muscovite culture for there were no fashion magazines in old Muscovy! Thus, another approach to the problem of what clothes to wear needed to be found.

Consequently, the *Fashion* columnist talked about "modern" rather than European culture. In this usage modern was a more neutral word because it did not refer to a specific nation or geographic area. Modern clothing could be worn both by individuals, who felt themselves to be Europeans, and also by those Russians who were proud of their ethnic heritage. This distinction was particularly important for conservatives because the government remained committed to European clothing as the style of dress for all government functions. To substantiate this claim for modernity, *Fashion*'s columnist invoked Peter the Great. The author claimed that Peter understood that Russians could give up their old clothing because it was superfluous to their sense of national identity. As the author appeared to be arguing that culture in the mid-nineteenth century was no longer European but modern, Russians were invited to participate in the creation of a modern, transnational, cosmopolitan culture and yet remain true patriots.

The logic of this argument called for some important changes in the Russian fashion magazine. If modernity was something to which all women could aspire, then there was no need for a distinctly Russian fashion magazine. Fashion magazines should reflect the latest trends regardless of their point of origin. Magazines like *Vase*, *Garland*, and *Fashion Store* could not meet the demand for this new kind of periodical. As a result, a whole new breed of publishers and magazines came into existence and transformed the Russian fashion press.

## THE RISE OF THE MODERN FASHION MAGAZINE, 1870–1917

European fashion magazines had continued to evolve throughout the nineteenth century. Advertising grew in importance as a major source of revenue. Virtually any product used by women could be found among advertisements in the second half of the nineteenth century. Publishers also continued their practice of offering free supplements with a magazine subscription. Patterns for clothing and needlework, books on household management, cosmetics, and child-rearing were regularly featured as bonuses to subscribers. By blending all of these features into one magazine, publishers were helping to create the ideal nineteenth-century woman. This ideal woman was first and foremost a mother and wife who devoted her life to the care of her family. She was also a consumer of both the magazines and the goods advertised in them. Thus, the fashion magazines presented women with two important roles to which they should aspire – one domestic, the other commercial.[40]

This type of European magazine served as the inspiration for Russian periodicals in the second half of the nineteenth century. Not wishing to limit themselves to fashion, publishers continued to expand their coverage to include those subjects thought to be of interest to all women, not just those of the elite. The goal of publishers was to raise the number of women subscribers, thereby enriching their firms. To do this, publishers needed to find a way to produce less expensive magazines that would have universal appeal. While many individuals tried their hand at publishing a fashion magazine, few were able to do so for more than a few years. The fashion press became a highly competitive business where only the shrewdest, most sophisticated publishers survived. Of all the Russian magazine ventures, three came to dominate the fashion media, *New Russian Bazaar* (*Novyi russkii bazar*), *Fashion World* (*Modnyi svet*), and *Fashion Herald* (*Vestnik mody*). Their history illustrates the rise of the modern fashion magazine in Russia.

In this new generation of magazines, French fashions became the sole focus of the news coverage since everyone agreed that Paris was the capital of the fashion empire. Because there was no need for Russian interpreters of French fashion, one relatively inexpensive way to bring published French fashion news to Russia was simply to translate already existing journals. Publishers did not have to hire a large staff of writers but could rely on a few translators and a good editor to create a Russian edition of a foreign periodical. The first magazine to do that was *New Russian Bazaar*. In August 1866 Sofia Ivanovna Leont'eva, the daughter of a government civil servant, petitioned the Central Censorship Administration for permission to publish a Russian-language translation of the German magazine, *The Bazaar* (*Der bazar*), which was already sold on Russian news-stands. The title for the new magazine was to be *New Russian Bazaar*.[41] The initial response from the censors was negative, but this elicited an angry letter from the real force behind the venture, Wilhelm Goldschmidt, a German subject who had recently moved to Russia. Confident that his publishing venture would be approved, he had already ordered 2,000 copies of the new magazine printed in Leipzig. He had even gone so far as to appoint a Russian to act as publisher on his behalf. When the Central Censorship Administration turned down his request, Goldschmidt demanded a reconsideration of his proposal.[42] Two weeks later, Vasilii Egorovich Genkel', clearly fronting for Goldschmidt, petitioned the government authorities again. This time, the Central Censorship Administration approved the proposal with Petr Ivanovich Eisner to act as editor.[43] Less than a year later, Goldschmidt assumed the role of publisher.[44]

Despite the initial difficulties, *New Russian Bazaar* quickly became popular with women readers. Its chief advantage was that it could present itself as a truly European fashion magazine, not a Russian imitation. Furthermore, the magazine could deliver the fashion news more rapidly since there were fewer delays in the publication process, primarily because the censors were able to approve translations more quickly than original texts. In 1870 after only three years of publication, the Central Censorship Committee reported circulation figures of 6,000 for *New Russian Bazaar*. Its closest competitor was *Fashion Store* with a print run of 5,000 copies. *Vase* was clearly losing ground with only 2,000 subscribers.[45]

*New Russian Bazaar* continued to thrive during the 1870s and 1880s when the magazine's success attracted the attention of the competition. In 1883 Herman Goppe acquired the rights to publish *New Russian Bazaar*, the first of three fashion magazines that his publishing house produced (to be followed by *Fashion Store*, which he took over from Sofia Mei, also in 1883). Goppe's business acumen helped to keep *New Russian Bazaar* as one of Russia's most successful fashion magazines. In 1892 the magazine received permission to publish a supplement called *Paris Fashions* (*Parizhskie mody*), which eventually became a fully fledged magazine in its own right. By 1895, *New Russian Bazaar* was the second most popular fashion magazine (after *Fashion World*) with circulation figures of 10,000 copies.[46]

*New Russian Bazaar*'s chief rival was *Fashion World* (*Modnyi svet*). This magazine's origins reveal the intense competition that existed in Russian publishing. In 1866, Ivan Afanasevich Solomka petitioned the Central Censorship Administration to start a new periodical, *Fashion Journal: A Journal of Fashions and News* (*Modnyi zhurnal: Zhurnal mod i novosti*).[47] In 1868 Solomka appointed a new editor, Iuliia Petrovna Pomerantseva. In November Herman Goppe and Pomerantseva declared their intention of publishing a new journal called *Fashion World* and discontinuing their work on *Fashion Journal*.[48] Before the censors could act upon this petition, they received an irate letter from Herman Karlovich Kornfeld, who identified himself as Goppe's business partner. He claimed that Goppe and Pomerantseva had stolen the material intended for *Fashion Journal* to place in *Fashion World* without his knowledge or consent.[49] The Central Censorship Administration tried to adjudicate this situation by refusing Pomerantseva permission to serve as editor of *Fashion Journal*. Despite this setback, she and Goppe continued to serve as the driving force behind the new magazine, *Fashion World*, during its early years, before she died in 1874.[50]

Like *New Russian Bazaar*, *Fashion World* began as a foreign edition of another German fashion magazine of the same name, *Die Modenwelt*.[51] All the plates and other illustrations were of foreign origin, and the fashion columns discussed only Parisian styles, rarely Petersburg trends. Before too long, however, it began to include stories and information of interest to its Russian clientele. The magazine came out weekly, each issue alternating between a fashion edition and a literary edition. As the magazine grew in popularity, Goppe added new sections

61 A portrait of Herman Goppe, the publisher of *New Russian Bazaar* and *Fashion World*. *Vsemirnaia illiustratsiia*, (16 December 1878), 17. Library of Congress Collections.

62 Goppe's rival, Nikolai Alovert, the publisher of *Fashion Herald*. *Vsemirnaia illiustratsiia*, (16 December 1878), 8. Library of Congress Collections.

dealing with music, family life, and other features. With Goppe's death in 1886, his wife, Adele, took over his publishing duties. She continued her husband's work until her own death in 1895, when her two daughters succeeded her. In 1901 Maksim Adol'fovich Mueller, another German émigré, became the new head of Goppe's publishing firm and continued to publish *Fashion World*. Already in the 1890s, the magazine was the most popular of the fashion periodicals with circulation figures of 12,500, followed by *New Russian Bazaar* with 10,000 copies.[52]

This "German" domination of the Russian fashion press did not go unchallenged. In 1884 Nikolai Pavlovich Alovert petitioned the Central Censorship Administration to start his own fashion magazine, *Fashion Herald: An Illustrated Magazine of Fashion, Housekeeping, and Literature* (*Vestnik mody: Illiustrirovannyi zhurnal mody, khoziaistva and literatury*). Alovert was the successful publisher of a number of technical journals, but now he

wanted to break into the women's market. In order to distinguish his magazine from *Fashion World*, Alovert played upon the patriotic sentiments of his readers. He claimed that Russian women did not receive their fashion news directly from Paris but rather through Berlin. This detour allowed German publishers to change the fashions according to their own tastes, or so Alovert claimed. Arguing that Russian women wanted their fashion news as quickly as possible without any alteration, Alovert promised to publish "real" French fashion plates with Russian text as soon as they appeared in Paris.[53] To hammer home his message, the masthead of *Fashion Herald* appeared in Slavonic lettering with Russian lace artfully draped around the name, and each issue was dedicated to "the Russian woman."[54] Ten years after its founding, the magazine with 9,000 subscribers was the third most popular fashion periodical after *Fashion World* and *New Russian Bazaar*, and claimed Empress Alexandra as a regular subscriber.[55]

There were numerous attempts to create fashion magazines to rival the three leaders, but most of the publications did not survive for more than a few years. Magazines with names such as *Dawn* (*Avrora*), *Fashions and Needlework* (*Mody i rukodelie*), *Parisian Fashion Patterns* (*Parizhskie modnye vykroiki*), and *Viennese Chic* (*Venskii shik*) appeared fitfully during the second half of the nineteenth century, but eventually they succumbed to the competitive pressures that characterized the Russian fashion press during this period. The growing interest in European dress coupled with the adoption of key marketing strategies marked the difference between those magazines that succeeded and those that failed.

## COMPETITION FOR THE FASHION MARKET

The history of the Russian fashion press during its second period of development is closely related to the rise of the publishing firms of Herman Goppe and Nikolai Alovert. These two men came from different backgrounds. Goppe was born in Westphalia in 1836. During his youth he served as an apprentice to printing firms in Germany, England, and Belgium before making his way to Russia. His first publishing efforts included *A Guidebook to Russia* (*Gid po Rossii*), *Petersburg Directory, 1863–68* (*Vseobshchaia adresnaia kniga S-Peterburga*), and *General Calendar* (*Vseobshchii kalendar'*). Then, in the late 1860s he began to work on the magazine that would become *Fashion World*. With the success of his fashion magazine, Goppe was able to fund another popular journal of the time, *Illustration of the World* (*Vsemirnaia illiustratsiia*).[56] His chief rival was Nikolai Alovert, a native of Voronezh and a member of the petty bourgeoisie. He came to St. Petersburg and actually worked for Goppe on *Illustration of the World* from 1869 to 1878.[57] A short time later, Alovert left Goppe and started his own publishing house. Like his former employer, Alovert established his reputation as a publisher of technical journals such as *Notes of the Russian Technical Society* (*Zapiski imperatorskogo russkogo tekhnicheskogo obshchestva*), *Photograph* (*Fotograf*), *Electricity* (*Elektrichestvo*), as well as fashion magazines.[58]

In many ways the rivalry between Goppe and Alovert was symbolic of the entire Russian fashion industry. Goppe, a German with substantial training as a printer, came to Russia to make his fortune in publishing. In his adopted homeland, he trained a gifted apprentice, the Russian Alovert, who eventually left Goppe's employment to set up a rival firm. This sharing of trade secrets and business expertise was essential if Russia was going to establish its own capitalist infrastructure to support a fashion industry. Nevertheless, Goppe must have been angered when he had to face competition from a former employee who used Goppe's German origins against him.

In spite of this intense rivalry, both men shared one feature in common – they had established themselves as publishers of technical publications. By the second half of the nineteenth century, fashion magazines no longer consisted of one or two fashion plates, but they contained large numbers of illustrations for clothing, embroidery, lacemaking, and cross-stitch as well as numerous advertisements. All of this pictorial material required great technical skill and capital to reproduce in large quantities. One of Goppe's admirers wrote:

> Let us not speak about the painstaking editing of a journal and the selection of talented coworkers without whom it is impossible to even think of creating a magazine. No, the publisher of *illustrated* magazines must give all his attention to the *outward appearance* of the publication. The paper, print, plates, drawings, and then the business part of the firm – all these demand the very organizational and administrative talents that G. D. Goppe possessed.[59]

These technical and administrative skills gave Goppe and Alovert a distinct advantage over their potential competitors.[60]

This emphasis on the technical and business aspects of publishing brought about an important change in the magazines themselves. Although the news from Paris might reach Russia more quickly due to the technical prowess of Goppe and Alovert, neither man ever wrote a fashion column. Foreign correspondents who were French or adopted French pseudonyms like "La Parisienne" ("Parizhanka") now wrote the commentary on dress. This change affected the tone of the magazines. The direct and intimate link between Russian publishers, journalists, and readers was lost in favor of a more modern, European tone. Instead of editor and publisher Sofia

Mei writing about changes in fashion, Goppe and Alovert confined their editorial presence in the magazines to occasional notices concerning subscriptions, publication delays, and other technical matters. Goppe's biographer stated that the German publisher was inspired by Adam Smith's well-known dictums about work and savings, not about the latest fashions.[61] For these men the fashion press served as a vehicle to make money for themselves and their firms – the fashion magazines were only one part of their growing publishing empires.

Nevertheless, it is important to stress that these men bore a tremendous responsibility for influencing not only how men and women dressed but also for shaping the gender order in imperial Russia. More was being imported from western Europe than merely news about clothing styles. The ideals of domesticity, which had taken shape in western Europe, came to Russia through the medium of the fashion magazine. Articles about clothes, cooking, and child-rearing became blueprints for how modern women should conduct themselves in society. Unfortunately, it is impossible to know how much publishers like Goppe and Alovert were aware of their role as arbiters of gender roles in Russia. Nevertheless, their contribution toward spreading the gospel of domesticity to their readers was vital.

The gender order also influenced the publishing business itself. While women continued to play important roles in the fashion industry as editors, writers, and translators, men now dominated publishing. The reasons for this are not hard to find. First, women were not given the opportunity to acquire the technical printing skills of the likes of Goppe and Alovert; most women who worked in the printing industry before 1906 served as proofreaders or binders (a skill that required sewing!).[62] Second, large amounts of capital were required to set up all the machinery and to hire the workforce necessary to publish an illustrated magazine. It was no longer a question of simply paying for a fashion plate or two from Paris. Most Russian women did not have access to large sums of money for such capital investment. Given the advantages that Goppe and Alovert had when they began their fashion magazines, it is no surprise that women publishers would have difficulty competing with them. The only exception to this trend was Adele Goppe who took over her husband's firm after his death. It is clear

from the continued success of Goppe's publishing venture that she was a talented publisher, but she acquired her position in the firm through her marital connection.

Goppe and Alovert had other advantages over their competition. Both publishers adopted marketing strategies, which were intended to corner the market for their magazines. Perhaps the most important of these was the price structure of the magazines. As was noted in chapter 3, the 1870s and 1880s marked the rise of ready-to-wear clothes in Russia. The availability of cheap copies of European clothing created an interest in fashion news, which spread from the elite to the middle and even lower ranks of Russian society. Therefore, Goppe and Alovert printed their magazines in multiple editions, each one targeted to a particular share of the market. To give some examples, in 1868 there were two editions of *Fashion World*, one with twelve pictures and the other with twenty-four. The cost of the first edition was four rubles for Petersburg residents, and five rubles and seventy-five kopecks for everyone else. The second edition was five rubles for residents of the capital and seven rubles for non-residents. Goppe advertised his magazine as "the most complete and cheapest fashion periodical."[63] In 1884, Alovert tried to lure customers away from *Fashion World* by offering three editions of his magazine at prices lower than his rival.[64] As the postal service in Russia improved, publishers were even able to offer consumers home delivery for an additional fee.

What distinguished each edition was the number of plates, supplemental brochures, and illustrations that were sent separately from the magazine itself. For instance, over the years subscribers to *Fashion Herald* received pamphlets such as "The Art of Dressing," "An Album of Ukrainian Designs," "Lessons in the Cutting and Sewing of Reformed Women's Clothing," and "An Album of Masquerade Costumes." These pamphlets, which were sometimes translations from western European authors, allowed publishers to feature specialized subjects not regularly discussed in fashion magazines.

Perhaps the most popular of the extras were sized paper patterns. In the United States, entrepreneurs such as Ebenezer Butterick and James McCall set up companies to manufacture these paper patterns for the retail market,[65] but in Russia magazine publishers went into the business of producing sized paper patterns. In 1885,

63  An advertisement announcing the best stores in St. Petersburg. From *Modnyi svet*, 2 (1871), 17. University of Illinois Library
Collections.

the readers of *Fashion Herald* complained that fashion
magazines provided only a few patterns to subscribers,
and frequently these patterns were for outfits that were
not that practical. In response, Alovert promised to supply his customers with full-size patterns of all the outfits
displayed in the magazine. Readers could also write to
a special workshop established by the publisher, and for
a nominal fee order other patterns.[66] At first, Alovert sent
the patterns by separate parcel but that proved too
expensive, so he later sent twenty-four patterns with the
magazine. In 1898 Alovert offered an additional bonus
to his subscribers – they could order patterns in eight
different sizes.[67] All this attention to paper patterns shows
their importance to the readers of *Fashion Herald*. Since
there was no Russian equivalent to Butterick or McCall

until the eve of World War I, the paper patterns of
fashion magazines provided a great service to dressmakers, seamstresses, and home sewers.

Another benefit that fashion magazines supplied were
the advertisements that proliferated during the second
half of the nineteenth century.[68] In 1868, *New Russian
Bazaar* charged eight kopecks a line for advertisements.
Other magazines charged as much as twenty kopecks per
line.[69] Whatever the actual costs, many business people
saw advertising as an important venue for publicizing
their stores and products. Interestingly, ads in the fashion
magazines were not limited to clothing and accessories.
Corsets, hats, shoes, cosmetics, health aids, magazines, and
books all received publicity on the pages of Russia's
fashion magazines. These ads benefited publishers
because the advertising revenues helped to offset rising
costs. At the same time, women subscribers obtained
useful information on a whole range of products and
services.

Readers clearly valued the extras that the fashion magazines provided. By the 1890s, all the major publications
had a mail column as a regular feature. Unfortunately, the
magazines did not publish the letters from readers, so it
is impossible to know what these women actually wrote.
The editors' answers to these queries suggest that virtually everyone wrote to obtain further information about
a product or topic that had been discussed in a previous
issue. Questions about patterns, cosmetics, and household
hints were frequent. In 1870 a rather irate editorial
appeared in an issue of *New Russian Bazaar*. The editor,
Ol'ga Aleksandrovna Blagoveshchenskaia, complained
that she received huge numbers of letters from readers
demanding a response to their queries in the next issue.
She carefully explained to them the intricacies of the
publishing industry, which precluded a quick response to
each individual letter.[70] This rather pedantic editorial
demonstrates the value that both publishers and readers
placed on the services the magazines provided.

Once the fashion market had developed sufficiently
in Russia, publishers of fashion magazines began target-
ing specific subscribers. The most important of these sub-
groups were the dressmakers. Russian dressmakers had
always relied on foreign and domestic fashion magazines
for their inspiration. Indeed, a successful dressmaker
could take a fashion plate and create a lovely confection

| | | | | | |
|---|---|---|---|---|---|
| Начатыя подушки по канвѣ, послѣднихъ узоровъ | | от | 3 р. 50 до | 6 р. | |
| » » » съ бархатными application | » | » | 9 » | — » | 14 » |
| » » » букеты гобленъ | » | » | 9 » | — » | 14 » |
| » » мохнатой матеріи Torvel, сѣрой | » | » | 5 » | — » | 6 » |
| » » » бѣлой | » | » | 7 » | — » | — » |
| » » суку во французскомъ вкусѣ | » | » | 6 » | — » | 12 » |
| » » атласу, съ кретономъ | » | » | 6 » | — » | 8 » |
| » составленныя изъ различныхъ матерій и | | | | | |
| цвѣтовъ, съ большимъ вкусомъ | » | » | 10 » | — » | 14 » |
| полоски для стульевъ, по сукну съ кретономъ | » | » | 5 » | — » | 6 » |
| полосы » креселъ Longchaise въ началокъ по сукну | » | » | 15 » | — » | 18 » |
| салфетки по сукну | » | » | 14 » | — » | 25 » |
| » лава и вафельной канвѣ, красив. узоровъ | » | » | 3 » | 50 » | 5 » |
| ковры новѣйшихъ узоровъ по канвѣ | » | » | 10 » | — » | 15 » |
| Экраны, вышитыя фигуры, безъ фона | » | » | 9 » | — » | 15 » |
| Подушки » бисеромъ, послѣдняя новость | » | » | 2 » | — » | 8 » |
| » » шерстью, букеты и съ арабесками | » | » | 2 » | — » | 6 » |
| » » высокимъ швомъ, плюшевыя | » | » | 5 » | — » | 9 » |

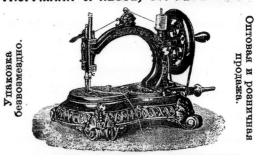
64 A typical page of advertisements. The goods being publicized are sewing machines, tape measures, pianos, cosmetics, maps, paper patterns, hair products, candies, and a shop selling needlework and embroidery. *Modnyi svet*, 78 (1876), 371. Russian State Library Collections.

65   This gown is an example of the bad taste of this young woman or the poor training of her dressmaker. The gown's proportions are simply wrong. State Central Archive of Documentary Films, Photographs, and Sound Recordings of St. Petersburg.

for her client, using her skills in measuring and cutting as well as her knowledge of fabric. These skills did not necessarily require the craftswoman to be able to read the accompanying text – she could see from the illustration what was required. Nevertheless, the expense of the first generation of Russian fashion magazines must have made it difficult for all but the most successful dressmakers to subscribe regularly. With the new technologies which allowed for cheaper editions of fashion magazines, publishers like Goppe and Alovert tried to provide the latest fashion news at a cost dressmakers could afford. In 1893, Alovert began a new publication called *Fashion Herald for Dressmakers* (*Vestnik mody dlia portnikh*), which began as a translation of *Moniteur de la Mode* (*Monitor of Fashion*), the

leading French fashion magazine of its day. Acknowledging that many dressmakers could not afford *Fashion Herald*, Alovert promised to create an edition just for them by eliminating the light fiction and decorative needlework in favor of more colored plates and patterns.[71] In 1903, Mueller, the head of Goppe's publishing house, asked permission to publish four editions of *Fashion World* specifically for dressmakers, ranging in price from four to twenty-four rubles. The chief difference among the different editions was the number of extras included.[72]

The only Russian magazines devoted to men's fashions were solely intended for tailors. Since these magazines were trade publications, they did not contain any light fiction, news stories, or anything else except information about men's dress. The earliest attempt at such a publication was *Russian Artisan* (*Russkii remeslennik*), published from 1862 to 1867. The magazine's purpose was to provide general enlightenment and practical information to the entire artisan community in Petersburg. Each copy of the magazine contained a fashion plate of men's clothing with detailed descriptions of the fashions. Another magazine, intended just for tailors, was *Men's Fashions* (*Muzhskie mody*) published from 1874 to 1884. Friedrich A. Iurgens, a Petersburg sewing-machine salesman, started the magazine.[73] *Men's Fashions* was just four pages, and the text was in German and Russian reflecting the prominence of German tailors living in the Russian capital. In 1875 the magazine introduced a new feature called "The Art of Cutting" to encourage journeymen to teach themselves to become cutters.[74] Despite these innovations, the magazine fell upon hard times. Iurgens blamed the devaluation of the Russian currency for his problems; a devalued ruble made it difficult to purchase the fashion plates from European publishers.[75] Other magazines that focused on men's fashions faced similar problems.

It is difficult to know for certain why these magazines failed. It may have been that Russian tailors were too poor to subscribe to specialized journals, or, because men's fashions did not change quite as dramatically as women's, tailors did not need the latest news from Europe in order to succeed in their trade. It is also quite possible that fashion magazines had become so thoroughly associated with women that men felt uncomfortable subscribing to periodicals that featured men's clothing. Whatever the reason, magazines intended for male tailors were short-lived in Russia. And unlike women dressmakers, who could subscribe to women's magazines to obtain fashion news, there was no comparable men's magazine that reported on men's fashion to which tailors could subscribe.[76]

In addition to pitching magazines to niche markets within the fashion industry, Alovert experimented with specialty fashion journals, which focused on the fabrication of a specific type of clothing for both professional and non-professional sewers. These magazines did not carry any of the features such as short stories and household hints that *Fashion World* or *Fashion Herald* included. Instead, these magazines focused on individual items in women's wear as well as children's clothing.

Although these more specialized periodicals were not as successful as the big three fashion magazines targeted for a general audience, the growing diversity among Russian fashion periodicals by the early twentieth century suggests that the market for fashion news was on the rise. Because the archives for publishing firms have not been preserved, it is difficult to calculate just how large this market was. Nevertheless, some clues remain as to the growing importance of the fashion press. In 1895, the Central Censorship Administration reported the following circulation figures for the leading fashion magazines:

| | |
|---|---|
| *Fashion Herald* | 9,000 |
| *Fashion Herald for Dressmakers* | 3,000 |
| *Fashion World* | 12,500 |
| *New Russian Bazaar* | 10,000 |

These figures do not include print runs from the other smaller fashion magazines. Even if there were a few subscribers to more than one magazine, the total is more than 34,000.[77]

Print runs also fail to reveal the social profile of the audience for fashion magazines. Nevertheless, a few points can be made. Moving beyond the elite market in the 1870s, the new generation of fashion magazines attempted to appeal to all women, but especially literate women of the middle ranks. For them the magazines served as a guide to respectability through dress, manners, interior decoration, cooking, and childcare.[78] The allure of the magazines was that if a woman followed the advice, she could improve her social status and affirm her femininity. At the same time, fashion magazines could also appeal to semi-literate or illiterate working women. Goppe's editorial staff acknowledged this in 1878: "Pictures of nature, types of dress, facial features, contours of buildings and their ornamentation – a picture communicates easier than words . . . it provides meaning even to an illiterate person, and that is why an artist's talented pencil serves as a pioneer for progress, a bearer of light into the kingdom of darkness and ignorance."[79] It was this "pioneering" role that the magazines hoped would allow them to expand the market for their magazines. Fashion illustrations provided even illiterate Russians with an opportunity to appreciate cosmopolitan living. For those working-class and peasant women who dreamed of a better life, the illustrations gave their dreams concrete form.

Fashion illustrations proved so popular that other magazines began to include this material. By the 1880s magazines included fashion supplements as part of a yearly subscription. The most successful of the fashion supplements was *Paris Fashions* (*Parizhskie mody*), the quarterly publication of *Cornfield* (*Niva*). *Cornfield* was the most widely read magazine in the second half of the nineteenth century with circulation figures of over 200,000 by 1900.[80] An illustrated weekly, its purpose was to bring fiction and news to a broad range of readers. A. F. Marx, *Cornfield*'s publisher, introduced *Paris Fashions* in 1872 and it continued uninterrupted until World War I.[81] In the early years, the supplement included rather inferior reproductions of French fashions along with the patterns to make the clothing. The growing financial success of *Cornfield* eventually allowed the publisher to provide better reproductions and more intricate patterns as well as recipes and household hints. Supplements such as these demonstrate that the desire to learn more about European fashion was no longer confined to the urban elites in imperial Russia, but had now spread to the rural intelligentsia and prosperous peasants who subscribed in large numbers to these magazines.[82] In 1883, a rural schoolteacher reported that village priests subscribed to religious periodicals unless they had daugh-

66   A fashion plate, 1887. Private collection.

ters, in which case they received copies of *Cornfield* as well.[83] It may very well have been that these young women encouraged their fathers to subscribe so that they could receive *Paris Fashions*.

The final indication that the market for fashion news was flourishing was the intense competition among the publishers to produce the magazines. In 1880, Goppe wrote to the Central Censorship Administration with a complaint. The censors had asked publishers to refrain from using the words, "the most complete" and "the best" in advertisements for their magazines. Goppe complied with this request, but the publishers of *Fashion Store* and *New Russian Bazaar* did not. He insisted that the censors enforce the regulation uniformly.[84] In January 1885 just a few months before his untimely death, Goppe wrote again to the censors, this time to complain about his rival, Alovert. Alovert claimed in his advertisements that *Fashion Herald* was the only Parisian fashion journal in Russia. This claim was blatantly untrue and Goppe demanded that the censors intervene. They refused to get involved.[85]

These complaints about false advertising were a prelude to the magazine takeovers that became a common feature of the fashion press in this period. Each publisher strove to become the tsar of the fashion press. By 1890 the Goppe publishing house controlled the two most popular fashion magazines, *New Russian Bazaar* and *Fashion World*, but Alovert remained determined to overtake his former employer. Clearly, the lucrative nature of the fashion market encouraged Alovert's dreams of establishing a fashion publishing empire. After the successful launching of *Fashion Herald*, which quickly began to rival the Goppe publications, Alovert added specialty magazines, and in 1898 he even started a new magazine, *Fashion Courier* (*Modnyi Kur'er*).[86] As late as 1903, government censors refused Alovert permission to publish his sixth journal, claiming that he already had enough fashion magazines.[87] This was only a temporary setback for the aggressive publisher. By the early years of the twentieth century, Alovert felt confident enough of his position that he took over *Fashion World* in 1905, and in 1911 he revived the defunct *New Russian Bazaar*.[88] By the outbreak of World War I, Alovert alone controlled all the leading fashion magazines in Russia.[89]

## GOVERNMENT CENSORSHIP AND PUBLICATION DIFFICULTIES

Despite the growing popularity and financial success of fashion magazines, publishing remained a tricky affair in tsarist Russia. As seen already, government censors continued monitoring the magazines and their content. Moreover, difficulties resulted from relying solely on foreign sources for fashion news. Both of these problems had an impact on how the fashion press developed during the second half of the nineteenth century.

The new government censorship regulations, promulgated in 1865, altered only slightly the rules affecting fashion magazines. As before, a publisher had to seek the approval of the Central Censorship Administration, and any changes in format or price also needed prior authorization. The one major concession to fashion publishers was that certain periodicals could and did receive permission to publish plates and lithographs without first seeking approval from the Central Censorship Administration.[90] In the increasingly competitive world of fashion journalism where publishers struggled to keep up with the ever-changing styles, the ability to publish fashion plates at the same time as they appeared in Europe had wide appeal, for it confirmed Russia's place as an active participant in European *haute couture*.

This freedom to publish fashion illustrations quickly relieved publishers of only one aspect of government surveillance. In the second half of the nineteenth century, Russian publishers included light and serious fiction in their magazines, as did western European periodicals. These stories posed problems for government censors, however. The ever-suspicious Russian government tried to prevent the publication of any story that could place the government in an unfavorable light or cause social unrest of any sort. So, when the publisher of *New Russian Bazaar* submitted a chapter from John Stuart Mill's *The Subjection of Women* for inclusion in the magazine in 1869, the censors refused permission.[91] In 1885 the same magazine was refused permission to print a story called "London Society," an account of the relationship between Queen Victoria and her nobility.[92] Two years later, censors deemed a story about a young woman's involvement in the French Revolution as "not suitable for a fashion magazine."[93] These stories, culled from European fashion magazines, reveal all too well the government's desire to limit discussion of any issue with political implications, even though the events took place in western Europe. Indeed, the only semi-political issue, which was regularly covered in the fashion magazines, was the women's dress-reform movement.

While it might be understandable that government censors would be nervous about articles dealing with political issues, they were equally cautious about short stories, which were a regular feature of the fashion magazines. The story that illustrates this best is "The Revenge of a Polish Catholic Priest" ("Mest' ksendza").[94] The tale incorporated themes that were to become typical of women's Gothic romances: A beautiful young Russian countess is married off by her family to a man many years her senior. She is deeply unhappy, dreaming of a better life, when she meets and falls madly in love with a young Russian gentleman named Dorin. Their affair culminates in the birth of a male child who is then given to a Polish Catholic priest to raise. The priest takes the child to Poland where he raises him to hate all things Russian. In 1863, during the Polish uprising, the Russian father and his now Polish son meet on the battlefield. Taken prisoner and sentenced to hard labor, the son fractures his skull in prison and dies. The priest then reveals to Dorin that he is the father of the dead prisoner, and Dorin promptly goes mad.

According to Amaliia Andreevna Lishke, the editor of *New Russian Bazaar* in 1874, the story concerned daily life in Russia and Poland, and did not constitute a threat to the government, nor did it involve any actual participants in the uprising. Furthermore, she claimed that the description of the Polish uprising was taken from a book the censors had approved in 1868. The censor Smirnov took issue with Lishke's assertions, claiming that the story was not about daily life but very much about the Polish uprising. Moreover, this kind of story was inappropriate for a fashion magazine with such a large audience. The Central Censorship Administration upheld the censor's decision to deny permission to publish the story.[95]

Thus, government censors were quick to sniff out the subversive content of any story, no matter how melodramatic. In this case, Smirnov was obviously concerned that no story publicizing Russia's ignominious role in the Polish uprising should grace the pages of a woman's magazine and encourage sympathy for the Polish cause. For this reason alone, he felt obliged to reject the story and knew he would have the support of his superiors if he did so. Nevertheless, he must have had additional concerns about a story that condoned a woman's flight from an unhappy marriage into an extramarital affair, undermining the Russian government's view of family life. If this was a story about daily life, as Lishke claimed, what did that say about marital relations in imperial Russia? For both of these reasons, the government was determined that this story and others like it should never be published.

Fiction was not the only part of the fashion magazine that drew the wrath of government authorities. Publishers often illustrated literary works with reproductions of famous paintings or other drawings, adding to the overall appeal of the magazines. At first, publishers had trouble gaining approval to publish such pictures. Goppe was turned down in 1871, but nine years later he finally gained permission to publish reproductions of famous paintings.[96] By the 1890s these lithographs were an integral part of the literary section of the fashion magazine.

Interestingly, the ecclesiastical authorities objected to many of the reproductions found in the fashion journals. In 1882 *Fashion World* published a picture of the Kazan' Mother of God icon. Konstantin Pobedonotsev, the Ober-Procurator of the Holy Synod, wrote an indignant letter to the Central Censorship Administration. He stated that the magazine was allowed to publish drawings of only dress and needlework, and furthermore, the Ecclesiastical Censorship Committee had the right to oversee the publication of all religious images, including the image of the Kazan' Mother of God. The minister of internal affairs himself replied to Pobedonotsev. He justified his censor's decision to allow publication of the holy image by arguing that *Fashion World* was allowed to publish holy images in their needlework section. Many women readers used these sacred images to create liturgical articles for Orthodox services. The Kazan' Mother of God had been approved for just such a purpose, and it was published separately from the fashion plates. Nevertheless, the minister agreed that from now on such images would not appear without approval from the ecclesiastical authorities.[97] There were at least three other occasions when the religious authorities criticized the reproduction of religious works in fashion magazines.[98] In contrast to western Europe where religious images were used to support a traditional view of family life, in Russia the religious authorities forbade the mixing of secular and holy images. Fashion magazines concerned themselves with ugly materialism, and the Orthodox Church wanted to maintain a strict division between the sacred and the profane.

These encounters with government censors give some indication of how the government understood the role of the fashion press in imperial Russia. In 1897, the Petersburg Censorship Committee argued that the purpose of fashion magazines was "to answer questions about fashion, dress, housework, and hygiene."[99] This definition did not permit any discussion of politics or social questions. Consequently, the editorial staffs of the magazines had a very difficult task. As the market for fashion magazines grew in the second half of the nineteenth century, editors and publishers wanted to include material that would entice more readers to buy their magazines. But at the same time they needed to stay within government parameters. For the most part, the magazines were able to achieve this balance. They continued to push the boundaries of what was permissible while trying to refrain from including discussions of political or social issues that would irritate their government overseers.

Not until the Revolution of 1905 did government censorship of printed material end. After that, publishers continued to petition for permission to begin new magazines or to take over failing ventures, but there was no more censorship of the stories and pictures published in the magazines. Despite the new freedom, the format of the fashion magazines barely changed. Publishers had discovered a successful formula mixing fashion and fiction, illustration and text. By the outbreak of World War I, they had created a modern magazine, which differed very little from its European counterpart.

Government censorship was only one of the hurdles that publishers faced in the production of fashion magazines. The other major hurdle was the continued reliance of Russian publishers on foreign sources for fashion news and illustrations. Unlike the fashion magazines of today or the Russian magazines published during the first half of the nineteenth century, publishers did not believe that their objective was to support the domestic fashion industry. Now that the readers of fashion magazines dressed exactly like other Europeans, there was no need to highlight Russian designers or manufacturers. As Alovert declared in 1886, ". . . Russian women through their own exquisite taste and understanding of the laws of fashion stand closer to French women than women from any other nation . . ."[100] Because all the experts declared that the French were the international arbiters of taste in clothing, access to French sources remained vital. No fashion magazine had any legitimacy unless it could declare a thorough knowledge of French trends.

This dependency on foreign sources created continual problems for Russian publishers during the second half of the nineteenth century. The production of colored fashion plates remained an expensive undertaking. The best plates were hand-painted and then made into lithographs, which could then be reproduced in the magazines. Furthermore, the French completely controlled the production of colored plates in the nineteenth century.[101] That meant Russian publishers had to establish foreign contacts in order to obtain the necessary plates. In the case of *New Russian Bazaar* and *Fashion World*, their German counterparts served as ready suppliers, but Alovert spent much time and effort in finding French business partners for his magazine. The demand for the costly plates grew significantly as publishers tried to include more plates in each issue of their magazine. In 1888, Alovert asked permission of the censorship authorities to raise the price of his magazine because the new protectionist tariffs had significantly raised the customs duties on fashion plates.[102] Throughout the 1890s the price of the fashion magazines continued to rise because of the expense of the illustrations. Although much of the printing industry was mechanized in Russia during the second half of the nineteenth century, lithographs were produced primarily by hand.[103] Rising costs put publishers in a difficult position because they feared losing their readers to less expensive magazines. At the same time, larger printing firms had an advantage over smaller ones since they could absorb the expense more easily.

While improved transportation and postal services meant a speedier delivery of fashion plates, any disruption in delivery caused frustrating delays in publication. In October of 1880, the German sales agent for *Fashion Store* informed readers that the steamship "Moskay" which was carrying fashion plates for the magazine was stuck in the ice at Kronshtadt, an island in the Gulf of Finland, not far from Petersburg! Until another way could be found to ship the plates to Petersburg, readers had to settle for short stories and fiction.[104] In 1888 heavy snowfall delayed the trains carrying fashion plates from Paris to Russia.[105] Weather was not the only reason for delays. Any outbreak of hostilities sent shock waves through the fashion press. In 1870 the Franco-Prussian War brought the export of almost all fashion plates to a complete halt when French communication with the outside world was cut off during the siege of Paris. Magazine publishers provided inferior substitutes until French production resumed in 1871.[106]

These problems paled, however, in contrast to the 1917 revolution which brought a temporary end to the fashion press in Russia. Alovert, now the tsar of fashion magazines, wrote about the difficulties all magazines faced during 1917. In January 1917 *Fashion Herald* ceased publication without notice. Six months later, another issue appeared. In a note Alovert promised that he would resume publication once a month with plenty of illustrations to highlight the new fashions. However, he went on to tell his readers of the desperate conditions under which he was operating. Since the beginning of the war, the price of fashion plates had risen between 800 and 1,000 percent, lithographs 500 percent, mailing costs 1,000 percent, and the price of paper between 600 and 1,000 percent.[107] In October, just days before the Bolshevik seizure of power, Alovert published a new price list for his magazine and warned his readers that if they wanted uninterrupted service, they should renew their subscriptions right away.[108] The next issue published a month later further outlined the desperate conditions of the fashion press. The price of publishing a magazine had risen almost twenty times. The company, which had supplied the paper for the dress patterns, now refused to send any more paper. Finally, a shortage of workers in France meant that *Fashion Herald* could no longer provide colored fashion plates to its readers.[109] Alovert published one more issue of the magazine before he was forced to cease publication. All the other fashion magazines collapsed for the same reasons. In the revolutionary cataclysm then engulfing Russia, the market for fashion news evaporated as Russians struggled to survive famine and civil war.

★　★　★

In 1878 Friedrich Iurgens, the publisher of *Men's Fashions*, lamented to his readers:

> As every tailor in Russia knows, we Russians sew European fashions, but we borrow those fashions from western Europe. It follows from this that every fashion magazine in Russia is totally dependent upon a few European firms from whom we receive all essential items for journals in Russia.[110]

67　A fashion plate from *Le Moniteur de la Mode*, summer 1887. Private collection.

For the most part, this assessment of Russian dependence upon foreign publishing firms remained true for the entire imperial period. So long as France remained the undisputed leader of European *haute couture*, magazines that could inform readers of Parisian modes of dress were essential. In fact, throughout the nineteenth century fashion magazines all over Europe were remarkably the same both in terms of their content and layout.

By characterizing the Russian fashion press as a dependent cousin of European magazines, however, Iurgens' statement masks the fascinating history of the fashion magazine in Russia. From rather humble beginnings in the late eighteenth century, fashion magazines had grown in number and popularity, and their success had helped to create a market for women's magazines of

68 A portrait of young couple in 1911. The man is elegantly dressed and groomed. Although his wife is not wearing jewelry, her black lace collar and perfectly coiffed hair indicate that she is a woman who pays attention to fashion. Private Collection.

all kinds in imperial Russia. From the very beginning publishers had vied with each other to see who could produce the most influential periodical. In the race for subscribers, Russian publishers had adopted techniques used by western European publishing houses to attract readers, thereby bringing marketing and other business strategies to Russia. The dynamic and competitive world of the fashion press had become an integral part of the emerging Russian business culture of the nineteenth century.

The history of the Russian fashion press also reveals how publishers sought to provide an education in dress and femininity. Initially, Russian publishers tried to create a fashion magazine that was not merely an imitation of French magazines but something unique and special. In presenting Russian women as arbiters of good taste, the journalists helped to make Russian tastes in fashion part of the wider world of European *haute couture*. The overall message was that Russians may have joined the European fashion world late, but they had quickly caught up to the French in terms of grace and style.

Once these feelings of inferiority had been overcome, Russian fashion magazines could give up reporting on the Russian *beau monde* and concentrate on European tastes and styles. This shift in focus brought about the transformation of the fashion magazine in two important ways. First, publishers no longer catered to the interests of the Russian elite alone. They expanded their market to include women from the middle ranks as well as dressmakers and seamstresses. Through the clever use of marketing, advertising, and other business strategies, publishers created a modern fashion magazine that appealed to growing numbers of women readers. In fact, the craving for fashion news became so widespread in Russia that many non-fashion periodicals carried information about clothing in order to attract women subscribers.

Second, by circumventing the Petersburg elite as the intermediaries through whom other women received their fashion news, publishers allowed all Russian women to participate more directly in the world of European couture. Now many more women could gain admission into the world of high fashion and find out how elegant French women dressed, styled their hair, shopped, and sewed. No expensive trips to Paris were necessary, just a quick stop at the local news-stand. Even if a woman could not afford to buy or sew a single outfit featured in the magazines, she could still participate vicariously in European *haute couture* by thumbing through the pages of Russia's many fashion magazines.

The ability of domestically produced fashion magazines to connect Russian women with a world outside of their own daily existence was as important as their educative role. Just as peasants could step out of their circumscribed lives by reading the popular press, as Jeffrey Brooks has argued,[111] Russian women could transport themselves from Petersburg, Tambov, or Omsk to the streets of Paris, London, or Berlin just by opening the pages of *Fashion World* or *Fashion Herald*. They read the same fashion columns, recipes, household hints, and fiction as women in other parts of Europe. Whether they were able to follow the dictates of the fashion magazines depended upon their individual financial resources. Nevertheless, every woman who sewed a skirt, baked a cake, or fashioned a hat based on information acquired through the fashion press could feel herself part of a modern cosmopolitan community of women who shared the same interests and tastes.

Finally, the fashion press helped to create a new identity for many Russian women, that of modern, sophisticated consumers. No matter how many home-sewing and craft projects the magazines included, their primary message was to go out and shop. The advice columns and advertisements taught women the etiquette of modern consumerism by recommending to them the best stores, fabrics, and clothing styles. In soothing tones, the magazines confidently assured Russian women that their participation in commercial life only enhanced their roles as wives, mothers, and household managers.

69 (*right*)    An elegant young couple, circa 1900. Her gown has a lace inset in the bodice, and cloth buttons. The buttonholes are hand stitched. Private Collection.

70   The inside of Aravin Textile Shop on the Catherine Canal Embankment in St. Petersburg. This photo shows the elegance of the western shops in the Russian capital. The silks are neatly arranged along the walls. The room is furnished with lovely chandeliers, mirrors, and woodworking. The clerks are tastefully dressed and treat their customers with the utmost civility. There are even chairs for clients to rest in while they make their purchases. From *Ves' Peterburg na 1910 g.*, XIX. Harvard University Collections.

# 5

# Clothes Shopping in Imperial Russia

THE FASHION INDUSTRY'S SUCCESS was dependent upon the development of a shopping network where consumers could purchase their wardrobes. During the eighteenth and nineteenth centuries, shops selling western fashions emerged alongside traditional Russian stores, fairs, and markets. These fashion shops introduced new forms of retailing – arcade shopping centers, department stores, and mail-order catalogues. With the development and proliferation of western European retailing came the need to define clothes shopping both socially and culturally, to institutionalize the "values and forms of relationships based upon the purchase and acquisition" of clothing.[1] In Russia, as elsewhere, gender gave shape to the discourse on production and consumption: men produced and women consumed. But, in addition, fashion critics used clothes shopping as a way of defining national identity by establishing a "western" and a "Russian" style of shopping. At the same time, there was an attempt to counterpoise the new urban world of the western stores with the traditional trading of the Russian markets. All of these oppositions – male/female, Western/Russian, and urban/rural – played a critical role in the development of the fashion industry and the creation of a Russian consumer culture.

★   ★   ★

## SHOPPING AND NATIONAL IDENTITY

In order to understand Russian retailing, it is necessary to say a few words about general European commercial developments particularly as they relate to clothes shopping. Retailing throughout Europe developed according to a common pattern. The first markets were open areas where traders hawked their wares displayed on the ground or on small carts. Since most clothing in the premodern period was handmade, these markets sold items such as shoes and hats, which were difficult to make at home but were desirable to wear. Those who could afford custom-made outfits purchased their garments from small tailors' workshops scattered throughout urban areas. These open-air markets and workshops frequently developed into more formalized trading rows. Trading rows were usually housed in large, unheated buildings where merchants and artisans would each have a small area to exhibit their wares. In the case of clothing, items necessary to dress properly – fabric, lace, shoes, and hats – could frequently be found in the same row. In an era when clothing was worn until the fabric frayed beyond repair, second-hand clothing was usually for sale in markets and trading rows. Finally, there were itinerant peddlers who roamed the cities and countryside in wagons, or on foot, selling whatever they could carry.

As the pace of commercial life quickened in the seventeenth century, new urban retail outlets developed. The first improvement was the creation of the specialty store.

These retail establishments improved upon previous shops in several ways: They were well lit, heated, and contained orderly displays of goods. The creation of these elegant boutiques particularly affected tailoring and dressmaking establishments. Sophisticated artisans created elegant anterooms where clients could discuss their clothing needs in comfort and style. These small specialty stores grew so rapidly in European urban centers during the eighteenth century that there was a need to create more retail space. This led to the development of the arcade shopping center. The arcade consisted of rows of elegant stores in a large, covered, multistoried space in which consumers could shop no matter what the weather. Arcades quickly became home to many stores dealing with fashion and clothing, as well as restaurants. Clustered in fashionable shopping districts, arcades were a place for the *beau monde* to see and be seen. The final retail innovation was the creation of the department store in the 1860s, which combined the goods sold at many smaller specialty stores under one roof. The department store was a boon for clothing manufacturers. Every store sold ready-to-wear, custom-made clothes, and accessories. Catering to a middle-class clientele, department stores offered the latest fashions at moderate prices. As the scale of retailing grew in Europe, many department stores and specialty stores opened up subsidiary retail outlets, creating large, and sometimes even multinational, commercial empires.

By the beginning of the twentieth century, most European cities contained shopping districts, which included specialty stores, arcades, and department stores. Typically, there was one central business area, where ateliers, boutiques, financial institutions, restaurants, and theaters served as a playground for high society. Outlets of the main specialty and department stores, which catered to the middle classes as well as small family-owned stores, could be found in the outlying shopping districts. Despite the growth of these stores and shopping districts, it is important to stress that open-air markets, flea markets, and trading rows had not entirely disappeared from urban areas. In fact, many working-class people continued to buy all of their possessions at these retail outlets well into the twentieth century, but by that time more modern retail establishments had come to dominate urban commercial life. In rural areas, most peasants shopped at markets and fairs, although increasing numbers traveled to the cities to do their shopping.

## THE INTRODUCTION OF WESTERN STORES IN RUSSIA

Russian retail development followed this European pattern. Before the eighteenth century, merchants sold their goods in open-air markets and trading rows, while peddlers roamed city streets and the countryside hawking their wares. Russians could also purchase goods at large fairs, which were held annually in different parts of the country. Nizhnii Novgorod was the site of the most significant of these fairs, but there were others as well, such as the Contract Fair in Kiev and the Palm Sunday Fair in Moscow. Since most clothing in Muscovite Russia was made at home, few clothing items were found at these venues.

The first stores to sell western clothes sprang up in the German Quarter in Moscow during the seventeenth century. These small tailoring enterprises clothed western European émigrés who had made their home in the Russian capital. Tailors in the Kremlin workshops also sewed western-style clothing for members of the court.[2] After Peter the Great's sartorial revolution, European tailors and dressmakers created elegant shopping districts located near financial institutions and homes of the wealthy.[3] In Petersburg, members of high society flocked to the upper part of Nevskii Prospekt to purchase their outfits, while in Moscow the fancy shopping area was located in the White City (Belyi Gorod) district, which included Tverskoi Boulevard and Kuznetskii Bridge not far from the Kremlin. In these two areas, Russian consumers could find all the essential stores that sold fabric, ribbons, lace, hats, shoes, and men's haberdashery to dress *à la mode*. In 1852, of the forty-four shopkeepers in the Miasnitskii section of Kuznetskii Bridge, only two had Russian last names. Although it is impossible to tell from the documents which shopkeepers were Russian subjects in 1852, the overwhelming number of foreign names suggests the preponderance of foreign capital at the beginnings of Russian commercial development.[4]

During the nineteenth century, Russia's other big cities developed exclusive shopping districts. In Kiev, the

71 (*left*) The inter-section of Nevskii Prospekt and Bolshaia Morskaia Street in St. Petersburg. It was this section of the city, close to the Winter Palace, that became home to many of the city's elegant dress shops and tailoring firms. Library of Congress, LC US262 101808.

72 (*below*) Kuznetskii Bridge in Moscow. The picture shows the mix of foreign and Russian stores, a common sight in all cities in the Russian Empire. Library of Congress Collections.

73　A. Kurtz's Shop of Women's Clothes on the Catherine Canal Embankment in Petersburg. The shop signs in three languages, the tasteful window displays, and the store's location were all intended to attract a well-heeled clientele. *Ves' Peterburg na 1910 g.*, xlvii. Harvard University Collections.

Khreshchatyk housed exclusive western stores, and in Odessa, Nikolaev Boulevard and De Ribas Street drew customers eager to purchase fine European clothing. As in the two capitals, foreigners came first and set up fashion boutiques. Russians who wanted to sell western fashions soon established their own stores next to their foreign competition.[5]

Two different types of stores dominated the sale of western clothing in Moscow and Petersburg in the eighteenth and early nineteenth centuries. The first were the tailors' and dressmakers' ateliers, described in chapter 1. The second was the fashion store (*modnyi magazin*).[6] According to one historian, "In the new [fashion] stores light replaced darkness, and space was substituted for exiguity, neat displays for piled-up goods, marked prices for haggling, and cash payment for usurious credit."[7] Increased sales allowed these store owners to spend more on overhead. In Russia, French tailors and dressmakers constituted the elite of the foreign craftsmen primarily because of their connections to Paris, but German and English garment makers also earned a handsome living in both cities, particularly in men's fashions.[8] Between 1792 and the great fire of 1812, well-heeled Muscovites could shop at Louis Ségur's tailoring establishment, Madame Goutte's and Madame Homette's fashion stores, and at Parisian Taste (Au Goût parisien) and Temple of Good Taste (Au Temple du bon Goût).[9] In St. Petersburg, two fancy-goods stores, the English Store (Angliiskii magazin) and a branch of the French store, DeLisle, became the

74  Arthur's Specialty Shop in Women's Lingerie and Men's
Furnishings, 23 Nevskii Prospekt. I. N. Bozherianov, *Nevskii
Prospekt, 1703–1903*, XLV. Harvard University Collections.

most exclusive shops for the purchase of high-quality,
imported textiles deemed most suitable for western
dress.[10] Foreign and especially French dominance of the
fashion trades in Russia persisted well into the nineteenth
century. In fact, many Russians who opened their own
boutiques frequently gave them foreign names to attract
customers. Shops named Madame Josephine, Louis
Kreitser, Vandrague, Société anonyme, Jacques, and
Maison A. Bogen lined the fashionable Petrovka Street
in Moscow, establishing a pattern found in all other
Russian cities as well.[11]

With the advent of ready-to-wear clothing, the fashion stores faced increased competition from retail outlets that sold clothes "off the rack." Most of these fashion
stores had their headquarters in Moscow, which was the
center of ready-to-wear production. The firms of M. and
I. Mandl', Rozentsveig, and the Petukhov brothers, all
had flagship stores in Moscow with numerous outlets in
Petersburg, Kiev, Odessa, and other provincial cities. The
Mandl' company had three retail stores in Moscow, including one on Tverskaia. The company also had stores
in Petersburg on Nevskii; in Kiev on the Khreshchatyk;
and one store in Tiflis. The Rozentsveig firm had five
Moscow stores, including one on Tverskaia and one store
in Samara.[12] The strategy was to have a store in the
exclusive shopping areas to attract the business of the
wealthy, and outlets in other retail districts where middle-
class men and women shopped.

The costs associated with maintaining western stores
in Russia were high. In 1841, one commentator complained that the annual rent for the smallest shop in

75 The House of New Paris Fashions was located on the second floor of 12 Nevskii Prospekt, just a few doors down from the M. and I. Mandl' store. I. N. Bozherianov, *Nevskii Prospekt, 1703–1903*, XII. Harvard University Collections.

Petersburg cost between 800 and 2,000 rubles, which helped to explain why there were only 137 western-style stores in contrast to more than 2,000 Russian shops.[13] By the early 1880s, rents in Moscow's fashionable arcades ran between 8,000 and 15,000 rubles per year. Furthermore, the municipal government imposed a tax on all stores with heated premises along with various other taxes. According to one shopkeeper, a merchant who rented a store in one of the fashionable arcades for 15,000 rubles could expect to pay 1,500 rubles for the heating tax and at least 500 rubles for his shopkeeper's license. These expenses totaled 17,000 rubles alone, and did not include the actual costs of heat and lighting, or the wages of the salesclerks. Russian merchants complained that the high rents and taxes reduced their profits so significantly that they were reluctant to open western stores.[14]

One document offers a rare glimpse into how Russian dress shops functioned. The Imperial Philanthropic Society set up an atelier in Petersburg to train indigent girls to become dressmakers. Despite its altruistic purpose, the shop was an integral part of the Petersburg fashion world. The workshop organizers had even hired French merchants to supply it with French fabrics and trimmings. In 1890 the shop produced gowns worth 42,035 rubles.[15] In 1892 a society official, unhappy that the shop used only imported French fabric to make the clothes, demanded an explanation from Princess M. F. Apakidze who supervised the boutique. Apakidze replied that French fabrics were essential for the success of the business. Although many women were initially put off by the high prices, they came running back to the atelier when they discovered that these fabrics were unavailable anywhere else in Petersburg. As Apakidze put it, "In the commercial world it is customary to pay for the goods using the customer's money, not one's own capital." Since prices for fashion goods only went up, never down, the consumer ultimately paid the cost of importing these goods. This policy was necessary because of the capriciousness of fashion. Apakidze wrote that since a shopkeeper did not know ahead of time what the new fashions were going to be, it was necessary to have a large inventory of fabrics on hand. She believed that this retail strategy worked quite well, since the atelier was highly profitable.[16]

Another problem for shopkeepers was collecting payment for purchases. As noted in chapter 1, many clothing establishments felt obliged to allow their customers to purchase clothing on credit. During the second half of the nineteenth century, payment at the time of purchase became customary, but even then, some clients were still able to buy on credit. At the Imperial Philanthropic Society's atelier, Princess Apakidze reported that several prominent actresses, society women, and wives of provincial factory owners who had shopped at the atelier for more than fifteen years kept running accounts at her store. By wearing these lovely confections at public occasions, these women then became walking advertisements for both the fashions and the shops. Some shops also hired models to stroll among customers to help encourage consumer spending.[17]

Petersburg, the home of the court and officialdom, remained the leading center of European fashions in Russia throughout the imperial period. One scholar has calculated that Petersburg had fifty-four western stores, or *magaziny*, that sold fashions in 1815.[18] By 1868 these numbers had grown considerably. One source lists 422 tailoring shops for men and 133 stores that sold men's ready-to-wear. For women there were 148 dressmaking shops and 142 ready-to-wear stores.[19] In the first city census conducted one year later, statisticians included both apparel makers and traders. Approximately 37,000 men and women listed their occupation as garment workers. Of these 2,800 were owners of clothing ateliers. Another 2,300 individuals were counted as engaged in the sale of apparel. The combined figure of 5,100 represents a very conservative estimate of those individuals engaged in the sale of clothing.[20] According to one

analyst, Petersburg had as many clothing manufacturers as London but fewer store proprietors than Berlin.[21] In the last census conducted before the 1917 revolution, census takers counted 7,751 tailors and dressmakers who owned their own shops, and 6,667 individuals involved in the sale of clothing, bringing the official total to 14,418 individuals.[22] Here, too, these figures are conservative estimates, for many individuals were reluctant to reveal their occupations to government officials in order to avoid paying taxes.

In 1897 a member of the Petersburg sanitary commission reported his findings on conditions in the city's clothing stores. He divided the stores and shops into five different categories, from the most luxurious fashion houses to the tiniest sweatshops. His description of one Petersburg designer's establishment provides a rare look inside the western *magaziny*:

> . . . the House of Brizak, founded in 1868, occupies a large, four-story building at No. 8 Malaia Koniushennaia Street. The first floor is divided into two parts by large colonnaded corridors . . . one room is the area used to take orders and two other rooms contain counters and cabinets filled with fabric, lining, and trimmings. All the rooms are lighted by three large Venetian mirrored windows below and nine windows above. The first floor is connected to the second by a carpeted wooden staircase with mounted mirrors. On the second floor is a gallery covered in carpet and mirrors where mannequins have been placed. In addition there are six other rooms of which two sunlit ones served as areas for taking measurements and three lighted ones are used to choose fabric for evening wear. The other rooms [in the building] are used for the sale of ready-to-wear. All the rooms are light and spacious with high ceilings; the entire house is lit by electricity. The furnishings are luxurious: comfortable furniture, carpets, and mirrors.[23]

The House of Brizak was certainly not typical of most clothing stores in Petersburg, but it served as a model for all others. In order to compete in the fashion business, store owners needed to expend large sums in creating well-appointed establishments.

The rise of retail clothing stores in Moscow developed in a similar manner. Outside of the Trading Rows the old

76 Nevskii Prospekt lined with shops and shoppers. The columned building on the left is Gostinyi Dvor and across the street is the Passazh. Library of Congress, US262 095769.

capital in 1829 had nineteen fashion stores, five stores that sold military attire, and five hat stores. Of these twenty-nine stores, Russians owned a mere seven. There were also thirty-eight apparel makers who owned their own ateliers.[24] According to the city census of 1882, there were 17,337 owners of clothing stores in Moscow. By 1902, the number had increased to 18,665.[25] These figures include owners of the important ready-to-wear firms plus tailors and dressmakers, who did business in their ateliers, as well as makers of umbrellas, corsets, hats, and shoes. One scholar has calculated that by 1890 almost a third of

Moscow's trading establishments dealt with textiles and clothing, second in number only to those that provided room and board.[26]

Perhaps the best indication of the growth of western shopping was the rise of the arcade. During the nineteenth century, shop space became scarce in the exclusive shopping districts in both Petersburg and Moscow. The solution was to build arcade shopping centers. In Petersburg, the first and most famous was the Passazh which opened in the spring of 1848 on Nevskii across from Gostinyi Dvor.[27] By the early twentieth century, Moscow had at least ten arcade shopping centers including the Golitsynskii arcade built between 1835 and 1839, Petrovskii and Solodovnikov arcades in the White City district, and the Popov, Aleksandrovskii, and Postnikovskii arcades.[28] Tailors, dressmakers, and purveyors of fashion-

able goods rented much of this prime retail space. The arcades also housed restaurants and stores that sold home furnishings and other luxury goods, increasing their appeal as shopping destinations for the carriage trade. One disgruntled Muscovite writing in the mid-nineteenth century, Ivan Kokorev, described this transformation:

> . . . specialty shops virtually ground the *lavki* [Russian shops] into the dirt; about ten more years passed – the depot [i.e., *le depôt*, essentially a fashionable, frenchified word for *le magasin*] arrived, and now, wherever you look, depo are everywhere. . . . Then appeared passazhes, galleries, little bazaars and à la, which, it appears, have a magical power to attract Russian purses and empty them à la this way or that.[29]

77   The interior of the Passazh shopping arcade. Shop 3 sold perfumes and Shop 5 was a haberdashery. Built in 1846, the glass ceiling protected shoppers from the elements as well as providing natural light. Central State Archive of Documentary Films, Photographs, and Sound Recordings in St. Petersburg.

The vital role of foreigners and foreign investment in the retailing of clothes continued in Russia with the introduction of the department store in the 1860s. The department store introduced a new kind of retailing enterprise which combined an abundance of goods under one roof, volume buying, and periodic sales to boost profits. Other retail outlets quickly adopted these measures in order to compete with the new emporiums.[30] Jules Picard started City of Lyon (Gorod Lion in

Russian after the French name, À la ville de Lyon) in 1842, while two Englishmen, Andrew Moore (Muir in Russian) and Archibald Merilees, founded their store in Moscow the following year.[31] Both stores began as fashion shops but evolved into department stores. While Muir and Merilees became the preeminent department store in Moscow, if not in all of Russia, Russians themselves established other department stores in the second half of the nineteenth century. In Petersburg, the Guards' Economic Society (Gvardeiskoe ekonomicheskoe obshchestvo) founded a store for military officers, which eventually became Petersburg's leading department store.[32] All of the department stores had large ready-to-wear as well as custom-made clothing departments for men, women, and children.

Foreign entrepreneurs brought to Russia new retail practices. In a western *magazin*, well-dressed, polite salesclerks assisted customers with their purchases in elegant, clean, and heated premises. Prices were fixed; no bargaining was permitted. This practice allowed customers to buy quality merchandise quickly, so that there would be time to gossip and promenade in their finery, which was also an integral part of shopping.

## RUSSIAN SHOPS AND TRADING ROWS

This network of western specialty stores, arcades, and department stores coexisted with traditional Russian trading rows and markets. Both Petersburg and Moscow had several open-air markets as well as seasonal ones. These markets sold everything from food to footwear. Most of the clothing for sale was second-hand, although some ready-to-wear stores had stalls at the Moscow markets. According to one Muscovite, "any poor man who cannot spend more than a ruble for a jacket or half a ruble for a pair of pants, can go to the flea market and immediately find everything."[33] Many of the working poor in both cities as well as peasant migrants relied on the markets to supply all of their material needs.[34]

It was the trading rows, however, which served as the main source of consumer goods throughout urban Russia. In the capitals, the most important of these trading rows were the Upper Trading Rows and Gostinyi Dvor located directly across Red Square from the Kremlin, and the Petersburg Gostinyi Dvor on Nevskii. The Upper Trading Rows stood in rather stark contrast to the elegant *magaziny* located on Tverskaia and Kuznetskii Bridge. In 1862, Alexander Ushakov, a bookstore proprietor and publisher who grew up in a Moscow merchant family, described the lethal atmosphere that prevailed in the Upper Trading Rows:

> The Rows occupy two huge sheds, buildings completely unsuitable for business. They are immense cellars or caves in the open air. Their dampness, particularly in the autumn and winter, is *murderous* even according to the merchants themselves. An individual not accustomed to their atmosphere, which can be compared to a Siberian goldmine for much of the year, may quickly develop rheumatism or continually suffer from colds.[35]

In Russia's long winters, customers and salesclerks alike had to suffer these freezing temperatures primarily because individual shop owners refused to pay the heating tax to the municipal government! The interior of these bitterly cold "caves" resembled a giant garage sale. Small stalls stacked one upon the other sold everything imaginable. The noise, smell, and sights of the place reminded both foreign and Russian visitors alike of an Asian bazaar.[36] In this damp, unheated, "eastern" emporium, Russian merchants began selling European fashions on the Knife Row in the early nineteenth century.[37]

Conditions in the two Gostinyi Dvors were slightly better. In Moscow and Petersburg lovely, multistoried, neoclassical buildings housed the hundreds of Russian petty traders who worked within those walls and protected customers from the elements. Here too, Russian traders sold European lace, fabric, and fashion goods.[38] While the neoclassical exteriors of the Gostinyi Dvors suggested similar shopping arcades in England and France, their interiors shared more in common with the Russian trading rows than with western stores.[39]

The differences between western and Russian retail outlets extended beyond the mere physical layout of the establishments themselves. In the Russian shop, or *lavka*, salesclerks greeted customers outside the store, expounding the glories of the merchandise contained within. Once the potential buyers entered the store, the owners demanded that customers buy something, but only after lengthy negotiations over the price.[40] Sales-clerks were frequently punished if a customer left the store without making a purchase.[41] Russian clerks were notorious for their exaggerated forms of polite address with which they conducted business and for lying to their customers about the quality of the goods and the prices. There are numerous stories about these encounters, but the following one is typical:

> Lady: I wish, if you please, to look at some French ribbons.
> Shopman: Horro sha, Sudarina (Very well, lady).

The shopman takes down a box, the contents of which are undeniably of Russian manufacture.

> L: These are not French – I want *French* ribbons.
> S: These are *real* French: they are from Paris.
> L: No, I am sure they are not.
> S: (After again most energetically repeating his assertion) Well! How much do you want?
> L: Show me the ribbons, and then I will tell you.
> S: How many arsheens did you say?
> L: Show me the French ribbons.

The shopman unblushingly puts back the box which he has so recently declared contained the real article, and takes down another, which is filled with ribbons of French fabrication.

> L: How much is this arsheen?
> S: (With a most graceful inclination) Seventy copecks.
> L: Seventy copecks! Why the price is only fifty, and that is all I will give you.
> S: (Quite indignant) Fifty! They cost us more than that; you shall have it for sixty-five.
> L: Fifty
> S: Bosha moia! No! I can't think of fifty – say sixty.
> L: Not a copeck more than fifty.
> S: By Heaven! I can't sell it for that price; you shall have it for fifty-five.
> L: Will you take fifty or not?
> S: I can't indeed. (He shuts up the box and puts it back into its place.) You shall have it for fifty-three.

The purchaser refuses to be cheated of even three copecks per arsheen (a length of 28 inches) and walks

78  The Ivan Kondrat'ev and Son Overcoat and Fur Store in Gostinyi Dvor in Petersburg. Although Gostinyi Dvor was often juxtaposed to the Passazh, by the early twentieth century, the small shops in Gostinyi Dvor had window displays, wooden counters, and other hallmarks of western shopping. *Ves' Petersburg na 1910 g.*, XXXI. Harvard University Collections.

out of the shop; she has perhaps gone half a dozen yards, when the shopkeeper's voice is heard calling out, "Barishna, Barishna! Come back, if you please!"

This transaction concludes only after further negotiations on the price. The buyer remained firm in her price, but the clerk still tried to cheat the customer on her change.[42] Hundreds of these complex and lengthy transactions occurred every day in the Russian trading rows and markets.

This lengthy haggling over goods and prices came to be seen during the nineteenth century as the Russian form of shopping. If western shopping was cold and formal, Russian shopping was informal with frequent heated exchanges between customers and clerks arguing over prices. Western shopping was standardized, predictable, and orderly. Russian shopping, by contrast, appeared unruly, unpredictable, and disorderly.[43] I. I. Ianzhul, a distinguished Russian political economist, described the situation by claiming that "Russian trade has preserved an Asian character in many of its features."[44]

## WESTERN VERSUS RUSSIAN SHOPPING

The division of clothes shopping along western and Russian lines meant that it became part of the larger cultural debate about the meaning of westernization in Russia. One journalist commented on this cultural division in Petersburg:

> Gostinyi Dvor is a Russian bazaar, a memorial to older times, an episode from Moscow life. The Passazh is a European commercial street, a copy of foreign customs, a scene from foreign morals and manners. The former reminds one vividly of Moscow, the latter automatically of Paris.[45]

For some individuals, Russia's attempt to modernize along western European lines meant the loss of her uniqueness, her national identity. The tearing down of the old Trading Rows in Moscow in 1886 and their replacement with an arcade shopping center became symbolic of the loss of the commercial customs and habits which characterized not only old Moscow but all of Russia. According to G. Vasilich, writing in 1912:

> The difference between the former *lavka* and the contemporary *magazin* is not a chance phenomenon. In it are the echoes of two changing systems of morals and manners. With the colossal houses, with the trams and automobiles, in general with the ascendancy of the machine, the former good nature, the conviviality, the appealing disorderliness and freedom is disappearing. The tenor of life is becoming disciplined, is being chained to the pace of the machine.[46]

As this quotation makes clear, for individuals like Vasilich, modernization equaled the wholesale rejection of Russian mores and values. Vasilich equates the cold, rational "pace of the machine" with western stores, and mourns the loss of "the conviviality" and "the appealing disorderliness and freedom" which he associates with the *lavki*. He expresses the fear shared by many Russians that in the government's attempts to modernize, Russia was losing crucial aspects of its traditional way of life and national identity.

For those Russians who embraced westernization and modernization, the pace of change was too slow and they welcomed any sign, no matter how insignificant, that Russia was becoming a part of the western world. These people frequented the *magaziny* in the fashionable shopping districts and whiled away the hours gossiping and promenading with other like-minded Russians. In their opinion, western goods, no matter what the cost, were of higher quality than similar, Russian-made goods. And, perhaps more importantly, western goods were always made according to the latest styles, whereas Russian goods often were not. One Russian had this advice for his countrymen:

> If you have just come to Moscow and you feel you need to have a suit made, then I implore you do not order it on the Pokrovka, or across the Moskva River, in Lefortovo or Gruzinakh; you will perish . . . they will make you a suit in accordance with a fashion which has never existed, you will be dressed worse than a newcomer from the provinces. Hurry to Tverskaia or Kuznetskii Bridge; address yourself to Zanftleben, to Samias, Reno, Otto, Muller, Tepfer, Lyuk. . . .[47]

Sophisticated Russians needed to wear western clothes to appear like westerners, and the primary way to do that was to rely on foreign-born and foreign-trained tailors and shopkeepers. Only they knew what was *à la mode*.

The persistence of this western/Russian opposition in discussions of shopping had complex implications for both buyers and sellers because it obscured the complex social reality that had developed in Russia over the course of the nineteenth century. By 1900 the boundaries between western *magaziny* and Russian *lavki* had become blurred. To give just one example, the Austrian clothing manufacturer, Mandl', made inexpensive copies of French fashion using Russian textiles and labor. Were these garments French or Russian? If consumers bought these ready-to-wear items from a *magazin*, a mail-order catalogue, or an open-air market for used clothing, were they supporting the development of native retailing or furthering the profits of foreign entrepreneurs? The intermingling of western and Russian capital, design, goods, and personnel thwarted an easy identification of western and Russian merchandise. The very complexity of Russian commercial development, particularly in the fashion industry, rendered any patriotic plea for consumers to buy Russian goods problematic.

## SHOPPING AS A SOCIAL PHENOMENON

The origin of modern consumerism in Europe is still a hotly debated topic among scholars. While some argue that the desire for luxury goods preceded industrial development, others believe that the ability to manufacture vast quantities of industrial products encouraged mass consumption. Whatever the eventual outcome of this debate, there is no question that industrialization and modern retailing transformed western Europe. One feature of this transformation to which virtually all scholars point is the democratization of luxury goods. Prior to the modern era, luxury goods had remained the preserve of the landed elite and the court. It was they and they alone who could afford to purchase handmade furnishings, carpets, and clothing. These luxury goods provided a visual marker between the elite and everyone else. Beginning in the seventeenth century, Europe underwent a profound economic and commercial transforma-

tion in which land no longer served as the chief source of wealth and power. Individuals who worked in trade and manufacturing began to accumulate large fortunes. Having achieved financial success, they wanted to display their new wealth through the purchase of luxury goods. In fact, many of the newly rich, such as Josiah Wedgwood of the Wedgwood China Company, had made their fortunes learning how to produce inexpensive copies of luxury goods. These shrewd entrepreneurs allowed the middle ranks of society to buy china, silver, furnishings, and fashions. The development of new industrial technologies coupled with modern retailing helped to create the mass-consumer market of the twentieth century.

The democratization of luxury goods did not create a democracy, however. Instead, it fashioned a new hierarchy of consumers. At the very top were the old landed elites and the *nouveau riche* created by industrialization. They were the only ones who could afford luxury items. Beneath them were the businessmen, professionals, civil servants, and their wives who purchased mass-produced copies of luxury goods. At the bottom of the pyramid were workers and peasants for whom an occasional purchase of a mass-produced item was all they could afford. What made this new consumerism different was that mass-produced products appeared to be within reach of everyone. Advertisers used their image in newspapers and magazines. Department and specialty stores invited everyone to gaze at luxurious displays. This vicarious participation proved to be the democratic element in modern consumerism. It cultivated in everyone the desire to buy luxury goods, even those who could not afford them. All Europeans could imagine themselves as modern consumers.

Entrepreneurs who wanted to introduce modern consumerism into Russia faced a Herculean task. With the exception of Petersburg, Moscow, Warsaw, Kiev, and Odessa, most Russian cities were merely administrative outposts with poorly developed economic and commercial infrastructures. And yet Russia's vast expanses were what proved so attractive to foreign and domestic businessmen. Russia was a market of gigantic proportions for those bold and brave enough to try. In order to succeed, these retail pioneers needed to overcome these serious impediments and challenges, and they did this by applying to Russian conditions the retail techniques learned in western Europe and the United States.

## URBAN SHOPPING

Petersburg became the model for how the rest of Russia adapted to the introduction of modern retailing.[48] The city's *magaziny* became *the* source for fashionable clothing during the eighteenth and early nineteenth centuries. The court, aristocracy, and high government officials strolled along Nevskii, where the elegant store signs frequently written in French or German beckoned them to shop in search of the latest fashions.[49] These French or German signs served to keep "undesirables" out of the *magaziny*. However, clerks, shopkeepers, artisans, and domestic servants also needed European clothing.[50] Shopkeepers in Gostinyi Dvor and the other Petersburg trading rows began to carry European goods primarily to meet this demand for inexpensive western items. Shopkeepers in the *lavki* favored shop signs with pictorial representations of their wares, a perfect lure for illiterate or semi-literate urban dwellers. In 1897 the government issued regulations requiring shop owners to translate any French or German shop signs into Russian to democratize shopping for those who did not read foreign languages.[51]

As demand increased among city residents of all social ranks for European clothing, Russians could shop in a variety of retail outlets from the swankiest foreign boutiques to the grittiest of flea markets. Unfortunately, retail records of who shopped where have long since vanished. Impressionistic evidence suggests some general patterns of consumption. Certainly the chic western stores remained the preserve of the elites. The atmosphere of formal civility and fixed prices that prevailed in these stores was intended to intimidate those customers who did not have sufficient income to purchase the goods displayed. In Moscow in the 1840s one commentator tells the story of a young seamstress who headed for the fashionable Kuznetskii Bridge to shop for a shawl for herself and her sister. She was humiliated by an indifferent salesclerk, by a society woman, and by the glamorous atmosphere of the store. Instead, she went to the Trading Rows where she was not only able to purchase scarves but to buy tulle, hairpins, and whalebone for a corset from an obsequious salesclerk. Although the shawls on Kuznetskii Bridge were more beautiful and of a higher quality than those in the Trading Rows, the young seamstress could not bring herself to endure the indignities necessary to buy the goods.[52] This young woman's experience was typical of the non-elite shoppers who attempted to cross the thresholds of western stores during the early years of Russia's retail transformation.

In the second half of the nineteenth century, arcades and department stores in particular served as a place where both elite and non-elite shoppers were welcome. Everyone was allowed to enter and browse in a department store with no obligation to buy. These stores stood in sharp contrast to the *lavki* where a customer had to make a purchase before leaving. Department stores with their myriad displays of reasonably priced, mass-produced luxury goods added a new dimension. Even though many of the customers never bought any goods on these shopping expeditions, they became participants in the world of modern consumerism. The department stores nurtured in the Russian public the desire to wear fashionable dress, which further stimulated the demand for such goods.

Individuals who could not afford the high prices of the western stores could shop in the sprawling Russian markets and trading rows. Merchants in the Upper Trading Rows in Moscow and Gostinyi Dvor in Petersburg sold both domestic and foreign fashion goods catering to a middle- and lower-class clientele. Those who could not afford new clothing could purchase second-hand garments instead. Tailors, dressmakers, milliners, pawnbrokers, peddlers, and petty thieves all traded in second-hand clothing. Individuals brought in old clothing or outmoded fashions to a dealer who, in turn, sold them to someone else. With regard to similar practices in eighteenth-century England, one scholar has observed:

> Exchanging new goods for old acted as a stimulus to productivity. The barter process implicitly accepted the resale value of clothing, thus extending the purchasing power of many more of the English population. This process connected an ancient barter tradition with the rising productivity. Non-cash payments widened the choices and selection of goods, drawing in a broader

79  An open-air market in the Kitai Gorod neighborhood in Moscow. Makeshift stalls line one side of the street where petty traders try to cajole or sometimes browbeat customers into making a purchase. Meanwhile, hat sellers and tailors selling trousers roam the street carrying their merchandise with them. The hats for the sale are the ubiquitous workers' cap that became a fundamental part of an urban worker's wardrobe by the late nineteenth century. Library of Congress, US262 023769.

80  An open-air market underneath the Kremlin Walls on Red Square in Moscow. Some traders brought their own makeshift shelters, but others simply placed their merchandise on the ground. Library of Congress, US262 29392.

spectrum of consumer into more active participation in the marketplace.[53]

The English experience foreshadowed events in Russia. The second-hand trade supplied individuals longing for fashionable clothing at prices they could afford. As a result, the fashion industry was able to influence all levels of urban Russia – from high society to the working poor.

This attempt to democratize shopping remained incomplete. While on the one hand the new urban elites in Russia were attempting to wrest cultural control away from the nobility, they were also trying to preserve their new cultural power and status from encroachment by the

81   A tailor selling ready-to-wear trousers in an open-air market in Moscow. In this photograph it is possible to see the social mixing that often occurred in these markets. While the women in the picture are dressed alike in their headscarves, simple skirts, and blouses, the men's clothing shows a greater range of styles. The tailor along with the other two men in the foreground are wearing the workers' peaked cap with simple trousers and coats, typical dress for urban workers. The other men wear nicely tailored suits, boaters, fedoras, and umbrellas, common attire for businessmen. Library of Congress Collections.

lower classes. Even though the western retail outlets were open to everyone, obviously only those with enough money could actually afford to buy the merchandise. Yet,

82  A second-hand clothing market in Moscow. Library of Congress Collections.

as poorer folk became familiar with western stores and shopping, snooty salesclerks and well-appointed stores no longer intimidated them. Trips to the central shopping districts to window-shop became outings for working-class families. The occasional purchase of a real French ribbon, comb, or other small trinket brought a bit of color and elegance, however briefly, into the monotony of working life. By the early twentieth century, social commentators identified a new social problem that they called "hooliganism." Unemployed workers, petty criminals, and young thugs, sometimes in outlandish costumes, invaded the social spaces of respectable Russians.[54] These young men articulated the resentment that the lower classes felt toward those who had money and power in imperial Russia. What better place to thumb their noses at their social "betters" than the elegant shopping districts?

By the beginning of the twentieth century, European clothing had become so widespread that Russian dress had virtually disappeared on city streets. One unhappy commentator described the changes in Moscow:

In general in the last few years the streets of Moscow have taken on a more "Europeanized" appearance. A kind of "chic" has appeared among the crowds in the street whereas in old Moscow the population had no

understanding of fashion. The dress and customs were regulated by tradition, daily comfort, and personal choice. But, the tendency toward impersonal "fashion," valued only because everyone follows it, is already growing with substantial progress in city life. This collective culture is leveling city dwellers by making them resemble factory-made products. Bowler hats, coats, monotonous in their black coloring – are conquering the Moscow streets. Long-waisted coats, Russian shirts, service caps, and colorful shawls – all have disappeared and have gone to the suburbs. This leveling of the various strata of the city population testifies to the general democratization of culture. Beneath the mask of imitation the yearning of the urban lower classes appears to join with the powerful flow of world culture. "Russian dress" is worn only by the Old Believers in the eastern part of Moscow, and even there "German dress" is sometimes worn for church services.[55]

This sartorial revolution was brought about by the development of an urban shopping network which allowed members of all urban social strata to purchase European clothes. If barriers remained between those who shopped in western and Russian stores, these barriers proved increasingly difficult to maintain as store owners encouraged customers, if not to buy, then at least to dream.

## EXPANSION OF SHOPPING OUTSIDE THE TWO CAPITALS

City folk, both high and low, dressed in city clothes not only to appear European but also to distinguish themselves from their less glamorous country cousins, to signal that they were no longer part of backward, rural Russia. This sartorial division between urban and rural Russia cut across existing social categories. In 1806 Ivan Krylov, the Russian fabulist and playwright, satirized the sartorial gulf between city dwellers and provincial landowners. In his play, *The Fashion Shop (Modnaia lavka)*, the action takes place in a fancy French boutique in St. Petersburg. The wily serf and salesclerk, Masha, sells out-of-date fashions to an unsuspecting provincial noblewoman simply by mentioning the names of a few prominent society women who supposedly shop at the store. Although her husband pontificates about the treachery of French retail practices and forbids the sale, nevertheless, his wife completes her purchases behind his back. She returns to her provincial estate dreaming of the sophisticated impression she hopes to make in her French fashions at the next ball, unaware that she has been duped into purchasing garments that are hopelessly out of date.[56] This story articulates the profound gap that existed between urban and rural Russia in the early nineteenth century, turning the existing social hierarchy on its head. According to Krylov, even an uneducated serf such as Masha, simply by virtue of living and working in a city, knew better what was fashionable than her social "superior" from the countryside.

Entrepreneurs were not content to maintain the cultural gap between town and country since this limited the profits they could reap from their retail establishments. Social pressures to dress *à la mode* and the increasing availability of fashion magazines served to stimulate the demand for fashionable clothing not just among city residents but among provincial landowning families as well. Individuals involved in the fashion industry wanted to meet this demand by expanding the existing retail networks in Moscow and Petersburg. In 1829 a group of Petersburg businessmen and -women organized the first exhibit of Russian manufactured goods which included fashion merchandise. They described their mission in rather dramatic terms that highlighted the cultural gulf between urban and rural Russia:

> In order to understand the truth, it is necessary only to look at, first, the poor, half-wild existence of this country's inhabitants where no industrial development has penetrated, and then, at the contented and luxurious life of the state where manufacturing and trade flourish. On the one side, poverty and none of life's necessities. On the other, a contentment with everything and even superfluous luxury. There, rank coarseness and ignorance. Here, civility, education, refined taste, and politeness. . . . [I]n short, there stands a coarse son of wild Mother Nature and here stands an educated citizen of civilized society.[57]

The goal was to "civilize" rural Russia by selling manufactured goods to the coarse sons of wild Mother

83  A group of young women in Murom, circa 1900. All three gowns have a great deal of detail, but the woman on the right has a bodice that does not lie properly. Private Collection.

Nature. A simple retail transaction promised to raise these individuals into the ranks of civilized society.

Retailers could not transform Russia overnight. They began by focusing first on provincial gentry families. Since many could not afford frequent trips to Moscow or Petersburg, enterprising individuals began to establish western stores in the provinces. In 1863 the Ministry of the Interior published a survey it had conducted of economic conditions in Russia's provincial capitals. Of the forty-two cities surveyed, ministry officials broke down the stores into western *magaziny* and Russian *lavki* for thirty cities. According to these reports, six cities had five or fewer western stores; nine cities had between six and ten western stores; four cities had eleven to fifteen western stores; three cities had between sixteen and twenty western stores; four cities had between thirty and forty

84 Bol'shaia Pokrovka Street in Nizhnii Novgorod. Located at the confluence of the Oka and Volga Rivers, the city was home to the enormous summer fair. Despite the preponderance of Russian-style trading in the city, this street shows the influence of western shopping on this provincial town. The store on the left is named the Viennese Shop of Fashions, Hats, and Lingerie. Library of Congress Collections.

85 A portrait of a middle-aged woman, perhaps a teacher, with four adolescents in Ekaterinburg. The girls' dress is similar in that they are all wearing a cap over their sleeves, but the gown of the girl on the far left has a very rumpled bodice, suggesting poor tailoring. Private Collection.

stores; and finally Nizhnii Novgorod topped the list with 154 western stores.[58] As these figures indicate, western shopping had established a foothold in most Russian provincial capitals by the mid-nineteenth century. Furthermore, in some cities, a new category of shopkeeper indicated the presence of the Russian fashion industry in these provincial towns – the modiste. Originally the modiste's job was to advise women on how to put together the perfect outfit, but frequently she was a dressmaker as well. The modistes, identifying themselves with European clothing and business practices, found enough work to support themselves in half of Russian provincial towns. Of the twenty-two towns that listed the presence of modistes, thirteen towns listed between one and ten modistes; six towns listed between eleven and twenty modistes; and four towns listed twenty or more modistes.[59] The modistes, western stores, tailors, and dressmakers all participated in expanding the market for European fashions into the provinces.

It is important not to exaggerate the extent of western shopping in provincial Russia. Many elite families continued to shop in Moscow or Petersburg, or relied upon serfs to make their clothes. Nevertheless, the rise of western stores in the provinces suggests a number of conclusions. First, western dress had become the norm for the provincial elite by the first half of the nineteenth century. Second, fashion magazines helped to popularize French fashions in the smaller towns. Elite women could take the patterns published in the fashion press to their modiste, who could create a beautiful gown. Third, the presence of western stores in the provincial towns served as a foundation around which other stores could build in the future. For those who desperately wanted to dress according to the latest styles but who could not afford an expensive trip to either capital, there were provincial alternatives.

## MAIL-ORDER CATALOGUES

Despite the presence of provincial stores, such outlets proved to be a costly undertaking for many retailers. Shopkeepers had to pay rent and utilities, wages for their clerks, and freight rates to ship merchandise. They also needed enough capital to be able to weather economic downturns when demand for consumer goods slackened. As more mass-produced goods became available during the second half of the nineteenth century and demand continued to grow, retailers began to seek other, less expensive means of supplying consumer goods to the smaller towns. Once again borrowing from western Europe, store owners began to publish mail-order catalogues which could be sent through the mail, creating an empire-wide market for products of the new industrial age.

The full history of the mail-order catalogue in Russia will never be known – most of the records have long since vanished. A few collections of the catalogues remain, however, allowing a glimpse into this remarkable retailing innovation.[60] The earliest catalogues from the 1860s were little more than handbills. They listed the products, their prices, and the address of the store where the goods could be purchased.[61] By the 1880s store owners began publishing more substantial pamphlets and booklets. Department stores, clothing stores, and even factory retail outlets invested substantial amounts of capital in mail-order catalogues. For example, in 1914 the Muir and Merilees department store spent almost 400,000 rubles at their publishing firm for catalogues and other printed material.[62]

Mail-order catalogues offered retailers a whole new way to sell their products:

Without a doubt the purchase of goods through a catalogue from a large factory center like Łodz is the most advantageous and handy method. You do not have to walk through provincial stores where you can find the latest fashions alongside goods long since gone out of style. And what about the prices? We consider it superfluous to point out the difference because everyone can easily understand that provincial stores having bought their goods from a third party (Rarely do they come to Łodz.) for which they pay a significant percentage more that must be passed along to the consumer. . . . We pay particular attention to the production of both men's and women's ready-to-wear, trying to include the customer's smallest instructions or wishes in the making of the garment, which we produce according to the most advanced methods . . . we are certain that our orders will be filled much better than can be done by local tailors.[63]

In this typical passage, the manufacturer captured the appeal of mail-order catalogues. They saved the consumer time, money, and labor. Even though catalogue shoppers did not live in a big city, they could shop as if they did. Mail-order catalogues represented modernity and urban life. This dichotomy between the urbane mail-order catalogue and the backward provincial store mirrored and reinforced those qualities that differentiated western and Russian shopping.

Retailers used catalogues to sell their wares for other reasons also. Publishing a catalogue was less expensive than opening up a retail outlet. Although retailers sent their publications free of charge, which meant that they absorbed all publication costs, they must have felt that these expenditures were worthwhile. A catalogue guaranteed a larger market than a single retail outlet alone could offer. Another important consideration was that mail-order catalogues could be sent to anyone. Residents of Petersburg, Samara, and Ufa all waited impatiently for the catalogue from Muir and Merilees. Just one publication could reach thousands of potential customers. It is difficult to know precisely where the mail-order catalogues ended up, but the catalogues themselves give some indication. The 1899 Muir and Merilees catalogue announced that goods could be sent cash on delivery by mail, rail, and steamship to all corners of European Russia, the Caucasus, and western Siberia (Tobol'sk and Tomsk guberniias). Packages intended for towns in Asian Russia could only be sent if they had already been paid for.[64] By 1908, the list of places where Muir and Merilees could send its goods had expanded to include Central Asia, eastern Siberia, and Manchuria.[65] The giant Moscow emporium was not the only store to deliver to remote places. Clothing manufacturers also indicated their willingness to send prepaid goods to Siberia, Asian Russia, and the Far East.[66] As in the United States, the catalogues and the goods followed the railroads. Russians who were stationed at the far outposts of the empire, but desired modern clothing and conveniences, ordered these goods from stores like Muir and Merilees, Mandl', and many others.

The mail-order catalogues provided Russian consumers with their entrée into western stores. Many catalogues had pictures of the flagship store on their covers. The compilers divided their publications into different departments just like the stores themselves. The 1890–91 Muir and Merilees catalogue displayed goods from twenty different departments, and clothing stores also arranged their catalogues by category as well.[67] Some manufacturers provided a brief history of their factories and retail outlets. The Zhirardovskii Company founded in 1829 produced high-quality men's and women's shirts and undergarments. The author of the company's cata-

logue regaled customers with the saga of the company's rise to the top of the lingerie business.[68] In addition to these manufacturing histories, retailers indulged in hyperbole to describe the wonders of their merchandise. A few catalogues went so far as to include poetry. A retailer of raincoats celebrated his product with the following ditty entitled "A Dream in the Hand":

> A glorious kingdom,
> A glorious kingdom,
> All-Russian.
> And in this kingdom
> There is a province,
> This province
> Is called Vitebsk;
> In this province,

Lies the city Dvinsk,
And in this city,
A young merchant
(By name
He is Khaikevich)
Sells Viksatinov raincoats.[69]

This light-hearted, optimistic verse beckons customers to enter the enchanted kingdom of plenty where all Russian subjects are welcome. Thus, mail-order catalogues served to proclaim not only the high quality of a particular store's merchandise but also the glories of Russian capitalism.

Each catalogue contained detailed purchasing instructions. In buying clothes, getting just the right fit was critical, so much attention was spent on sizing. Clothing manufacturers usually included instructions for taking measurements in their catalogues so that customers could ascertain their size. For custom-made clothing, retailers suggested that customers send in same-size well-worn garments which could assist their cutters in creating the perfect fit.[70] Another important consideration in selecting a garment was the cost. The prices listed were usually just for the medium sizes in ready-to-wear departments. Anyone who was larger or smaller had to pay extra. The Mandl' firm gave a price range for its clothes, and virtually every catalogue had a clause which indicated that prices were subject to change without prior notice.[71]

The mail-order catalogues printed in the 1880s were rather simple. The clothing was not particularly well described, and there were few pictures. In the 1890s catalogues began to include more pictures, so that in the Muir and Merilees catalogues printed in the early 1900s almost every item for purchase was pictured in some way. At the same time, the Muir and Merilees store informed its customers that it sent its own fashion experts to Paris, Berlin, Lyon, and London to ascertain the latest trends in women's clothing.[72] According to the Mandl' Company, consumers requested more pictures and more detailed descriptions of the clothes, and therefore, by 1895 the Mandl' catalogue, with its large format and multitude of pictures, looked very much like a fashion magazine, but, unlike in fashion magazines, these items were actually for sale.[73]

87    A guarantee from the Popova and Company mail-order catalogue. The Popova Company sold sewing machines, and this document assured their customers of the proper working order of each machine the company sold. The fine print at the bottom of the page revealed that this guarantee was good only for two years rather than the full life of the machine. The medallion in the middle is from the Shah of Iran while the others recognize the company's participation in several universal exhibitions. *Preis-kurant shveinykh, viazal'nykh i drugikh mashin i prednadlezhnostei s nim Russkogo Tovarishchestva torgovli shveinimi mashinami Popova i Ko. v Moskve*, 10 and 11. Russian Public Library Collections.

The expanded use of pictorial representations undoubtedly increased the success of the catalogues. Prior to the 1890s, customers who ordered goods could never be certain of their purchase until it arrived, but now they could see what they were about to order. Well-illustrated catalogues also had the potential to attract semi-literate or even illiterate consumers. These individuals could use the pictures to decide what goods they wanted and with the help of a literate friend actually make a purchase. Beyond this, mail-order catalogues served as a celebration of the new industrial age. For those who could not afford to buy, the sheer abundance of goods allowed them to dream about a richer material life.

The catalogues also offered modern services and conveniences to their customers even though they were many miles from the stores. Many clothing firms provided free cleaning and ironing.[74] Most promised to make the clothing within two weeks of the initial receipt of the order; one firm even offered twenty-four-hour tailoring![75] Muir and Merilees had occasional sales of out-of-season merchandise.[76] Perhaps the greatest service that the stores offered was their return policies. Most stores were happy to accept returns for ill-fitting or flawed garments. But retailers also stipulated that they could not accept garments that had been worn or were simply out of fashion. If items were returned within two weeks, the store paid the shipping costs; otherwise, the customer had to pay to send the merchandise back to the store.[77] In every way possible, store owners tried to make their mail-order customers feel that they could enjoy the privileges of shopping in their store even though they were hundreds or thousands of miles away. Each Muir and Merilees catalogue announced the store's motto: "The basis of our trade is to sell all of our goods honestly and at the most modest prices."[78] In the world of modern retailing, the customer always came first.

## THE SINGER SEWING MACHINE COMPANY IN RUSSIA

Provincial society represented just a very small portion of rural inhabitants as the vast majority were peasants. Since peasants were specifically excluded from Peter the Great's initial dress decrees, western clothing quickly became an easy way to identify city folk from peasants, and modern, "civilized" Russia from traditional, "backward" Russia. Nevertheless, as the provincial nobility became more westernized, they tried to modernize their entire way of life which included dressing their house serfs in European clothing. Sometimes, members of the provincial nobility gave outmoded fashions to their serfs as gifts. In other cases, serfs like the wily Masha who worked in Moscow or Petersburg returned to the countryside bearing information about life and customs in the city. Whatever the mechanism, peasants developed a desire to wear such clothes themselves.

The emancipation of the serfs in 1861 marked an important watershed in the history of the Russian peasantry. Freed from bondage, peasants were burdened with heavy tax and redemption obligations, and few opportunities to become successful farmers. The implications of the emancipation decree are still being debated by scholars, some identifying greater immiseration of the peasantry after 1861 and others growing improvement. Whatever the outcome of that debate, there is substantial impressionistic evidence that suggests peasants, whether they could afford to or not, began to buy city clothes in the years immediately following emancipation.[79] Shoes, hats, aprons, ready-to-wear garments, and factory-produced cloth transformed the way peasants dressed. Their desire for city clothes only increased during the second half of the nineteenth century. In provinces with heavy male outmigration to Russia's urban centers, observers reported that peasant girls frequently needed entire dowries of city clothes in order to attract suitable spouses.[80] And even if peasants bought only one piece of clothing each year, this represented a huge market for clothing manufacturers and retailers, particularly since Russia experienced a population explosion after emancipation. Consequently, the rural market presented retailers with an opportunity for considerable profits. At the same time, this rural population was scattered over thousands of miles with an inadequate transportation system. The problem then was how to integrate the rural and urban markets into a unified system which would allow anyone with money to buy western fashions.

As the railroad network grew and credit became more available, retailers experimented with other methods of selling their wares. The first innovation was to bring western goods to the annual fairs that attracted thousands of peasants each year. The most important of these fairs was held each summer in Nizhnii Novgorod. Because of its nearness to Russia's new textile centers, the city proved to be an excellent venue for the sale of cotton goods which accounted for nineteen percent of the total goods sold at the fair in the 1880s. Initially, textile manufacturers sold their fabrics to merchants and itinerant peasant traders. By the turn of the century, wholesalers replaced itinerant traders, and ready-to-wear clothing manufacturers had established their own stores at the fair.[81] Peasants who journeyed to Nizhnii Novgorod could now buy inexpensive French fashions at this most famous of the Russian fairs.[82]

One company that wanted to create a truly national market became the envy of all Russian and foreign firms. The Singer Sewing Machine Company, founded in 1851, was known throughout the world not just for its sewing machines but also for its sales operations. In Russia, the Singer Company accomplished two important tasks. First, it was able to integrate Russia's urban and rural markets by creating a complex network of administrative centers, retail outlets, and village sales personnel. Second, the company furthered the development of the Russian fashion industry. Inexpensive factory-produced textiles, readily available paper patterns, and a sewing machine were all the tools necessary to make European clothes at home. There was no need for expensive trips to the city or to the fairs. The Singer Company allowed French fashions to be sewn in peasant huts all across the Russian Empire.

As remarked in chapter 2, sewing manufacturers began marketing sewing machines for women in the nineteenth century. Initially, Singer simply shipped its machines manufactured in Scotland and the United States to Russia, where licensed agents were responsible for the sale of merchandise. Anxious to gain the upper hand over its competition, the company started a wholly owned subsidiary in 1897. The Russian Singer Company built a factory in Podol'sk which made almost all the sewing machines intended for family use; other specialty machines were imported from the United States. In fact, Singer was the only manufacturer actually to make sewing machines in Russia, which gave it a huge advantage over its competitors. It could supply new machines

and replacement parts more quickly than any other company.

The distinctive feature about Singer was less the machine itself than the company's retail operation. Fresh from its marketing triumphs in western Europe and America, Singer was ready to apply these same techniques in Russia. Once they had established a prominent place in the home-sewing market among middle-class women, company officials set their sights on expanding the market to reach all garment workers, especially those who toiled in city sweatshops and peasant huts. According to a company document from World War I:

> The business operations of The Singer Company in Russia are undertaken on the same line as those of the American Company, the basis of which is *the sale of all articles in their own shops and through their own employees direct to the consumer*, i.e. private persons, artisans and owners of factories, thus eliminating all re-sales and agents. Thanks to the wide credit which The Singer Company offers to the public, sewing machines, previously considered as articles of luxury which could only be purchased by wealthy people, have now become accessible to all classes of the population, including the poorer people . . .[83]

By handling its own manufacturing, retail operations, and credit, Singer saved money, savings that it passed along to the consumer by offering the lowest-priced sewing machines on the market.

In order to do this, the company had set up an elaborate retail network. The board of directors for the new Russian subsidiary established its headquarters first in Petersburg and later in Moscow. From there, the directors broke the Russian Empire down into districts which were based on the size of the population. By 1914 there were thirty-nine central offices. The central office was responsible for all of the stores and employees in its jurisdiction and reported to the company's headquarters. For instance, in Kiev province, the central office was located in the city of Kiev along with ten retail stores. In addition, there were forty-two stores scattered throughout the province – some in small towns, others in tiny villages.[84] In these more remote areas, Singer usually rented space from local peasants or officials. In Ekaterinoslav province, Singer rented some rooms for three years from Dr. V. N. Bragin in the village of Ivanovka, and from the peasant P. D. Barkdak and his wife in Irkleevo.[85] In the village of Beloomut in Riazan' province, Singer rented rooms in the home of Ivan Kuzmin Gordunov.[86] Each of these retail outlets or depots was responsible for a particular area, again based on the size of the population. In 1914 each manager served between 1,000 and 2,500 customers.[87] The manager also supervised sales people who worked in the retail outlets, clerks who completed the paperwork, and packers and mechanics who delivered and repaired the machines. In addition, each depot manager employed special collectors whose job it was to collect installments and provide parts and labor to keep the sewing machines in good working order. These individuals had clearly defined districts so that they would not compete with each other. A Singer representative regularly visited all areas within these sales districts – no village was too small. Agents were paid a salary plus a commission.[88] In 1914 one employee who headed a depot in Ekaterinoslav district received eight rubles a week plus a three-percent commission; his total income that year was 1,126 rubles. Another depot manager received twelve rubles plus a three-percent commission. He received 539 rubles for the first half of 1915.[89] In Beloomut, the salesclerk earned 1,500 rubles in 1900 from sales and commissions.[90] According to the terms of their employment, agents were not to work for any company except Singer. Their salaries compare quite favorably with the 600 rubles per annum that skilled workers and schoolteachers received in Petersburg.

Singer company policy was to employ local residents at all levels of its operation. The company needed individuals familiar with the regions in which they worked, in part because of the way in which credit was distributed. As the company readily admitted, determining which customers should be allowed to pay for their sewing machines on the installment plan was a tricky business in Russia. In the case of peasants, Singer agents needed to find out the regular income of the person plus some indication as to what kind of a harvest was predicted. For workers, agents asked for length of service at a particular factory or workshop plus wages. Agents also needed to be familiar with local economic conditions in order to determine which clients were good credit risks.[91]

Having hired individuals because of their knowledge of local conditions, Singer proceeded to train them in the ways of their company. Given the size of the operation, the board of directors demanded frequent reports from all of their retail outlets. Depot directors were required to collect regular information from their employees. These reports were then sent to the central district office where a report for the entire region was composed and forwarded to company headquarters. In order to facilitate the writing of these reports, the company had forms that the employees filled in with the appropriate information. Much time and effort was spent getting the Russian employees to fill in the forms accurately and in a timely fashion. There were constant letters from the company headquarters chiding the district offices about the tardiness of these reports. In addition to these bureaucratic duties, all Singer agents learned how to operate the machines. In fact, a demonstration was a fundamental part of the sales pitch; agents gave sewing and embroidery lessons on the machines.[92] In the cities, young women employees sat in the store windows and sewed on the machines, attracting crowds of awed admirers.

Very little is known about the Singer employees. The few records that have survived suggest that most were in their twenties and thirties on the eve of World War I. Despite their youth, these men and women had been employed with the company for many years, working their way up through the business. To give one example, twenty-seven-year-old Gigel' Iankelev Gen'kin began working for Singer as a collector. Three years later he became a senior collector and worked at the Nizhnedneprovsk depot. In 1916 his superiors recommended him for a new position as head of the Amur depot.[93] In return for loyal service, the company tried to retain these workers in whatever capacity it could. The central district manager for Ekaterinoslav province, A. M. Rudnik, wrote to the company headquarters with frequent requests either to find other jobs for faithful workers or to give subsidies to those who were disabled by illness or injury. One worker, Gersh Nusev Berdianskii, began working for Singer in 1901. Like other employees, he moved quickly from one post to the next within the Ekaterinoslav sales district. In November 1916 he was mobilized, serving in the Russian Army until he was wounded. After his return from the front in the spring of 1917, he asked his former employer for another position at Singer and indicated his willingness to move to Turkistan or Siberia. The company was unwilling to hire any new employees during that tumultuous year, so they gave him 250 rubles instead, a paltry sum given wartime inflation.[94]

The company assisted its agents by spending significant sums on advertising and mail-order catalogues. By 1913 Singer had spent over 120,000 dollars on advertising of all kinds. In addition to ads in major magazines and newspapers, the company ordered calendars, knives, scissors, and pencils engraved with the company name.[95] The company also printed mail-order catalogues for use by its agents. By 1895, it had distributed 149 Russian-language editions of its catalogue.[96] By 1909 the Singer catalogues had changed significantly. They now contained very little written text. Black-and-white numbered photographs matched numbers on the price lists.[97] This new design helped unlettered individuals order from the catalogue.

Singer's successes did not go unchallenged. Other sewing-machine retailers attacked the company in their mail-order catalogues, hoping to attract customers for their own products. K. G. Tsimmerman declared: "[O]ne well-known firm calls its sewing machines real American machines, while in reality they are from Glasgow (England)[sic]. This same firm has the temerity to call its family machines the best in the world, while it has been proven that the production of the machines has died, and from a technical perspective they are very far away from modern innovations."[98] The owner of the Krauzel'burg firm complained bitterly:

> It is well known to everyone that the entire market for sewing machines in Russia is exploited by an American company through its multiple outlets and agents. It has been very difficult to compete with this company for a long time, for its network of exploitation has spread over all of Russia. In all cities and towns there are Singer Company stores, and the villages and hamlets swarm with touring agent-benefactors, selling sewing machines on the installment plan or as the agents say with no money down (*bez deneg*). It is also well-known that the main users of the sewing machines are the working class and peasants for whom these machines are not some form of high society luxury but a source for earning a living. And here are these poor folk, intoxicated by Singer's many powerful ads and wily agents for many years humbly satisfying the insatiable appetite of that company, paying as much for each machine as the company asks; in reality twice as much as they are worth.[99]

Of course, the only solution to this problem was to buy German sewing machines from Krauzel'burg, Tsimmerman, or the other sewing-machine manufacturers who made virtually the same claims as Singer did about its machines. But these companies could not offer their customers the same service or credit that Singer could.

Singer's elaborate network of stores and agents proved to be enormously successful. One historian has determined that the Russian Singer Company was poised to overtake the American Company in sales by 1914. According to company records, the Russian Singer Company posted a profit of over one million dollars in 1910 and almost nine million dollars in 1914.[100] Singer did so well in Russia primarily because it was able to integrate the urban and rural economic sectors into a national market. All customers, no matter where they lived, received the full benefits that the company offered. And as Singer's competitors readily acknowledged, peasant and working-class families were eager to buy this new machine which saved garment workers and home sewers hours of tedious hand sewing. Peasants, in particular, were introduced to new forms of retailing such as installment buying which introduced modern concepts of time and money into villages. For some peasants these lessons in consumerism were hard to learn. Those who could not keep up with the payments had their sewing machines repossessed. According to company records, the company lost almost 800,000 dollars due to bad credit; by 1914 this number approached one million dollars.[101] Individuals who overextended themselves financially quickly learned that modern retailing had a darker, uglier side. Whatever the outcome, however, these transactions indicate that peasants were fast becoming active participants in modern retailing.

The Singer sales organization presented a powerful model to those entrepreneurs who wanted to expand

88    The Singer Sewing Machine Company's advertisement in Russia. Private collection.

their retail operations, but who saw the backward state of rural Russia as a hindrance to their plans. The business climate in Russia continued to suffer from turbulent economic conditions as well as a difficult political situation. But the Singer Company demonstrated that the Russian market could be integrated in such a way that interested firms could reap considerable profits, breaking down the gulf between urban and rural Russia. By the early twentieth century, Russian consumers were hungry for modern conveniences not just in the cities but also in the countryside, and the Singer Company served as a model for how to satisfy that demand.

When the Singer Company created its new subsidiary in Russia, it needed a logo for its advertisements. The company chose to russify the logo that was used elsewhere. In the European and American ads, a young woman in European dress sat at a sewing machine while the letter "S" for Singer curled around her. The new Russian logo placed the Cyrillic letter "Z" in the middle of the field to represent the company name, Zinger. Ad executives placed a young woman dressed in Russian national costume at a Singer machine in the middle of the "Z". This use of Russian national dress on the female figure can be read two ways. On the one hand, her dress was an ethnic marker – this woman represented all Russian consumers. At the same time, the only individuals who wore Russian dress in this period were peasants. By placing this woman in ethnic costume in front of the sewing machine, the company's advertisers were creating a logo that appealed to peasants as well as city folk.

What is also interesting about the company logo is that a female figure was used to represent Russian consumers. In Russia, as elsewhere, both men and women purchased sewing machines throughout the nineteenth century, but the company chose a female as its symbol. As other historians have pointed out, Singer targeted women for its advertising campaigns in the United States and Europe even though thousands of men purchased the machines for their work.[102] Singer was not alone in its advertising appeals to women, however. Just as sewing was being gendered as female, so, too, was shopping. And it was women's role as consumers, particularly of high fashion, that proved as troubling for Russian society as it was elsewhere.

★　★　★

89　The three-story building housed the J. Block Company Store in Moscow. The store sold sewing machines including Singer models. Library of Congress Collections.

## SHOPPING AS A GENDERED PHENOMENON

Once fashionable shopping districts were established, well-to-do Russians flocked to places like Nevskii Prospekt and Kuznetskii Bridge to make their purchases. For Russian men, the sartorial choices were fairly straightforward. Most military personnel and civil servants wore uniforms to work. Tailors made the uniforms according to the specifications of each individual branch of service. Men not in government service wore suits, which had become the uniform for men in business and the professions. In addition, elite men needed outerwear to protect themselves against the elements, and a more festive suit for evenings at the theater or other such occasions.[103] For elite women who wanted to dress fashionably, the situation was more complex. In order to dress *comme il faut*, these women changed clothing several times during the day, and it was necessary to have seasonal wardrobes as well. Thus, a good deal of a woman's thought, time, and energy was necessary in order to dress fashionably.

In addition to the actual purchase of goods, an important aspect of western shopping was to see and be seen in the exclusive shopping districts.[104] Wealthy women gathered in the shops and the surrounding streets

143

to gossip and show off their sartorial splendor. Shopping became an elaborate ritual with its own etiquette. As commercial advertising matured during the second half of the nineteenth century, advertisements were increasingly aimed at women, encouraging them to go out and shop.

As more and more women attempted to partake of shopping, it became defined as a woman's occupation. No less a theorist than the Norwegian-American sociologist and economist Thorstein Veblen built an entire economic theory around the assumption that women consumed so as to enhance their husband's status by appearing in expensive clothing, and to indicate to everyone that they were not engaged in any form of productive labor. Women's role as consumers became indicative of their husband's wealth and status.[105] At the same time that women were being encouraged to shop for more beautiful and expensive clothes, some critics began to denigrate their "obsessive" concern with clothes and shopping.

The growing concern over women's role as consumers can be seen in the changing images of women in the Russian attitudes toward shopping. One such "true" story can be found in the December 1851 issue of *Fashion*. The story begins in St. Petersburg with a beautiful young woman dressed for an afternoon's outing. While waiting for her carriage, she meets her husband who suggests a visit to the fashion store DeLisle on Nevskii Prospekt. According to her husband, the store has just received goods from the 1851 Crystal Palace exhibition in London. Delighted at his suggestion, the happy woman departs with her husband. Inside the emporium she beholds a magnificent bazaar with goods from all over the world. Amazed at the splendor she sees, she finally comes upon an exquisite velvet outfit. When the young wife asks the price of the "velvet poem," she is quickly informed that it has already been sold. She screams and promptly faints into the arms of her husband. In order to bring back "her smile of pleasure," the husband races around the store buying the most expensive goods he can find. The wife leaves the store with many handsome packages but also with a slight tinge of regret about the loss of the "velvet poem."[106]

This story reveals the important elements in the gendering of shopping. Both husband and wife are con-

90  An elegant gown from the late 1860s. A partial overskirt with a pattern in velvet coupled with a few ruffles adds visual interest to the soft green of the dress. The State Hermitage Museum, St. Petersburg.

cerned about the wife's appearance. Her beautiful clothing and carriage convey to everyone they meet that her husband makes enough money to clothe his wife in the latest styles, purchased from the most exclusive stores in Petersburg. The story also shows how the wife uses her feminine wiles to get her husband to buy the goods she desires. Overcome by her passion for beautiful clothing, she faints and this spell emphasizes that she is a member of the "weaker sex," a woman who cannot cope with any difficulty because of the delicacy of her physical and emotional health. She needs a man to act decisively for her in her weakened condition, to buy the goods that she desires. Shopping, then, was seen as a release for women's passionate natures. Women literally lost their senses upon entering a store and needed men to act rationally for them.

Shortly after this story was published, Russian women began to seek a greater public role in society, as seen in chapter 2.[107] No longer content to remain delicate creatures dependent upon men, they sought employment outside of the home. This greater public presence of women in the workplace as well as the marketplace caused concern in some circles about the New Woman and her quest for greater equality, which began to find expression in the literature on shopping. One example can be found in Leo Tolstoy's *The Kreutzer Sonata*, the story of one man's sexual obsession and the resulting tragedy. Written in 1889 and published in 1891, *The Kreutzer Sonata* was widely read and discussed.[108] One of Tolstoy's themes in the work was the connection between women's clothing and their manipulation of men's sexual desires. According to Pozdnyshev, the story's narrator:

> Women, especially those who get their learning from men, know very well that conversations on important subjects are mere talk, and that what a man really wants is the body and whatever adds to the seductiveness of the body, and so that is what they offer him. If we could rid ourselves of this disgraceful habit which has become second nature to us and look at the life of the upper classes as it really is, we would see that it is a veritable brothel. . . . If people have different aims in life, if their inner lives are different, the outer forms of their lives will be different too. But look at the unfortunate women whom we despise and then at young ladies from the very highest society: the same clothes, the same styles, the same perfumes, the same bare arms, shoulders and bosoms, the same exaggerated behinds, the same passion for precious stones and expensive, glittering ornaments, the same amusements – dancing,

music, and singing. All the same means of enticing men are used by one as by the other. No difference at all. To make a strict distinction between them we can only say that short-term prostitutes are usually despised whereas long-term prostitutes are respected.[109]

The difference between Tolstoy's view of women and clothing and those expressed in the 1851 *Fashion* magazine story is stark. Whereas the woman in the earlier story was portrayed as delicate and weak, in Tolstoy's tale high-society women have become prostitutes – they are still passionate creatures but this time in a cold and calculating way. Upper-class women ensnare men with their provocatively dressed bodies, and like prostitutes they receive money in exchange for sex: high-society women marry for the money their hapless spouses possess. Once married, these women/prostitutes continue to shop and spend money:

> Go through the shops in any large town. Millions of hands – more than can be counted – have labored over the things displayed there and just see! Can anything for men's use be found in nine-tenths of these shops? All the luxuries of life are demanded and consumed by women. Count the factories. A huge portion of them are engaged in making useless ornaments, carriages, furniture, and knickknacks for women. Millions of people, generations of slaves, perish at this cruel factory labor to satisfy the whims of women. Women, like queens, have forced nine-tenths of the human race to labor for them as their slaves. And all because they have been humiliated and deprived of equal rights with man.[110]

Thus, Tolstoy makes explicit the connection between women's sexual passions, their greed as consumers of modern luxury goods, and their desire to seek revenge for men's unwillingness to grant them equal rights. What had been feminine delicacy in 1851 became women's revenge forty years later.

Both *The Kreutzer Sonata* of 1891 and the 1851 story were written at a time when shopping in fancy western stores was a relatively rare occurrence in Russia, something that only the wealthy could afford. By the end of the nineteenth century, however, these shops and stores had proliferated in Russian cities so that more and more

91 With her fur hat, collar, and muff, this young woman from Narva was dressed for a winter shopping trip. Private collection.

*Fashion*.[112] Surveying the social crisis that was engulfing Russia in 1914, Elets blames the financial and moral decline of the Russian family upon women's desire to dress *à la mode*. If Tolstoy described women's obsession with shopping and clothes as the poison in male/female relations, Elets expanded upon this attack to claim that women also neglected their children and their education because they were too busy planning their wardrobe. To illustrate his point, he claimed that many times women left their children behind in stores because of their preoccupation with their purchases. These women either returned to the stores once they realized that their children were missing or the store owners returned the children to their mothers.[113] As if this literal abandonment of children was not bad enough, Elets condemned women for spending their husbands' or fathers' hard-earned money. He stated that seventy-five percent of family unhappiness was due to fashion, and he regaled his readers with innumerable stories of men who lost most of their money due to their wives' insatiable clothes shopping: rapacious wives and daughters victimized helpless Russian men.[114]

Moreover, this "epidemic insanity" was not limited to elite families any longer but affected working-class women as well. According to Elets, working-class women spent virtually all of their wages buying fancy clothes, or else they turned to prostitution to earn the money necessary to finance their purchases. The only women in Russia who were immune from relentless shopping were peasant women who remained in the village. Elets wrote, "Peasant women and girls, going to a party or wedding, never think about whether they will be dressed better or worse than the others, because all [peasant women] dress more or less the same."[115] Thus, what had begun as a discourse on aristocratic women and their shopping habits had now been expanded by 1914 to include women of all social classes who stepped foot into the city.

There was another dimension to this concern about women and shopping. Elets was extremely worried about women's moral purity, which he and others claimed was being destroyed by their obsession with clothes and shopping. While Elets believed there still were respectable women in Russia, the marketplace was a dangerous place for them. It was filled with all sorts of unscrupulous individuals who tempted virtuous women

Russians could experience the wonders of modern consumerism. In addition, the early years of the twentieth century saw an increase of female peasant migration into the cities. These women continued to seek work as domestic servants and seamstresses, but they also began to look for work in Russia's new factories and stores.[111] The proliferation of stores and women shoppers caused a change in men's attitudes toward women and shopping. One example of this change appeared in Russia in 1914. Iulii L. Elets, a decorated military officer, journalist, and self-appointed social commentator, published a book entitled *Epidemic Insanity: Toward the Overthrow of the Yoke of* to give into feelings of avarice, greed, and passion. The cast of characters who attempted to corrupt innocent women included virtually everyone with whom women had contact while they were shopping.

According to Elets, the first danger to respectable Russian women was the saleswomen who worked in the dress shops. Many Russians assumed that these women were prostitutes, as indeed some of them were. Poorly paid, overworked saleswomen, recruited primarily from the lower classes, often turned to prostitution to supplement their wages so that they could afford the nice clothing required for work. More importantly, even those saleswomen who were not prostitutes were seen in the same light, particularly when shopkeepers subjected their employees to lewd and lascivious comments.[116]

Elet's second set of sleazy characters who were part of the world of commerce, were the shop owners themselves. Shopkeepers' advertising and window displays enticed honorable women into their stores and encouraged them to buy goods they could not afford. According to Elets, shopkeepers sometimes blackmailed their unsuspecting clients, leading to the downfall of innocent young women. In one such story, he described how a respectable maiden moved to Petersburg to live with her relatives. One day she admired a beautiful new hat, and the woman shopkeeper urged her to take the hat without paying for it. The young woman demurred but finally accepted the offer because she looked so perfect in the hat. These events were repeated two more times and then one day the shopkeeper presented her client with the bill for the hats, which amounted to more than 400 rubles. The young woman was devastated, for she did not have the money. The angry shopkeeper used the debt to blackmail the young woman into becoming involved with a certain prince who had become infatuated with her. The young woman agreed in the end and succumbed to her inevitable downfall, the loss of her virginity. This sad story, Elets concluded, was typical of the evil nature of many shop owners who specialized in women's fashions.[117]

The final set of dubious characters who inhabited Elets' world of fashion and shopping were the customers themselves. Many clients who frequented the exclusive boutiques were part of the *demi-monde* – actresses, dancers, and singers – who were sometimes the mistresses

92    The wife and daughter of a high government official dressed for a day's shopping in 1914. The elegance and beautiful tailoring of their gowns suggest that these two shopped at the best establishments. Central State Archive of Documentary Films, Photographs, and Sound Recordings in St. Petersburg.

of powerful men. The actresses Savina, Slavina, and Figner shopped at the Imperial Philanthropic Society's atelier where they were allowed to purchase gowns on credit.[118] The *demi-mondaines* played a prominent role in the world of fashion. They often helped to publicize the latest fashions by being the first to dress in the newest styles, either on the stage or in the restaurants to which they retired after their performances. At the same time, some of these women, although still dependent upon men in varying degrees for their success and notoriety, did not live by conventional moral codes of behavior, and therefore provided an alternative example of how women could conduct their lives. There was great concern that respectable women might rebel against conventional moral standards simply by rubbing elbows with the *demi-mondaines* on their shopping trips.

Elets believed that these unwholesome characters made the world of clothes shopping an extremely dangerous one for the respectable Russian woman. At every step along the way, she came into contact with women who had been corrupted by sexual licentiousness, passion, and greed, as these were the characteristics that united saleswomen, shop owners, and customers. The respectable Russian woman was seduced into buying items that she did not need, and she, in turn, used these garments to seduce her unsuspecting husband or lover. All these women had abandoned appropriate female behavior emphasizing modesty, restraint, and self-sacrifice to participate in the world of commerce. Thus, a simple commercial transaction became, in the eyes of many commentators, a defiant and deviant expression of a woman's sexuality. Consequently, it was women who were corrupted and sullied by wanton consumerism, not men, who remained the hapless and innocent victims of their female companions' greed and passions.

The discomfort felt by some Russian commentators and authors on the subject of women and shopping paralleled the same concerns of many western authors and social commentators. Theodore Dreiser in *Sister Carrie*, George Gissing in *Eve's Ransom*, and others provided commentary on women and consumerism, but the most influential work was Émile Zola's novel, *Ladies' Paradise* (*Au Bonheur des dames*).[119] In this work Zola chronicles the rise of a department store in nineteenth-century Paris. Significantly, Zola's fictional store is called Ladies' Paradise, a store whose sole purpose is to release women's alleged passion for luxury goods, gossiping, and spending money. Much of the novel concerns itself not just with the shopping habits of the store's clientele but also with their sexual lives. The upper- and middle-class women who shop at Ladies' Paradise are buying goods to enhance their beauty to please their lovers. The female salesclerks occupy their time with thoughts of their lovers who are often male store employees. The heroine, Denise, is virtually the only virgin in the story, and much of the novel chronicles her attempts to save her purity in the midst of the sexually depraved world of the department store. The language of the novel is saturated with sexual

imagery – the same types of images that Elets would use in his work.[120]

The use of sexual imagery to describe women and shopping reflects a deep concern Russians shared with other Europeans over the changes that industrialization and urbanization had brought about in gender relations. Wealth in Russia was no longer based upon titles and serfs, but upon the accumulation of capital, creating a new moneyed elite desirous of purchasing the new manufactured goods. Although mass consumption still eluded many Russians and Europeans, the *magaziny* created a public space where customers could look at the new industrial goods and sometimes buy whatever they desired.[121] Because of their prominent role as the new mass consumers of industrial goods, women and their supposedly passionate, sexual natures became the locus of anxiety expressed by those Russians and Europeans who did not like mass consumption.

Moreover, this gendering of shopping and its equation with seduction was part of a larger cultural image that Russians and Europeans used to characterize the impact of urbanization on European life. According to Elizabeth Wilson, an entire male discourse developed equating urban life, control of disorder, and women. Wilson writes:

> Woman is present in the cities as temptress, as whore, as fallen woman, as lesbian, but also as virtuous womanhood in danger, as heroic womanhood who triumphs over temptation and tribulation. . . . many writers. . . . posed the presence of women as a problem of order, partly *because* their presence symbolised the promise of sexual adventure. This promise was converted into a general moral and political threat.[122]

To use Elets' metaphor, clothes shopping was an urban mental illness which attacked women of all social classes foolish enough to enter the city. Thus, women shoppers and salesclerks symbolized the dangers for Russia and Europe inherent in urbanization.

*   *   *

Gender was only one component of the Russian discourse on shopping. As this chapter has shown, another element of shopping was its reflection of national identity. For Russians the changes in retailing were an integral part of their country's drive to modernize and industrialize. Mass consumption and production went hand in hand. And, here too, there are striking similarities between Russian and European descriptions of that process. Vasilich, who compared the rise of the *magaziny* with "the ascendancy of the machine," is really only mimicking Zola who also used the language of industrialization to describe his fictional department store. According to Zola, the department store was a machine – built of iron and steel, and run with the labor of hundreds of Parisian men and women, just as factories were.[123]

By using the language and metaphors of industrialization to describe mass consumption, Russian and European writers introduced the third important component to shopping, namely, how it increased the gulf between modern, urban life and the tradition-bound life of the countryside. For most members of the Russian and European lower classes, the "dream world" of mass consumption remained exactly that – a dream. Nevertheless, entrepreneurs worked continually to devise technologies and sales operations to expand the markets for their goods. Just at the moment when firms like Singer, Mandl', and Muir and Merilees were breaking down the urban/rural divide in Russian life, however incompletely, individuals such as Elets were trying to resurrect it to preserve their own place in the social hierarchy.

Because this democratization of luxury appeared to be changing society, it caused many members of the Russian and European intelligentsia to question the role of consumerism in modern life. The new stores brought with them some serious concerns. In her study of late nineteenth-century France, Rosalind Williams has written about the debate among social thinkers between those who wanted to encourage consumption as part of a general democratization of luxury and those who felt guilty about mass consumption. In her words, "this ambivalence formed a serious fault line in bourgeois culture."[124]

For Russians this fault line in bourgeois, urban culture was even more serious because many of them regarded this culture as western and therefore alien to Russian life. While many French people were also disquieted by retailing developments, they understood them to be an inevitable part of their own capitalist development: at

93  A pair of young women dressed to go out. The woman on the right wears a black suit which perfectly fits her corseted figure. Her hat and white collar adds drama to her otherwise austere suit. Her friend is wearing a beautifully made coat. Her long gold chain for her glasses and her hat add a further touch of class. Private collection.

least Frenchmen ran French department stores. In Russia, however, capitalism was seen as an external imposition upon Russia by the West. By juxtaposing western shops with Russian forms of retailing, Russian commentators were asserting the alien nature of western retail and capitalist developments in their native land. They did so at the precise moment when modern retailing was making serious inroads into Russian commercial life. This discomfort with shopping, coupled with the role of women in the new consumerism and the resulting change in gender relations, gave many Russians some compelling reasons to fear just such a capitalist order and its consumer culture.

# 6

## *Adorned in Dreams: Clothing and National Identity*

ONE OF THE GOALS OF THE FASHION industry is to celebrate the role of clothing as an aesthetic experience of the self. Like other forms of artistic expression, dress encourages individuals to fantasize, to dream, to give expression to their inner feelings and desires. The body becomes an artist's easel upon which to express the varied shadings of human experience and longings. In Elizabeth Wilson's words, "[Dress] links the biological body to the social being, and public to private."[1] At times, fashion highlights an individual's need to fit into a larger group, whether that is a social class, an ethnic group, or a religious community. At other times, fashion helps individuals reject the social status quo. Refusing to wear the uniform of one's particular social group has proven to be a powerful tool in European political life. Fashion allowed individuals to create imagined communities in Europe, whose sartorial nonconformity frequently led to political confrontation.

It was precisely this idea of fashion as an expression of the self that underlay Peter the Great's sartorial decree.[2] The tsar insisted that Russians imagine themselves as Europeans, step out of their own cultural traditions and

imitate those of their European neighbors. Peter's dream for himself and his countrymen was that Europeans would see them as cultural equals rather than uncouth barbarians from the east. If the Russian government hoped to maintain control of the symbolic and manipulative qualities of fashion, however, it was to be sorely disappointed. Fashion served as a powerful tool in imperial Russia precisely because it was so difficult to control. Even an autocratic government could not hope to eliminate the idiosyncratic choices that individual Russians made when they decided what to wear each day. And yet, what they chose to wear became a powerful statement. Sartorial choices gave shape to individual and collective dreams about the Russian past, present, and future. New identities were coalescing while visions of the past tightened their grip on the public imagination.

### EIGHTEENTH–CENTURY DEBATES ABOUT DRESS

Peter the Great's sartorial revolution essentially created two categories of dress: traditional Russian clothing and European fashion. Like all symbolic systems, they were subject to revision and interpretation, making apparel a vital and contested aspect of Russian life. Debates about clothing styles helped Russians grapple with complex

94 *(facing page)*  A woman in Russian court dress in 1913. Central State Archive of Documentary Films, Photographs, and Sound Recordings in St. Petersburg.

cultural questions as clothing became a visual metaphor for more abstract ideas. In his 1916 book *The History of Russian Clothing*, P. K. Stepanov summarized the fundamental question that shaped not only sartorial debates but also Russian identity politics in general: "What kind of culture did the ancient inhabitants of our country give us . . . [and] what relationship do we, the contemporary inhabitants, have to this culture?"[3] At stake was the very essence of Russianness. Could a French corset stifle a Russian heart? Somehow Russians had to grapple with this question to create a coherent national identity.

Not much time elapsed after Peter's sweeping cultural reforms before Russians began to question and critique them. The historian Hans Rogger has argued that over the course of the eighteenth century Russians developed what he calls "national consciousness" in response to the government's adoption of western European culture. This appropriation of European dress, manners, and lifestyle forced Russians to consider what was unique and special about their own culture. Although most of the educated public understood the need for Russia to become an integral part of European economic and political life, what troubled some intellectuals was the slavish imitation of western dress and manners. The Frenchified coquette and dandy became stock figures in Russian plays and satires of the time. Zealous attention to the latest fashions identified these characters as vain, superficial egotists. Forgetting the duty they owed to their families and country, they thought only of their own pursuit of pleasure. As Rogger points out, these intellectuals were not offended by European culture per se. Rather they "deplored the loss of identity on the part of Russians who mistook imitation for Europeanization and as a result were neither Russian nor European." Thus, by the second half of the eighteenth century, excessive attention to fashion by both sexes had become a trope in Russian culture to identify those who had lost themselves to an alien culture.[4]

This growing national consciousness intensified during the reign of Catherine the Great. Although the empress herself was German and not Russian, she encouraged and participated in these attempts to define Russianness. As part of her campaign to exalt Russian culture and to control the outrageous sums that women spent on their gowns, Catherine declared that all female courtiers must wear her version of Russian dress at certain ceremonial occasions. This court uniform for women combined the sarafan and a type of Russian headdress called a *kokoshnik*. While Catherine's declaration might appear a radical departure from Peter's decrees, it was not. The sarafan rather closely resembled the high-waisted, empire-style gowns that were all the rage in Europe at the time. These gowns, in turn, had been inspired by Grecian clothing styles from antiquity.[5] One Russian called the gowns "English-Greek-Russian" dress, highlighting the artificiality of ethnic designations for dress designs.[6] Nevertheless, this sartorial sleight of hand allowed aristocratic women to express their Russianness at court without having to sacrifice their allegiance to European *haute couture*.

This reintroduction of native designs into Romanov court ceremonies gave a certain legitimacy to ethnic dress that Peter's decrees had denied it. Now it was acceptable to use Russian design elements with *haute couture*, thereby combining and harmonizing Russian and European cultures. Indeed, Russian women's court dress signified one of the earliest attempts to bridge the cultural divide that resulted from Peter's westernization policies. The initial feelings of inferiority that Russians had felt toward their western European neighbors were replaced by a growing sense of comfort and confidence.

These changes in court dress occurred at the same time as gender roles were being redefined. As we saw in chapter 2, Catherine the Great's reign marked the introduction of the cult of domesticity into Russia. The Frenchified coquette who thought only of her own pleasure gave way to the virtuous wife and mother. Traits that eighteenth-century Russians identified as part of their ethnic heritage – simplicity, generosity, kindness, sincerity, diligence – were the very same attributes associated with women's natures.[7] These similarities between Russian and feminine qualities allowed elite women's bodies to become the perfect vehicles with which to represent those traits. And yet, while noblewomen wore Russian dress to ceremonial occasions, drawing attention to the empire's unique contribution to world civilization, their male partners continued to wear European-style uniforms, reflecting universal cosmopolitan tastes and masculinity. Those characteristics that defined masculinity – duty, physical courage, loyalty, and rationality

– were closely associated with westernization. By wearing European dress in public, male aristocrats showed their acceptance of westernization as well as European definitions of masculinity. The War of 1812 further reinforced these cultural dichotomies. When France became Russia's enemy, elite women abandoned their French fashions for Russian sarafans to demonstrate their patriotism. When their husbands and brothers marched into Paris after the defeat of Napoleon, they did so wearing garments that harmonized with the uniforms of the other European armies.[8]

## THE RISE OF ROMANTIC NATIONALISM

Napoleon's defeat ushered a new era of political reaction and cultural experimentation into European life. Frightened by the excesses of France's revolutionary experiment, monarchs were restored to their thrones across Continental Europe. Meanwhile intellectuals rejected universalist Enlightenment appeals that had led the French to revolutionary violence. Romantic writers sought to identify those qualities that made each nation state or ethnic group unique. One of these writers, the philosopher and poet Johann Gottfried Herder, created the doctrine of cultural nationalism, urging Europeans to study "the folk" and their culture, and dress played a crucial role in this development. Paris fashions became associated with the evils of the cosmopolitan city, while folk dress remained the signifier of pastoral village life.[9]

Cultural nationalism had a profound, multifaceted effect on Russia. Tsar Nicholas I's government formulated its own brand of nationalism with the doctrine of Official Nationality in 1834. Official Nationality declared that autocracy, Orthodoxy, and nationality were the essential features that made Russia unique among nations.[10] In the same year, Nicholas I reformed court dress as part of his attempt to encourage national sympathies at court. Russian dress became the official uniform for ladies-in-waiting at all court ceremonies, while European design formed the basis of men's court uniforms. The tsar, who adopted the trappings of European family life to characterize his relationship to his people,[11] further reinforced the association of aristocratic women with Russian and feminine virtues, while Russian noble-

men appeared as the embodiment of European masculinity. These court uniforms continued in use with only minor changes until the fall of the Romanov dynasty in 1917.[12]

In addition to these government measures, many intellectuals and artists began to explore the concept of nationality, building upon the work of their eighteenth-century predecessors. The poet, novelist, and dramatist Alexander Pushkin, combined European literary forms with Russian folk themes and became the father of modern Russian literature. While neoclassicism dominated Russian architecture in the first quarter of the nineteenth century, native architects began to incorporate Russian motifs into their work in the 1830s. They called this new style "Byzantine," although its sources were Muscovite. In the fine and decorative arts, artists began depicting rustic rural scenes, romanticizing the enserfed Russian peasantry. All of these artists created something new by blending Russian and European cultures together.[13]

These attempts to integrate Russian and European cultures suffered a setback in 1836 when Petr Chaadaev published his "Philosophical Letter." Chaadaev represented the best and brightest of Russian intellectual life. Raised in a thoroughly Europeanized environment in Russia, he had served with the Russian Army during the Napoleonic invasion and had traveled in Europe after the War of 1812. Well versed in European Romantic thought, Chaadaev had become despondent over what he perceived to be a profound chasm between Russia and the West, making it impossible for Russia to contribute significantly to European civilization:

> Nothing from the first moment of our social existence has emanated from us for man's common good; not one useful idea has germinated in the sterile soil of our fatherland; we have launched no great truth; we have never bothered to conjecture anything ourselves, and we have only adopted deceiving appearances and useless luxury from all the things that others have thought out . . .[14]

This thoroughly pessimistic, even nihilistic, view of Russia could not go unchallenged, since Chaadaev was calling into question the government's entire westernization program. The government's response was immediate and swift. Chaadaev was placed under house arrest and declared insane for his views. Russian intellectuals gave a more measured response. One group, the westernizers, angered by Chaadaev's rejection of Peter the Great's reforms as ineffectual, argued that they had not gone far enough. Russia needed more westernization if it was going to contribute to European civilization. Another group, the Slavophiles, was incensed by Chaadaev's complete disavowal of Russian culture and history. Consequently, they began to extol pre-Petrine life. These conservative utopians insisted that Peter the Great's westernization policies had shattered the communal, organic wholeness of Muscovite Russia, creating a gulf between educated society and the people. In order to restore this lost world, Russians needed to rediscover those features, which made them unique.

To publicize Slavophile views, Konstantin Aksakov took the radical step of appearing at public gatherings in the clothes of a Muscovite nobleman. While Chaadaev joked that ordinary Russians mistook him for a Persian,[15] Nicholas I and many members of polite society were shocked. As we saw in chapter 1, Nicholas I demanded that Russian officialdom, their women, and their servants be dressed properly at all times. To that end, the tsar personally oversaw the creation of new uniforms for all branches of government service. In 1834 Nicholas decreed that elite women were to wear "Russian" dress – a combination of Russian traditional dress with European fashions of the 1830s – to court functions. Elite dress for men consisted of European-style uniforms – any form of ethnic dress barred them from official circles. Outside of official functions, men were expected to wear European suits. Elite women were encouraged to wear European dress in the city and Russian traditional dress on their country estates. Despite this carefully laid out sartorial plan, Aksakov chose to wear Russian dress. He concurred with Chaadaev that European clothing represented "deceiving appearances and useless luxury." He wanted Russia to return to its native traditions freed from European cultural norms and influence even though this violated the government's own dress code. Consequently, Aksakov's defiance of the tsar's wishes placed the government in an awkward and hypocritical position. How could the government that espoused Official Nationality as its ruling ideology be opposed to an elite male wearing national dress? At the same time, his sartorial protest underlined the double standard inherent in the government's uniform regulations – only elite women were supposed to wear ethnic dress. Since Aksakov did not hold an official government position, the government could not punish him in any way for his sartorial choices except to mock him. Nevertheless, he had added a new layer of meaning to Russian dress by making it a weapon in the *male* arsenal of social protest.

The intellectual ferment of the 1840s both in Europe and in Russia had raised the question of the role of dress in modern life and, in particular, the relationship between fashion and ethnicity. Essentially three positions emerged in these discussions. The first was that of Peter the Great himself: Russians could dress in European fashions without jeopardizing their national identity. The problem with this approach was that some Russians appeared to lose their sense of ethnic identity when they tried to copy European manners and dress too closely. This gave rise to the second position. Those Russians who accepted westernization as essential to the future development of the empire, but wanted to preserve some part of their ethnic heritage, adopted an integrative approach to dress. By incorporating Russian folk elements into the western design vocabulary, Russians could express their national spirit and collective identity while still appearing sophisticated, chic, and, above all, European. The third position was that, for some Russians, neither approach was acceptable. They rejected all forms of European dress, preferring instead the clothes of their ancestors.

## DRESS IN THE AGE OF REALISM

The death of Nicholas I in 1855 ushered in a new era. Nicholas's son, Tsar Alexander II, eased censorship and encouraged educated society to participate in a reinvigoration of public life. It was to be an "Age of Realism" in which the government and educated society together grappled with Russia's serious economic, social, and political problems. Alexander's government attempted a series of reforms that included the emancipation of the serfs, the creation of a modern European judiciary, educational system, and military, and measures intended to foster industrial development. Unfortunately, these reforms promised more than they delivered. The peasants remained tied to the land despite their emancipation, and the tsar's unwillingness to create a more democratic political system frustrated members of the Russian educated elite.

Some members of the younger generation quickly became disillusioned with Alexander II's reform initiatives. Rejecting individual acts of protest as ineffectual, they banded together and publicly rejected the rules which had governed their parents' lives. These rebels, called nihilists, used dress as a way of identifying themselves. The young men gave up the elegant custom-tailored suits and uniforms of their fathers, preferring the shabby chic of western European bohemians and artists. Others, having become involved in the agrarian socialist movement called populism, identified with the peasantry whom they hoped to guide to a better life. As a result, some of Russia's best and brightest young men began appearing on city streets dressed in embroidered peasant shirts and loose pants tucked into their boots, looking like peasants. Their parents were appalled.[16] When these same young men went out into the Russian countryside and attempted to preach revolution to the rural inhabitants in the early 1870s, the peasants were also appalled. They contacted the police and had their "liberators" arrested for sedition.

While this attempt to arouse the peasantry into political revolt failed, sartorially it established men's use of dress as a form of protest for those on the political left. The nihilists' rejection of the political status quo was linked to an equally vehement critique of Russian social life. These men felt intense guilt at the privileges that their birth had afforded them. As a result, the idea of dressing as a Muscovite nobleman, as Aksakov had done, was anathema to them. They chose instead to identify themselves with the peasants that their families had long exploited. Later in the century, the individual who came to personify this rejection of noble status and dress was Leo Tolstoy. Although he was neither an agrarian socialist nor a nihilist, Tolstoy chose to dress as a peasant. In doing so, he made clear his rejection of aristocratic privilege and his condemnation of a government that was so callous in its treatment of the peasants. In the 1880s and 1890s when disaffected young men turned to Marxism as

a cure for Russia's social, economic, and political problems, they too used clothing as a form of social protest, this time adopting the attire of Russian workers. Whether dressed as peasants or workers, radical men blurred social boundaries and with their bodies made the educated elite conscious of the problems of the laboring classes by appearing in public out of the uniform of their social class.

Educated young women who wished to join the lifestyle revolt of the 1860s and 1870s did not have the same options as their brothers. Inspired by the women's movement in western Europe, these young women rejected Russian patriarchy. Women radicals wanted the freedom to live their lives as they saw fit, not in the shadows of their fathers, husbands, and brothers. And yet, even though they empathized with the plight of peasant women, they did not seek to emulate them in their dress. Wearing Russian dress or incorporating Russian folk elements into European design served as elite women's uniform at court and represented female patriotism and support for patriarchy. To display their unhappiness with Russian patriarchy in whatever guise it was found, women radicals wore dark, plain woolen frocks, cut their hair short, smoked cigarettes, and wore blue glasses, the uniform of women radicals in Europe. In creating this unadorned form of dress, Russian female radicals rejected the sumptuous world of high fashion that enticed women to spend hours shopping and primping so that they could remain attractive to men.[17] They understood that a return to Russian folk culture could not lead them to the independent lives they craved.

## DRESS AND THE DISCOVERY OF THE *NAROD*

Nicholas I's doctrine of Official Nationality, the utopian writings of the Slavophiles, and Alexander II's Era of the Great Reforms encouraged the further development of cultural nationalism in Russia. As nationalist sentiments gripped the public imagination, the newly emancipated peasantry became an important focal point for both the Russian government and educated society. These groups believed that the peasants had preserved Russian culture from nefarious western influences. Educated society began to look for authentic sources of Russian culture among the peasants whom they now identified as "the people," or *narod*. The relatively new scientific disciplines of archeology, anthropology, ethnography, and geography gave Europeanized Russians tools with which they could explore their country's past and traditions.

One of these tools was the collection and analysis of traditional Russian dress. Rather than seeing clothing as an expression of an individual's aesthetic sensibilities and social status, nineteenth-century ethnographers saw dress as a visual metaphor for the abstract qualities and attributes that made each ethnic group unique, privileging the collective over the individual sense of self. Because these scholars believed that ethnic dress changed very slowly in contrast to fashion, they postulated that the stability of folk designs expressed the essence of Russianness. The very timelessness of Russian dress made it an excellent source to study native culture. The military historian Viskovatov articulated this commonly held view when he reported that "Russian dress from the founding of our state to Peter the Great did not experience significant changes and the Russian people were almost as constant in this respect as they were in their feelings of loyalty to the Throne and their religious faith." Inspired by Viskovatov, Johann Georgi, Peter Pallas, and others, a new generation of scholars set out to discover how Russian peasants dressed.[18]

In 1845 a group of scientists formed the Russian Geographical Society whose purpose was to study the Russian land and its people. In 1863 another group of professional and amateur scientists formed a rival organization, the Society of Lovers of Science, Anthropology, and Ethnography (Obshchestvo liubitelei estestvoznaniia, antropologii i etnografii, or OLEAE). Local historical and archeological societies also began to salvage artifacts from the past and to construct histories based upon this new information.[19] In 1848 and 1853, the Russian Geographical Society sent out an ethnographic survey to collect information about dress throughout European Russia. Local elites sent back the surveys with descriptions of typical peasant garments.[20] The data collected by these groups encouraged writers and artists to give more realistic portrayals of peasant life in their work. The new style of visual art, called the "Russian style," incorporated folk motifs observed in real life or in

historical documents into the fine and decorative arts. Scholars began to publish beautifully illustrated treatises on folk art, architecture, and dress. Artists and architects would then take the designs they found in Russian embroidery and clothing, and use them as decorative elements on buildings, jewelry, and china.[21]

In addition to providing invaluable information about the past, these scholarly writings had another purpose. The corruption of the native folk culture by modernity alarmed many social scientists. These researchers argued that changes in clothing styles provided visual evidence of the transformation of peasant life. In 1865, ethnographers from OLEAE issued the first of many warnings about the changing nature of peasant wardrobes: "The collection and preservation of typical dress of the various tribes and regions is virtually impossible at the present time because with every year in the various locales of Russia more and more people give up their use of those clothes which from time immemorial have made up their characteristic feature."[22] As this quote makes clear, ethnographers and other intellectuals were horrified that European dress was becoming popular among the very people who were supposed to preserve Russian national identity. This was particularly true now that ethnic dress had all but disappeared among the upper and middle classes. The ethnographers deplored peasants' willingness to abandon their traditional dress worn since "time immemorial" in favor of fashion, even though the ethnographers' ancestors had done precisely the same thing a hundred years earlier. Because they believed that *peasant* clothing represented ethnicity, the scientists worried about the implications of these changes. Russia was losing its unique identity because the peasants were becoming "westernized." Who was going to preserve Russianness if the peasants abandoned their traditional way of life?

It is important to point out that Russian peasants did not wake up one morning and decide to put on frock coats, silk gowns, and corsets, thereby making themselves indistinguishable from the ethnographers who studied them. The situation was more complex than that. Because these intellectuals saw *any* change as undermining the timelessness and stability of folk dress, even small changes represented westernization. As we have seen in examples from earlier chapters, the ethnographers

observed that peasants used factory-made cloth instead of homespun to make their clothes. Some peasant women no longer knew how to sew and therefore could not supply their families with clothing. Peasants had also begun to purchase factory-made hats, ribbons, and sometimes ready-to-wear work clothing. These simple purchases marked their abandonment of traditional clothing and cottage industries, and their entry point into the fashion industry and industrial capitalism. And even though peasants' purchasing power remained limited throughout the imperial period, the ethnographers and others who studied this gradual transformation of the Russian peasantry believed that every change, no matter how small, marked a loss for Russian national identity and culture. Traditional ways were giving way to modernity.

At the same time, scholars' attempts to understand Russian folk culture were yielding some unexpected results. As archeologists, ethnographers, and geographers explored the Eurasian plain, home of the Russian Empire, they returned with artifacts that challenged the very idea of a Russian culture preserved since "time immemorial." The discoveries they made about the origins of Russian dress were central to this new view of folk culture.

One of the most vocal proponents of the "Russian style" in the arts was Vladimir V. Stasov. Stasov grew up in the European environment of the Russian elite. He held several governmental positions as a young man, but his real passions were music and art. After an extended stay in western Europe, he returned to Petersburg in 1854 and took a position as the head of the art and Russian culture department at the Imperial Public Library. In his job, he collected and read an enormous amount of material dealing with all aspects of artistic endeavor. He also became acquainted with a number of artists and musicians for whom he served as a patron. Not content with increasing his own understanding, Stasov wanted to share his insights with other Russians. As a result, he became the chief publicist for Russian national art and was often seen in public wearing peasant dress to demonstrate his love for his native culture.[23]

Although Stasov is known in the West primarily for his music criticism, he also produced two scholarly works on Russian ornament. Like other nationalists, Stasov began his book on Russian folk ornament by lamenting the loss of peasant culture:

> Meanwhile objects employed in domestic folk life are rapidly disappearing from use yielding to objects of newer origin and form which without a doubt meet the circumstances and needs of modern life. But these newer objects are losing those qualities of artistic creativity from earlier epochs: distinctive originality, naiveté, and beauty. Therefore, now is the time to collect and publicize these objects: it is already very clear to every observer of folk life that within a decade or even a few years that these objects of domestic folk life will completely disappear without a trace.[24]

As Stasov looked at the sources of this "distinctive originality," however, he discovered that Russian folk culture was an amalgam of design elements that originated in Finnish, Persian, and even Indian cultures. In regard to ethnic dress, Stasov declared that, strictly speaking, there was no such thing as Russian clothing. The garments typical of Russian dress came from other cultures. The Russians adopted the caftan from the Tatars, the *kika* (headdress) from the Finns, and the sarafan from the Persians.[25] He even noted that the swastika which sometimes appeared in Russian folk designs was a common folk ornament in ancient India, Tibet, and Siberia, from where it made its way into Russian folk design.[26] This led Stasov to conclude that "in our needlework patterns a not insignificant influence of various other lands: Finnish, Persian, and occasionally Buddhist is visible."[27]

In 1881 Vasilii A. Prokhorov published the first volume of a multi-volumed work entitled *A History of Russian Dress and the Folk Way of Life*. Prokhorov was a prominent archeologist, scholar of ancient art, and one of the founders with Stasov of the Geographic Society's Ethnographic Museum.[28] In this work, he expanded upon and gave further credence to Stasov's arguments about the ancient origins of Russian culture. Prokhorov argued that Russians should use archeological and ethnographic data to construct their past rather than foreigners' accounts.[29] After years of examining fragments of cloth, vases, frescos, and other artifacts, Prokhorov identified two ancient civilizations as the sources for Russian dress, the Scythian-Slavs and the Byzantine Greeks.[30] The Scythians were a nomadic warrior tribe who had migrated from Central Asia to the shores of the Black Sea in the seventh century BCE. They established a large military state in southern Russia, Ukraine, and the Balkans which survived until the third century BCE. Noticing a remarkable similarity between Scythian dress and Russian garments, Prokhorov concluded:

> In general the character of Scythian clothing is Eastern, in the same family as Assyrian, Persian, and others. . . . [M]any Asia Minor artifacts completely resemble Scythians ones; this resemblance is reflected chiefly in dress, its decoration, etc. And just as the Scythians adhered to the strong and immutable ancient traditions of their ancestors, so a few similar garments have preserved their distinctive character not only for many centuries and thousands of years, but they have survived among their descendents – the Slavs and especially the Russian Slavs (*Slaviano-Russami*). . . . [T]he ancient dress of women from Asia Minor completely resembles current Ukrainian and Russian dress: Ukrainian *plakhty* or Russian *ponëvy* with their decorative designs, *koftochki*, and headdresses. Such a resemblance or general character we find in both men's and women's clothing.[31]

Despite the thousands of years that separated the Scythians from nineteenth-century Russian peasants, certain garments remained the same, connecting the two cultures.

At the same time, Prokhorov observed unmistakable Byzantine influences on the Russian artifacts, beginning in the twelfth century CE:

96   A sketch of Scytho-Sarmatian clothing. P. K. Stepanov, *Istoriia russkoi odezhdy*, 18–19. University of Illinois Collections.

In Rus' they wove material only from the coarsest linen and wool; they received other kinds [of material] from the East and sometimes from the West, but the richest works were Byzantine because Byzantium was the arbiter of fashion, taste, and culture [*obrazovannosti*] for the entire Christian world. Byzantine art ruled East and West.[32]

This Byzantine connection was crucial to Russian nationalist sensibilities. Byzantium was not simply the most powerful empire of its day but it was also the heir to the power and glory of ancient Greece and Rome. Imitating Byzantine art and clothing styles, Russians could lay claim to that reflected glory.

Thus, the Scythian and Byzantine influences on Russian dress connected the Russians to two powerful empires. The Scythians were known for their military

prowess, while Byzantine culture linked Russians to their religious faith and classical learning. Prokhorov's history of Russian dress implicitly tells the story of how the Russians had melded the influences of the Scythians and the Byzantines into their own unique culture and dress. Russians had forged East and West together to form a new alloy that was stronger than either one separately. Moreover, Prokhorov's work was scientific. No longer based upon impressionistic foreigners' accounts, the archeologist used scientific facts to demonstrate the origins of Russian dress.

Prokhorov's *History* appeared at a critical juncture in Russian life. In 1881, a group of terrorists assassinated Alexander II in the hope that his death would demonstrate the government's vulnerability, which, in turn, would precipitate a peasant uprising in Russia. Instead, his son Alexander III (1845–1894) took the throne, arrested and executed the assassins, and established a regime that was avowedly reactionary and nationalistic. Nationalism was on the rise all across Europe so that Alexander's renewed emphasis on Russian nationalism was in some ways a response to this pan-European trend. But, at the same time, these nationalistic policies did not reflect a profound shift in official policy – the government remained committed to westernization and industrialization. And while the government vigorously opposed the introduction of any limitation upon its political power, nevertheless, it relied upon and worked with a number of organizations such as the Geographical Society and OLEAE to promote its policies and initiatives.

Upon his accession to the throne, Alexander III attempted to create an image of himself as a true Russian who was trying to restore his empire to its Muscovite past.[33] Since the tsars often wore military uniforms for public occasions, Alexander undertook a reform of the Russian Army uniform, which would help him to repackage his own image as well as that of his army. For most of the imperial period, the Russian Army uniform closely resembled that of the Prussian Army. Now, Alexander III decided to create an ensemble combining western and Russian design elements. In November 1881 the new uniform was introduced. It consisted of three supposedly Russian design elements: a caftan, loose black pants worn inside boots (a sartorial tradition among peasant men), and a round, lambskin cap

97 Russian head coverings from the fifteenth and sixteenth centuries. V. A. Prokhorov, *Materialy po istorii russkikh odezhd i obstanovki zhizni narodnoi*, xxvii. University of Illinois Collections.

Alexander III's government. At the same time, there was an important difference from earlier attempts to incorporate Russian elements into western fashion. A decade earlier, Stasov had identified the caftan as originating with the Tatars.[35] The round lambskin hats were fundamental elements in the folk dress of the Christian and Muslim peoples of the Caucasus and Central Asia.[36] While Cossack and Siberian regiments had worn the lambskin hat for a number of years, the introduction of the redesigned *papakha* coupled with the caftan in 1881 was not accidental. For most of the nineteenth century, the Russian Army had waged an intense struggle to incorporate the vast territories of the Caucasus and Central Asia into the empire. The peoples of these regions proved to be skilled fighters, and they thwarted Russian efforts at every step along the way. However,

98 Russian folk designs. Vladimir Stasov, *Russkii narodnyi ornament: Shit'e, tkani, kruzheva*, xiv. University of Illinois Collections.

which was a variant of the *papakha*, a hat worn in Central Asia and the Caucasus. The change in uniform allowed Alexander III's army to present itself both at home and abroad as the embodiment of Russian military ideals and masculine prowess.[34]

This Russification of army uniforms was a complex process. Alexander III took his cue from the integrative process initiated by Catherine the Great in her designs for women's court dress. Russian elements changed the look of the western-style military uniform. Russian military men could now feel themselves to be a part of European culture and yet still express their ethnic pride through dress, reflecting very nicely the same blend of westernization and nationalist policies espoused by

99　A Russian army officer wearing his *papakha* and great coat. Private collection.

with the annexation of the Transcaspian in 1881, the Russians had managed to establish a colonial administration in these areas. The adoption of the new uniform served as a symbol of Russia's military prowess and status as a colonial power, a military force to be reckoned with both in Europe and in Asia.

A few months after the uniform regulations were announced, judges at the 1882 Industrial Exhibition in Moscow chided clothing manufacturers for failing to design clothing that expressed Russian national identity:

> Above all, almost all of these luxury goods . . . were lacking any kind of typical national characteristics and revealed themselves as slavish and insipid imitations of

the tyrannical arbiters [of fashion] in Paris, Vienna, and other cities. Fashion and taste terrorize the elite of all European societies, but in particular the newly rich but poorly educated classes (bourgeois upstarts, *les parvenus*), who with particular cupidity throw their money after every expensive new fashion.[37]

The judges went on to say that western Europeans included folk elements in their clothes, so why did Russians refuse to do so? They urged clothing manufacturers to include Russian design elements in their garments. At the very least, the bourgeois upstarts, those desperate slaves to fashion, would look Russian!

This nationalist call to produce fashions that incorporated folk culture created a problem for Russian designers. How were they to design fashions that combined western *haute couture* with Russian folk elements, especially now that the eastern roots of Russian dress were becoming better understood? It was one thing to design a military uniform that blended these elements together, but quite another matter to design clothing for the diverse consumer market. The key to the resolution of this dilemma lay in the new western European art movement called modernism.

## DRESS AND THE RISE OF RUSSIAN MODERNISM

Modernism was a complex artistic movement, which emerged in western Europe in the 1870s. Weary of realism, artists wanted to initiate forms of artistic expression that captured the spirit of the world in which they lived without having to construct a mirror image of that world. As a result, the artists who initiated modernism drew inspiration from a variety of contradictory sources which reflected the profound changes that Europe was undergoing. While some artists wanted to highlight Europe's rapidly growing cities with their trams, electric lights, and skyscrapers, other artists hoped to capture in their work the world that was being lost to industrialization and urbanization. Other artists rejected a materialist worldview and pursued a more spiritual path, while still another group embraced exotic, non-European cultures as a way of critiquing their own civilization. The interplay between these contradictory forces –

100　A display of different styles of women's dress worn in the Russian Empire. The mannequin second from left in the first row is wearing what was called neo-Russian dress. Central State Archive of Documentary Films, Photographs, and Sound Recordings in St. Petersburg.

western/non-western, urban/rural, material/spiritual – gave way to modernism.

Nowhere were the contradictory elements of modern life more apparent than in imperial Russia during the second half of the nineteenth century. Having emancipated the serfs as late as 1861, Russia was attempting to transform itself from a traditional agrarian society to a modern industrial economy virtually overnight. Eco-nomic gains could quickly be lost due to Russia's precarious position in the world market. Furthermore, the government refused to consider sharing political power in any meaningful way with elected representa-tives, and popular discontent was growing. Workers and peasants toiled away to achieve the government's economic objectives, but reaped few material benefits from their labors. Russian artists looked to modernism to provide new ways of thinking about Russia's place in the world.

The history of the Mamontov Circle provides a case study of how Russian artists moved from realism to modernism. A wealthy railroad magnate, Savva Mamontov had a dream to foster the development of

101   The Kharchevnikov family in 1904. While the woman and child are dressed in European fashions, the man retains some native traditions by wearing a Russian embroidered shirt and by tucking his pants into his boots. Private collection.

102   A mother and her teenage daughters. The mother has maintained the Russian sartorial tradition of a woman completely covering her body and head so that only her face and hands are visible. However, her daughters are dressed in contemporary fashions with their distinctive hats. The mother undoubtedly allowed her daughters to don European dress so that they would have a better chance to catch an eligible marriage partner. Private collection.

Russian opera. In 1885, he did just that when he opened his Private Opera Company. Italian opera was very popular in Russia,[38] but Mamontov wanted to popularize the efforts of Russia's nationalist musicians – Tchaikowsky, Rimsky-Korsakov, Musorgsky, Borodin, and Glinka. The musicians took folk melodies and worked them into classical compositions, blending western and Russian musical forms together. In the operas, old Russian folk tales and stories supplied the narrative structure. Throughout the 1880s and 1890s the Private Opera Company performed, among other works, Rimsky-Korsakov's *Snow Maiden* and *Sadko*, Glinka's *Ruslan and Ludmila*, Musorgsky's *Boris Godunov*, along with European operas. What made these performances

so extraordinary was the art that accompanied the music. Russia's leading artists – Victor Vasnetsov, Mikhail Vrubel', Konstantin Korovin, Sergei Maliutin, and Valentin Serov – used their knowledge of folk art to create colorful sets and costumes, recalling Russia's past. But this new generation of artists turned away from ethnographic verisimilitude and imbued western artistic forms with more subjective expressions of the Russian spirit.[39]

The development of the neo-Russian style, as this first modernist impulse was called, had an important effect on the fashion industry. First of all, it led to the revival of served as designs for other forms of art. Many artists took patterns used in embroidery for animals, birds, and other objects, and incorporated them into their work, thereby greatly expanding the grammar of ornament available to artists.[41]

Finally, the costumes for the Russian operas helped to publicize the beauty of Russian ethnic dress. Some of Russia's leading artists lavished great care on creating costumes that would reflect the "Russian spirit." Set against the backdrop of equally stunning sets, the costumes coupled with the glories of the music swept audiences up in dramas about Russia's mythic past. To nationalists, these operas reflected their personal dreams for their native land presented in all its splendor on the stage. Convincing themselves that the neo-Russian style was an exact replica of the Russian past, they sought to re-establish Muscovite culture on their native soil. Russia would no longer slavishly imitate western Europe, but would return to the cultural and spiritual values that made it unique. In their quest for a newly revitalized Russia, the nationalists looked to and received support from the tsar himself.

103    A family portrait. The woman on the left is wearing a neo-Russian-style blouse. Private collection.

THE 1903 WINTER COSTUME BALLS

In 1894, Alexander III died unexpectedly after a short illness and his son, Nicholas II (1868–1918), became what was to prove Russia's last tsar. Nicholas's upbringing reveals the paradoxes that were increasingly evident in Russian life. He lived in luxurious European palaces; he often visited his relatives in western Europe; and he married a German princess, Alexandra who was a granddaughter of Queen Victoria. He was completely at home in European high society. At the same time, his father and mother found tutors to prepare him for his role as a Russian tsar. Chief among these was Konstantin Pobedonotsev who encouraged Nicholas to believe that God alone had given him his autocratic power. Having accepted his responsibilities as autocrat, Nicholas II's job was to preserve the Russian Empire that he had inherited from his father. His dream was to create a bond between himself and the Russian people, which meant bypassing the restive, educated public, and appealing directly to the peasantry. Despite all of the political turmoil and revolu-

lacemaking and embroidery.[40] Workshops in central Russia at Abramtsevo, Solomenko, and Talashkino sought to preserve ancient designs as well as create neo-Russian patterns. As we have seen, the Russian government furthered the revival by sending examples of women's needlework to major exhibitions and worlds' fairs such as the 1893 Columbian Exposition in Chicago. The women who spearheaded this revival set up retail outlets to sell these peasant handicrafts in Russia's big cities, and the fashion magazines published patterns so that urban women could create these works of art at home. Just as crucial, these bits of Russian lace and embroidery could be worn with European fashions. This allowed women to express patriotism in their dress, but without having to sacrifice their allegiance to fashion. Furthermore, the folk patterns typical of Russian lace and embroidery often tionary violence that occurred during his reign, Nicholas II continued to encourage the development of a national mythology which featured as its centerpiece the bond between the tsar and his people. According to Richard Wortman, Nicholas II followed the example of other European royal houses in using historical occasions and other public events to present his image of himself to his people and the outside world.[42] One such occasion presented itself in 1903.

The winter months in Russia had always been a time for weddings and other forms of entertainment. Festive celebrations brought relief from the long, cold winter. Like other Christian societies, Russian folk culture had set aside a week called Maslenitsa for all forms of merriment before the austerity of the Lenten season. As the court and the aristocracy had become more Europeanized during the eighteenth century, they had combined the folk traditions of Maslenitsa with European Mardi Gras.[43] In Petersburg all members of Russian society – young and old, rich and poor – would gather to skate on the frozen Neva river and to sled down Russia's famous ice hills. The elite would rub elbows with clerks, servants, and ordinary working people to watch Punch and Judy shows, and other forms of street theater. Vendors in decorated booths sold food and drink to the spectators.[44] In addition to participating in these popular celebrations of carnival, members of high society organized costume balls and masquerades following the western European tradition.[45]

The year 1903 was a special one for the residents of Petersburg. It marked the bicentennial of the city's founding. Although the official celebrations were scheduled for May, there were events throughout the year commemorating the city and its founder. For Nicholas II this proved to be a difficult moment. The tsar was not an admirer of Peter the Great, believing that his ancestor had been too infatuated with western Europe.[46] The bicentennial could not be ignored completely, so he arranged for two costume balls to be held in February during Maslenitsa at the height of the winter social season. These balls were intended, however, to showcase Muscovite culture, to project the power and the glory of the culture that Peter had destroyed. In one week, Nicholas II presented his personal vision of himself and his country. The results were evenings rich in paradox.

104 A Petersburg couple in evening dress, circa 1900. The clothes fit this pair beautifully and suggest a kind of elegance necessary for a night at the opera or the ballet. State Central Archive of Documentary Films, Photographs, and Sound Recordings of St. Petersburg.

In order to understand the significance of the 1903 Winter Costume Balls, a word should be said about court practice. During Nicholas II's reign, the court usually held a number of balls during the winter season. According to one member of Petersburg's high society, there was a "Big Ball" to which three thousand guests were invited. There were also several other events: Concert Balls, which featured a musical program, and Hermitage Balls, which included theatrical performances in the Hermitage Theater. These gatherings included supper and dancing.[47] Both of the 1903 Costume Balls followed the established etiquette.

An Hermitage Ball preceded the Costume Balls on 7 February 1903. Nicholas and Alexandra invited members of the court and high society to the Hermitage Theater, which adjoined the Winter Palace. The newspaper account of the event reported that the tsar wore a naval uniform while his wife donned a black evening gown. The evening began with Eugène Labiche's one-act French farce, *Permettez, Madame*. After the entr'acte, the company watched a performance of Joseph Bayer's ballet, *Die Puppenfee (Feia kukol)*, a story about an enchanted toyshop. The Legat brothers created the choreography for the piece, and Matilda Kshesinskaia, one of Russia's great ballerinas and the former mistress of Nicholas II, danced the lead. A young artist, Lev Bakst, designed the sets and costumes. Bakst decided to russify the ballet by changing the scene from mid-nineteenth-century Vienna to modern-day Petersburg. He placed the action in a well-known toyshop on Nevskii Prospekt where large crowds would gather during Palm Week in order to see fantastic displays.[48] After the ballet, the guests of Nicholas II sat down to an elegant supper. At the conclusion of the meal, they entered the Pavilion Hall where they were greeted with birdsong and a wonderful fountain set up for the occasion. The guests were invited to dance and the opening number from the orchestra was a waltz. Both Nicholas and Alexandra danced that evening.[49]

All the glories of European culture found in Russia were present at that one event. Nicholas II and his court presented themselves as connoisseurs of European theater and ballet. The play was performed in French, a language that all members of the Russian aristocracy learned at an early age and the lingua franca of international diplomacy, European high society, and the fine arts. The performance of *Die Puppenfee* also suggested the cultural sophistication of the Russian court. Bakst's change of scene from Vienna to Petersburg without any significant change in the meaning of the ballet visually demonstrated that Petersburg was on a par with other European capitals. In keeping with the spirit of Maslenitsa, which was about to begin, an entertaining farce and a light-hearted ballet encouraged Nicholas II and his guests to think of themselves as part of the popular festivities going on outside of the Winter Palace. The evening celebrated the interplay between high and popular culture, which

was an essential element of the upcoming Maslenitsa activities.[50]

For the elite, no Maslenitsa festivities would be complete without a costume ball. It was here that Nicholas II gave complete rein to his nationalist vision by organizing two such balls. Rather than honor the memory of Peter the Great, he proposed to commemorate Peter's father, Aleksei Mikhailovich (1629–1676). On 11 February, just four days after the Hermitage Ball, the court and high society arrived at the same theater dressed as Muscovite courtiers. Nicholas and Alexandra wore the actual clothes of Tsar Aleksei and his first wife, Maria Miloslavskaia.[51] Everyone else wore copies of Muscovite court dress. The entertainment that evening consisted of a performance of the second act of Musorgsky's opera *Boris Godunov*, with the famed Russian bass Fedor Chaliapin playing Godunov. B. L. Persiianinova's *The Female Philanthropist*, and the last act of Marius Petipa's ballet, *La Bayadère*, entitled "The Kingdom of the Shades," completed the entertainment. After a tasty supper, the imperial couple led their guests once again to the Pavilion Hall where a Russian choir and dance group greeted them. The singers and dancers performed Russian folk songs and dances accompanied by a man playing a bandura, a Russian folk instrument. Both the choir and dance group were dressed in seventeenth-century costumes.[52]

Two nights later, this Muscovite spectacle was repeated, but this time the festivities took place in the Concert Hall of the Winter Palace. The guest list now included foreign ambassadors and their wives. The imperial couple, court, and high society wore Muscovite dress while their ambassadorial guests wore European evening dress.[53] The night began with a procession of the Russian guests who bowed before their imperial majesties. Immediately following the procession, a Russian dance group performed. Princess Zinaida Iusupova, a prominent member of Russian high society, led one of the folk dances, the *khorovod*. This was then followed by a waltz, a quadrille, and a mazurka. This time only the Empress Alexandra joined in the dancing, her husband remaining among the spectators. At midnight all guests were invited to the Nicholas Hall dedicated to Nicholas I. Here a choir sang a variety of Russian choral works which included the liturgical hymn, "Slava na Nebe," songs by Russian composers Dargomyzhskii and

Tchaikowsky, and a number of folk tunes. The final song of the evening was a Slavic polka sung in Czech. After an elegant supper, the Russian dance group performed again. At 3 am, the imperial family retired and their three hundred guests went home.[54]

According to the newspaper, *Saint Petersburg News*, "The sumptuous women's sarafans made of brocade, silver, and silk, and the various costumes from the era of Aleksei Mikhailovich transported the imagination to the pre-Petrine period." One participant, V. N. Voeikov, wrote, "it [the evening] gave the impression of a living dream." Nicholas II himself was so pleased with the ball that he entertained the idea of reinstating Muscovite dress at court, a plan that was not carried out due to the expense.[55] Instead, to preserve the memory of the evening, the court published a three-volume album with photographs of all the participants in their Muscovite robes. These photographs were frequently reproduced during Nicholas II's reign.[56]

But if these evenings were "a living dream," what kind of a dream was it? In keeping with the spirit of Maslenitsa, the balls celebrated the conjunction of high and popular culture. The sumptuous costumes provided an elegant backdrop to the performance of Russian folk songs and dance. What Nicholas II had done on this occasion was to substitute Muscovite culture for a European masquerade and entertainment in the court's celebration of Maslenitsa. But these balls were not simply recreations of seventeenth-century Muscovy; rather the court participated in a theatrical spectacle. The first ball was performed for domestic consumption and for the court itself, while the second night's performance for the ambassadorial community represented Nicholas II's attempt to display his vision of Russianness to the rest of the world. Nevertheless, in both cases, it was Russia's artistic community and fashion industry that made these spectacles possible. While Nicholas and Alexandra wore the clothes of real people, their guests did not. Instead,

105   Countess Varvara V. Musina-Pushkina in a seventeenth-century noblewoman's costume. This gown clearly shows the unusual sleeves that formed part of the sartorial tradition of Russian women's dress. *Al'bom kostiumirovovannogo bala v Zimnem Dvortse v fevrale 1903 g.*, 102. Library of Congress Collections.

Petersburg high society hired Russia's premier tailors and dressmakers, all trained in European design, to create their costumes. These men and women did what they had always done in designing costumes – they copied their designs from paintings and other artifacts from the Muscovite period. One guest asked Sergei Diaghilev, the ballet impresario and a prominent member of the Petersburg art world, to design her attire. Grand Duke Sergei Mikhailovich, the director of the Imperial Theaters, allowed a number of guests to use the wardrobe staff at the Mariinsky Theater to create the costumes. The House of Fabergé made the bejeweled headdress of at least one participant.[57]

In addition to the contributions made by Russia's artists, the stunning costumes celebrated Russia's success as a textile manufacturer and industrial power. The beauty of Muscovite dress lay in the luxurious fabrics and jewels used to adorn what were essentially simple flowing robes. In the seventeenth century the imperial couple's clothing was undoubtedly made from brocades and silks imported from China, Persia, and Italy, since the Muscovite court ordered only the finest fabrics for court dress. In 1903, the fabric was almost certainly of Russian manufacture. Garment workers would have worked day and night to finish the costumes in time for the ball.

Furthermore, Nicholas II employed the new system of modern publicity to advertise these court festivities, a system that the fashion industry had helped to create and refine. Both evenings were discussed in the print media and photographed for posterity. But, at the same time, this publicity exposed the evenings for what they were – costume balls. The purpose of a costume ball was to come in some sort of disguise, to dress up as someone else. In this case, the Russian court and high society came "in costume" as their Muscovite ancestors, suggesting that this was not who they really were. Anyone who read the accounts of the balls or saw the photographs knew that each individual exchanged their Muscovite robes for European dress as soon as they returned home. It appears

106  Prince Alexander S. Dolgorukii wearing the costume of a sixteenth-century Russian nobleman. Robes such as these would have been worn at home. *Al'bom kostiumirovovannogo bala v Zimnem Dvortse v fevrale 1903 g.*, 29. Library of Congress Collections.

that only Nicholas II deluded himself by believing that he alone was not in costume. Nevertheless, his appearance at the balls underscored the idea that he too was hiding his real identity.

The venue of the balls further enhanced the artificiality of this recreation of the Muscovite court. They were not held in the Moscow Kremlin, but in Petersburg's Winter Palace, an excellent example of baroque architecture designed by the Italian architect, Bartolomeo Rastrelli. The Muscovite court was entertained with Russian song and dance in this elegant, European-style palace, thereby accentuating the theatrical quality of the two events. When the time came to photograph the participants for the album commemorating the evening, the photographers used artificial backdrops and props designed to replicate old Muscovy. Thus, the photographs offer a stylized version of the Russian past created in part by the Russian fashion industry. This "living dream" was preserved for posterity by the camera, one of the great new inventions of the western publicity and advertising machine.

This mingling of Russian and European cultures can also be seen in the entertainment that Nicholas II provided to his guests. While he wanted them to think of the evening as a celebration of Russian song and dance, the program was a curious mixture. While the dance group performed Russian folk dances, the guests and the empress herself executed waltzes, quadrilles, and mazurkas, dances that had come to Russia from Europe. Indeed, the idea of the empress waltzing in her Muscovite robes was precisely the social gaffe that Nikolai Grech had warned Russian women against fifty years earlier. One guest even commented that many of the women had difficulty waltzing in Muscovite clothing.[58] The performance of Musorgsky's *Boris Godunov* represented a Russian musician's attempt to integrate Russian themes into European opera.[59] Petipa's production of the last act of *La Bayadère*, a European ballet about India, celebrated the Asian roots of Russian culture. It presented

107  Count Sergei D. Sheremetev wearing a costume that was fashioned from a portrait of one of his ancestors, Field Marshal Boris P. Sheremetev. *Al'bom kostiumirovovannogo bala v Zimnem Dvortse v fevrale 1903 g.*, 44. Library of Congress Collections.

the audience with yet another view of Asia as the eroti-
cized East, with female dancers swirling around the stage
and bewitching the audience with their sensuous
beauty.[60] Even the dreams of the Pan Slavs, who advocated the unification of all Slavic peoples, were recognized by the inclusion of the Czech polka.

The balls were not recreations of the pre-Petrine
period when Russia was supposedly uncontaminated by
western influences. Rather, they represented the spirit of
Russian art as interpreted by some of the leading artists
of the day. Like Mamontov's Private Opera Company,
these evenings were theatrical spectacles dedicated to
the neo-Russian style, that melding of European and
Russian art forms. This time the performance occurred
not on the stage of a private company but in the Winter
Palace itself. But if Nicholas II thought that his patron-
age would make the neo-Russian style the only expression of Russian cultural identity, he was mistaken. The
final irony of the evening was that traditional Russian
dress had now officially become costume – clothing
worn for masquerades and theatrical performances –
whatever Nicholas II's intentions might have been. By
ordering his guests to come in costume as Muscovites,
the tsar unintentionally acknowledged the success of
Peter the Great's dress revolution. One guest reported
that she never again wore her costume after the festivities.[61] Modern Russians felt too encumbered in their
traditional garments to participate actively in modern
life. They were in search of other forms of dress that
could present a more contemporary and sophisticated
vision of themselves to the world, a vision that encom-
passed Russia's complex cultural identity.

## LEV BAKST AND THE BALLETS RUSSES

The ethnographic verisimilitude that prevailed in the
costume designs for the 1903 Costume Balls no longer
satisfied many Russian artists. A year later, the artist Sergei

108  Kapitolina N. Makarova, wearing the costume of a seventeenth-century noblewoman. *Al'bom kostiumirovovannogo bala v
Zimnem Dvortse v fevrale 1903 g.*, 61. Library of Congress Collections.

Makovsky complained, "We have fallen in love with [folk art], forgetting that the resurrection of national motifs is not an end in itself, but that these motifs are just material to be used in creating a style that corresponds to the conditions of a European-wide culture."[62] It was precisely this sentiment – that Russian art should make its own contribution to European art – that defined a new artistic movement on the Russian art scene.

In 1889 a group of Petersburg high-school students critical of what they saw around them formed a club that they named the Nevskii Pickwickians. According to Alexander Benois, the founder of the group, "We objected to both the Russian coarseness and to the decorative complacency that many Russians love to parade."[63] To rid Russia of both coarseness and complacency, Benois and his confrères rejected the didactic populist sentiments that dominated Russian art in the 1870s and 1880s. They wanted to revive the idea of "art for art's sake." Under this umbrella, Benois recalled in his memoir, "Each one had his own sympathies, but all of us were far from any kind of doctrine."[64] This benevolent eclecticism encouraged these young men to pursue the modernist turn in European art in literature, painting, graphic arts, and stage design.

To accomplish their ambitious goals, these artists set out to revive western European art in Russia. They held a number of exhibitions which showcased both Russian and European art together, as well as revived an interest in eighteenth-century Russian art. In 1898, they established their own art journal called *Mir iskusstva* (*World of Art*) with the financial support of Savva Morozov, a wealthy industrialist, and Princess Maria Tenisheva, who was an important supporter of the revival of women's handicrafts.[65] The magazine included articles about the latest trends in Europe, as well as commentary on the arts in Russia. Its beautiful illustrations introduced Russians to Art Nouveau and Symbolism. Although *Mir iskusstva* ceased publication in 1904, it became a model which other art magazines quickly copied.

Before the *World of Art* group could consider its next move, revolutionary violence rocked the Russian Empire. Following the Russo-Japanese War of 1904–1905, the Russian revolution of 1905, which created Russia's first constitution and parliament, had serious repercussions among artists. Tired of the heavy hand of imperial censorship, bureaucracy, and conservative artistic values, a new generation of artists wanted to break free of imperial tutelage so that they could explore their own individual paths of artistic self-expression.[66] These young men and women joined forces with the *World of Art* group. They wanted to challenge tsarist artistic hegemony and revolutionize Russian *and* European art in the process. Some of these artistic dissidents – the choreographer Michel (Mikhail) Fokine, the ballet dancers Anna Pavlova, Tamara Karsavina, and Vaslav Nijinsky, the musician Igor Stravinsky, and the artists Lev Bakst, Nikolai Roerich, and Alexander Benois – banded together to form a new theatrical company. The head of the new company was Sergei Diaghilev, the former editor of *Mir iskusstva*. His connections with the artistic and commercial world facilitated the funding of the new group, which became known as the Ballets Russes.

Although Diaghilev & Company put together a major exhibit of Russian art in 1906 and staged a performance of Musorgsky's *Boris Godunov* in 1908 for French audiences, their greatest achievement lay in their radically new approach to the ballet. European ballet had begun in France in the eighteenth century, but like the decorative arts it had never achieved the status of a fine art. The Russians, however, fell in love with ballet. In 1738, the Russian government had established the Imperial Theater School, and had invited European dancers and choreographers to train Russians in the art form. The greatest of these choreographers was Marius Petipa, who worked for over half a century creating ballets that are still performed today. Petipa's contribution to ballet was the creation of the full-length story ballet. It was he who choreographed Tchaikowsky's *Swan Lake, Sleeping Beauty,* and *The Nutcracker.*[67] Although the narratives for these ballets were often formulaic, Petipa continually transformed the dance steps used in ballet. By the early years of the twentieth century, however, one of Petipa's pupils, Michel Fokine, had developed his own ideas for how ballets should be performed. Fokine's new approach to ballet fit in very nicely with the views of Diaghilev and Benois, and they named him chief choreographer for the Ballets Russes.[68]

The dance historian Lynn Garafola has identified an essential ingredient in the success of the Ballets Russes. She argues that the organizers of the new company had been influenced by both the overly bureaucratic and formulaic stagings at the imperial theaters and the highly unstructured world of private artistic organizations:

> This contradictory experience prepared them to work within a collective framework, while at the same time impelling them toward the creation of democratized structures in which each member functioned essentially as an individual. It was this collectivist-individualist impulse that enabled the former *miriskusstniki* to achieve the exemplary consistency and high artistic merit that distinguished the company's best works.[69]

This collective of musicians, dancers, artists, choreographers, and designers had one goal in mind for their productions. According to Fokine, ballets should take place within a particular historical epoch. The costumes, sets, dance steps, and music should follow the local customs and express the "emotional content" of the times.[70] This emphasis on ethnographic reality represented a strong line of continuity between the Mamontov Circle and the artists of the Ballets Russes. Nevertheless, their attempts to capture the spirit of the times, the "emotional content," really set the Ballets Russes productions apart from their predecessors. Rather than rely upon the simple retelling of a folk tale or legend, the Ballets Russes artists, heavily influenced by Symbolism, used the ballets to interpret these tales, mining them for deeper meaning. Diaghilev and his collaborators searched for stories whose deeper meaning would resonate with modern artists and audiences alike. The "emotional content" of these narratives – ancient tales of love and death, passion and duty, freedom and oppression – connected ancient and modern peoples together in that universal human search for the meaning of life.[71]

Diaghilev assembled a number of Russia's leading artists to create the scenery and costumes for his productions, but it was Lev Bakst's designs that captured international attention. Bakst had joined Benois and the other *miriskusstniki* in 1890, having studied at the Imperial Academy of Art. In his early years as an artist, he painted portraits and landscapes, and was the chief graphic designer of *Mir iskusstva*. As a result of his association with the *World of Art*, Bakst became interested in

stage design. In 1902 he designed a production of the French pantomime *Le Coeur de la marquise* for the Imperial Court's Hermitage Theater. As we have already seen, in February 1903 he created the sets and costumes for Joseph Bayer's *Die Puppenfee*, a ballet that made his reputation as an innovative stage designer. Although he continued to work for the imperial theaters, Bakst, like other artists of his generation, felt frustrated by the cultural conservatism of the imperial ballet productions.[72] He later remarked, "For a long time the idea came to me to render the ballet equal in importance to the other arts. That is, I felt that it could hold within it the thoughts and feelings which trouble our soul and which we express in the other arts."[73] So when Diaghilev invited him to work on his productions, Bakst readily accepted.

In order to reconstruct past periods for the ballets, Bakst did a prodigious amount of research. He took trips to North Africa, Greece, and Cyprus where he researched the ancient art forms of the Mediterranean world.[74] He also took advantage of the libraries and museums in Petersburg. The Hermitage had a world-class collection of ancient antiquities and western European art; the Oriental Museum and Library contained superlative examples of Asian art.[75] Bakst would also have been aware of Russian research in the arts, including the work of Stasov and Prokhorov on Russian dress. At the same time, Bakst studied the latest trends in western European art during frequent stays in Paris in the 1890s. He knew of the work of Henri Matisse and was influenced by the Fauves.

For Bakst, as well as Fokine, the "emotional content" was the real focus of his designs. While remaining true to the look of the past, Bakst managed to transcend it by his use of line and color. He had developed his own theory of color, which he used to convey the emotional content of ballets:

> I have often noticed that in each color of the prism there exists a gradation which sometimes expresses frankness and chastity, sometimes sensuality and even bestiality, sometimes pride, sometimes despair. This can be felt and given over to the public by the effect one makes of the various shadings. . . . There are reds that are triumphal and there are reds which assassinate. There is a blue, which can be the color of a St.

109    Leon Bakst's costume design for Daphnis and Chloe, Villageoise, 1912. 36 × 25.5 cm. Howard D. Rothschild Bequest, Harvard Theatre Collection, Houghton Library.

110　Leon Bakst's costume design for Scheherazade, the Blue Sultan, 1922. 87 × 68 cm. Watercolor, pencil and gold paint on paper. Howard D. Rothschild Bequest, Harvard Theatre Collection, Houghton Library.

111    Leon Bakst's costume design for Scheherazade, the Eunuch, 1922. 87 × 68 cm. Watercolor, pencil and silver paint on paper. Howard D. Rothschild Bequest, Harvard Theatre Collection, Houghton Library.

Madeleine, and there is a blue of a Messalina. The painter who knows how to make use of this . . . can draw from the spectator the exact emotion which he wants to feel.[76]

Bakst's genius was to know precisely which colors to use and how to combine them in ways never before seen on the stage. At a time when muted colors predominated on the stage and in the fashion houses, Bakst introduced his audiences to vivid oranges, purples, reds, blues, and greens.

Bakst also focused on the line of the garment: "It is in line as well as in color that I make my emotions."[77] According to John Bowlt, ". . . Bakst regarded the body as a kinetic force that was to be exposed and amplified in its movements, not enveloped and disguised."[78] His purpose was to create garments that would allow his dancers complete freedom of movement. Bakst also had an uncanny gift for understanding how the line of the garments would look against the scenery and managed to harmonize the two throughout an entire ballet: "My *mise-en-scène*s are the products of a deliberately designed arrangement of splashes of color against the background of the sets. . . . The costumes of the leading players dominate and blossom within the bouquet of the other costumes."[79]

Each spring from 1909 until 1914 Diaghilev took his troupe to Paris to perform. The company staged productions of the "Polovtsian Dances" from Borodin's *Prince Igor* (1890), Frédéric Chopin's *Les Sylphides*, Stravinsky's *Petrouchka* and *Firebird*, Rimsky-Korsakov's *Schéhérazade*, and many others. The dancers Anna Pavlova, Tamara Karsavina, and Vaslav Nijinsky became international celebrities. The Ballets Russes productions also popularized the music of Rimsky-Korsakov, Stravinsky, and other Russian composers. These ballets both shocked and delighted the Parisian audiences. One enthusiast reported her reaction to Michel Fokine's *Cléopâtre*:

When I entered the box to which I had been invited . . . I realized that I was seeing a miracle, something that had never before existed. Everything that could dazzle, intoxicate, seduce, arrest seemed to have been dredged up and brought to the stage to luxuriate there. . . . On the stage of the Ballets Russes, the kings

of India and China, skillfully clasped to the center of a slender and violent drama, appeared in the enormous luxury of palm trees spreading their greenery against indigo skies. Their costumes, gold with heavy embroideries . . . amplified them in such a way as to make their sovereignty formidable and superhuman. The angel, the genius, the triumpher of the spectacle, the divine dancer Nijinsky took hold of our hearts, filling us with love, while the soft or sharp sonorities of the Asiatic music completed this stupefying and luxuriant work.[80]

While Nijinsky captivated the audience with his dancing, it was Bakst who created the "luxuriant" setting and costumes of the ancient world.

Of all the ballets that the company performed, the "Oriental" ballets captured the hearts of the Parisian audiences, especially *Schéhérazade* and *Cléopâtre*. The reasons for this are not hard to find. Western Europeans had always been fascinated with the East, a term by which most Europeans meant the rest of the world. Western Europe's understanding of the Orient consisted primarily of a field of binary oppositions – masculine/feminine, civilized/barbaric, familiar/exotic, rational/erotic – which reappear constantly in both written and

112   "Influence of the Russian Ballet on Bathing Designs," *Punch* (27 August 1913), 197. This cartoon satirizes the English embrace of the Ballets Russes.

INFLUENCE OF THE RUSSIAN BALLET ON BATHING DESIGNS.
(*Salome and The Faun.*)

visual texts.[81] In *fin-de-siècle* Europe there was renewed interest in the exotic East, particularly in France. A craze for Japanese decorative arts had developed.[82] In 1891 Paul Gauguin left France for the South Seas where he developed a neo-Impressionist style, using Tahitian women as his subjects. But, as a commentator for the French newspaper *Le Figaro* declared, "The taste for oriental art came to Paris as a Russian import, through ballet, music, and decoration . . . Russian artists have acted as intermediaries between the East and us, and they have given us a rather greater taste for oriental color than a taste for their own art."[83] In her study of the Ballets Russes, Lynn Garafola has argued that the audience for Diaghilev's productions consisted of bankers, lawyers, artists, and émigrés from all over the world. This cosmopolitan mixture of *nouveaux riches* and *déclassé* aristocrats supported the Ballets Russes because their productions shocked polite society with their sensuality and eroticism. These sophisticated men and women were challenging the cultural hegemony of France's ruling elites just as the Ballets Russes challenged traditional dance and theater through its "blend of sumptuousness, decorative harmony, and historical veracity."[84] The emotional content of the ballets converged with the emotional needs of the audiences.

But herein lies the paradox of the Ballets Russes's Orientalism. As the correspondent for *Le Figaro* makes clear, the Russian artists "acted as intermediaries" between East and West. But, how could the Russians mediate between East and West? Most Europeans considered Russia part of the East. And yet, the Orient as seen on the Parisian stage consisted of Russian music, sets, librettos, costumes, and dancers. Rimsky-Korsakov, Stravinsky, and many other Russian composers supplied the "sonorities of the Asian music." Sets designed by Bakst, Alexander Golovnin, and Nikolai Roerich provided glimpses of Egyptian pyramids, Persian harems, and Oriental palaces. European audiences did not notice the incongruity because the ballets upheld their own views of Russians as Orientals.

At the same time, the situation was more complex than that. While some of the Ballets Russes's Oriental ballets took place in Russia, the majority of them were set in lands that formed part of Russia's own encounter with the East – Persia, the Caucasus, Central Asia, Turkey. As Stasov, Prokhorov, and other cultural nationalists had

definitively shown, these ancient civilizations had profoundly influenced the development of what Russians considered their own native culture. However, Russia's expansionism had not ended in ancient times but had continued throughout Russian history. During the eighteenth and nineteenth centuries Russia had expanded its southern and eastern borders, bringing it into conflict once again with the East. In the early years of the twentieth century, the Russian government pursued an increasingly aggressive foreign policy in Asia. The Russians attempted to establish a firm foothold in Manchuria, fought with the Japanese in 1904–5, and engaged in serious struggles with the British in Persia and Afghanistan. In fact, while Bakst was designing the costumes for *Schéhérazade*, Russian troops were participating in a bloody counter-revolution in Persia. Thus, Diaghilev's ballets expressed Russia's dream of becoming an Asian colonial power on a par with Britain and France. They expanded upon the vision of Russian colonial strength that Alexander III had formulated with his redesigned Russian Army uniforms in 1882. Just as the British and the French had mined African and Asian cultures for the exotic, the Russians expropriated foreign cultures, created their own interpretation of them, and exported these colonial fantasies to Europe, where they found receptive audiences accustomed to similar colonialist cultural presentations. Diaghilev's genius was to understand that Russia's cultural role was to serve as intermediary between East and West precisely because Russia represented Asia and Europe simultaneously.[85] Thus, the Ballets Russes productions were a kind of masquerade. The Russians came to Paris dressed as Orientals, but their real purpose was to present themselves as legitimate interpreters of the western cultural tradition. As Benois stated, "I felt from the very first days of our work in Paris, that the Russian Savages, the Scythians, had brought to the 'World Capital,' for judgement, the best of art that existed in the world."[86]

And yet, the Ballets Russes productions were more than just another presentation of Orientalism on the European stage. They also marked a defining moment in the creation of modernity.[87] The British photographer Cecil Beaton observed "a fashion world that had been dominated by corsets, lace, feathers and pastel shades soon found itself in a city that overnight had become a seraglio

113   A couturier gown by the House of the Worth, early 1900s. This gown reveals the trends that were popular before Bakst helped revolutionize women's fashion. The dress and corset underneath create an hourglass look. The muted beige, pink, and grey colors in the fabric give the dress softness. The State Hermitage Museum, St. Petersburg.

114   A Paul Poiret gown from 1913. This gown reinterprets Bakst's Orientalist ballet costumes for evening wear. The fur and the bright colors in the jacket, embroidery, and beadwork add brightness to the simple white dress. The designer also began to move away from the hourglass to the slim silhouette. The State Hermitage Museum, St. Petersburg.

of vivid colours, harem skirts, beads, fringes and voluptuousness."[88] Bakst's radical costumes helped to free women from the tyranny of cloth and corset, allowing them greater mobility. The fluidity and color of the costumes captured the excitement and fast pace of modern life as much as they recreated Oriental splendor.

Nijinsky's performances challenged European definitions of masculinity by combining traditional masculine physical prowess with an indeterminate sexuality, encouraging some men to challenge the status quo by adopting a new look.[89] The military uniform and staid business suit gave way to greater freedom of expression in male dress.

115 An evening dress by Nadezhda Lamanova, 1913–1915. Russian designers under the influence of Poiret and Bakst created their own interpretations of the new exotic look. By covering her green gown with sheer black chiffon and gold thread embroidered flowers, Lamanova created a shifting column of color and pattern reminiscent of Bakst's ballet costumes. The State Hermitage Museum, St. Petersburg.

116 A gown of the 1910s by the Russian House of Brizak. It is devoid of any color, but the layers and beading give the garment both elegance and and an air of exoticism. The State Hermitage Museum, St. Petersburg.

While these men did not stroll the streets of Paris in harem pants and beads, their new vision of the suit updated the fashionable look for men: ". . . the stiff, outmoded elegance . . . crimped by a high, stiff collar and top hat . . . turned the new look into a naughty, mannered, provocative chic – small busts arching under a high, nipped waist, low collars, bowlers worn low over the eyes."[90] As Peter Wollen has argued, Bakst's Oriental costumes helped to alter the image of the body, creating the "modernist body," fashioned out of the cultural encounter between East and West during the Ballets Russes seasons in Paris.[91] Europeans loved Bakst's re-

117  A young woman in evening dress in 1915. Her gown reflects the new slim silhouette which Bakst and Poiret helped to popularize. Private collection.

interpretations of the human body because he, like all great artists, managed to articulate their own longings for beauty, comfort, and freedom by encouraging movement and individual self-expression. And this modernist body attracted the attention of fashion designers who could now engage with Bakst's costumes to create a radically new look for their clients. Paul Poiret, the self-proclaimed king of Paris fashion, acknowledged his debt to the Russians when he visited Russia in the winter of 1911/12 to meet Nadezhda Lamanova and other Russian fashion designers.[92] His highly publicized trip essentially welcomed Russian couturiers into the world of European *haute couture* as equal partners.[93]

★  ★  ★

The integration of the Russians into the highest circles of the fashion industry furthered the development of what Mica Nava has called commercial cosmopolitanism.[94] As noted in chapter 4, the nineteenth-century fashion magazines encouraged their readers to think of themselves as part of a transnational community of consumers. In the early years of the twentieth century, the fashion industry joined forces with the art world to present a modernist vision of cosmopolitanism intricately linked with the marketplace. Fashion designers, store owners, and advertisers encouraged consumer spending through a sophisticated manipulation of cultural forms as East and West combined to create "modernism." For western Europeans, this commercial form of cosmopolitanism offered the "allure of difference," a desire to abandon traditional ways of thinking and embrace the new, the exotic, the "Other."[95] For Russians, commercial cosmopolitanism replaced their self-image as semi-Asiatic, backward barbarians, and confirmed that they were "modern, urban, and 'cultured.'"[96] At the same time, modernism and commercial cosmopolitanism healed the breach in Russian culture. Modernism transcended narrow definitions of European and Russian culture articulated by the westernizers and Slavophiles. Under the banner of modernism, Russian intellectuals redefined their culture to include *both* European and Russian artistic and intellectual traditions. In the commercial realm, the fashion industry as well as the other consumer industries played an important role in popularizing this new modernist vision of Russian identity. Russians could feel proud of their native cultural heritage, their industrial progress, and their embrace of westernization, which together allowed them to feel a part of a wider cosmopolitan community.

At the turn of the twentieth century, there were competing dreams for Russia's future. There was a capitalist vision of a modern, urban, cosmopolitan Russia. Another vision was of an autocratic, Orthodox Russia steadfast in its loyalty to its native traditions, culture, and religious rituals. The Russian government supported both visions. It encouraged industrial and commercial development while desperately clinging to its traditional political authority. The government's duplicity created political and social instability as Russia lurched between tradition and modernity. Ordinary Russians grew restive under these difficult conditions. Having been encouraged to imagine a better world for themselves, they were no longer willing to allow their government to speak or act for them. It was time to make their dreams a reality.

118   Workers and their employers could tell each other apart by the clothes that they wore. In this photograph the bosses wear three-piece suits, leather shoes, bowlers, and boaters; to complete their outfit, two have canes, and all three are wearing watches. The workers are identifiable by their caps and their belted peasant shirts worn over their trousers. Private collection.

# 7

## Adorned in Dreams: Fashion, Labor, and Politics

By THE MIDDLE OF THE nineteenth century, disaffected members of the educated public began to oppose their government's social and economic policies, and the political philosophy that undergirded this opposition was socialism. For many Russians, socialism appeared to offer a clear explanation for what was happening to their country. A new group of people – industrialists and businessmen – were challenging the social status and privilege of the landed aristocracy. The rise of this new bourgeoisie depended upon the exploitation of workers who toiled in huge factory complexes that were springing up in Russian cities and even in the countryside. If for many Russians socialism provided a clear explanation for what was happening, it also offered a plan of action to make life better for all Russians – a revolution that would sweep away the old and create an egalitarian society. Although disagreements arose among Russian socialists as to how to implement this vision of the future, all agreed that the intelligentsia must educate and organize the lower classes to prepare them for their role as revolutionary actors. To that end the radical intelligentsia created an underground movement whose aim was the overthrow of the tsarist government. Intellectuals introduced workers to the weapons of the proletarian revolution – strikes, trade unions, and other forms of labor protest.

Most socialist writings focused on factory workers and did not address the problems of artisans directly. Never-theless, artisanal workers were deeply affected by socialism's trenchant analysis of the worker's plight. Masters controlled all aspects of their employees' lives, including where they slept, what they ate, and how much sugar they put in their tea. Furthermore, this exploitation began during childhood when apprentices needed to obey every whim of their masters if they wanted to survive. The very intimacy of workshop relations made artisans such willing pupils of socialism.[1]

Socialism also offered artisans new weapons with which to confront their employers. The time-honored tradition of resolving labor disputes within the artisanal system was for a disgruntled journeyman to find another employer, or to leave and set up his own shop. Indeed, the purpose of the artisanal system was not to create a stable force of permanent employees, but rather to provide a way for each artisan to become an independent shop owner. For the more intractable problems, a journeyman could turn to arbitration boards run by the artisans' guild, but this was only an option for those whose masters were actual members of the guild.

In the case of the fashion industry, the traditional approach to labor disputes became increasingly inadequate. As we have seen, ready-to-wear manufacturing was the growth sector of the clothing trades, not custom tailoring. The competitive environment between the two manufacturing sectors exerted intense pressure on needleworkers. As custom tailoring began to lose business to ready-to-wear, garment workers could no longer rely upon finding employment at another bespoke shop or setting up their own shops. The only practical alternative was to become a subcontractor for a ready-to-wear firm. However, this option simply replaced one boss with another, and the conditions in the subcontracting shops – the notorious sweatshops – were worse than in traditional artisanal shops. With their backs against the wall, garment workers looked to socialism to provide them with alternative strategies for improving their lives. The result was the creation of a garment workers' labor movement whose powerful protests rocked the fashion industry in the years preceding World War I.

To describe fully the garment workers' labor movement is beyond the scope of this book. My purpose is to highlight the critical moments in that movement: the first recorded strike in 1870, the activities of Jewish workers in the Pale of Settlement in the 1880s and 1890s, the participation of garment workers in the Petersburg General Strike of 1905, and two citywide strikes in 1906 and 1913. By examining these events in some detail, it is possible to chronicle the growing frustrations of garment workers all over Russia, and their attempts to create a safe and secure workplace. This particular chapter in the history of the fashion industry once again highlights how class, ethnicity, and gender were giving shape to and being shaped by the garment workers' dreams of a better life.

## THE ORIGINS OF THE GARMENT WORKERS' LABOR MOVEMENT

The first garment workers' strike recorded in the sources occurred in St. Petersburg in May 1870.[2] On 26 May, the Petersburg newspaper *Stock Exchange News* reported that journeywomen at a leading dressmaking shop, joined by some workers from some smaller tailoring establishments, struck against their employers. All the workers demanded higher wages, but the women included an additional demand of two days of rest per week instead of one.[3]

The timing of the strike is highly suggestive. The spring season which ran from February through May was the busiest time for tailors and dressmakers. During these months, the city's upper- and middle-class clientele ordered outfits to celebrate Easter and the secular festiv-

ities that accompanied it. Once these celebrations were over, many of these same individuals prepared to leave Petersburg for the summer, moving to family estates or renting rooms in the countryside. Their departure necessitated ordering their summer wardrobes before they left, making May the most onerous month for garment workers.

The fact that women workers initiated the strike is also important. As we saw in chapter 2, by 1870 the deskilling of sewing was taking its toll on garment workers of both sexes. As employees of a leading dress shop, the striking women would have felt this loss of status keenly. Moreover, the journeywomen's instigation of the strike suggests that these women were less committed to the traditional artisanal system than male workers. Male artisans dominated the artisanal administrative structures established in Russia, leaving women on the margins of the craft. Given their inevitable domestic responsibilities, they did not have the time or the capital to go off on their own, making it essential for them to improve working conditions at their current place of employment. This was why they chose the radical step of striking – they must have thought they had no reasonable alternative.

Whatever their reasons, the journeywomen's strike demands reflected their exhaustion and frustration with their employers. Garment workers were supposed to receive one day of rest, but most shop owners refused to allow any time off during peak periods, forcing their employees to work eighteen-hour shifts and to sleep at the workshops. Unable to endure such conditions any longer, these Petersburg journeywomen demanded two days of rest along with higher wages, calling attention to women workers' double burden – artisanal work and domestic duties. By bringing their grievances to the attention of newspaper reporters, the needlewomen used the new medium of the mass-circulation press to insist that their employers and the Petersburg educated public regard them as talented artisans, not beasts of burden.[4]

The results of this strike are not known.[5] Given that shop owners deplored any negative publicity which might encourage their clients to take their business elsewhere, it is likely that the masters gave in to some of the demands so that the needleworkers would return to work as quickly as possible. Once the season was over, the shop owners had more options – they could either refuse to rehire the strikers or they could offer them prestrike wages. Whatever the outcome, the conditions in these shops improved only temporarily, if at all.

Despite the uncertain outcome, the May 1870 Petersburg strike established a precedent for other garment workers to follow. To maximize their power with their employers, garment workers typically stopped work during the busiest moments of the season. Moreover, their strike demands reflected an emerging "craft consciousness," an awareness of the special working conditions unique to the needle trades.[6] While most shop owners would initially refuse workers' demands, they had to settle these labor disputes quickly. Otherwise, their own livelihoods were in jeopardy. And yet, despite the leverage the strikes gave workers, employers retained the upper hand. They could fire "troublemakers" and lower wages with impunity. Between 1870 and 1904 neither Petersburg nor Moscow, the two centers of the Russian fashion industry, experienced any highly publicized forms of labor unrest among garment workers. Strikes and labor unrest were bad for business, and shop owners tried to deal with their employees' demands out of the public eye.

This is not to say that all was quiet in the fashion industry. Tailors and dressmakers were less worried about their own employees than they were about the rise of ready-to-wear manufacturing. The introduction of subcontracting, the sewing machine, and sweatshops undermined one-hundred-year-old labor and business practices in the bespoke industry. Interestingly, workers' attempts to address those changes in a sustained way did not begin in Russia's fashion capitals. While Petersburg journeywomen might have organized the first strike in May 1870, another marginalized group, Jewish garment workers in the Pale of Settlement, crafted their grievances into a powerful labor movement.

## LABOR UNREST IN THE PALE OF SETTLEMENT

The histories of labor unrest among Jewish and Russian workers have remained separate and distinct, with little attention being paid to how they intersected.[7] And yet, this separation cannot be maintained in the case of the garment workers' labor movement. The activities of Jewish garment workers were central to the development of a garment workers' labor movement in imperial Russia. The Pale of Settlement became a kind of testing ground for the development of tactics that garment workers would later use to confront their employers all across the empire. Their story also reveals how Jewish labor activists used ethnicity and religion to help foster a sense of community and identity among garment workers. From this sense of solidarity grew the determination of Jewish workers to do battle with their employers.

In the eighteenth century, as a result of the Partitions of Poland, large numbers of Jews had suddenly become Russian subjects. In response, the Russian government decreed that Jews would not be allowed to leave these areas except by special permission.[8] This enforced segregation encouraged the development of a distinctive Jewish language and culture, making Judaism both a religious and an ethnic designation in the Russian Empire. Furthermore, because Jews were prohibited from participation in agricultural pursuits by an imperial decree in 1882, most crowded into the cities, towns, and villages where they established small artisanal workshops. By the end of the nineteenth century, almost three fourths of the artisans in the Pale were Jewish, and almost 40 percent of these were garment workers.[9] In fact, one economist claimed that there were enough Jewish tailors "to supply clothing for half the urban population of the Russian Empire."[10]

As the Jewish population in the Pale began to grow, conditions worsened particularly for those who lived in Belorussia and Lithuania.[11] With few factories to provide jobs for the growing population, Jewish workers were essentially forced into the artisanal trades, hoping someday to own their own shops. For most, these dreams were unrealized. The large number of workers allowed for the development of a vast network of small workshops creating intense competition, which only exacerbated the worst aspects of artisanal production. Furthermore, the masters themselves found it difficult to survive in the competitive atmosphere of the Pale of Settlement. They, in turn, hired themselves out to stores, thereby relinquishing their independence to become subcontractors. In the Pale, these horrible conditions forced many Jews to emigrate to western Europe and the United States in the hope of finding better conditions there.[12] For those who could not or would not emigrate, something needed to be done to ameliorate their lives. Some masters and a few philanthropic societies helped individuals temporarily, but charity could not deal with the systemic problems that caused the poverty and labor exploitation endemic in the Pale. To begin to address these problems, workers with the assistance of Jewish radical socialists organized themselves into a labor movement.

In the 1870s the Haskalah (Enlightenment) movement which encouraged greater secularization among Jews found a receptive audience in the Russian Pale of Settlement.[13] This, in turn, encouraged Jewish parents to send their children to Russian schools, where they came into contact with the underground socialist movement.[14] Their exposure to socialism allowed these Jewish students to see the ugly underbelly of capitalism. A certain number of them dedicated their lives to eradicating labor exploitation. Having rejected the Judaism of their fathers, they saw themselves as part of a large international movement. Returning to the Pale, where there were few factories, these young men and women quickly recognized the same exploitative system at work among the artisanal workshops. Determined to help their co-religionists break out of their enslavement as they had done, they established illegal educational circles "to create small cadres of enlightened, progressive workers who would be dedicated to the idea of revolution and willing to devote their lives to bring about a new order in society."[15]

These circles proved popular with workers, but the Jewish intellectuals grew frustrated. Because these young men and women had become secularized, the language of instruction in the circles was Russian rather than Yiddish, the native language of the workers. Many of the best workers used the circles and their Russian language instruction to take the entrance exams to obtain a higher education outside of the Pale. In order to reach the vast majority of artisanal workers, these intellectuals realized that they had to be able to speak to the workers directly about how to improve their lives. The way to do that was to use Yiddish in their propaganda efforts. Only after they had reverted to their native language and re-established their cultural link with the Jewish workers could they then set about creating workers' organizations.

The change of language proved critical. In the 1890s intellectuals together with artisanal workers transformed the mutual-aid societies set up by the educational circles into nascent trade unions, organized along craft lines. This new workers' movement developed a series of weapons – strikes, boycotts, vandalism, and physical intimidation – to achieve its goals. A strike movement began in Vilna, Lithuania's largest city, and quickly spread to the smaller towns of Lithuania and Belorussia.[16] Finally, in October 1897 intellectuals and workers formed the Bund (General Union of Jewish Workers in Russia and Poland) to coordinate and lead the Jewish workers' movement.[17] Although Jewish workers and intellectuals remained committed to the idea of an international workers' movement, the essential first step was the creation of a worker's community that emphasized ethnic ties.

THE STRIKE MOVEMENT IN GOMEL'

Garment workers were active participants in the Jewish labor movement. As early as 1893 tailors organized a seven-week general strike in Vilna, which marked the transition from educational activity to direct confrontation with employers and government authorities.[18] Other towns also saw an increase in strikes directed against the garment manufacturers.[19] The southern Belorussian town of Gomel' provides a typical example of how the Jewish labor movement evolved among garment workers. In 1891 the Russian government expelled Jews who had been allowed to reside in Moscow. Many of these refugees came and settled in Gomel'. The result was the rapid development of artisanal trades in the Belorussian city.[20] Taking advantage of this new influx of labor, ready-to-wear manufacturers from Ekaterinoslav, Kiev, and Kremenchug set up sweatshops in Gomel' in the late nineteenth century, threatening the livelihood of the city's tailoring establishments and forcing many independent artisans into subcontracting in order to stay in business.[21] Jewish radicals set up educational circles in Gomel' in the mid-1890s, but little resulted from these initial efforts. In 1897 the radicals began propagandizing among workers in Yiddish instead of Russian, and the number of circle participants grew significantly. According to Aron Groznyi, a participant, in 1900 the Bund organized trades unions among a number of crafts including garment workers.[22]

As was true in other parts of the Pale of Settlement, the needleworkers' chief complaint was the length of the working day. Shop owners had complete freedom to set the workday schedule and found other ways to exercise their control over their employees' time. Groznyi complained that owners' wives took workers' meals out of the oven a half hour early so that they would not lose any time waiting for the food to cool.[23] Furthermore, employers attempted to exercise their authority outside the workshops. According to Groznyi:

> The only free time workers had was Saturday. (Tailors, owners as well as workers, were almost exclusively Jewish in Gomel'.) On this day workers together with owners conducted themselves to the synagogue to recite the prayer, "King of Kings," thanking Him for this Saturday rest. But not all of Saturday was at the disposal of the worker. After evening prayers (*mikhno*) the owner sent his workers to light the lamps and to start work. He himself stayed to listen to the rabbi's sermon.[24]

This grievance is quite telling. Despite the distinctly secular cast of the intellectuals who helped organize the Jewish workers' movement, the Gomel' garment workers clearly valued their faith. Unfortunately, their employers, members of the same synagogue, thwarted their desire to fulfill their religious obligations. This patriarchal exercise of power symbolized the profound economic, social, *and* religious inequalities that existed in the Jewish communities in the Pale.[25]

Between 1900 and 1903 the Bund established a meeting place on Kuznechnaia Street in Gomel' where radicals and workers could mingle.[26] The masters warned their workers that such meetings would lead to exile, but the workers paid no heed. At these meetings workers learned that in 1785 Catherine the Great had established a twelve-hour workday with a half-hour break for breakfast, and one and a half hours for lunch for all artisans. This information galvanized the Gomel' workers. Those who had been frightened of involvement in an illegal trade union now justified their actions by arguing that they were correcting an injustice by forcing their employers to live up to the law.[27]

In the fall of 1902 labor activists introduced new tactics in their battle with employers. Workers employed at the best tailoring establishments in Gomel' demanded an end to Saturday evening work. The owners refused to consider their proposals. Fearful of what might happen next, the employers went to the police who refused to help. According to Groznyi, the workers repeated their demands, saying "We are not beasts of burden. We are people and we want to live."[28] On the next Saturday, they stayed away from work and the synagogue, once again linking their workplace and religious grievances in this act of protest. The employers responded by calling for a lockout. In retaliation, the workers barred strikebreakers from entering the shops, and one worker, Eli Oberman, hit the tailor, Ber Baskin, on the head with a beer bottle. This violent act scared the other owners, and they quickly gave in to the workers' demands.[29]

If the owners thought this would be the end of the labor unrest, they were sorely disappointed. The workers presented them with a new set of demands: a twelve-hour workday with breaks, a food allowance so that workers could supply their own meals, and the freeing of apprentices from domestic chores so that they could spend their time learning the trade. The owners once again refused their demands, but this time the police arrested the labor militants, sentencing them to prison for three months. At that point the strike collapsed. When the activists had served their sentences, however, they immediately returned to Gomel'. During the busy Easter season in 1903, garment workers struck against the largest shop owners. Police arrested a few individuals but the strikers refused to return to work. The strike dragged on for three long weeks. Desperate but determined to win, a group of workers beat up two tailors. The badly beaten tailors agreed to the workers' demands, ending the strike. Having achieved "a complete victory," needleworkers at the smaller workshops organized their own strike, and, according to Groznyi, the entire process repeated itself.[30]

The workers' victory was short-lived. In September 1903 a pogrom broke out in Gomel'. The Bund encouraged Jews to form self-defense units to protect Jewish residents and property from the wrath of the pogromists. Although a number of Jewish labor activists were killed in the ensuing days, this marked the first time that Jews had tried to protect themselves. Having stood up to their employers and defended their interests as workers, it seems clear that the working men and women in Gomel' felt more confident in defending themselves as Jews, suggesting once again a link between religious, ethnic, and work identities in the Pale of Settlement.[31]

Strikes such as these in Gomel' and other towns in the Pale of Settlement served as an important training ground. In addition to striking during the height of the season, radicals and garment workers developed other tactics. Strikes usually began first against the most successful bespoke shops. If workers could effect changes in these workshops, other masters would follow their lead in order to remain competitive. When owners balked at their employees' demands, needleworkers sometimes resorted to vandalism or physical intimidation to help them achieve their goals. After just a few successful strikes, garment workers became more interested in forming illegal trade unions. With the help of these organizations, workers could then plan boycotts and city-wide general strikes, shutting down the garment industry for extended periods of time.

## A RADICAL GARMENT WORKER

The last decade of the nineteenth century was critical in the development of the garment workers' labor movement. Jewish garment workers were learning how to fight against what appeared to be the overwhelming power of their employers. However, these individual strikes and boycotts were not enough. Gains won through strike activity were frequently lost months later. Workers understood that in order for the systemic problems inherent in the garment trades to be eliminated, they needed to form a much wider alliance with workers all across the Russian Empire. This was a daunting task because the Russian government viewed with suspicion any attempts to organize. Nevertheless, a group of dedicated men and women took upon themselves this dangerous mission of broader organization, hoping to create an empire-wide garment workers' movement.[32]

At the same time that Jewish students were setting up circles in the Pale, their Russian counterparts were doing the same in central Russia. These educated men and women shared their experiences with each other in clandestine meetings or in coded communiqués. Because these underground revolutionaries were constantly on

the move to avoid the police, they drifted from city to city bringing information and practical experience wherever they went.

Workers too participated in agitational work. One such person was Avram G. Iusim whose life story illustrates how radicalized workers contributed to an organized labor movement. Iusim's career also provides a concrete example of how the Jewish and Russian labor movements intersected and developed, revealing how an illiterate Jewish apprentice could become a dedicated labor activist.[33]

Born in a small village outside of Simferopol' in 1872, Iusim found work as a journeyman tailor in Odessa in 1895. At that time he struck up an acquaintance with a woodcarver who encouraged him to give up Judaism and introduced him to the dressmaker, Olga Vol'fson. Finding him an eager pupil, Vol'fson encouraged Iusim to join her revolutionary circle. At the end of 1896, the police arrested Vol'fson, and Iusim went to Kiev where he quickly joined the revolutionary underground and began propaganda work. At this point, Iusim, a native speaker of Yiddish, learned Russian.

When arrests once again threatened Iusim's work, his colleagues suggested that he go to work among the Don Cossacks. This was a bold move since Jews were forbidden to reside in the Cossack lands. The ever-resourceful Iusim went to the Mikhailovskii monastery in Odessa where he spent a month preparing to convert to Orthodoxy. After his "conversion," which allowed him to change his nationality on his passport from Jewish to Russian, Iusim moved to Rostov-na-Donu in southern Russia in 1902. Agitation among the workers there proved disappointing. One member of a workers' circle betrayed Iusim to the police, but he escaped to Khar'kov in time to avoid arrest. For the next few months, Iusim moved from town to town, organizing garment workers and fleeing to avoid arrest.

Arriving in Ekaterinoslav, Iusim worked as a journeyman tailor for over a year and continued his labor agitation. At one point during his tenure there, labor organizers wanted him to work among the Jewish garment workers. Iusim claimed that he was Russian, and more to the point, that he had forgotten his Yiddish. His comrades insisted. After his speech to the workers, they remarked that for a Russian, he spoke good Yiddish, but for a Jew, well, he needed more study. This remarkable story is quite revealing about the fluidity of ethnic identity in late imperial Russia. While Iusim's conversion to Orthodoxy was certainly suspect, his years of living outside the small villages of the Pale in the big cities of southwestern Russia, and even among the Don Cossacks, coupled with his involvement with the revolutionary underground, had made him "Russian." He clearly wanted to forget the milieu from which he sprang – he identified himself as Russian and had a passport to prove it. Only with deep reluctance was he willing to communicate with Jewish workers in Yiddish, thereby revealing his true origins. But it was precisely his ability to speak both languages that made Iusim and other workers like him invaluable. They could operate in both worlds at once, bringing their experiences as labor organizers from the Pale of Settlement into other parts of Russia.

Iusim's agitational work finally brought him to the attention of the authorities. One day at work, his employer called the police and had him arrested. While the owner went to get his coat for the trip to the police station, the officer told Iusim to run away. Perhaps foolishly, Iusim remained in Ekaterinoslav, where a few months later the police searched his room. At this point, Iusim moved to Kiev but was quickly apprehended. Sentenced to six weeks in jail, he shared his cell with a student arrested at a revolutionary gathering. According to Iusim, the student advanced Iusim's education in revolutionary ideology. Released from prison, Iusim was sent to Novocherkassk in southern Ukraine where he was under constant surveillance. When he was finally free of police supervision, Iusim decided to try his luck in Petersburg where he arrived on 4 January 1905, just days before the start of the Revolution of 1905.

Avram G. Iusim was exceptional. A participant in the Jewish workers' movement, he understood the need to create an empire-wide labor movement if garment workers were going to be truly successful in realizing their dreams for a better life. Giving up any kind of personal life, he abandoned his religious beliefs and ethnic identity to adopt the identity of a Russian worker. Just as some members of the elite were redefining "Russian" to represent a modern, cosmopolitan identity, at the same time the assumption of a Russian identity among non-ethnic Russian workers often served to

119   An artisan recently come to Petersburg from his village to make his living. His attire reflects his peasant/worker status. He wears bast shoes, and his tattered sleeveless jacket is also something a peasant might wear. However, he is sporting a peaked worker's cap, a wool coat, and trousers, typical clothing for Russian urban workers. Central State Archive for Documentary Films, Photographs, and Sound Recordings in St. Petersburg.

delineate those who believed in the internationalist goals of socialism. As Iusim's story illustrates, his commitment to the cause never wavered, and he eventually became one of the organizers of the garment workers' union in Petersburg.

If Iusim's rise to prominence in the workers' movement was exceptional, the path he took was typical of other worker activists. Although constantly harassed by employers and the police, these men and women worked hard to explain to other garment workers the need for a strong labor movement to achieve better working conditions. Beginning in 1905 these worker activists were finally given an opportunity to bring their grievances before the Russian public. What had been a labor movement on the periphery among marginalized workers shifted to the very center of Russian life.

## THE 1905 PETERSBURG GENERAL STRIKE

On 9 January 1905 government forces fired upon a procession of unarmed workers and their families who had wanted to give a petition to Nicholas II. This attack upon innocent men, women, and children, known as Bloody Sunday, ushered in a new era in Russian life. Chronic famines, economic recession, and a disastrous war with Japan in the years and months preceding that terrible tragedy, highlighted the government's inability to provide effective leadership. In the aftermath of Bloody Sunday, ordinary Russians decided that change was essential. Since the government was unwilling to engage in a peaceful dialogue with its subjects, it was time for Russians to force change upon the government through revolutionary means.

The Revolution of 1905 consisted of a series of overlapping revolts among the educated public, peasants, and workers. Of all three groups, the workers sustained their revolutionary assault upon the existing order the longest. There were waves of strikes and other forms of labor protest throughout 1905, culminating in the October General Strike. When the government granted concessions to educated society but not to workers, Moscow laborers organized an armed uprising in December which was brutally put down by government troops. In March of 1906 the government finally permitted the creation of legal trade unions, which resulted in another series of strikes and protests. Unfortunately for Russia's workers, the government's strategy of granting some concessions and using force to restore order proved successful in defusing the revolution. By June 1907 when Prime Minister Stolypin dissolved the newly created Parliament (Duma) in order to replace it with a more docile one, the revolution was over.

The labor unrest that accompanied the 1905 Revolution deeply affected the Russian fashion industry. In May 1905 approximately two hundred salesclerks from ready-to-wear shops gathered on Moscow's Lubianka Square, and marched through the heart of the city's chief commercial district decrying their working conditions. The leader of the demonstration worked in one of the M. and I. Mandl' ready-to-wear stores. In the fall salesclerks working for Russia's largest fashion outlets – Mandl', Muir and Merrilees, Gostinnyi Dvor, Apraksin Dvor – and many smaller shops, struck for a reduced work week and higher wages. Salesclerks formed unions during the fall, and in December police reported that over 1,500 of them gathered in Moscow at various meetings in the days leading up to the December uprising.[34]

The greatest area of unrest in the fashion industry was between garment workers and their employers. By 1905 a significant number of garment workers knew about western European trade unions. In workers' circles, members of Russia's revolutionary parties and activists like Avram Iusim encouraged them to use an organized labor movement to help them fight for a better life. To realize this goal, garment workers created labor unions and organized a series of successful citywide strikes during the 1905 Revolution. Needleworkers in Baku, Odessa, Nizhnii Novgorod, and other cities scattered across the Russian Empire demanded higher wages, better working conditions, and greater respect. For the purposes of this story, we will look at developments in St. Petersburg and Moscow. Events in these cities reflected what happened in other Russian cities, and at the same time inspired garment workers in other regions to join workers in St. Petersburg and Moscow in their protests.

The spring and summer of 1905 have been aptly described as a "meeting epidemic."[35] Thousands of Russians gathered to discuss their concerns and to create organizations to represent those concerns to the authorities. Garment workers were no exception. Angry needleworkers gathered together to discuss strategies in the coming confrontations with their employers. In Petersburg, a group of journeymen radicalized by their participation in workers' circles conceived a bold plan to organize a series of strikes and a trade union to defend their interests after the strikes were over. Drawing upon the lessons learned from the Pale of Settlement, their plan was to strike simultaneously against the city's leading tailoring establishments during the height of the fall season.

As it turned out, their timing could not have been more auspicious. In September and October, labor unrest escalated dramatically all over Russia, but particularly in the two capital cities. Laborers saw the collapse of governmental authority as an opportune moment to express their anger at the government and their employers. The key moment came when Moscow railway workers issued a call for a general strike, which began on 9 October and quickly paralyzed the country. The strike shut down both Moscow and Petersburg, and forced Nicholas II to issue the October Manifesto on 17 October, in which he announced the creation of the Duma, or the elected parliament.

Before Petersburg journeymen could put their plan into action, however, the tailor Solov'ev murdered a policeman and wounded two watchmen not far from his shop in the city center. Although Solov'ev was arrested, he was quickly released after being ruled mentally unstable. According to one account, the incident rattled the city's tailors.[36] The negative publicity tarnished their image as respectable shopkeepers, and connected the tailoring community with the collapse of law and order in Russian society.

A few days later, on 12 October, more than fifty journeymen at the elite shops of Lidval', Ganri, and Grenfel't went out on strike, demanding higher wages. The strike shocked their masters since these firms paid the best wages in the city. Furthermore, the strike could not have come at a more inauspicious moment for the tailors just as their clients began ordering their winter clothing. An October strike could seriously jeopardize the financial well-being of any tailoring establishment. Lidval' and Grenfel't settled the strike immediately, but the master at Ganri, Eduard E. Foilenverden, held out a

120   A worker reading a newspaper announcing the founding of the Duma, 19 August 1905. His attire combines peasant and worker sartorial conventions. Central State Archive for Documentary Films, Photographs, and Sound Recordings in St. Petersburg.

few days longer until he, too, acceded to the workers' demands. The next day, at the height of the October General Strike, workers at the prestigious Kalina, Tedeski, and Novotny shops as well as some dressmaking establishments, went on strike as well. According to one source, journeymen's wages increased from 10 to 30 percent in 1905 as a result of the October strikes.[37]

On the foggy, rainy morning of 17 October 1905, the nineteen-year-old journeyman A. Voronov was standing on a Petersburg street corner reading Nicholas II's October Manifesto that announced the creation of the Duma, when someone tapped him on the arm. Voronov recognized a fellow artisan who said, "Forget it. It's all nonsense. Let's go somewhere else." The two young men went to the Leipzig tavern where they joined twenty other tailors. Over steaming cups of tea, a thirty-year-old journeyman tailor named F. I. Ozol explained that the only way for workers to achieve their goals was to reject the tsar's false promises of freedom. According to Voronov, this was the first meeting of the new union.[38] Embroiderers, furriers, corset-makers, milliners, seamstresses, and knitters established their own unions in the days and months that followed.[39]

121   Some of the delegates to the August 1906 tailors' conference in Moscow. In the first row, seated second from the left is F. I. Ozol, a leader among Petersburg journeymen. In the second row, standing third from the left is the Mandl' employee Maksimov who led the negotiations between Mandl' and the striking workers in 1906. S. I. Gruzdev, *Trud i bor'ba shveinikov v Peterburge, 1905–1916*, 58. Library of Congress Collections.

This first impulse to unionize reveals the problems that union leaders faced. Not only were garment workers employed in small workshops scattered throughout the city, but craft divisions further divided them. Although all garment workers used needle and thread, making corsets, hats, and fur coats required different skills and training. The division of the garment workers' unions into craft specialties, emphasizing the differences rather than the similarities among needleworkers, thwarted the efforts of the labor activists to create a unified labor movement. It was only with the legalization of trade unions in March 1906 that union leaders attempted to establish organizations that included individuals from all of the needle trades. In Petersburg the union registered in March as the Union of Men and Women Tailors and Furriers (UTF), while in Moscow the union was called the Union of Men and Women Workers in the Manufacture of Clothing in the Moscow Industrial Region (UMGW). The UTF had a peak membership of approximately 1,500 while over 3,000 individuals belonged to the Moscow union.[40]

In her magisterial study, *Roots of Rebellion*, Victoria Bonnell has pointed out that journeymen formed the radical core of many workers' organizations. Because of their apprenticeships, these men were long-time residents of Russia's cities, and many of them had learned to read and write in workers' circles or adult literacy programs.[41] Consequently, they imagined for themselves a comfortable life in a clean apartment as respected members of Russian urban society. Working as they did in custom tailoring put them into direct contact with their dream world. As apprentices they had run errands for their

masters, which included delivering packages to the clients at their tastefully furnished apartments. Each day these men saw the elegant carriages that delivered the equally elegant customers to their doors. And yet, while many of these journeymen tailors dressed in dapper clothes, they could not afford the food, furniture, or housing that symbolized the good life. In Russia's capital city, the sights and sounds of modernity surrounded them, but they remained on the margins.

By 1905 the deleterious effect of ready-to-wear on custom tailoring could no longer be ignored. Large quantities of men's shirts, trousers, and other accessories

122  A sewing workshop producing army overcoats in 1905. The photograph shows how some workers used sewing machines while others performed hand sewing in the traditional way by sitting on tabletops. Central State Archive for Documentary Films, Photographs, and Sound Recordings in St. Petersburg.

were now available from ready-to-wear stores. Consumers preferred the convenience of buying these prefabricated garments, and the store owners preferred to hire subcontractors rather than set up artisanal workshops. Many journeymen realized that their dreams of becoming respected independent artisans were fading quickly. They could either remain as journeymen for the rest of their working lives, or they could work as subcontractors for ready-to-wear manufacturers. In either case their hope of a better life was shattered, and it did not take these workers long to identify those individuals who thwarted their dreams.

As a result, when Petersburg journeymen began organizing their new unions, they specifically excluded the owners of bespoke shops and ready-to-wear subcontractors from membership. For journeymen, these two groups were the enemy. The masters failed to provide their employees with a decent life and stood in the way of their dream of independence.[42] The journeymen had even more bitter feelings toward the subcontractors who had sold out to ready-to-wear manufacturers and posed the most serious threat to the journeymen's livelihood. While subcontractors might have been bosses of their own sweatshops, their independence was illusory since they themselves were employees of the manufacturers.[43] Other unions in Moscow and elsewhere organized in a similar manner.[44] Thus, tailors' unions were much more narrowly defined organizations than their names suggest. They represented only one segment of an increasingly complex form of manufacturing.

In addition to the specific prohibition placed upon masters and subcontractors from union membership, the unions remained overwhelmingly male. Despite the active role played by Petersburg journeywomen in organizing the 1870 strike, by 1905 both intellectuals and male journeymen, with few exceptions, perceived women workers as notoriously difficult to organize. At no point did female membership in the UTF, for example, rise above 15 percent.[45] Despite the dramatic rise in numbers of female garment workers from 1900 to 1914, they remained a woefully under-represented group within the union. The reasons for this are not hard to find. Women's domestic responsibilities after a full day at work meant that there was little time for participation in workers' circles which might have helped women feel part of the larger garment workers' movement. Furthermore, women workers received lower wages than their male counterparts. This meant that women could not afford to participate in any kind of labor unrest, as every kopeck was needed to feed themselves and their families. Since employers often fired individuals who were involved in strikes, women were naturally reluctant to participate.

## THE 1906 MANDL' STRIKE[46]

Developments among Moscow needleworkers paralleled those of their co-workers in Petersburg during 1905. After a series of successful work stoppages during the October General Strike, on 4 November approximately one thousand garment workers held their first public meeting of their new union. According to N. Shevkov, a garment worker and later historian of the movement, "The union was the fighting center of Moscow needleworkers. The chief means of realizing its goal was not mutual-aid but struggle. The weapon in that struggle was the strike." Shevkov reports that from the beginning 75 percent of the union's resources were placed in a strike fund.[47]

With the legalization of trade unions in March 1906, the UMGW leadership was able to recruit members for the new organization. And yet, despite the calls for unity, the UMGW excluded masters and subcontractors from membership, just like the UTF in Petersburg. Here, the inexperience of journeymen as labor organizers prevented them from understanding the reality of the situation they faced. The socialist rhetoric that provided the ideological underpinnings of their labor movement divided the world of work into two camps – exploiter and exploited. But the fashion industry presented no such easy dichotomy. In order to end worker exploitation in the garment trades, Moscow journeymen needed to do battle not just with the masters in bespoke tailoring but also with ready-to-wear manufacturers. As we will see, by excluding subcontractors from union membership, union leaders had rejected an essential ally in their battle with employers.

On 26 August, UMGW leaders hosted the first All-Russian Conference of Tailors in which union representatives from all over Russia gathered to discuss mutual concerns. Although the official reports about the conference do not mention strike tactics – public discussions of strikes would certainly have attracted the attention of the police – it seems likely that plans to strike must have taken shape during those days.[48] At the very least, the Moscow union representatives learned in private conversations about the successes and failures of needleworkers' strikes in other cities.

Before the Moscow union could organize its membership into strike action, another group preempted them. Having been excluded from the UMGW, subcontractors had formed their own union (MSU). On 24 August, two days before the start of the journeymen's conference, one thousand city subcontractors and their employees met. At that time, they asked for a raise in piece rates, which they then circulated among the ready-to-wear retail stores located in the Sretenskii section of Moscow, giving the store owners three days to reply.[49] On 30 August, the MSU met again. Not one store owner had replied to their demands; some had even refused to read them. The angry subcontractors called for a strike, and asked rural subcontractors in the outlying provinces to support them. The MSU then voted unanimously to send their demands to all ready-to-wear stores in Moscow. If the owners did not respond, the MSU would call for a citywide strike against ready-to-wear manufacturers.[50]

This radical step on the part of subcontractors galvanized the UMGW and its membership. Individual strikes began at popular Moscow stores. On 3 September union members called for a strike at three stores – Gurevich, Zaglukhinskii, and Firgang – because they had not responded to the strike demands. At the same meeting journeymen called for the creation of an All-Russian Tailors' Union and artisanal courts, to replace the existing but ineffective arbitration boards. A few days later all three stores acceded to the strikers' demands. In retaliation, the management at Firgang fired the eight workers who had led the strike at their establishment.[51]

As the largest employer of garment workers in the city, the M. and I. Mandl' firm became the chief target of garment workers' hostility. Workers had nicknamed the company "the All-Russian exploiter" (*vserossiiskii eksploatator*) with good reason.[52] By 1906 the Mandl' company had twelve departments in its Moscow stores that employed two hundred and seventy journeymen and women. The store also employed six hundred subcontractors plus their employees, and twenty thousand home workers in Moscow and Riazan' provinces. Union

leaders believed that if they could gain concessions from the Mandl' company, then the other ready-to-wear manufacturers would have to follow suit in order to remain competitive. The union focused its attention and resources on the Mandl' strike even though there were strikes at all major centers of clothing manufacture in the city.

The trouble at Mandl' began in the spring of 1906. Once again, conflict arose over owners arbitrarily controlling their employees' time. In April the company's management had announced that it was abolishing the daily lunch break during Lent in order to keep up with the demand for clothing. The firm agreed to pay each worker seven rubles and fifty kopeks at Easter to compensate for the removal of their lunch break. After Easter, Mandl' decided to eliminate the lunch break completely and pay workers fifteen kopeks in return. Journeymen at the Tverskaia men's department went on strike, demanding the return of their lunch break. This launched a series of strikes against the firm, with demands for higher wages. Eventually six company departments and two hundred workers were involved, but the strike ended with only a partial victory for the workers.[53] As a result, they began to plan for a strike during the fall season.

On 3 September the Mandl' journeymen submitted individual lists of grievances to the UMGW, and on 9 September union leaders and workers drew up a single list of demands. They included the end of piece rates and the introduction of hourly wages; the abolition of subcontracting and home work; the creation of new workshops to perform work that had been sent out to subcontractors and home workers; the appointment of worker representatives to help run the workshops by overseeing the hiring and firing of workers, and investigating conflicts between workers and their employers; and a raise in monthly and daily wages – a forty-five ruble minimum for journeymen, thirty-five rubles for female journeymen, and a minimum daily wage of two rubles and fifty kopecks.[54]

These demands represented the Moscow journeymen's dreams of a better life and a complete restructuring of the system of clothing manufacture in Russia. The end of subcontracting and home work would have eliminated ready-to-wear manufacturing and sweating completely. All manufacturing would occur in the radically revised artisanal workshops. Indeed, it seems from these demands that workers wanted to create factory-like settings. In the new centralized workshops, masters would no longer have complete authority over their employees. They would share their power with worker representatives, and together master and journeymen would establish the work regime. What had been a hierarchical and very decentralized relationship was to become one of power-sharing. If journeymen had to give up their dreams of owning their own shops, then at the very least they could have a greater say in running the workshops.[55]

Written accounts of this strike agree that the most important demand was the end of piece rates. Piece rates had become the norm in both bespoke and ready-to-wear manufacturing, and it was this system of payment that violated the very nature of artisanal work. Emphasizing quantity rather than quality, piece rates denied garment workers the opportunity to demonstrate their mastery of the craft. The only way to stop this degradation of their work was to eliminate piece rates and sweating in favor of daily and monthly wages. Furthermore, male craftsmen, as family breadwinners, would receive higher wages than women workers, but all would benefit from a regularized work schedule, the abolition of overtime and fees, sanitary improvements, and paid leaves. In contrast to the subcontractors whose sole demand was an increase in piece rates, the Moscow journeymen and their union presented management with a dramatic revisioning of the artisanal workshop as a partnership of equals.

In order for their strike to succeed, the UMGW belatedly realized that they would need the support of Mandl's rural employees. On 10 September they sent representatives to Beloomut in Riazan' province, the center of a vast network of home workers. Union officials spoke to villagers in the area and told them about the events in Moscow. The rural workers agreed to strike on 18 September, demanding a meeting with company representatives from Mandl', Rozenstvaig, Neishtadt, Petukhov Brothers, and other ready-to-wear manufacturers who had employees in the region.[56] Thus, the vast networks that the manufacturers had so painstakingly created were now being mobilized against them in what appeared to be a defiant show of solidarity.

On 11 September a delegation of Mandl' workers and the secretary of UMGW presented their demands to the company. Informed that they had until 13 September to reply, the managers countered by telling their employees that the head of the company was out of the country and they could not deal with the workers' demands without him.[57] As the deadline passed without any response, two hundred journeymen and women went out on strike and met to discuss their options. After some discussion, the majority voted to continue their strike.

This growing militancy terrified the journeywomen who worked at the Mandl' shop on Tverskaia Street. According to one source, they refused to support the strike, fearing the wrath of their supervisors.[58] However, the women's defection is more complicated than that. Why should they have been any less afraid of their supervisors than their male co-workers? A more nuanced answer would point to the strike demands themselves. In allowing wage differentials to remain between men and women workers in the new workshops, women had little to gain from the strike. By ignoring the concerns of women workers, the journeymen demonstrated their indifference to their concerns.

Despite this initial defection, the Mandl' strike entered a new phase on 18 September when the vast majority of the company's employees joined the original strikers. The company's managers quickly tried to defuse the situation by driving a further wedge between journeymen and sweatshop employees. In the city, they refused to make any concessions until Ludwig Mandl' returned from his trip overseas. They also tried to determine the identities of the strike leaders and to give work to subcontractors.[59]

123 (*facing page top*) Leaders of the union and strike movement in Petersburg. S. Gruzdev who later wrote a history of the movement is in the top row on the right. S. I. Gruzdev, *Trud i bor'ba shveinikov v Peterburge, 1905–1916*, 97. Library of Congress Collections.

124 (*facing page bottom*) Petersburg union leaders. S. Kitavin, an active participant in the strike movements in 1905 and 1913, is pictured in the top row on the right. S. I. Gruzdev, *Trud i bor'ba shveinikov v Peterburge, 1905–1916*, 96. Library of Congress Collections.

Верхний ряд: 1) П. Пирогов, б-к — предс. прав. в 1908 г.; 2) И. Богданов с. д. — казначей 1910—11 г.; 3) Е. Силина—чл. правл. 1909 г. (б-ка); 4) С. Груздев—секрет. с-за 1910—11 г. (б-к). Второй ряд: 5) М. Выборнов—б-к секретарь с-за 1912 г.; 6) В. Лебедев—б-к секрет. 1913 г.; 7) И. Ионов—б-к секр. 1913—14 г.; 8) Сумичев—б-к редактор журн. „Прол. Иглы".

Старые работники союза.

Верхн. ряд слева направо: 1) Корсак—перв. секретарь с-за б-к; 2) Я. Шаров—чл. правл. и руковод. груп. б-в; 3) А. Еремина—чл. перв. правл. союза; 4) С. Китавин—предс. рев. ком. с-за с. р. Второй ряд: 5) Серяков; 6) К. Волков—организаторы с-за в 1908 г.; 7) П. Базаров—пред. правл. в 1911 г.; 8) М. Лейтис—чл. правл.

They took a different approach with their rural employees. In Beloomut the villagers were in an uproar on 18 September. Some women, mostly wives of the rural home workers, had smashed the windows of the manufacturers' distribution centers. Others had sent their men off to meet company representatives after much weeping and praying, fearful that they would not return. The workers gathered in the village square in front of the district offices. When the company representatives arrived, they told the workers that if they went home peacefully, they would give them vodka. The vast majority of those present rejected this humiliating bribe and announced that they had come to negotiate a raise in piece rates. A delegation of five workers was then appointed, and deliberations began in earnest. By the end of the day, the home workers had a raise although it was not as much as they had wanted.[60]

Having averted a strike among their rural employees, the manufacturers turned their attention to the two-week-old strike among subcontractors that was still going on in Moscow. These men and women could not sustain a long strike against their employers who, seeing the determination of their subcontractors to win better piece rates, began negotiations. On 27 September fourteen manufacturers out of seventy-one agreed to raise their piece rates by 25 percent. The strike continued at the other fifty-seven shops. Finally on 30 September, a month after the strike had begun, those shop owners agreed to increase piece rates although these new wages were between 35 and 50 percent less than the subcontractors wanted.[61] Nevertheless, the subcontractors accepted the new terms and called off the strike. Despite their inability to force the manufacturers to accede to their demands in full, they demonstrated to all of Moscow their ability to organize and sustain a strike. Moreover, they indicated to both owners and journeymen that they were a force to be reckoned with in any restructuring of the garment trades.

Mandl' and the other ready-to-wear firms now entered into a period of protracted conflict with their journeymen. Having discovered that Ludwig Mandl' had now returned to Moscow, the workers arranged to negotiate directly with the head of the company. On 30 September he met with representatives of the striking workers and two UMGW officials. He agreed to raise wages to thirty-five rubles for men and thirty rubles for women workers and to grant personal leaves, but he categorically refused to consider the abolition of piece rates.[62] On 1 October the UMGW called a meeting to which 1,000 of the 2,600 members attended.[63] In an attempt to establish the principle of collective bargaining, the UMGW rejected the company's offer and set up a strike fund to provide financial aid for the duration of the strike. It also made clear that the demand for an end to piece rates was the chief purpose of the strike. As Mandl' was the largest employer in the city, such changes in that company would mean changes in other ready-to-wear firms.[64]

By the end of September it was clear to both workers and their employers that this strike was like no other in their experience. Most garment workers' strikes occurred in small workshops employing five or six people, but the Mandl' Company found itself doing battle against almost all of its more than twenty thousand employees at once. Furthermore, the newspapers were giving almost daily accounts of each side's moves. What had once been a private negotiation between master and journeymen now became news, open to public discussion and debate.[65] For the workers, this publicity proved beneficial, particularly in their struggle against strikebreakers. When the Mandl' Company tried to bring rural home workers into the city, they quickly realized that they would be strikebreakers and left immediately.[66]

On 2 October the Mandl' workers met to decide how to proceed. For the first time, they approved a change in their demands. They authorized their delegates to make the abolition of piece rates their third demand rather than their primary one. It looked as though the journeymen might now begin serious negotiations with their employer. That same night, however, a group of unidentified individuals broke into the Mandl' store on Bol'shoi Cherkasskii Lane. The intruders stole three furs worth thousands of rubles, and eight gold pieces worth a thousand rubles from an adjacent store. Unable to break open the safes, the thieves departed, leaving behind the tools of their trade.[67]

This one act transformed the strike. On 3 October, the owners of ready-to-wear stores and tailoring shops, 120 in all, gathered together to form their own union, the Society of Owners of Tailoring Shops (SOTS) and changed their tactics. The members of the new union began by expressing their support for Mandl'. To make that support a reality, they agreed to a lockout of all employees if the Mandl' workers did not return to their jobs by 6 October. In exchange for this support, Ludwig Mandl' drew up a blacklist of strikers that he sent to all members of the SOTS, guaranteeing that the troublemakers would not find another job. With the support of his colleagues, the next morning Mandl' announced that he was withdrawing his concessions of 30 September, and those employees who did not return to work would be removed from the payroll as of 18 September.

When these actions did not elicit a response from the workers, the SOTS met again on 5 October and composed a letter to the strikers, demanding an immediate resumption of work. Arguing that "[s]ome of the demands led to the destruction of the master's authority and power in the workshop," the owners refused to honor any demands not already approved. Indeed, the owners must have felt that they had no choice. Low overhead costs were essential to the survival of both bespoke and ready-to-wear manufacturing. Workers' demands for a shorter workday with no overtime, paid leaves, and other demands would have meant increasing the overhead costs which certainly threatened the profitability of most clothing manufacturers. The SOTS insisted that workers choose representatives for an arbitration board composed of both workers and management to resolve the issues in the strike, and that both sides had to honor whatever agreement was negotiated. If they did not approve these demands by 9 October, the owners would proceed with a lockout for which they had already received the approval of the Moscow police.[68] This vacillation between confrontation and conciliation was typical of owners' unions in 1906–07.[69]

Representatives of both sides met on 7 October to determine whether they could resolve the conflict. Since neither side was willing to back down, the stalemate continued. Adding to the crisis, rural subcontractors went on strike again for higher piece rates. In Moscow, the UMGW appealed to the Central Trade Union Bureau, an umbrella organization for all of the city's trade unions, asking for other workers to support the strike and calling for a consumer boycott of ready-to-wear manufacturers.[70]

Despite this expression of solidarity, support for the strike began to crumble. On 11 October, UMGW leaders met and concluded that the situation was very bad. The owners had refused to negotiate, and there was growing police interference on the side of management. Twenty journeymen had returned to work, and Mandl' had employed fifty strikebreakers. The final blow to the UMGW was that it was running out of money to support the striking workers. It had distributed over one thousand rubles to those in need but only had six hundred rubles left in its treasury.

On 13 October the store owners met once again to approve the rules for their union. They also agreed to publish their blacklists of striking workers so that these individuals would not be able to find a job anywhere in Moscow. Yet, despite this show of strength, the owners tabled their plans for a lockout and tried to placate their employees by calling for the creation of a mutual-aid society for both owners and workers. At the same meeting, Ludwig Mandl' announced that he would not accede to any of his employees' demands, but he would offer his workers new piece rates.

On 15 October the UMGW organized a meeting of its membership. During the course of the meeting, the Mandl' workers voted to end their strike, declaring that they "do not consider themselves completely defeated . . . and will prepare for a more aggressive battle."[71] In response, Ludwig Mandl' agreed to authorize new piece rates for his workers and to eliminate the blacklist he had compiled during the strike. The Mandl' piece rates were then adopted at other ready-to-wear stores. In an ironic twist, the subcontractors had the last public word on the strike when the MSU issued an appeal to Moscow consumers. Rumors had been circulating that ready-to-wear manufacturers were going to raise prices as much as 40 percent, using the strike as their excuse. However, the subcontractors informed consumers that the improvements in the wages of garment workers were so insignificant that they could not possibly be responsible for such a sharp hike in prices.[72]

The month-long strike yielded important lessons for Russian garment workers and their unions. Organized sustained strikes by both subcontractors and journeymen demonstrated an impressive show of strength on the part of needleworkers. The unions had supported their members financially and reached out to other workers' organizations to help them in their struggle, which made it difficult for their employers to find strikebreakers. Russian newspapers aided the strike by making sure that the public was aware of what was happening. Even consumers were called upon to support the strikers. Perhaps the best indication of the strength of the needleworkers and their cause was that custom tailors and ready-to-wear manufacturers were forced to join forces in order to defeat them.

Beyond that, the Moscow strike revealed the obstacles that unions had yet to overcome. As a result of the strike, union leaders decided that the shorter spring season was a better time to strike – owners would have less time to mount a coordinated response. Union leaders were also forced to acknowledge their numerical weakness. Simply put, the UMGW represented only a minority of Moscow garment workers. In order to accomplish their goal of abolishing piece rates and sweating, the union needed to build a stronger base. The crux of the matter lay with the need to include *all* garment workers in one organization, but here there was serious dissension among union members. While some argued that subcontractors and their employees, as the most exploited of needleworkers, should be incorporated into the UMGW, many journeymen still believed that the subcontractors were worse exploiters than their masters.[73] Moreover, women needleworkers were conspicuously absent from the membership rolls. As the strike revealed so clearly, the discrepancy in wages between those working at the subcontracting shops and those employed at bespoke establishments made it difficult for any one union to come up with a single list of demands that would cover the rights of all workers equally. Indeed, during the strike, some owners were presented with a demand for higher wages that were actually below the rates they already paid.[74] Finally, if the journeymen had won their strike, thousands of garment workers would have lost their jobs.[75] Without any concrete plans to provide employment during the transformation of clothing manufacture, the poorest-paid laborers could ill-afford to support the radical vision of the journeymen.

Despite these problems, garment workers resolved to continue the battle with their employers. In May of 1907 the Moscow union called for a boycott against the Matveev tailor shop. Despite this show of strength, the tide was turning against the workers by this point. Local and state officials had begun to clamp down on "improper" activities. So, after the initial call for a boycott, the police intervened. Declaring that the union did not have the right to call for a boycott, the police shut it down.

The closure of the union marked the end of the participation by garment workers in the Revolution of 1905. There had been some successes. The strikes against custom-tailoring shops in Petersburg had ended with an increase in piece rates. The Moscow citywide strike had not achieved what the journeymen had wanted, but it had allowed them to articulate their vision of a radically new relationship between themselves and their employers. Perhaps most importantly, clothing manufacturers understood that relations with their employees had entered a new phase. Not content with higher wages alone, journeymen wanted to become equal partners in the production of clothing.

## THE 1913 PETERSBURG CITYWIDE STRIKE

The immediate post-revolutionary period proved to be a very difficult one for garment workers. After the disastrous Russo–Japanese War of 1904–05, government officials and business leaders demobilized from wartime to a peacetime economy. Poor harvests in 1906 and 1907 made this process all the more difficult. As Russians struggled through another recession, the demand for clothing declined. Garment workers who had fought so hard for higher wages and better working conditions now found themselves unemployed. Until the economic climate improved, there was little that garment workers could do to improve their status.

As a result, the years 1908–11 marked a slump in labor activity as well. The government had shut down garment workers' unions. In most cases, the unions reopened a year or two later, but they lacked the energy that had characterized the first organizations. In Moscow, the situation was made worse when rank-and-file members discovered that the treasurer had absconded with five hundred rubles of UMGW funds.[76] According to one union organizer, this financial scandal had sown a deep mistrust of the union among ordinary workers.[77] Their financial situation was too precarious to give money to organizations that could not be trusted. Despite these problems, some garment workers pressed on in their struggle to improve working conditions. Developments in Petersburg, the center of bespoke trade, served as a model for other garment workers to follow. A new union, the Union of Men and Women Workers in the Tailoring Trade (UWT) opened in that city in October 1908, and for a while labor activists tried to sustain a cooperative workshop (artel'). The Fifth Tailors' Artel' began operation in the spring of 1908. The journeymen who worked there instituted an eight-hour workday and paid daily wages rather than piece rates. According to the artel's regulations, its purpose was "the development and raising of the spiritual and economic well-being of the members." The journeymen tried to create ideal working conditions as well as a special school and library for union members. Unfortunately, problems quickly arose. According to one account, the journeymen spent too much of their day debating with each other, while others began to drink. The cooperative did not make enough money to pay back its start-up loan, and it was forced to shut down in 1910.[78]

The 1910 fall season was also marked by the revival of strikes, all of which ended in defeat for the workers. In August 1911 the UWT organized a conference of union representatives. At this meeting in the Russian capital the delegates first discussed a citywide general strike in Petersburg. Having had time to absorb the lessons of the 1905 Revolution and the 1906 citywide strike in Moscow, union leaders must have realized that they were still not strong enough to take on Moscow's ready-to-wear manufacturers. However, journeymen had been much more successful in Petersburg in their battle with bespoke manufacturing. In order to keep the garment workers' movement alive, they needed to strike where they had a chance of success.

Shortly after the meeting, perhaps as a preparation for the planned general strike, there were a series of strikes organized with the help of the UWT against some of Petersburg's prominent establishments – Kalina, Ganri, and Tedeski – the same firms that had been targets in 1905. Kalina was sufficiently concerned that he called in the police who arrested the strikers. Only Tedeski agreed

to workers' demands in full, but those concessions gave union leaders hope that they could soon organize a much bigger protest that would benefit all garment workers in the city.[79]

By 1912 the Russian economy had pulled out of recession and began to grow again. According to one journeyman, the demand for clothing was livelier than it had ever been. Just as the economy was beginning to take off, however, the Russian government in April 1912 fired upon a group of protesting workers in the gold fields of Siberia. The Lena Gold Fields Massacre served as a bitter reminder to all workers of how little their government valued them and the work they performed. This tragedy galvanized workers' organizations all across Russia including garment workers. Journeymen in Petersburg organized 14 strikes with 278 participants in the fall of 1912.[80]

During the winter of 1912–13 Petersburg journeymen began to prepare for their general strike against bespoke manufacturing. Union officials decided that they would not simply ask for higher wages but for an actual change in the wage structure. Although piece rates in Petersburg had risen by 25 to 30 percent since 1906, prices for the basic necessities of life had also increased, preventing much improvement in needleworkers' standard of living. Journeymen especially resented piece rates with their emphasis on quantity, not quality. Instead, Petersburg garment workers proposed to replace piece rates with hourly or monthly wages – "the American system," as it was sometimes called. This would allow journeymen to produce well-sewn garments that displayed mastery of their craft. The same pride in their craft that had motivated Moscow workers in 1906 now underlay in 1913 the central demand of Petersburg journeymen – to replace piece rates.

At the same time that the journeymen and the UWT were preparing for a general strike in the spring season, the owners of Petersburg's bespoke establishments were making their own arrangements. These men had formed a union in 1907, the Society of Tailoring Shop Owners (STSO), to defend themselves against their employees, just at the moment when the needleworkers' movement had collapsed. As a result the STSO remained moribund, but it had never officially disbanded. With the economic revival in 1912, it began to meet again. On 11 February

125  A member of the Petersburg journeymen's union in 1913. This individual has abandoned all forms of peasant and working-class dress. He wears the uniform of bourgeois respectability – three-piece suit, boater, cane, and leather shoes. Central State Archive for Documentary Films, Photographs, and Sound Recordings in St. Petersburg.

1913 an article entitled "The Tailors' Union against Clients" appeared in *Stock Exchange News*. According to the article, it had long been "chic" for Petersburg's "golden youth" not only to purchase clothing from an excellent tailor but to refuse to pay the bill. Having grown weary of this practice, the STSO decided to act. The first proposal was to create a blacklist of recalcitrant clients. Some artisans argued that this measure would be too demoralizing for their customers, so the union agreed to hire two lawyers to help them determine what means they could use to receive prompt payment for their services.[81]

It is not hard to see that this notice would have encouraged Petersburg journeymen in their attempts to organize a general strike. The usual response of store owners to strike demands was to claim that they did not have the money to implement whatever changes their employees wanted. With a booming economy, a growing demand for clothing, and prompt payment for services, the owners could no longer argue that they too were short of money.

The general strike in Petersburg began incrementally so as not to alert the owners as to the workers' real intent. On 3 March 1913, thirty-five workers at a military uniform workshop went out on strike for higher wages. The strike lasted four days and on the fifth the owner capitulated. On 16 March, four workers went on strike against the dressmaker Vasil'eva. Soon workers went on strike at other firms – Tedeski, Lidval', Novotny. During the strike against Fal'strem, workers demanded an end to sweating and the introduction of "the American system."[82]

At this point the position of both sides hardened. The STSO met and refused to accede to workers' demands, even though their losses due to the strikes were beginning to mount. In response, the UWT also convened its membership. Rather than negotiate with each individual owner, workers authorized the union to present their demands to the STSO. In their official set of demands, UWT officials insisted upon a number of changes: the end of sweating and piece rates; the introduction of daily and monthly wages; the approval of all individual strike demands that had not been resolved since March; and finally the appointment of a UWT delegate for each workshop. The membership agreed to call a general strike to begin on 23 April. To help coordinate activities in the workshops, the UWT set up a strike committee. Thus, the 1913 general strike had two main goals: the end of sweating and piece rates, and the establishment of collective bargaining as the standard for labor negotiations in the garment trades. With the introduction of collective bargaining, Petersburg journeymen added another feature to their radical restructuring of the artisanal workshop.[83]

As the strike deadline loomed and tensions mounted between owners and workers, a tragic event occurred. On the afternoon of 22 April, thirty-two-year-old Ivan Izmailov shot nineteen-year-old Anna Smelkova with his hunting rifle at point-blank range. While murders were not uncommon in Petersburg, this one caused a sensation. Smelkova was a journeywoman working for Izmailov's wife, a dressmaker, and the murder occurred in his wife's garret workshop in the Rozhdestvenskaia neighborhood. The investigation into the murder revealed that Smelkova was the oldest daughter of a printer. Her father had apprenticed her to Izmailova so that she would always be able to support herself. Unfortunately for Anna, her employer's husband, a former manservant, became attracted to her. Her co-workers told reporters that he began to grope and fondle Anna at the workshop. While resisting Izmailov's advances as best she could, Anna kept quiet. Frightened by what was

happening, on the advice of her friends, she told everyone at the workshop that she was engaged and even wore an engagement ring. This news further inflamed Izmailov. One day he cornered Anna and a friend in the workshop, and said, "You know, my beauties, I have loved many, but they have been fleeting. . . . I even laughed when people said that it is possible to love a woman to death. . . . But now I believe. And if such a woman would resist me – all the same I would kill, cut, and smother [her]!" On Holy Saturday, 13 April 1913, Anna went home to her parents and told them what was going on. For four days, her father forbade her return to the workshop. At that point, the dressmaker Izmailova telephoned Smelkov, insisting that he allow Anna, her best worker, to return to the workshop. She promised

126   A cartoon that appeared during the 1913 strike following the murder of Anna Smelkova. The gentleman is the head of the guild, presumably A. I. Tkachenko who says, "Don't come to us with your complaints!" In Madame Sina's shop the owner upbraids her young employees and pulls their hair while yelling at them. In Madame Nina's shop, the owner's husband molests a young girl while his wife looks on smiling. In Madame Lina's shop the owner's husband shoots a young woman worker dead. *Peterburgskaia gazeta*, (27 April 1913), 3.

Въ мастерскихъ модныхъ нарядовъ

M-me Sina        M-me Nina,        M-me Lina

ЦЕХОВОЙ СТАРШИНА: — Къ намъ жалобъ не поступаетъ!!

Smelkov that nothing untoward was going on. Five days later Anna was dead.[84]

A popular daily newspaper, *Petersburg Gazette*, provided extensive coverage of the murder, coming as it did after a month of labor unrest and at the beginning of the general strike. One reporter sought out the head of the tailors' guild, A. I. Tkachenko, for his reaction to the crime. Tkachenko stated that there were few legal measures the guild could take in this case, but it was possible for garment workers to file an official complaint with the guild. Tkachenko did acknowledge that complaints from apprentices and journeymen, "revealing the secrets of their workshops," were rare.[85] In fact, groups of women needleworkers wrote to *Petersburg Gazette*, thanking the paper for publicizing the horrors occurring in dressmaking workshops. The same article called for the creation of an artisanal workshop inspectorate, similar to the one for factories, which could prevent such situations in the future.[86]

Nikolai Breshko-Breshkovskii wrote the most sensationalist piece for the newspaper, which he entitled "White Negroes in Dressmakers' Shops." He described the desperate conditions in the workshops. The women worked hard, "losing their sight and wasting away" in the process. But because "they ate [their masters'] bread," owners had complete control over their workers. "And if they take their labor, time, and the best years of their lives, why not take their honor, innocence, and youth?" What made the situation at Izmailova's workshop worse was that the other workers knew what was going on and did nothing to stop the harassment because they too "ate their master's bread." He called these young women "white Negroes," declaring "Has there not been an eternal war between planters and white Negroes? A loud shot has been heard. All of Petersburg has heard it."[87]

Breshko-Breshkovskii's use of racial and sexual imagery suggests how the newspaper and presumably its readers interpreted Smelkova's murder. His commentary on the "eternal war between planters and white Negroes" and "eating their master's bread" recalls socialist rhetoric, the language of class struggle found in Marxist tracts. Although garment workers were not legally slaves, they were still "owned" by their masters who controlled all aspects of their lives, a constant complaint among the workers. Thus, the eternal war between master and slave was not meant to invoke the American Civil War or other slave revolts as much as it was a veiled reference to the war between haves and have nots, between capital and labor. And the shot fired at the innocent Smelkova was a call for revolt against such an exploitative system.

Bresho-Breshkovskii's evocation of slavery had another meaning as well. During the nineteenth and early twentieth centuries there were constant worries expressed in Europe and America that young women were being handed over to brothels where they were forced into prostitution. These unfortunate young women were called "white slaves."[88] Here, Smelkova's story illustrates the fears that many Russians had for young women who worked in the cities. Removed from the protection of her parents, Smelkova found herself subjected to unwanted sexual advances. In her case, Anna was not harassed by her employer, but by her employer's husband who technically had no power over his wife's employees. Nevertheless, in the cramped quarters of a sewing workshop, there was no clear boundary between the workplace and living quarters, making it easy for Izmailov to prowl the crowded workshop looking for victims. Given the close quarters, it is hard to imagine that Izmailova did not know about her husband's harassment of Anna, but either she turned a blind eye to his desires or acted as a pimp for his uncontrolled sexual appetites. By describing the sexual dimensions of the crime in great detail, Breshko-Breshkovskii's article was a reminder to everyone of the dangers that awaited young, unattached females as they entered the workforce. One way or the other, their masters would enslave them.

At the same time that the press was covering the Smelkova murder, reports about the general strike began to appear. On 24 April, four hundred workers were on strike against twenty-nine firms.[89] On 26 April, the owners attempted to explain their situation to the Petersburg public. They claimed that their workers received on average sixty to eighty rubles a month for a ten-hour workday, but during the busy months of the fall and spring season wages increased to 100 to 120 rubles. Furthermore, the owners claimed that they had voluntarily raised wages "not long ago." And while it was true that owners could raise wages again, it was consumers who would end up paying for this. The owners were quoted as saying, "Of course, the public partly suffers, but what is to be done?" The journalist concluded his report with this very revealing comment from the owners: ". . . about three years ago there was a strike of a similar nature, but then the owners of the workshops had their own way and gained the upper hand. In this strike the owner's union will firmly defend its rights." As this article reveals, the owners were trying to gain public support for their unwillingness to give in to workers' demands. The rules of the marketplace decreed that higher wages meant higher costs for custom-made clothing. In a not so subtle threat, owners were clearly warning their customers that any financial improvement in workers' wages would come out of their pockets. Furthermore, tailors wanted to protect themselves from what they saw as demands of an increasingly "dictatorial nature." They expressed concern that workers would not just strike every season, but every month. To forestall this kind of labor unrest, private negotiations between master and journeyman were no longer acceptable. To help them defend their interests and authority, owners too would negotiate only through their union.[90]

The owners were sorely disappointed if they thought that this plea to consumers and an assertion of their rights would discourage garment workers. On 27 April an article in *Petersburg Gazette* appeared with a large headline reading: "Tailors Strike! The majority of journeymen at the best shops and stores have struck. Petersburgers are without summer clothes. The owners' union black list." The reporter revealed that tailors' shops were only able to fill a third of their orders because of the strike. In an interview with the head of the guild, Tkachenko once again claimed that Petersburg journeymen were very well paid and predicted that the strike would last only five to ten days. Claiming that only a minority of Petersburg's needleworkers refused to work, Tkachenko announced that owners were sending their orders to firms that were not involved in the work stoppage, and the strikers had been blacklisted. Next to this article was a cartoon entitled "In a Fashionable Workshop," which retold the story of Anna Smelkova's murder. Underneath the drawings there was a caption: "Head of guild: We don't get complaints!!"[91]

In the glare of all this publicity, the garment workers continued their struggle against the owners. On 29 April in an article entitled "Women are without their summer clothes!," a reporter revealed that some owners had brought in strikebreakers. In fact, the tailor, Leopold Kalina, had imported ten workers from Austria to work during the strike. They turned out to be very poor craftsmen who spoiled the garments. And yet, Kalina not only had to pay them high wages but he also had to send them back to their native land at company expense. As one worker commented, it cost Kalina more to pay the strikebreakers than it would have to accede to workers' demands.[92] Terrified of losing customers, the STSO issued an appeal. They asked their clients to delay placing new orders so that there would not be any "unnecessary price increases." Nevertheless, some shop owners had already doubled prices for alterations and other services. When asked whether the owners would be willing to negotiate with the workers, a member of the artisanal administration replied, "Never! An owner has a private agreement with a journeyman. Owners regulate the prices for work."[93]

That same evening seventy members of the STSO met to discuss the situation. After passing a resolution refusing to consider any improvements, the owners discussed the introduction of hourly wages and abolishing piece rates. When the meeting broke up at 4 am, no agreement had been reached. The workers' response was swift and unequivocal. The next day every sewing workshop in the city was on strike, including subcontractors and even home workers. One owner complained bitterly, "Imagine, I have journeymen who did not have any economic demands, but announced that they were striking only in solidarity!" Coat manufacturers simply had to stop taking any new orders.[94] On 1 May, striking garment workers joined other workers to celebrate the socialist holiday. Over 110,000 men and women went on strike on that day, of which almost 10,000 worked in subcontracting shops.[95]

The owners now became desperate to end the strike using whatever means they had available. On 4 May they introduced new piece rates "to pacify our journeymen," and one newspaper even declared that the strike was almost over.[96] The battle continued, however. Having discovered the identities of the UWT strike committee, the owners handed that information over to the police who promptly arrested the union members on 6 May.

The police also conducted a search where they found a list of striking workers.[97] The UWT held a meeting of its membership and demanded the release of their co-workers. The strike committee was released the next day. On 9 May the strike continued at sixty-seven firms, with almost nine hundred workers on strike. That evening a huge meeting of needleworkers demanded that the owners immediately abolish piece rates, giving them a deadline of 12 May to reply.[98] The owners replied by calling for a lockout against striking workers.[99]

A few days later *Petersburg Gazette* ran a cartoon with a man in a bowler hat grabbing a man in a top hat and cane by his coat. The caption read:

Tailor: Ah, Pimenov, finally I caught you! Don't you want to pay off your old debts?
Dandy: Uh, uh. . . . I am in solidarity with your workers and . . . I'm on strike.[100]

As with all good caricatures, this one pulled together the entire history of the general strike. What had begun as an attempt by tailors to get their customers to pay their bills promptly had erupted into three months of labor unrest, affecting not just masters and journeymen but consumers as well. And as the cartoon slyly suggested, consumers were supporting the workers, not the tailors whom the newspaper had gone to great lengths to portray as unfeeling, morally corrupt exploiters.

By the middle of May both sides were exhausted. Owners and their employees met on 22 May and came to an agreement to end the strike. The owners refused to abolish piece rates but agreed to hire back the striking workers.[101] A few days later strike committee members were rearrested and exiled from the city. Perhaps in retaliation, on the night of 27 May, thieves broke into the Viennese Chic clothing store located on the corner of Nevskii Prospekt and Sadovaia in the very heart of Petersburg. They smashed display cases and shelves, and broke into a cash register removing a few hundred rubles in cash. They stole thousands of rubles-worth of goods and destroyed the merchandise that they left behind. After an extensive search of the railroad stations, the police found the stolen goods at the Nikolaevskii Station, but not the thieves.[102] At the firms where the trouble began – Fal'strem, Kalina, and Lidval' – the strike continued until July. One participant calculated that the average worker lost sixty-eight rubles in wages. For owners, the losses were very heavy, over 54,000 rubles.[103]

The Petersburg General Strike indicates the complex position that garment workers occupied in 1913. On the one hand, the strike was an enormous success. The garment workers had demonstrated their ability to organize and sustain a prolonged strike. In late April and early May the strike affected every sewing workshop in the city. Owners simply could not portray the unrest as the work of a few malcontents. Instead, after Anna Smelkova's murder, the local press publicized the horrors of garment workers' lives, so that all city residents knew what was going on and why, thereby creating bad publicity for the owners. In addition to gaining public support through the press, needleworkers demonstrated an incredible degree of solidarity during the strike. Garment workers from all over Russia and even some from Paris had sent money to help their Petersburg comrades. This show of strength and solidarity clearly startled their employers, who continually underestimated their employees' determination.

As impressive as this show of strength was, the owners did not accept attempts by workers radically to revise conditions in the workplace. The owners categorically rejected the demands for collective bargaining, and the end of sweating and piece rates. The most the owners' union offered the strikers was the return of their jobs. Paradoxically, after the official end of the strike in late May, both sides entered into a period of intense private contract negotiations, the one element that both sides had so vociferously rejected during the early days of the strike. Some shop owners withdrew from their union, so that they would be free to negotiate their own terms with their employees rather than abide by what their union dictated. They may also have been afraid that union membership would make them a target in future strikes. Many other owners attempted to restore good relations with their employees and avert any further problems by voluntarily raising piece rates and improving material conditions in the workshops.[104] For their part, striking workers seemed to understand that their dreams of a reformed artisanal workshop would take time and further effort.

After a fall season with only a handful of strikes, garment workers renewed their battle with employers in January 1914. According to one participant, the spring of 1914 resembled the strike movement of 1905, with work stoppages occurring all across Petersburg. This time workers in the smaller and less prestigious workshops also participated in the labor unrest. Journeymen joined other artisans and factory workers in Petersburg during the first half of 1914 in yet another wave of strikes and protests. On 1 May 1914 more than five thousand needleworkers participated in the May Day celebrations. These strikes once again took a financial toll on their employers, forcing them to work through the summer months.[105] Moscow, too, saw its share of garment workers' strikes in 1913 and 1914, but there was nothing comparable to the events in Petersburg. Wherever the strikes occurred, workers focused on the same fundamental demands: the abolition of sweating and piece rates, an eight-hour work day, and safer workshops.[106] They aspired to create a working environment where mutual respect existed between labor and management, and where quality craftsmanship was the standard for excellence. It was these hopes that lay at the heart of the garment workers' strikes. As workers grew more practiced in labor agitation tactics, they became increasingly determined to see their dream of a new workplace become a reality.

127  "A Panorama of Spring Fashions," from a Moscow magazine during World War I. The caption reads: "Elegant costumes for male officials – the latest fashions for theater and walks along Kuznetskii Bridge." V. Ruga and A Kokorev, *Voina i moskvichi: Ocherki gorodskogo byta, 1914–1917* gg., 304.

# The War on Fashion

IN THE SUMMER OF 1914, long-simmering inter-national tensions exploded into violence as Serbia, Russia, England, France, and Belgium, united to fight against Austria-Hungary, Germany, and the Ottoman Empire. "The war to end all wars," as World War I became known, it shattered the European status quo with four long years of brutality, economic dislocation, and political turmoil. With the call for a general mobilization on 18 July 1914, Nicholas II led his empire into a conflict for which it was ill prepared. Between 1914 and 1917, millions of Russians died at the front while their families suffered from the serious economic dislocations that combat placed upon the Russian economy. With no real leadership at the front or at court, the unresolved issues from the 1905 Revolution burst forth once again with renewed intensity.

At the same time that Russian soldiers were fighting against the armies of Germany and Austria-Hungary, another war was also occurring – a war against fashion. This war had two fronts. First, the cultural debates between the nationalists and the modernists discussed in chapter 6 did not remain confined to artistic and court circles, but reverberated in popular culture. A multi-faceted discussion of fashion and its place in Russian society emerged following the 1905 Revolution and continued through World War I. In an age of intense nationalist feeling, how were modern Russian men and women to dress? Nikolai Grech's question posed during the Crimean War emerged again with renewed intensity: Could a French corset stifle a Russian heart?

A second front in the war on fashion developed in the commercial sphere. The trade disruptions that World War I generated made Russia's prewar economic relationships difficult to sustain. The demand for war materiel placed a huge burden on a growing but fragile economy. But the Russian government and business leaders made the situation worse by declaring an economic war that targeted German, Austrian, and Turkish businesses oper-ating within the Russian Empire. This economic war had a profound effect on the Russian fashion industry. At issue was who was going to lead the industry in the twentieth century. Were foreigners going to continue to shape the fashion industry in their own image, or were Russians finally going to assume control over it? Now more than ever, the questions raised by Peter the Great's dress revolution over two hundred years earlier demanded resolution.

## FASHION AND ITS CRITICS

For those in Russia on the political Left, their attitude toward fashion was clear. An individual's resources should be used for the betterment of society and should not be squandered on fashion. The duty of those radicals who came from the monied elite was to set an example for others to follow. Ever since the nihilist revolt of the 1850s, members of the radical intelligentsia had refused to follow fashion's dictates and so created their own anti-fashion statements. Their hope was that by abandoning

fashionable dress – a class barrier – they could forge closer links with workers and peasants, and encourage them to reject fashion as well.

Because so much pressure was placed upon women to follow fashion's dictates, Russian feminists became the most outspoken critics, enlisting other arguments to provide a more sweeping critique of fashion. One approach they used was to draw on scientific discourse to discourage women from wearing clothing that harmed their bodies. While dress reform had been much discussed in Europe and America at mid-century, it received renewed publicity in 1881 with the founding of the Rational Dress Society in England. Members of the society attacked the wearing of corsets and the use of chemical dyes. They believed that these products interfered with the normal development of the female body.[1]

In Russia, M. M. Volkova founded the Society for the Protection of Women's Health and made dress reform one of the organization's goals. In 1899, she published a book outlining her views on the deleterious effects of fashion on women's lives. After presenting the usual arguments against high fashion, she observed that Muscovite aristocratic dress was more hygienic than contemporary garments. However, as a feminist, Volkova could not recommend clothing associated with Russian patriarchialism. Instead, she believed that Russian women needed a modern approach to dress, one that obeyed the "general laws of hygiene."[2] A few years later, in January 1905, an anonymous physician furthered this line of argument in an article in the new feminist journal, *Women's Herald* (*Zhenskii vestnik*). The doctor expressed concern about women's skirts, arguing that they were unhealthy. Long skirts dragged on the ground, bringing all kinds of dangerous microbes into the home. This bacterial invasion endangered not just the women who wore the skirts but their families as well. According to the physician, the new trend for shorter skirts worn with high-heeled shoes was not any better. Scientific evidence demonstrated that high heels endangered women by placing abnormal pressures on their skeletons and internal organs.[3]

Feminists also employed moral and philosophical arguments in their appeals to women to reconsider their relationship to their clothing. In an article entitled "Woman and Fashion," M. Novikova wrote:

When a woman's life changes, widening her sphere of participation, and [when] her influence on her surroundings takes on a different character, we think that she will not have time to worry about the fashion for "scalloped edges," nor will she want to adapt to other's demands. She will follow her own taste. Woman, we hope, will understand that each person must respect not only their own spiritual "I," but also their physical self. And if, with time, an aesthetic sensibility begins to penetrate further into people's lives, the need for the beautiful, in the widest and most serious sense of the word, will ennoble the human personality, creating physical and spiritual harmony. And then the yearning for beauty . . . will be dictated by individual motives and not the unnatural tastes of the masses.[4]

According to Novikova, women should seek to integrate physical and spiritual beauty in their lives in order to become fully human. This quest should not involve the search for the latest fashions. Rather it should entail widening women's participation in life. No longer slaves to "the unnatural tastes of the masses," women should be free to discover their own individual sense of self, which could find physical expression in their choice of garments but must not be limited to that alone. For reformers like Novikova, a woman's style of dress should reflect not just her sense of hygiene or her financial resources but also her profound expression of individual identity. Clothing choices marked another step along the road to modernity, reflecting women's individuality and their true sense of self, unencumbered by society's views of what their nature should be or how they should look.

Dress reform and the feminist call for women's self-realization created an inevitable backlash that became an important, if overlooked, component in the emergence of Russian conservatism and right-wing politics. Most historians agree that Russian conservatism developed very slowly because of its complex relationship with the government. After all, the Russian autocracy by its very nature embodied many of the principles that conservatives held dear. There was no need for the representative bodies that liberals and radicals continued to clamor for – the tsar alone represented the will of the Russian people. And yet, as Hans Rogger has observed, there existed "individuals or small groups convinced that there

129  Two young women in July 1914. The woman on the left is wearing a simple blouse and skirt that dress reformers advocated. This woman's only adornment is a pair of small earrings. Private collection.

were better and more imaginative answers than those given by the government . . . to the threat of liberal reform, democratic aspirations, or revolutionary upheaval."[5]

The first officially sanctioned conservative organization to form was the Russian Assembly, a group of intellectuals, bureaucrats, and landowners. Established in 1900 in St. Petersburg, its purpose was to stop "the spreading cosmopolitanism of the upper strata of Russian society." To that end, their chief activity was to acquaint Russians with their cultural heritage. The Assembly organized lectures, dramatic readings, and recitals.[6] Moreover, dress, that quintessential sign of cosmopolitanism, played a key role in the Assembly's activities. According to its charter, ". . . [R]ussian dress, bringing artistic taste to our modern times, must be worn first at the holiday celebrations of the Assembly and then spread to everyday life."[7]

The role of dress in the Russian Assembly reveals how entwined the notions of personal and national identity had become for some Russians in the late imperial period. The cultural nationalism of many artists coupled with the imperial court's own sartorial politics encouraged conservative nationalists to use dress as a weapon in their war with those who would transform Russia. Like the Slavophiles, members of the Russian Assembly rejected European fashion as cosmopolitan, masking their true identity as Russians. And yet, how could modern Russians who lived in a world of automobiles and bicycles comfortably wear seventeenth-century Muscovite robes? It was one thing to wear their ancestral garments to balls and other social occasions, but it was quite another matter to drag these cumbersome robes and headdresses onto the stock exchange or government offices. This was the conundrum that the Russian Right had to resolve.

When Tsar Nicholas II made known that he was considering the establishment of a legislative body in February 1905, the Right finally entered the political fray to save the government from its own mistakes. The Russian Assembly became more politicized, and a number of other right-wing groups emerged. The most notorious was the virulently anti-Semitic Union of the Russian People (URP) founded in October 1905. Unlike the Assembly, the URP expanded its base of support beyond the aristocracy and the bureaucracy to include professionals and those involved in commerce. It also attempted to recruit workers and peasants with promises of easy credit, improved working conditions, and land resettlement. While it is unclear how successful these membership drives were, the URP garnered a great deal of publicity through its participation in violent street demonstrations and pogroms.[8]

Despite political differences between the Russian Assembly and the URP, they collaborated in a number of ways during and after the 1905 Revolution. One such effort was the creation of a women's auxiliary, the Union of Russian Women (URW), in November 1907. Earlier in

the year, four female members of the Russian Assembly approached its chairman, Prince M. L. Shakhovskoi, with their idea of setting up a new union whose purpose was "the unification of all Russian women in the area of social and economic life." As was true for other right-wing organizations, Jewish women were the only group not permitted to join.[9] With Shakhovskoi's support, the organizers received a government charter and established their headquarters in Petersburg. The Empress Alexandra became the patron of the URW.

In order to achieve their goal of female solidarity, the founders of the Union of Russian Women created an ambitious, multi-layered program for their organization that reflected the enormous complexity and diversity of Russian women's lives at the beginning of the twentieth century. First, they wanted to establish workshops, cafeterias, stores, and manufacturing enterprises as well as theaters, schools, libraries, and reading rooms. Second, they wanted to create charitable organizations such as day-care centers and shelters for the homeless. Third, the founders hoped to publish newspapers, magazines, books, and brochures as well as to present lectures, readings, and concerts. Finally, the URW wanted to create a mutual-aid society, a credit union for its members, and to build a church. In order to raise money to finance these projects, the founders would rely upon annual membership dues of fifty kopecks, a percentage of the sales from the union's retail outlets, and profits from its various cultural gatherings.[10]

After such a bold beginning, the Union of Russian Women quickly floundered. The annual dues were not enough to fund the projects that the organization had envisioned. In November 1910 the head of the URW and one of its founders, A. P. Chebysheva, resigned her post due to illness. In her place the membership elected Maria Nikolaevna Ditrikh, a writer, who had been born Countess de Rochefort.

Ditrikh wanted to revitalize the URW, but in doing so she altered the nature of the organization. In 1912 she submitted a new charter for government approval. This document offered a radically different view of the organization and demonstrates how the Right had evolved in the years since the 1905 Revolution. The new purpose of the URW was "the maintenance and understanding of the beauty of the national spirit." The charter went on to

130 A party given by the Union of Russian Women. The participants are wearing different forms of national dress. Central State Archive for Documentary Films, Photographs, and Sound Recordings in St. Petersburg.

say that because women's main vocation in life was to raise the next generation of "faithful sons of the Fatherland," Russian women should encourage the "development of knowledge of the Motherland" in their sons. Lest women of the URW felt empowered by such a noble mission, the new regulations made clear how women were supposed to accomplish the task laid out in front of them: ". . . members of the URW, nevertheless, must remain apolitical, considering any active participation in the political arena incompatible with the high ideal of womanhood." Russian women should try "to find for the construction of their beliefs in life, a more beautiful form, closer to their nature."[11]

With political participation deemed unfeminine, the URW decided to pursue more beautiful endeavors, and, not surprisingly, they involved clothing. The outbreak of the First Balkan War in 1912 between the Balkan League (Bulgaria, Serbia, Greece, and Montenegro) and Turkey encouraged many Russian patriots to send aid to their fellow Slavs. Members of the URW, a significant number of countesses and baronesses among them, gathered together at Ditrikh's apartment in Petersburg to sew clothing for the war victims. In one month, they raised over 1,000 rubles to purchase the fabric necessary to make the warm coats, socks, and blankets that they sent to the Balkans. In 1913 the URW received permission to build a school for young girls in St. Petersburg province, in order to teach them traditional handicrafts which they would then sell in kiosks located throughout the capital. Through these endeavors, the URW heralded sewing as both a patriotic and feminine act.[12]

Sewing clothing for war victims did not address the larger mission of the URW to increase "knowledge of the Motherland." To that end, in 1912 the organization began a series of "evenings of our native land" at bazaars selling Russian arts and crafts. A number of members wore Russian national dress which they had made themselves for these events. Their purpose was "to revitalize Russian costume, to adapt it to modern requirements, and to give it a wide distribution." To modernize native dress, these women chose dark colors for their gowns and light-weight headdresses. The women who wore the gowns stated that they looked and felt completely Russian. However, there was nothing particularly original in attempts by the URW to modernize Russian dress. Ever since the late eighteenth century, court dress for women was intended to represent an amalgam of European and Russian design vocabularies. What the URW had in mind was that women should wear modernized Russian dress not just at court but in all of their daily activities.[13]

In the winter of 1914 the Union of Russian Women received support for their work with the publication of a new book. As we saw in chapter 5, Iulii Elets' book, *Epidemic Insanity: Toward the Overthrow of the Yoke of Fashion*, sought to medicalize the discourse on shopping and connect it with his theory of social degeneration. In his introduction, Elets declared his intention:

> This book about the most burning and painful question in modern social and family life appears as a sincere howl of despair about how women disfigure themselves with ugly and absurd fashions, how they extort countless sums of money, how debauchery and disintegration are introduced into the family by constant yearnings for the newest fashionable nonsense,

how colorful rags cultivate emptiness in women's minds and hearts, how many crimes are committed because of the mindless laws of fashion, and how many people perish because of them!![14]

Declaring "war on the entire beautiful sex," Elets argued that the vast array of Russia's social ills – adultery, divorce, debauchery, prostitution, child neglect – could be blamed on women's obsession with fashion. As evidence for his views, Elets combined pithy quotations from western philosophers, personal anecdotes of Petersburg high society, and the language of the biological sciences. Accordingly, the purpose of the female of the species (*samka*) was to attract the male for reproductive purposes. Women's "nature" evolved with an emphasis upon physical attraction, but this evolution had led to debauchery, "the step-sister of fashion." In Elets' scenario, women's desire to attract men became so strong that they were not content with just the admiration of their husbands, but became obsessed with attracting other males as well. This led to a ceaseless search for the perfect outfit so that women could remain attractive to all males. "[Woman] spends [money] without purpose, spends it because it is in her nature, as it is a bird's nature to sing."[15] Russian women tortured their hapless husbands into spending far more money than they had to keep them and their daughters dressed in the latest fashions. The women repaid their husbands' generosity by neglecting their children and household obligations to gad about town, flirt, and commit adultery. Furthermore, Elets saw little difference among women:

> Neither poverty, nor wealth, nor social position influence women's coquetry. All women – both millionaires and workers – express themselves in almost identical ways. The poor seamstress who is preparing to eat stale bread . . . to save money for a flower or ribbons for her hat is no different in her soul from rich and distinguished women who decorate themselves with precious stones and pearls.[16]

Women's selfishness and subsequent vicious corruption led directly to the breakdown of family. Their brains had no place for anything except thoughts of themselves and how they looked. Furthermore, women's debauchery did not remain in the home but corrupted the public sphere as well. Elets reported the shameful appearance of beautifully dressed women in Petersburg restaurants and theaters following the Russian naval defeat by the Japanese at Tsushima in 1905. Seeking only individual pleasure, these women had no time to mourn their country's defeat.

Despite his bleak views, Elets had some clear proposals to end the "epidemic insanity." He claimed that fashion lacked logic, based as it was upon women's animal instincts. To provide some badly needed practicality, Elets proposed that clothing should be modest, simple, inexpensive, and mindful of climatic conditions. While Elets praised the nihilists for trying to encourage such clothing, he condemned the feminists of his own day for ignoring nihilism and abandoning family life completely. Not surprisingly, the clothing that met all of his requirements was native Russian dress. Echoing Volkova's earlier claims, Elets argued that Russian dress was easy to make, covered the body, and was suited to both the climate and working conditions of the peasantry. As proof of his solution, Elets naively reported that peasant women were indifferent to fashion. They wore whatever clothes they had and did not fret about what their neighbors were wearing.[17]

Regarding native dress as the proper inoculation against "epidemic insanity," Elets proclaimed, "Women of the world unite and organize national costume leagues."[18] Co-opting Karl Marx's fiery call to revolution, Elets had an equally dramatic agenda in mind, the liberation of all women from the yoke of fashion. The demise of the fashion industry would result in a restoration of morality and goodness to women, their families, and to Russian society as a whole. As proof that his plan would work, Elets pointed to none other than Maria Ditrikh, the president of the Union of Russian Women. According to Elets, Ditrikh always wore seventeenth-century Russian aristocratic dress, and her motto was that a Russian woman must always remain faithful to her country in her dress.[19]

Elets' book provided a sensationalist and controversial critique of the role of European fashion in Russian life. With its emphasis on vanity and sexual attractiveness, fashion had distorted women's true nature. Russian women were no longer willing to submit to their husbands' authority and to care for their children. Instead,

131   A young woman photographed in Yalta, November 1915, showing her at a beach in a peignoir. Private Collection.

they fought over money and its allocation within the family, went on endless shopping sprees, conducted adulterous affairs, and, most importantly, raised their daughters to follow in their footsteps. The only cure for this epidemic insanity was to return to traditional values and gender roles. For Elets and other Russian conservatives, a European corset did stifle a Russian heart. The only remedy was to remove the corset and don Muscovite dress.

Yet Elets' plan posed its own set of problems. How could the president of the Union of Russian Women, a woman whose maiden name was de Rochefort and whose married name was Ditrikh, consider herself Russian? At the very least, Maria Ditrikh was ethnically only half Russian, but this was clearly the half with which she *chose* to identify. Did simply declaring herself Russian make her so? At a time when ethnic nationalism was on the rise, Ditrikh's complex family history made her suspect in the eyes of some Russian nationalists who saw ethnicity as a birthright, not a choice. Indeed, Ditrikh's ethnic heritage, a European transplanted into Russian soil, was precisely the kind of cosmopolitan whom the nationalists hated. While the resurgence of national dress was an attempt to eliminate the problem of cosmopolitanism in Russia, nevertheless it raised even more troubling questions in a multi-ethnic empire about who was entitled to wear national costume.

*Epidemic Insanity* antagonized a number of people who tried to refute Elets' arguments. The first to comment was E. Likhacheva who wrote a review of his book for *Women's Herald* in 1914. Apparently, Elets sent Likhacheva a copy of the book with the inscription "to the one exception." Unmoved by his flattery, Likhacheva proceeded to challenge Elets' view of women and fashion. She argued that fashion was not a stepsister of debauchery but an art form comparable to a painting or poem whose purpose was to brighten the grayness of human existence. Because women could interpret fashionable dress as other artists did, it allowed them to express the many sides of their individuality rather than present a uniform appearance to the outside world. This individuality would be lost with the reintroduction of native costume. Contrary to Elets' claims of practicality and beauty for traditional dress, Likhacheva believed that it was totally unsuited to modern life, nor did all women look good in

it. Furthermore, she pointed out that the fashion industry was a fundamental feature of Russian economic life, and it employed thousands of men and women in textile factories and sweatshops. If Elets' scheme was adopted, these workers would lose their jobs, furthering the immiseration of the lower classes. Finally, Likhacheva decried Elets' misogyny. His book, she argued, was really about high-society women. Middle- and working-class women were too busy taking care of their families and housework to waste time acquiring fashionable dress. And while she acknowledged that some upper-class women behaved as Elets described, Likhacheva concluded angrily by asking, "Who is going to write the book about epidemic drunkenness and men's depravity, which not only costs large sums of money, but also the health of entire generations?"[20]

In the very next issue of *Women's Herald*, A. Khlebnikova, a strong supporter of women's dress reform, added her voice to this debate about women and fashion. Khlebnikova sent in a poem written in 1865 that had recently been discovered in the archive of a women's high school. The poem called for women to abandon French fashion and devote themselves to improving their native land. In her preface, Khlebnikova reminded her readers, "At that time of enthusiasm among the young and the rise of civic spirit, the very idea of fashion appeared *sinful . . .*" Sadly, fifty years later, Khlebnikova saw fashion's influence everywhere and demanded its liquidation. Russians had become hypnotized, and "such a condition of society – is it not 'an epidemic insanity,' is it not 'a psychiatric epidemic'?" Thus, Khlebnikova agreed with Elets about the tyrannical role that fashion played in women's lives. Nevertheless, she rejected his patriotic call for a return to native dress and traditional gender roles. Instead, she reminded women that a rejection of fashion marked a return to the values of the 1860s when patriotism had included women's emancipation and civic responsibility.[21]

Shortly following these critiques in *Women's Herald*, a new book appeared written by the mysterious Adov. Clearly a pseudonym, Adov entitled the book *Insane Epidemic (Answer to the Book of G. Elets)*, providing a chapter-by-chapter rebuttal of Elets' argument. Adov took fundamental issue with Elets' insistence that fashion must be logical, declaring that "Women's questions need to be examined and decided not logically, but psychologically."[22] According to Adov, "To expect logic from women is ridiculous and funny! 'I cannot not love him' is the best female logic! Nature made woman the tsaritsa of feelings and man the tsar of thought."[23] Despite these differences, Adov claimed that both the male and female of all animal species, including humans, were biologically programmed to seek a partner for reproduction. However, the author went on to state, "A naked woman is not a woman, but the female of her species. Naked, she arouses only erotic feelings rather than aesthetic ones . . . dressed, she arouses in [a man] aesthetic delight which in turn gives him erotic pleasures when undressed."[24] In this view, clothing distinguished humans from other animals by acting as an essential agent of culture and civilization. Furthermore, because of this complex interrelationship between the sexes, Adov argued that men, too, worried about their appearance: "[T]he older the man, the longer he stands in front of the mirror trying to smooth his bald spot . . . and it is possible to find in a side pocket a small mirror and mustache comb – Ah, those mustaches! How many inner thoughts, feelings, and daily worries are concealed in them."[25] Adov concluded that clothing and its relationship to human existence was identical in both genders, making women no more slaves to fashion than men.

Finding Elets' biological and philosophical explanations inadequate, Adov also rejected Elets' call for national costume leagues. Repeating earlier arguments, Adov stated that native dress did not allow for individuality. While it might be patriotic to wear traditional clothing, these garments were not intrinsically more beautiful than European fashions. Adov also believed that women were quite capable of spending just as much money on native dress as they did on high fashion. And since fashion in 1914 was quite self-consciously composed of elements of folk dress from many different countries, how could national costume leagues bring about the end of fashion? The fashion industry had already included folk costume within its design vocabulary, making folk costume part of fashion. In Adov's view, Elets categorically failed to articulate a sensible plan or rationale for why women should give up fashion.

Despite the range of opinions expressed in this debate, there were some common themes. At the heart of this discussion was women's search for individual self-expression. Between 1850 and 1914 an increasing number of Russian women yearned to be more than just wives and mothers. Women from all social classes were taking up positions as teachers, doctors, factory workers, servants, seamstresses, and market sellers. They frequented stores, restaurants, theaters, and sporting venues. Magazines and newspapers gave voice to an incredible range of women's ideas, hopes, and dreams, and politically active women organized clubs to articulate their demands for a better and richer life. Since most of these venues required "city clothes," women's search for the appropriate way to express their individuality, whether it be in charity work, teaching in a school, or working in a factory, necessitated their participation in the fashion industry. Thus, fashion became inextricably linked with women's search for individual satisfaction and happiness, a search that often took women out of the home and away from their families.

At a time when women's bodies were emerging from underneath corsets and heavy fabrics to reveal their natural contours, Russians became increasingly nervous about women's physicality and sexuality. The French corset was indeed stifling the Russian woman's heart, not by suppressing her ethnic identity as Russian conservatives would have it but by not allowing her to embrace her many-sided nature which now included a freer expression of her sexuality. While fashion in the early twentieth century literally liberated women's bodies from corsets and heavy clothing, Elets and the other critics used fashion to contain this emancipatory impulse. Both Elets and Adov referred continually to the biological drive to mate and give birth as the defining feature of women's sexual identity. Since clothing served to attract a mate for reproduction, this gave it unprecedented importance in human society. And yet, the terms "epidemic insanity" or "insane epidemic" suggested that women's biological drives were sick or diseased. At the very least, women behaved irrationally. They could not control their physicality because they were ruled by their hearts, not by their minds as men were. Weak creatures, they gave in to their desires for luxury and lust, and debased themselves in acts of adultery and greed, which in turn shook the foundations of family life and Russian society.

132 A young woman with the androgynous look that Bakst advocated. She is wearing a simple man-tailored blouse with a bow tie and a dark skirt. Private collection.

There was one way out of this "epidemic insanity." If science identified what the problem was, culture would save women and society. Likhacheva and Adov agreed that fashion was an expression of aesthetic values – it tamed intense biological urges by providing a means to express the goodness that resides within the human heart. In the case of Elets and Khlebnikova, their only disagreement was about which culture would provide a cure for fashion. Elets believed that only pre-Petrine Russian culture could serve as an antidote for the ills that modernity had visited upon the Russians, while Khlebnikova argued that the mid-nineteenth-century revolutionary aesthetic could break fashion's spell.

The fashion industry did not remain quiet during this debate. Too much was at stake to allow non-experts to dictate fashion's role in Russian society. To make its case, the industry looked to Lev Bakst, Russia's most influential fashion designer who, as we have seen, had helped revolutionize European *haute couture* with his ballet costumes. In 1914, he wrote two important articles about fashion. The first appeared in a February issue of *Petersburg Gazette* (*Peterburgskaia gazeta*). The pretext for the article was a recent ball to which some society women had worn blue, green, orange, and red hair. Bakst's purpose was to defend these women from their detractors: "Alas, in Russia there still survives a shortsightedness and arrogance which decides everything relating to Fashion and fashionable dress . . ." According to Bakst, new theoretical work on fashion argued that dress was a reflection of current philosophical trends, making the sartorial choices of elegant women vital to understanding any society. Applying this insight to his own country, and taking careful aim at Elets and the Union of Russian Women, he declared, "From this perspective, I find that if there is a genuine ideology, eternally living in the 'Institute of Progress Is Not Necessary,' then dress as its agent must be strictly national – traditional headdresses and sarafans . . ." But, for those who lived in the real world where men and women were struggling for equal rights, fashion dictated other clothing. Bakst prescribed for women's daytime wear sporty, man-tailored outfits that would allow them to travel with ease to work and school. For evening, he preferred colorful feminine clothing: "Modern evening dress will equalize the battle in which the 'evening' woman presents herself to the man, winning him over with her sex's entire arsenal of line and color for the future victory in the battle for equal rights for women."[26]

If Bakst answered his nationalist critics in *Petersburg Gazette*, two months later he further refined his views on fashion and art for *Capital City and Country House* (*Stolitsa i usad'ba*), a magazine dedicated to the good life in Russia. He argued that there were two groups in art, the antiquarians and the futurists. Bakst had no patience with either one, describing himself as "an enthusiastic modernist." He condemned those who revered antiques simply because they were old: "We live in a [nineteenth-century] building among old furniture, upholstered with shabby materials among paintings with a valuable 'patina' or yellowed with age. We look at ourselves in faded, dim mirrors with charming spots and rust where it is possible to examine our disgraceful modern figure, arrayed in an outfit made from an ancient piece of cloth." The contrast between the old furniture and textiles with the modern body repelled the fashion designer. And yet, he was equally scornful of the futurists. ". . . I don't want [to think] that my day was only a small step toward the single, authentic, significant tomorrow."[27] Instead of looking to the past or the future, Bakst wanted art and fashion to reflect the immediate concerns of his life and times.

In these short pieces, Bakst clearly opposed the nationalist agenda of the Russian Right, and became the champion of fashion and women's desire to wear it. Fashion was about living in the moment and expressing that moment in dress. There was no reverence for the past – the past was simply a reference point from which to define the present. Bakst's genius was his ability to translate these abstract principles into beautiful clothing. He believed that all corsets, not just French ones, stifled the heart. The twentieth century, the modern age, demanded a new look which he labeled "the fully emancipated androgyne."[28] To live in the world of the tram and automobile, women needed to be free to move about, and so Bakst liberated them from clothes that bound their bodies and suppressed their heart's desires. In doing so, he became an ally in the women's movement not by espousing suffrage or any other specific political goal, but rather by embracing the male and female aspects of women's personalities, by allowing women to become androgynous. Indeed, the editors of *Stolitsa i usad'ba* found Bakst's modernism so radical that they issued a disclaimer so as not to offend the sensibilities of some of their more conservative readers.[29]

Thus, by the summer of 1914 the cultural debate about fashion that had begun just over two hundred years earlier reached a critical point. Lev Bakst had given women a brand-new look, one that redefined themselves and their bodies. In Bakst's view, women should be free to follow their hearts, equal to men in rights and opportunities. Men by day and women by night, women's clothing should reflect their new life as "emancipated androgynes." Nothing could have been more abhorrent

133   A young couple's wartime portrait. While her husband wears the usual three-piece suit, the woman's dark suit and plain blouse show how many women gave up any kind of ornamentation during World War I. Private collection.

to Russian conservatives like Elets and Ditrikh. They saw their world crumbling before their very eyes. Familiar objects and ways of doing things were giving way to commercial capitalism with its factories, automobiles, and advertising. The only way to stop the collapse of their beloved Russia was to return to the ways of their ancestors, to reverse the Petrine reforms. In demanding that women don Muscovite robes, conservatives believed that women would once again return to their supposedly natural roles as full-time wives and mothers, rarely venturing into the public sphere. In 1914 this battle played itself out in the press and in ballrooms, as women bedecked in Bakst's colorful, Orientalist outfits exchanged incredulous glances with women in Muscovite costume. It must have been a spectacular sight, reflecting as it did the growing polarization and politicization of Russian society.

## THE ECONOMIC WAR

Before another salvo could be fired in the culture wars between conservatives and progressives, World War I intervened. In the first days and weeks after Germany declared war on Russia, life suddenly became more serious and purposeful as all resources were redirected toward the war effort. From July 1914 to 1917, over fifteen million Russian men were called up for military service. Since Russia's enemies were imperial Germany, the Austro-Hungarian Empire, and the Ottoman Turks, her long border with these empires was now closed to the transfer of goods and people. This fact coupled with a naval blockade of the Baltic and Black Sea ports meant that Russia was completely isolated from Great Britain and France, both militarily and economically. Furthermore, Russia simply did not have the railroad stock or network to move domestic goods where they were needed most. The disruption of trade and its concomitant loss of customs revenues was further compounded by the government's decision to prohibit the sale of alcohol for the duration of the war. Because the government had maintained a monopoly on the sale of alcohol, it is estimated that this one decree alone reduced government revenues by over seven hundred million rubles. This staggering loss in revenue coupled with an equally staggering increase in expenditures were not problems that could be easily fixed. Although the government created new taxes and took out loans, these changes failed to stop the economic crisis that was developing. In yet another ill-considered but desperate measure, the government devalued the currency, which only created runaway inflation as prices jumped dramatically and real wages declined.[30]

Against this backdrop of growing economic chaos, the fashion industry had to find a way to do business. There were two immediate problems that needed resolution. With the outbreak of war, fashion had become unfashionable. The cultural debates about fashion resonated in new ways as men and women said their goodbyes, uncertain whether they would ever see each other again. One magazine, *Women's Affair* (*Zhenskoe delo*), briefly renamed its bimonthly fashion column "Instead of Fashion." Writing on the eve of war, fashion columnist "Irma Laurent" declared: "Scarcely any of our readers will be thinking about fashionable dress now when the entire country is anxiously living through events of such historic importance."[31] When the lives of fathers, sons, husbands, and brothers were at stake, women's frustrations over which hat to buy or wear seemed petty indeed.

On a more practical level for those who wanted to think about fashion, Russians were literally cut off from Paris, the source of all fashion news. The French colored fashion plates, lithographs, and advice columns could no longer be sent via Germany to Russian publishers. Without these items, the journalists had no fashion to discuss. On 1 September 1914, Nikolai Alovert, Russia's leading fashion publisher, alerted his readers that the Hanchette Publishing House, his French source for lithographs and colored fashion plates, was no longer going to supply these materials for the duration of the war. To compensate for this devastating loss, Alovert announced that he would use a British company that would send the material through neutral Sweden to Russia.[32] He warned his readers that these new drawings would reflect English taste in fashion, and thereby change the character of the magazine, but he hoped that they would continue to subscribe during these difficult times.[33]

A number of fashion magazines perished during the war years. Many women had to give up their subscriptions as the cost of living rose precipitously. In addition, there was a paper shortage that limited production and prevented magazines from providing those free copies of books and patterns that were popular with subscribers.[34] Magazines able to sustain production were reinvented to account for the new wartime situation. Deprived of their Parisian fashion plates, editors solicited sketches from native artists to use alongside the few French drawings that managed to arrive from Sweden. Not as finely drawn as the earlier plates and lithographs, these Russian illustrations provided enough information for dressmakers and home sewers to use in their work. Publishers also began utilizing photographs, adding an aura of verisimilitude and a modern feel to the magazines.

134 Even mourning could be fashionable. A lovely crape and cashmere mourning dress with kimono sleeves and a veil. *Damskii mir*, no. 11 (November 1913), 29.

135 An elegant coat, with hat and muff, drawn by the fashion illustrator Erte. *Damskii mir*, no. 1 (January 1913), 19.

While these modifications solved some of the technical problems associated with wartime, editors and publishers also addressed the issue of fashion's place in wartime. Advice columns encouraged readers to pay attention to their clothing, hair, and makeup even while dressing modestly and frugally. Bakst's bold colors were out, replaced by somber grays, browns, and blacks. Since there was not as much fashion news from Paris to fill the pages of their magazines, the editors provided subscribers with valuable information on how to economize with limited household resources, patriotic stories to sustain them during difficult times, and information about women's wartime activities in western Europe. An issue of *Fashion World* from 1914 included on its first page an article with instructions on how to sew a soldier's shirt.[35] In this way, publishers tried to provide a support network for Russian women as they strove to survive in increasingly difficult circumstances. Another article that enumerated ways to save money concluded with an appeal to patriotism, "Be thrifty and you will perform a great service to your Motherland, faithful daughter that you have always been."[36] Thus, the fashion magazines reinvented themselves as women's cheerleaders during the war. At a time when many women had to curtail their clothing expenses, the magazines offered them friendly advice, hoping to ensure a faithful readership once the war was over.

Although some of the fashion magazines were able to deal creatively with the challenges presented by the war, the manufacturing sector had a much more difficult time. During the first six months of the war alone, over five million men were drafted into the military, and every single soldier needed uniforms, boots, and bedding. Military hospitals also required bed linen, bandages, and clothing for patients and medical personnel. How were clothing manufacturers to respond to such an enormous rise in demand?

Prior to World War I, the Russian military acquired uniforms from two sources. Some bespoke tailors in Russia's cities specialized in military uniforms, while other tailors were assigned to sew or repair uniforms for entire regiments. As we have already noted in chapter 3, military uniforms were the first ready-to-wear garments. Before 1914, Moscow had two factories producing military uniforms: Karl Til' and Company, and Mandl' and Raits. Unlike the cramped artisanal workshops, these factories employed hundreds of workers under a single roof. There were plenty of sewing machines to increase worker productivity. Furthermore, workers no longer stitched one piece of clothing from beginning to end. Instead, work was subdivided so that each item passed through several workers' hands before completion.[37] In addition, the factories producing military uniforms hired hundreds of home workers and subcontractors to perform many smaller sewing tasks.

Although these factories with the help of military tailors might have produced enough garments for a peacetime army, they could not produce enough uniforms to match the sheer scale of the 1914 mobilization. Initially, the pre-existing uniform manufacturers simply hired on new workers, subcontractors, and home workers to replace those who had been drafted, but soon new enterprises were created. In Moscow alone there were twelve factories, each employing between one hundred and three thousand workers. Ready-to-wear manufacturers like Mandl', Rozentsvaig, and others also responded to the call for military clothing. Since there was a dramatic drop in the demand for men's civilian dress, they shut down their men's ready-to-wear workshops in the Russian countryside and opened military workshops instead.

Outside of industry, philanthropic organizations stepped in as well. The Russian Red Cross and members of the royal family established sewing workshops dedicated to the war effort. In Moscow, Grand Duchess Elizaveta Fedorovna, the widow of the former governor general and sister of the Empress Alexandra, funded a workshop that employed five hundred workers with three hundred sewing machines and eleven thousand home workers. These dedicated workers produced one hundred thousand items per day. At the same time, two war relief agencies, the Union of Zemstvos and the Union of Towns, also became involved in clothing production.

These "distribution centers," whether they were set up by philanthropic organizations or local government officials, were modeled after the subcontracting operations of ready-to-wear manufacturers. Tucked into urban neighborhoods and rural villages, the centers consisted of one room for storing fabric, another for cutting, and a reception room to distribute and collect the finished products. Those in charge distributed pre-cut fabrics to individuals looking for work. Initially, these distribution centers were charged with making shirts, underwear, and bed linen, but eventually they began producing more complicated items such as overcoats and trousers. Between August 1914 and January 1916, approximately 11,500 Moscow residents employed by the Union of Towns produced over twelve million garments. As one tailor remarked, ". . . they distributed [the goods] to anyone with a sewing machine."[38]

The army mobilization had another profound effect on the production of clothing. Of the fifteen million men who served in the Russian Army, a disproportionate number of them were skilled workers and artisans. The government had used the mobilization as an excuse to end the labor unrest that had plagued Russian commercial life since 1912. Indeed, Petersburg was in the midst of a general strike just days before the declaration of war.[39] In the garment trades, the government shut down the labor unions and newspapers, and proceeded to conscript the activists into the army. Instead of fighting their employers, these men found themselves in the trenches staring down the Germans. For those who were not drafted immediately, many lost or left their jobs in bespoke tailoring to work in the production of military uniforms.

The wartime mobilization meant that for the first time women needleworkers were hired en masse, revealing the full impact of the gendering of sewing. By 1914 the Russian government and educated society had expended a great deal of effort to teach all young girls to sew. World War I now called upon Russian women to perform this universal female task for the greater glory of the motherland.[40] Wartime conditions demanded that women serve their country by sewing in the uniform factories, sweatshops, and in their own homes. These goods could then be shipped both to complete strangers and to their loved ones, allowing women to continue to perform their female role of caring for their male relatives despite the great distances. Russian women entered the workforce knowing that they were both doing their patriotic duty and performing women's work, just as their menfolk performed their gender role in fighting and dying for their country.

When these women entered the labor force, however, they were not greeted as valuable and skilled craftswomen but as unskilled or semi-skilled laborers, the universality of their sewing abilities undermining the very notion of skill. Since bespoke tailoring and ready-to-wear manufacturers had long regarded women workers as inferior to male workers, these same attitudes now governed the hiring of female needleworkers. Although

clothing manufacturers received lucrative military contracts, they did not pass the extra money along to their employees. In fact, employers saved money by paying their female replacement workers less than the men who left for the front. As the war dragged on, employers hired more women to work in sweatshops and as home workers, resulting in reduced overhead costs for employers. This had the effect of further lowering women's wages, since they now had to pay for housing and meals that had once been provided by their employers. Thus, World War I marked a decisive turning point in the history of Russian clothing manufacture. Bespoke tailoring never recovered its competitive position vis-à-vis the ready-to-wear industry. The old artisanal world gave way to the sewing machine, the sweatshop, and a "semi-skilled" female workforce. While the journeymen tailors were off fighting the Germans, the battle that they had been waging against the encroachment of ready-to-wear manufacturing was lost.

## THE WAR AGAINST GERMAN DOMINATION

Another equally serious problem complicated Russia's transition to a wartime economy. As the history of the Russian fashion industry so clearly illustrates, foreigners – French, Germans, Austrians, English, and Americans – had provided capital, artisans, and technological and commercial innovations to help create a domestic industry. The fashion industry was not alone, as virtually every Russian industry had benefited from foreign capital and expertise.[41] At various points throughout the nineteenth century, Russian businessmen had sought to influence their government's economic policies to protect them from foreign encroachments. By 1903, however, many industrialists had grown increasingly disillusioned with the government's reluctance to adopt their views.[42] As a result of loosening strictures on public debate and assembly following the 1905 Revolution, a group of like-minded Russian businessmen decided to create an organization that would help them publicize their views. Believing that economic autarky, or complete self-sufficiency, was the panacea for all of Russia's economic ills, the Association of Industry and Trade (AIT), founded in Paris, proposed a three-pronged program to end economic dependence: high tariffs, a reduction in railroad and shipping rates, and support for domestic purchases.[43] To that end, the organization realized that it needed to conduct a "buy Russian" campaign. As one of the founders of the AIT, Adolf Volskii, remarked:

> Russian society views its own affairs, including the products of domestic industry, with a surprising kind of mistrust and even contempt. Of two objects that are completely identical in price and quality, our society prefers the one that carries a foreign label. . . . Obviously, it is necessary systematically to influence our public opinion with the aim of developing in the population a healthy and patriotic attitude toward native work.[44]

Although the AIT remained opposed to all foreign influence on Russian economic life, the Germans were the chief target of the organization's enmity. By 1900, imperial Germany had become Russia's primary importer and also the principal market for its exports. According to Ruth Roosa, the AIT believed that an 1894 treaty had fixed Russia "in its traditional colonial role as a backward country providing German industry with cheap food, fodder, and raw materials as well as a market for its products."[45] Although this viewpoint did not accurately reflect Russia's complex economic relationship with Germany, the AIT found enthusiastic support for its anti-German views from the venerable Moscow Merchant Society. The society set up a special commission which sent questionnaires to all parts of the Russian Empire asking detailed questions about the role of foreigners in the economy. Based on an analysis of the responses, the commission concluded that the reasons for the popularity of German and Austrian goods were the high quality of the merchandise, competitive prices, and the commercial infrastructure of their firms, which emphasized the use of mail-order catalogues and advertising in Russian.[46]

As tensions among the European powers increased, the AIT, the Moscow Merchant Society, and other business leaders became increasingly concerned about Russia's dependence on German trade. How could Russia sustain itself economically if war with Germany became a reality? As one AIT member commented, "The first rule of a well-organized military program must be the manufacture of all necessary equipment and all military supplies in one's own country."[47] At the very least, an economic war appeared to be a sure way to free Russians of their colonial oppressors.

Given the increasing hostility toward German subjects doing business in Russia, it should not come as a surprise that a Russian military uniform factory became one of the first victims of the campaign against German domination. On 3 May 1914, the firm of Mandl' and Raits, a company with stock valued at 2,800,000 rubles, held a general shareholders' meeting. Present at the meeting was the company's board of directors: Lev Raits, Lev Lur'e, and Ludwig Mandl', directors of the company; their wives; Victor Mandl', Ludwig's son; and three other Austrians. Although the M. and I. Mandl' Company and Lev Raits had established the factory together, it was an unequal partnership. Ludwig Mandl' was the majority stockholder (over 1,000 shares out of 2,800) with family members on the board to provide him with greater leverage. Furthermore, his position as director of the M. and I. Mandl' ready-to-wear company made him the most powerful figure in Russian clothing manufacture, dominating both military and civilian production. And yet, his prominence made him a target for those who would rid Russia of "Germans," as Mandl' was an Austrian subject. According to a report that was filed after the fateful May meeting, Russian stockholders, with the help of some Moscow banks, were able to remove Mandl' and his family members from the board. Raits became the new director and 85 percent of company stock now rested in Russian hands. In September 1914 the company was renamed "Mars" after the Greek god of war.[48] When Russian soldiers marched off to war, they did so in uniforms produced by their fellow countrymen.[49]

The large numbers of German and Austrian subjects living in Russia created a dilemma for the government. Ever since the Napoleonic Wars, it had refused to prosecute enemy nationals, but with anti-German sentiments running at an all-time high in 1914, something needed to be done. In August 1914 the Council of Ministers declared that actions taken against enemy nationals were contrary to international law and would be harmful to Russia's overall economy.[50] However, the Council of Ministers quickly retreated from this position due to domestic pressures. In the words of one scholar, "The War was simply a convenient moment for achieving certain aims of domestic foreign policy."[51] Businessmen continued their attacks against Germany's dominant role in Russian economic life. The newspapers whipped up anti-German feeling by publishing all kinds of rumors and gossip. Three scurrilous articles appeared in the fall of 1914 accusing Mandl' of having masterminded the hostile takeover of Mandl' and Raits by changing the name but maintaining financial control of the business.[52] Another newspaper reported that a Herman Mandl', the forty-two-year-old co-owner of the M. and I. Mandl' Company, had been found among the Austrian prisoners of war taken to a hospital in Kiev where he was in a serious condition.[53] The All-Russian National Union published a list of German and Austrian firms in Moscow, calling for a boycott of their products. The Union then distributed the pamphlet throughout the empire, gathering genuine popular support for the boycott.[54]

The campaign against German dominance of Russian economic life gained a powerful ally in October 1914. At that time the Russian commander-in-chief, Grand Duke Nikolai Nikolaevich, demanded that the Council of Ministers respond to German and Austrian atrocities at the front. He called for immediate retaliation against enemy nationals. The Council of Ministers quickly drafted a law, dated 22 September 1914, banning enemy nationals from buying property or businesses. In November of the same year, the Council of Ministers appointed a committee under the jurisdiction of the Ministry of Trade and Industry to examine all companies owned by enemy aliens in Russia. After a careful investigation, the committee would recommend either shutting such a business down or transferring it to those who supported the Russian war effort.[55] In January 1915, another decree prevented enemy nationals from receiving commercial licenses and, more importantly for our story, demanded the liquidation of any firm in which enemy aliens formed part of the leadership. The original date for the liquidation of these firms was 1 April 1915, but this was quickly changed to 1 June.[56] The government ministers declared that "The leading principle underlying all these measures is twofold: it is aimed, on the one hand, at the exclusion of the foreigner and of foreign concerns from the probable zone of military operations;

on the other, at the release of the economic system of the country from German influence."[57] Thus, the nationalist arguments for economic independence now became government policy with disastrous consequences for all concerned.

## THE MOSCOW POGROM

In the spring of 1915 anti-German hostility reached a fever pitch as a massive pogrom broke out in Moscow. The confluence of a number of factors help to explain the origins of the violence. In April of 1915, the German and Austrian armies delivered a series of crushing defeats, forcing the badly decimated Russians to retreat. Against this backdrop of military failure, rising costs, inflation, and an actual shortage of goods created a consumer crisis that was especially acute in Russia's biggest cities. This crisis occurred at a time when Moscow's population was growing, as refugees fleeing the front poured into the city looking for work and housing. On 1 May, Prince Feliks Iusupov, a man well known for his anti-German sentiments, was appointed as the city's new military governor. One of his first acts was to begin deportation proceedings against German and Austrian subjects as the June deadline for the liquidation of enemy firms approached. Lists of the deportees appeared in the newspapers. At the same time, the press published rumors that the company running the city's power plant was threatening to curtail electricity to city factories. Although this firm had been founded by Germans, they had handed over control of the firm to the Swiss prior to World War I. Nevertheless, many considered the rumors as an attempt at German sabotage.[58] A few days later, the newspaper *Russian Word* (*Russkoe slovo*) featured a story on the Moscow Merchant Society's investigation into the German influence on Russian economic life, which was to be presented on 15 May to a meeting of the Moscow Merchant Society along with proposals intended to overcome the German competitive advantage.[59] On 14 May about two thousand metalworkers gathered together outside the Kremlin for a patriotic demonstration, carrying pictures of Tsar Nicholas II and King Victor Emmanuel III of Italy. Singing folk songs, they proceeded to Prince Iusupov's residence where he joined the demonstrators.[60] Just days before the pogrom began, rumors spread throughout the city that German employees had poisoned the water supply causing some striking workers to fall ill with cholera.[61]

On 26 May, Russian women workers gathered on Tverskaia Street, in the heart of Moscow, to receive their sewing work from the distribution center of the Committee of Grand Duchess Elizaveta Fedorovna. The official in charge told the women to go home. There was no work that day because the center's supply of fabric had been sent to the German Mandl' company. The women, who were mostly war widows and soldiers' wives, became deeply upset. They begged the official to give them some work as they had no other source of income. Shouting and cursing erupted as onlookers confirmed that they had seen the fabric carted away. By this time, the crowd had swelled well beyond the original group of women. The police arrived and suggested that the angry workers report to Prince Iusupov precisely what had happened. Before they left for his residence, however, they declared that if the authorities would not rid Moscow of Germans, then they would do it themselves, not realizing that Ludwig Mandl' and his son, Viktor, had been deported the day before.[62]

That same day, Russian workers at a German printing factory went on strike, demanding the dismissal of foreign employees. In the evening these workers, carrying flags and portraits of the tsar, and singing patriotic songs, marched to the factory where the workers had died from cholera. They were met by the police who dispersed the crowd. In an ominous sign of things to come, individuals broke into the Sokolov ready-to-wear store on Malaia Sukharevskaia Square that night, destroying the store and two thousand rubles' worth of merchandise.[63]

The following day the pogrom continued. Organizing patriotic demonstrations, rioters attacked Germans at their workplaces or in their homes. Some German tailors and dressmakers shut down their workshops and vanished from the city to avoid the angry mob.[64] Although the police tried to rescue Germans from the pogromists, they had not been given orders to use force. As a result, a number of Germans died at the hands of the mob. Moscow's governor general believed that it would be dangerous to shoot at "patriotic" demonstrators. Nevertheless, he ordered the dismissal of all German and Austrian employees in the city, which can only have lent official approval to the workers' cause.[65]

The next day at 2 pm, patriotic demonstrations from all parts of the city converged on Red Square. The crowd that gathered represented a cross-section of the city. Professionals, students, and businessmen mixed with working-class men, women, and adolescents. Having gathered together to express their support for the tsar and the army, the crowd carried out its own war against the Germans. The first targets were the retail outlets for Einem chocolates and Tsindel' fabrics next to Red Square. From here, the crowd smashed windows and looted the stores of the Upper Trading Rows. At this point, the leaders of the pogrom distributed the pamphlet published by the All-Russian National Union identifying German and Austrian shops located in Moscow. They urged their fellow pogromists to break up into groups so that they could cover the city's entire commercial district.[66]

One of the chief targets was the M. and I. Mandl' company. Its three retail stores in central Moscow stood in the path of the raging mob. The Mandl' store across from the State Bank on Petrovka Street was emptied of merchandise by the mob and the premises badly damaged.[67] The second store on the corner of Sofiika and Rozhdestvenskaia Streets was also looted. A crowd stood and watched as suits, coats, and trousers came flying out of the broken windows. At one point, the protesters detained a young man wearing three overcoats that he had stolen from the store. Not wanting to enrage the crowd any further, he handed over his loot.[68] At the Tverskaia women's store, looters threw the clothing out onto the street where the angry crowd waited to rip it to shreds. They also tore up accounting books, correspondence, and other business papers, filling the air with shredded paper. Onlookers complained bitterly about German insolence toward the Russians and how they oppressed their Russian employees. The mob demanded that the store be destroyed and the looters happily obliged.[69]

These scenes of looting and destruction of property repeated themselves all across Moscow that day. In the resulting chaos, some stores that had once belonged to enemy nationals but were now in Russian hands suffered the same fate as the German firms. Adolf Bogen, a Hungarian, had sold his ready-to-wear store to the Russian

Friedrikh Filipp in March 1915. At that time the business was worth 390,000 rubles. During the pogrom, this Russian business was utterly destroyed.[70] This tragic mistake may have been due to the many errors contained in the list of German firms that the rioters had with them – the Bogen store was listed by the name of its original Hungarian owner.[71] However, even firms that had always been Russian were sacked during the pogrom, suggesting that the crowd's destructive impulses simply got out of hand. More than seven hundred firms suffered serious damage with losses estimated at almost forty million rubles. On 29 May, Russian troops finally intervened, restoring order to the city.[72]

In his recent study of the Moscow pogrom, Eric Lohr has argued that workers' participation in the May riot was motivated as much by a strong desire to eliminate Germans from the economy as it was by workplace antagonisms, or as he puts it, "enemy-alien categories had influence and often trumped class."[73] In the case of the fashion industry, it might be more accurate to see the categories of enemy aliens and class as intertwined. Ever since the Mandl' family had opened its first workshop in Russia in 1877, they had made themselves the enemy of their employees by introducing sweatshops and subcontracting. In 1915, a factory inspector's report to the Ministry of Trade and Industry indicated that garment workers at the former Mandl' and Raits uniform factory had not received a raise since 1911.[74] And yet, Ludwig Mandl' had purchased a hotel in Piatigorsk, a resort town, valued at one million rubles.[75] Underneath the flags and pictures of the tsar in these patriotic demonstrations during the pogrom were longstanding grievances about exploitative labor practices. In 1906 garment workers had set out to force Mandl' and the other ready-to-wear manufacturers to deal with them as equal partners, using labor unions and strikes to help them in their negotiations. The owners had ignored their employees, and the closure of employees' unions at the start of the war meant that these men and women were driven to take their revenge. They smashed the windows and machinery, tore up the ledgers, and ripped the clothes so that their employers could no longer benefit at their expense. The ruthless employment policies of Ludwig Mandl', the all-Russian exploiter, as much as his Austrian birth made him a prime target in the Moscow pogrom.

If the May violence was a pogrom against outsiders and employers, it was also a consumer revolt. Although there were certainly some factories that were damaged during the three-day rampage, the chief targets were Moscow stores that sold ready-to-wear, chocolate, perfume, textiles, watches, and other modern conveniences. It was precisely these goods that were heavily advertised in late imperial Russia, and as a result of these advertising campaigns they had come to represent for city residents the key to a better life. While none of these items were essential for human survival, they provided small moments of beauty and comfort. But the war took all that away. As more Russians migrated to the cities in search of work and improved living conditions, they found only substandard housing, low wages, and spiraling prices that kept these goods just out of reach. What was the point of working in unsafe factories and workshops if workers could not buy a piece of calico, a hat, or even some chocolate to brighten up their difficult lives? The enormous sacrifices that the government demanded from its people also demanded some kind of reward, and the frustrated consumers of Moscow decided to take their revenge upon an unsympathetic retail establishment.

Their revenge was short-lived. The Mandl' company consolidated its operations into the Sofiika store as the other shops were closed and workers dismissed. The destruction of the Moscow retail outlets forced the company to lay off its vast network of rural garment workers. Thousands lost their jobs in a matter of days. In October the company shut down its two stores in Petersburg, laying off more employees and making it even more difficult for people to find affordable ready-to-wear clothing.[76] The biggest blow to the Mandl' company occurred when the government seized its assets and sequestered them for military use. On 1 June, Ludwig Mandl' lost his right to trade in Moscow, and the government appointed a trustee to oversee the conversion of the company to a military workshop.[77] Working conditions in the new workshop replicated those introduced by Mandl' in the 1880s. Thus, the employees benefited little from the Russian ownership of the firm. Even when Ludwig Mandl' was removed and deported, those charged with running the uniform factory failed to respond to workers' demands for a raise.[78] Russian employers had replaced German ones but the rules of employment – sweatshops, piece rates, and subcontracting – remained the same. The enemy was still in place.

## THE SINGER SEWING MACHINE COMPANY

The Moscow pogrom marked the beginning of the Russian government's liquidation of businesses belonging to enemy aliens, coming as it did just days before the June deadline. Those companies not destroyed in the pogrom came under government scrutiny in the summer of 1915. Because wartime legislation specified that any company with even one enemy-alien board member was subject to liquidation, the government had the power to interfere in the affairs of all firms located in the Russian Empire. The hunt for "Germans" now became an excuse to rid Russia of all foreigners.

One company that fell victim to this campaign was Kompaniia Zinger, the Russian subsidiary of the American Singer Sewing Machine Company. The trouble for Singer began in the fall of 1914. At that time, company officials had dismissed for embezzlement S. Levitskii, a manager of a depot in Aleskin, Tula province. When the company tried to retrieve the embezzled monies, Levitskii threatened in a letter to reveal that the company had not paid its taxes. Receiving no response, the conniving employee sent a second letter dated 12 November 1914. He demanded that the company stop trying to get its money back, or he would go to the right-wing organization For Russia (Za Rossiiu) and various government agencies, and he would reveal documents demonstrating that Kompaniia Zinger was a German enterprise engaged in espionage. "[W]hat is better for you," he wrote, "to pay out a one-time payment of 7,000,000 rubles or to leave me alone?"[79]

The company ignored Levitskii, but soon articles began appearing in the Russian press claiming that Kompaniia Zinger was a German business. The right-wing newspaper *Russian Banner* (*Russkoe znamia*) claimed that "all of the sales personnel in this firm from the smallest to the most powerful are either pure German or German Jews." Supposedly headquartered in Hamburg, Kompaniia Zinger had established a "monopolistic exploitation of our consumers." Conservative and right-

wing newspapers claimed that Singer's sales operations were a "spider's web that covered all of Russia," selling German machines instead of American ones at exorbitant prices. ". . . Singer agents travel primarily among the rural and working-class populations of the Empire, promising them wonders and selling machines on credit." When individuals fell behind in their payments, these same agents came back with the bailiff.[80] These articles were intended to discredit Singer while at the same time show that the Russian business community was looking out for the best interests of workers and peasants. Over the course of the winter and into the spring of 1915, these false accusations continued to circulate in the press and right-wing circles. The All-Russian National Union included Singer on its list of German companies published in 1915.[81] These scurrilous attacks in the press coupled with the new anti-German legislation forced the company to fire all German employees in February 1915, a total of 125 employees out of a workforce of 31,000.[82] The greatest casualty of these mass firings was Albert Flohr, the general sales manager and architect of the company's success in Russia.[83] A few weeks later, Flohr's replacement, the Latvian Oskar O. Kel'pin received a letter from an Aleksandr Gur'ev. Gur'ev said he had proof that Flohr was still running Kompaniia Zinger and he, Gur'ev, was prepared to go to the authorities. Kel'pin ignored the letter.[84]

Meanwhile, the Russian military high command (Stavka), which had supreme authority over all aspects of life along Russia's western frontier, found the time to conduct its own investigation into the company and uncovered a number of disgruntled employees who claimed that some Singer agents had collected "military data," and that Singer's decision in 1912 to move the headquarters from Petersburg to Moscow meant that Germans now controlled the company.[85] Without any attempt to corroborate these accusations, the Stavka ordered local government officials to begin shutting down Singer stores.[86] On 3 April 1915, the company was placed under government inspection at the insistence of the military authorities.[87]

The government inspector, Prince Zubar D. Avalov, immediately verified that Singer was not a German company, and, in fact, had received a Russian corporation charter in 1897. This prompted the minister of trade and

ШВЕЙНАЯ КОМПАНІЯ

industry, Prince Vsevolod Shakhovskoi, to ask for the removal of government inspection in June 1915. Before the Council of Ministers could rule on this, the Petrograd[88] military authorities, determined to have their way, authorized a raid on the Singer stores in that city. They arrested Kel'pin at the company's sales headquarters on Nevskii Prospekt and the managers of the other twenty-eight retail outlets. The latter were quickly released, but the unfortunate Kel'pin remained in jail.[89] Shakhovskoi quickly sent off a letter to General N. Ruzskii, the commander of the northern front, asking once again for the removal of government inspection. He reminded Ruzskii

136    This poster was part of the campaign against German dominance. It attacks the masculinity of German soldiers and the "German" Singer Sewing Machine Company. V. Ruga and A Kokorev, *Voina i moskvichi: Ocherki gorodskogo byta, 1914–1917* gg., 311.

that Singer was engaged in war work. The company's factory in Podol'sk had manufactured shells, gauges, stands, and other goods valued at four million rubles, with more government contracts on the way. Furthermore, the company had provided half a million rubles of relief to soldiers' families, ten thousand free sewing machines to organizations engaged in war work, and the company itself had produced one million pieces of clothing for the war effort.[90] Despite Shakhovskoi's pleading, General Ianushkevich, chief of staff of the army, issued an order to shut down all Singer operations in those eight provinces directly affected by the war. During two weeks in July the government shut down five hundred stores, and six thousand workers lost their jobs. This partial closure jeopardized the company's ability to pay its debts to its parent company in the United States, to which it owed 102 million rubles. Moreover, since Singer was the only sewing-machine company still in business in 1915, this placed the war effort in serious jeopardy.[91]

The company was now in deep crisis and used all of its connections to resolve the situation. On 8 August, Singer representatives met with leaders of the Union of Zemstvos and Towns to resolve the crisis. During these meetings, they opened up their private business affairs to the union leaders and discussed the various attempts at blackmail. They denied the charges of espionage, explaining that soliciting economic and commercial information was a longstanding company policy to outsell their competitors. The senior Singer official, Walter Dixon, reported that the American parent company was having difficulty understanding why the Russians had shut down the stores. The United States was a neutral country and had done nothing to support the Central Powers during the war. He further warned that the American company was prepared to shut down the Russian subsidiary if the situation did not improve. At the end of the hearings, the union leaders declared all the charges against the company to be false. They asked that the Army Chief of Staff General Ianushkevich be given a copy of their findings and allow Singer to resume normal operations.[92] At the urging of the American ambassador, the minister of foreign affairs also joined the fray by asking the army to remove government inspectors.[93]

Finally, in late August the minister of war asked the Council of Ministers to determine whether or not Singer should be shut down completely as the conflict between military and civilian officials over the fate of the company needed resolution. On 18 September the council ruled that the military commanders could decide the fate of the stores in those areas near the front, but it ordered the reopening of those retail outlets not directly affected by the war.[94] This confirmation of what was already the status quo only exacerbated the situation. Provincial inspectors wrote to government officials that Singer's business practices baffled them. One admitted that he was having trouble determining how to collect money from Singer's customers and send it on to Moscow.[95] This dramatic disruption in sales caused firstly by the war but secondly by government inspectors' incompetence in supervising daily operations meant that Singer's losses during the war amounted to over seventeen million rubles.[96]

The campaign to shut down the Singer Sewing Machine Company brings into sharp relief the conflicts present in the fashion industry and in Russia itself during World War I. The attack on Singer reveals how elastic the category of "German" had become. By the summer of 1915 it is clear that the government with the support of the Russian right wing began to use the campaign against "German dominance" to rid Russia of all foreign entrepreneurs. In the case of Singer, the Stavka together with "patriotic" businessmen and right-wing organizations began a smear campaign against the company, accusing it of espionage, monopolistic practices, and exploitation of Russia's laborers with the introduction of credit buying. These charges speak to the real issue that many Russian businessmen had with the company. The sewing-machine market was dominated by Singer and German manufacturers whose business strategies included high-quality merchandise at competitive prices, installment purchasing plans, extensive advertising, and detailed research into the social and economic conditions of the market. Just as important, these innovations had proven enormously successful for the manufacturers. In 1914, the Singer Sewing Machine Company was one of the most successful multinational corporations of its day. Its incredible success made other Russian businessmen angry and envious. They realized that they would have to give up familiar ways of doing business and adopt this foreign business culture if they were going to succeed. The sewing-machine market served as a model for future economic development in Russia, but these conservatives sought to postpone the inevitable changes for as long as possible. To this end, they solicited the government to help them in their battle against the evil Singer company by conducting a vicious campaign of lies and innuendo in the newspapers and the halls of government. Even when government officials realized that the charges were false, they did not wish to antagonize business interests or the army by going against their wishes. Government inspectors remained in place. Their inability to operate successfully within Singer's business culture, coupled with worsening wartime conditions, managed to crush the once-powerful company. Conservatives and nationalists within the Russian business community allowed the government to rid them of their competition rather than viewing government overseers and military authority as a danger to the entire business community.[97]

## THE BAN ON LUXURY GOODS

The campaigns against Mandl' and Singer were just part of the larger story of economic chaos that enveloped Russia in 1915 and 1916. During those years the Russian government essentially allowed for the creation of two markets – one civilian and one military. As the war dragged on, the army's needs placed huge burdens upon Russian industry. The only way for industry to meet the demand was to redirect raw materials and labor into war work. The inevitable result was that the civilian economy experienced skyrocketing prices and, eventually, a lack of many consumer goods. By 1916 prices for basic goods had more than doubled. The rising prices of and shortages in textiles were of particular concern to the fashion industry. One report on cloth production from 1915 painted a grim picture: "The retail trade is beginning to feel the effects of the three months' decrease in output. The stock intended for the towns and for the peasant population will shortly be exhausted, and the warehouses are no longer overcrowded with goods as they used to be. In consequence of heavy demands from the Army Supply Department there is hardly any stock on hand."[98] With 70 to 80 percent of textiles going to the army, there was not much cloth for the civilian market.[99]

This lack of consumer goods could not have come at a worse time. Despite the mobilization of millions of male peasants, the 1914 harvest was a good one and

peasants consequently had sufficient funds to spend on consumer goods. Furthermore, peasants had extra cash that year. Money that had previously been spent on alcohol could now be used in the purchase of "city clothes," samovars, and other goods. However, when peasants came to make their purchases, there was little to buy and what was available was very expensive. They responded by producing enough grain to feed themselves and their families, but not enough to sell to the urban markets.[100]

Inevitably, the growing crisis encouraged the development of profiteering and speculation. In a belated attempt to institute state controls over industry, the government introduced price controls on requisitioned goods in the summer of 1915. This measure created a dual price structure. As one historian observed, "Favoritism and bribery flourished during the War . . . [they] seriously hampered the successful control of prices, and of equitable distribution. When goods could be obtained by means that eluded fixed prices and all rules, the Government's regulations lost all of their efficacy, and remained only a dead letter. In such cases the law of supply and demand ruled the market and the circulation of goods depended upon the success of those who were most determined."[101]

Consumers – both rural and urban – responded in a number of ways. Before World War I, Russia had the largest number of cooperative societies in the world. In the economic dislocation caused by the war, these societies became even more popular, attracting "the conservative and the radical, the well-to-do and the poor."[102] Cooperatives attempted to supply their members with regular supplies of foodstuffs, textiles, clothing, and other goods at reasonable prices. However, given the collapse of some of Russia's most successful wholesale businesses, the dearth of raw materials and foodstuffs, and inflation, these societies suffered from the same problems that ordinary consumers experienced.

The result was a number of violent confrontations between merchants and consumers. Following the May 1915 pogrom in Moscow, consumer revolts spread to other cities. The mobs smashed windows and looted merchandise from shops selling sugar, cotton goods, meat, and other items. Once again, these attacks suggest how far the laboring classes, and especially those outside the two capitals, had been drawn into the "dream worlds" of consumer capitalism that the business community had so carefully crafted. In an earlier generation, sugar, factory-produced cloth, and meat would have been considered luxuries which few peasants or working people could afford. By 1915, ordinary Russians defined these goods as necessities and were demanding their right to consume them at affordable prices.[103] At the same time, the dramatic increase in the cost of living demonstrated quite clearly that the government and the business community could not organize the economy to fight a war and meet the needs of ordinary people. The whole country appeared to be mired in a battle for survival both at the front and at home.

In this difficult environment the government recognized that something had to be done to improve economic life and, just as important, the morale of the country. It responded by increasing its regulation of industry and additional price controls.[104] In particular, it targeted "speculators," those parasites who were reaping enormous profits while the rest of Russia suffered. Indeed, in the consumer revolts of 1915–1916, protestors often blamed these people for their misery.[105] While Russia certainly had its share of war profiteers, nevertheless they provided a convenient scapegoat for the government's own failures. Along with "Germans," speculators and war profiteers now became the enemy on the home front. An amorphous social category, speculators included those who had enriched themselves during the war, and flaunted their wealth by spending it lavishly on clothing, meals, automobiles, and entertainments. Conspicuous consumption became all that more grotesque as the war dragged on with no end in sight.

Against this backdrop of the campaigns against German businesses and wartime speculation, the government and Russian business leaders pressed forward with their own agenda of economic independence for Russia. One weapon in this war was the trade embargo. During the first months of World War I, the government prohibited imports from Germany, Austria, and Turkey, but these sanctions were frequently ignored, especially in the case of Germany. Russia continued to receive badly needed chemicals, metals, and machinery from German manufacturers throughout 1914 and 1915. Only at the beginning of 1916 did the government finally decide to

prohibit all trade with the enemy, although that law did not take effect until 24 October 1916.[106]

The Association of Industry and Trade (AIT) had even greater ambitions than the government for the trade embargo. In the spring of 1916 A. A. Bublikov, who was a member of the AIT and the Duma, introduced legislation that would prohibit the importation of luxury goods. The legislation was to take effect on 1 June 1916 and remain in place for three years. The list of banned goods was a long one and included food, wine, sweets, umbrellas, watches, jewelry, china, fabrics, cosmetics, and women's and children's clothing.[107] Interestingly, the Russian legislation was introduced at the same time that similar bans were being enacted in Austria-Hungary, France, England, and Germany.[108]

In connection with this new legislation, the AIT polled its member organizations to solicit support for the proposed ban. Eighty percent of the organizations surveyed approved of the ban. By ending the competition between foreign and domestic goods, the ban was clearly giving a huge boost to Russian industry and would go a long way in eliminating the Russian consumer's predilection for foreign goods. Not all Russian businesses were happy with the legislation. Representatives of the candy and perfume industry argued that it was not possible "to establish a proper distinction between luxury goods and goods of 'comfort' which had become or would become essential for the population."[109] The fur industry, which had exported furs worth over ten million rubles to western Europe every year since 1905, complained bitterly against the proposed ban. The furriers feared a trade war as western Europeans retaliated against the Russian ban.[110] In fact, the Moscow Stock Exchange calculated that Russia would lose eighty-two million rubles if the ban were enacted.[111]

Journalists who discussed the pending legislation in the press made clear that the ban was intended to punish speculators. The first article to appear claimed that the ban had two goals: the first was postwar support for the ruble and domestic industries, and the second was "a 'wartime' measure directed against the extensive and intolerable expenditures on luxury goods by a certain part of the public at a difficult time in the survival of the motherland." The author, writing in March 1916, believed that the ban would be ineffective in punishing specula-

137　An outfit that was part of a spring 1916 collection. At a time when so many Russians were wearing mourning clothes, this white confection symbolized the wartime speculators' callous disregard of ordinary Russians' suffering. N. Shebuev, "Modoborchestvo," *Sol'ntse Rossii*, 329/23 (May 1916), 13. Library of Congress Collections.

138　Another spring 1916 ensemble. The ribbons, lace, and frills on this outfit emphasize the pampered existence of any woman who purchased this dress. N. Shebuev, "Modoborchestvo," *Sol'ntse Rossii*, 328/22 (May 1916), 5. Library of Congress Collections.

tors, since those who had profited the most were those individuals engaged in war work rather than in the luxury trade. Instead of instituting a ban, the author proposed raising taxes on certain items. These higher taxes would increase government revenues at the expense of the war profiteers.[112]

As the economic crisis deepened, the idea that speculators must be punished gained in popularity. In April the

prominent Petrograd daily *Stock Exchange News* published a translation of German wartime dress regulations, in the hopes of encouraging the adoption of similar regulations in Russia.[113] It is possible to see here the connection that was being made between fashion, speculation, and women. Since fashion was a female preoccupation, it made sense that women should be punished for their extravagant outfits in a time of war and hardship. Women's

Она. — Какое великолѣпное платье у вашей жены!
Онъ. — Да, я отдалъ за него весь мой гонораръ за три лекціи о борьбѣ съ дороговизной дамскихъ нарядовъ...

139   A cartoon from a Moscow journal. The caption reads: "She – What a magnificent dress your wife has! He - Yes, I gave up my entire honorarium for three lectures on the war against the high prices of women's clothing for it." V. Ruga and A Kokorev, *Voina i moskvichi: Ocherki gorodskogo byta, 1914–1917* gg., 288.

fashions became the symbol of conspicuous consumption. Fashionable Russian women were attacked for having the leisure and the money to continue to dress *à la mode* while poorer Russians scrambled to make ends meet. Consequently, fashionable women increasingly became scapegoats in the campaign to punish speculators. The money made through war profiteering by their husbands and lovers was enabling these women to focus their attention on their wardrobes.

In May an article in *Russian Sun* (*Sol'ntse Rossii*), a magazine for the well-to-do, merged the prewar critique of fashion with the discourse about speculators and conspicuous consumption, providing yet another twist to the story. The author, N. Shebuev, began by suggesting that the war years were a time of "insane" bodily extravagance, particularly in Russia's big cities. The shortages of dress patterns and fabrics encouraged some Russian women to obsess about fashionable clothing to an unhealthy degree. Particularly obnoxious to Shebuev was the idea that certain women should desire frippery when others of their sex wore mourning or nurses' uniforms. Women pursued fashion until they "lost consciousness," prompting the Duma to introduce its ban against imported luxury goods. According to Shebuev, a Duma member had declared that luxury was now a crime! Even in Paris, the fashion capital of the world, women had given up luxury for modest dress. However, the evil dressmakers in Russia misrepresented the latest fashions to their unsuspecting clients, encouraging them to dress extravagantly while the dressmakers pocketed the money.[114] Thus Shebuev, echoing Elets' earlier descriptions of female insanity and mental instability, blamed these foolish women for falling into the hands of those dreadful war profiteers, dressmakers. The only way to stop these ruthless craftswomen and restore women's sanity was to join the fight against conspicuous consumption. Presumably without access to foreign designs, dressmakers would no longer be able to attract enough business to remain financially solvent. In Shebuev's view, women remain flighty, passionate creatures who have no self-control. They mindlessly pursue fashion while their country is engulfed in a difficult war. The real villains were the dressmakers, working women who had no scruples. Their profits grew while Russian men were dying on the battlefield. It was for these reasons that the war on fashion must be pursued by punishing women and their dressmakers.

Government officials had their own reasons for supporting the trade embargo. To help them assess the legislation, the Council of Ministers set up a special subcommittee to study the ramifications of Bublikov's ban. One member of the subcommittee was M. Langevoi, who believed that it was essential for Russia to ban imports from all countries, not just Germany. For Langevoi, the purpose of war was to rid Russia of all foreigners.[115] Although the other committee members agreed with Langevoi, nevertheless they worried about the impact of the ban on their wartime allies, primarily France and Italy. Although the ban specifically violated trade agreements with both countries, the committee members decided to overlook this, declaring that wartime concerns overruled the earlier trade agreements. Like the businessmen who proposed the ban, it is clear from the discussions conducted among representatives of various government industries that these officials wanted to create a favorable balance of trade with western Europe by decreasing foreign imports and providing greater protection of certain Russian industries, particularly as Russia transitioned from a wartime to a peacetime economy.[116] The Council of Ministers approved the ban on 13 September 1916.[117]

★ ★ ★

The ban on imported luxury goods was the final salvo in the economic war on the fashion industry, an industry that had grown and prospered as a result of intense collaboration and competition between foreign and Russian entrepreneurs. During World War I, the government and a significant number of Russian industrialists worked to realize their goal of economic independence, and the fashion industry became one of their chief victims. With the encouragement of various sectors of the Russian business community, the government shut down Mandl', the most successful of the ready-to-wear manufacturers, and so crippled Kompaniia Zinger that the company never recovered, shutting down its retail operation in 1917 and its sewing-machine factory in 1919. And while the ban on luxury goods presumably denied elite women and war profiteers the high fashions that they craved, the loss of ready-to-wear and sewing machines meant that "city clothes" – the unpretentious, ordinary garments that Russians wore to work and at home – were also difficult to find. But the Russian government and business community did not care. They were determined to rid Russia of "foreigners," and in 1916 it appeared that they had succeeded. Once the war was over, Russian companies using Russian textiles, machinery, and labor could fill the void left by foreign business concerns and establish a truly national fashion industry.

№ 328 (22).     Май 1916 г.               Цѣна № 25 коп., на ст. жел.

**СОЛНЦЕ**
РОССІИ

140     The cover of the magazine, *Russian Sun*, with one of the Russian-inspired fashions from the May 1916 fashion show. The model's hat and veil are reminiscent of Russian women's headdresses. *Sol'ntse Rossii*, 328/22 (May 1916), cover. Library of Congress Collections.

# Epilogue

AS GOVERNMENT OFFICIALS WERE considering the merits of the ban on imported luxury goods, a fashion show took place in Petrograd's Palace Theater on 14 May 1916. Organized by the Union of Russian Women, the evening consisted of two parts. In keeping with their goal of maintaining "the beauty of the national spirit," the URW had sponsored a contest among students from the Imperial Society for the Encouragement of the Arts to determine who could draw the most attractive Russian fashions, offering a five-hundred-ruble prize. The results of the contest were displayed on the walls of the theater that night.[1] To further the celebration of Russian dress, artists – both neo-Russian stylists and modernists – collaborated to create a series of tableaux. The first was entitled "In a Dressmaker's Workshop," in which some of Russia's leading ballerinas appeared in various gowns and hats. This was followed by readings of works by Mikhail Kuz'min and Aleksei Tolstoi, Ukrainian folk songs, and dances choreographed by Vsevolod Meyerhold. There was also a brief skit called "Russian Fashion" and the evening closed with Tamara Karsavina dancing a tango.[2] On that spring evening, the fashions and the tableaux revealed modern Russianness to be an amalgam of native and western cultural traditions.

Such an elaborate production captured the attention of the press. Not surprisingly, the show was condemned for its extravagance during wartime. A reporter for *Petersburg Gazette* complained, "Is now the time to create an entire spectacle devoted to women's fashionable dress and hats? Everywhere there is talk about the battle against luxury and the high cost-of-living . . ." In the article from *Russian Sun*, Shebuev complained, "We thought we were going to see Russian beauties in costumes prepared by Russian dressmakers from sketches by Russian artists using Russian fabrics, taking care not to spend large sums during wartime." Instead, the outfits on display cost between 250 and 2,000 rubles.[3] As a result, the fashion show reinforced the view that Russian nationalists were hopelessly out of touch with ordinary Russians as they struggled to clothe and feed their families during World War I.

The journalists also attacked the design of the clothes. The *Petersburg Gazette* reporter complained that one of Karsavina's outfits was more eastern than Russian, and the ugliest fashions of the entire show appeared in the Russian fashion portion of the program. The chief criticism of these garments was that native folk elements were too obviously grafted onto French fashions. As Shebuev put it, despite the wartime alliance between France and Russia, French fashion did not harmonize well with Nizhegorod folk costume. Nikolai Alovert, the publisher of Russia's leading fashion magazines, concurred, pointing out that "A sarafan, since it does not vary, will always be a sarafan" and could not be successfully combined with anything but other Russian folk elements.[4]

The one outfit that the commentators considered a success was a dress inspired by a Lev Bakst design from one of his ballet costumes. Bakst was not present at the show because he was in America selling his dress designs. And yet, he had emerged as the "poet" who understood the Russian spirit and translated it into beautiful fashions that even French women wanted to wear.[5] Not satisfied with merely copying traditional dress, he integrated Russian concepts of beauty, line, and color with those of Parisian high fashion to create something new. Indeed, it was the creative tension between western and Russian that allowed talented artists like Bakst to create chic fashions popular wherever fashion reigned supreme. Because Bakst's designs had revolutionized *haute couture*, Russian women had no need to parade around in folk costume as the URW advocated. They could wear French fashion knowing that it reflected Russian sensibilities. The student sketches that lined the walls of the Palace Theater confirmed this. No crude imitations of folk costume, these designs gracefully integrated Russian design vocabulary with French fashion.

The May 1916 fashion show represents a defining moment in the history of the fashion industry, revealing the profound changes in the Russian sartorial landscape since 1700. First of all, peasant clothing came to represent the essence of Russianness and became categorized as national costume. The long-suffering common people supposedly preserved those qualities that made Russians unique from other ethnic groups, and that uniqueness found expression in Russian peasant dress. Consequently, elite Russian clothing became suspect, particularly when it became so closely associated with right-wing cultural politics. With the defeat of the Right in the 1917 Revolution and Civil War, elite clothing disappeared from Russian life, as discredited as the people who had worn the garments.

Yet, as Nicholas II himself had unintentionally demonstrated in 1903, sarafans, kaftans, and *kokoshki* could be worn to masquerades and folk festivals, but not in everyday public life. The fashion press, high society, and even ordinary consumers rejected wearing folk costume or modernized versions of native dress that the URW advocated. They were able to do this in large part because fashion itself had become more cosmopolitan in the early years of the twentieth century. Although fashion, centered in Paris, had always borrowed designs from other cultures, the industry now embraced "the exotic" much

more self-consciously at the beginning of the twentieth century. The success of Bakst's ballet designs marked western Europe's embrace of Russian design and culture. Russian sensibilities became an intrinsic part of French *haute couture*. In turn, modern Russians had been liberated once and for all from the need to appear in their national costume. The cultural conundrum created when Peter the Great first introduced European fashion into Russia in 1700 had been resolved. And even though the fascination of European designers for Russian ethnic dress would fade, Russians could wear fashionable clothes confident that they were now equal citizens in the cosmopolitan empire of fashion.

The resolution of Russia's cultural conundrum was only one part of the revolution in dress. The second was the creation of a fashion industry to manufacture and sell European fashions for the Russian market. Here too, the Russians succeeded in creating a mirror image of the fashion industry found in the West, due in large part to the influx of foreign entrepreneurs. Beginning in the eighteenth century and at every step along the way, these men and women brought their business skills, labor practices, and innovative technology to Russia. In their adopted homeland, these European entrepreneurs laid the foundation for the development of the fashion industry. At the same time, they found the Russians to be eager pupils. Before too long Russians trained in the art of European tailoring were setting up shop next to their European teachers. Russians established a vibrant fashion press and retailing practices to publicize and sell the latest fashions well beyond the borders of Russia's major cities.

The fashion industry's achievements can also be measured by what happened to it during the early years of the twentieth century. Ready-to-wear appeared to promise a better life for all Russians, but many workers and peasants struggled to purchase items for themselves or family members. Indeed, the industry proved better at raising expectations than in meeting them, in large part due to the uneven development of the Russian economy which the fashion industry could do little to improve on its own. These rising expectations coupled with notoriously poor working conditions within the industry itself spilled over into a series of bitter and often violent confrontations between owners and garment

141  A dress from the May 1916 fashion show. The embroidery on the bodice and skirt pockets is done in the Russian style. *Sol'ntse Rossii*, 329/23 (May 1916), 13. Library of Congress Collections.

142  A modern version of the Russian sarafan shown at the May 1916 fashion show. *Sol'ntse Rossii*, 329/23 (May 1916), 14. Library of Congress Collections.

143  Some of the student sketches that were on display at the May 1916 fashion show. Each outfit successfully integrates Russian and western design vocabularies and aesthetic sensibilities, winning the admiration of critics and consumers alike. *Sol'ntse Rossii*, 329/23 (May 1916), 15. Library of Congress Collections.

workers. During the 1915 Moscow pogrom, workers took their revenge upon stingy employers, and middle-class consumers vented their frustrations about the rising cost of living by pillaging the city's clothing stores.

The Moscow pogrom also marked a very public confrontation between the fashion industry and Russian right-wing nationalists. By the eve of World War I nationalists saw their old familiar world collapsing. Dress was redefining gender, class, and ethnicity, undermining all that was good, true, and "immutable" in Russian life. As the sewing machine and ready-to-wear became tangible symbols of modernity, the liquidation campaigns

directed against Mandl' and Singer show how the nationalists blamed these foreign businessmen and their merchandise for their sense of loss. It was precisely because the nationalists took dress so seriously – as being fundamental to ethnic identity – that they exacted their revenge upon the fashion industry during World War I. Fashion's very success made it vulnerable to attack.

In his August 1916 article critiquing the May fashion show at Petrograd's Palace Theater, Alovert concluded by remarking that when Russia quieted down after the war, his magazines would be the first to participate in the re-building of the fashion industry, now that the foreigners had been eliminated.[6] This proved to be a promise that he could not keep. In late February 1917, consumer protests and workers' strikes in Petrograd mushroomed into a fully fledged revolution against autocracy. When the new Provisional Government formed in March after the abdication of Nicholas II, failed to take Russia out of the war or solve any of the empire's serious economic problems, the Bolshevik Party under the leadership of Vladimir Lenin took control of the government in October, setting up the world's first socialist state.

Not surprisingly, there was no call during the years of revolutionary turmoil for Russians to return to the dress of their ancestors. Modern clothing, that synthesis of European and Russian, became the uniform of the new Soviet state. During the Civil War, the Red Army wore garments that combined western design and Russian folk elements. In the 1920s fashion designers and artists, following in Bakst's footsteps, elaborated upon modernism in dress. Nadezhda Lamanova won first prize in Paris in the 1925 World Exposition for her dress designs which combined Russian folk elements with the flapper look. Alexandra Exter, Liubov Popova, Sonia Terk Delaunay, and others created clothing and textiles for the new Soviet man and woman, which in turn had a profound influence on *haute couture* outside of Russia. This integrative approach merely echoed a process that had begun with Catherine the Great.[7]

Nonetheless the integrative approach has proven very popular in the west down to the present day. In their never-ending search to come up with something new, western designers periodically rediscover Russian dress and use it as a source of inspiration for their own "Russian season". The result is successful precisely because the consumer can feel Russian and chic all at the same time. Just as Russians can consider themselves European in clothing that combines European and Russian design elements, so too can Europeans create a Russian identity for themselves. Fashion's ability to be both ethnic and cosmopolitan is fundamental to its success.

Yet, as comfortable as most Russians were in clothes that integrated Russian and western styles, Soviet ideology opposed any luxuriousness in dress or excessive attention to personal appearance, seeing it as a remnant of the bourgeois world that they had destroyed. Bolshevik propaganda now transformed the prewar discourse about the wastefulness and mindlessness of fashion into an attack against "bourgeois morality" and "philistinism." This anti-fashion discourse became particularly strong during the New Economic Policy of the 1920s. After years of war, revolution, and deprivation, the relative economic prosperity that occurred in those years encour-

144   An advertisement for mourning dress. Far too many women had to abandon colorful garments in favor of mourning during World War I , the Russian Revolution, and the Civil War. *Damskii mir*, no. 2 (February 1917), 2.

aged the more affluent Soviet citizens to spend their money on fine clothing and other consumer goods. Echoing the earlier attacks on war profiteers, the Bolsheviks condemned those Soviet citizens for becoming slaves to fashion once again.

One challenge that the Soviet government faced was rebuilding the fashion industry after the economic war perpetrated by the tsarist government and business leaders had all but destroyed it. Mandl', Singer, and other foreign businesses had been swept away along with most of their Russian competitors. They simply could not survive as the Russian economy collapsed under the weight of war, revolution, and civil war. Fashion magazines had disappeared during World War I owing to a lack of information on the latest styles, subscribers, illustrations, patterns, and paper, shortages that only grew worse during the 1917 Revolution and the Civil War. Custom tailoring and dressmakers' shops had also gone out of business as a result of shortages and a lack of clients. Many journeymen tailors died in the trenches or were too disabled by their war wounds to return to their physically demanding craft when they were demobilized. Furthermore, in the journeymen's absence the labor practices of the ready-to-wear industry emerged as the most productive way of manufacturing clothing for a mass market. The old artisanal world of bespoke tailoring began to give way to modern manufacturing.

The creation of a workers' state provided the Russian fashion industry with a new beginning. Ordinary Russians expressed their preference for wearing modern clothing like their European counterparts, and the Soviet government committed itself to providing it. There would be no divide between European fashion and traditional Russian clothing as had existed under the tsars. Everyone would dress in "city clothes." And while there were certainly some individuals who wore Russian dress in the Soviet period, these people were the exceptions that proved the rule. The Soviet fashion industry also had the opportunity to reconstruct itself without any foreign "interference." Industry leaders could use Soviet fabrics, machines, and designs to create comfortable, affordable clothing for their fellow citizens. In this new workers' state, labor would work together with employers and government officials to create a safer, healthier working environment for all needleworkers, realizing garment workers' dreams of a radically new workplace that they had first articulated in the 1905 Revolution. Unfortunately for Soviet consumers, the task of establishing a new fashion industry proved harder to achieve than anyone imagined.

# Notes

## INTRODUCTION

1   Tsars Alexis and Fedor forbade Russians from wearing foreign fashions in 1675 and 1680 respectively. See Lindsay Hughes, *Russia in the Age of Peter the Great* (New Haven: Yale University Press, 1998), 280.

2   *Polnoe sobranie zakonov Rossiiskoi imperii* (*PSZ*), vol. 4, no. 1741, p. 1, and no. 1887, p. 182.

3   The literature on Peter the Great and his reforms is vast. Recent works include Hughes, *Russia in the Age of Peter the Great*; Paul Bushkovitch, *Peter the Great* (Lanham, MD: Rowman and Littlefield, 2001); and Evgenii V. Anisimov, *The Reforms of Peter the Great: Progress Through Coercion in Russia*, trans. John T. Alexander (Armonk, New York: M. E. Sharpe, 1993). Older works include Vasili Klyuchevsky, *Peter the Great*, trans. Liliana Archibald (New York: Vintage, 1958); and B. H. Sumner, *Peter the Great and the Emergence of Russia* (New York: Collier, 1976).

4   In the eighteenth century Russians used the adjective "German" (*nemetskii*) to describe foreign goods imported from western Europe, which explains why Peter called European fashions "German dress." The word derived from the Russian for "deaf" (*nemoi*), meaning that foreigners were "deaf" to Russian speech. Vladimir Dal', *Tolkovyi slovar' zhivogo velikorusskogo iazyka* (Moscow: Russkii iazyk, 1981), II: 562.

5   The best work that discusses Peter's controversial role in Russian history is Nicholas V. Riasanovsky, *The Image of Peter the Great in Russian History and Thought* (New York: Oxford University Press, 1985).

6   Andrzej Walicki, *The Slavophile Controversy: History of a Conservative Utopia in Nineteenth-Century Russian Thought*, trans. Hilda Andrews-Rusiecka (Notre Dame: University of Notre Dame Press, 1989).

7   For an introduction to some of the major theories about fashion's role in human life, see Thorstein Veblen, *The Theory of the Leisure Class: An Economic Study of Institutions* (New York: Viking, 1931); Roland Barthes, *The Fashion System*, trans. Matthew Ward and Richard Howard (Berkeley: University of California Press, 1990); Alison Lurie, *The Language of Clothes* (New York: Vintage, 1983); Georg Simmel, "Fashion," *International Quarterly*, 10 (October 1904): 130–55; Anne Hollander, *Seeing Through Clothes* (New York: Penguin, 1988); and Elizabeth Wilson, *Adorned in Dreams: Fashion and Modernity* (Berkeley: University of California Press, 1987).

8   For a more detailed discussion, see Wilson, *Adorned in Dreams*, 16–26.

9   Natalie Rothstein, ed., *Four Hundred Years of Fashion* (London: Victoria and Albert Museum, 1984), 62–64; Farid Chenoune, *A History of Men's Fashion*, trans. Deke Dusinberre (Paris: Flammarion, 1993), 30 and 34; and Aileen Ribeiro, *The Art of Dress: Fashion in England and France, 1750–1820* (New Haven: Yale University Press, 1995), 107 and 222–30.

10  For further discussion of these complex issues, see Michael Khodarkovsky, "'Ignoble Savages and Unfaithful Subjects': Constructing Non-Christian Identities in Early Modern Russia," and Yuri Slezkine, "Naturalists versus Nations: Eighteenth-Century Russian Scholars Confront Ethnic Diversity," in *Russia's Orients: Imperial Borderlands and Peoples, 1700–1917*, ed. Daniel R. Brower and Edward J. Lazzerini (Bloomington: Indiana University Press, 1997): 9–26 and 27–57.

11  Alison Hilton, *Russian Folk Art* (Bloomington: Indiana University Press, 1995), 96.

12  David Kuchta, "The Making of the Self-Made Man: Class, Clothing, and English Masculinity, 1688–1832," in *The Sex of Things: Gender and Consumption in Historical Perspective*, ed. Victoria de Grazia with Ellen Furlough (Berkeley: University of California Press, 1996), 54–78.

13  Marshall S. Shatz, ed. and trans., "'Evgenii Onegin and his Ancestors' by V. O. Kliuchevskii," *Canadian-American Slavic Studies*, 16, 2 (Summer 1982): 241.

14  These include the draped costume, slip-on costume, closed

sewn costume, open sewn costume, and sheath costume. See François Boucher, *20,000 Years of Fashion: The History of Costume and Personal Adornment* (New York: Abrams, 1987), 12.

15 On Turkish trousers for men, see Chenoune, *A History of Men's Fashion*, 76–77. On bloomers, see Wilson, *Adorned in Dreams*, 209; Lois W. Banner, *American Beauty* (Chicago: University of Chicago Press, 1983), 86–105; and Nancy G. Isenberg, *Sex and Citizenship in Antebellum America* (Chapel Hill: University of North Carolina Press, 1999), 48–55, 100.

16 Wilson, *Adorned in Dreams*; Judith G. Coffin, *The Politics of Women's Work: The Paris Garment Trades, 1750–1915* (Princeton: Princeton University Press, 1996); Daniel Roche, *The Culture of Clothing: Dress and Fashion in the "Ancien Régime,"* trans. Jean Birrell (Cambridge: Cambridge University Press, 1994); Beverly Lemire, *Fashion's Favorite: The Cotton Trade and the Consumer in Britain, 1660–1800* (Oxford: Oxford University Press, 1991); and Jennifer M. Jones, *Sexing La Mode: Gender, Fashion, and Commercial Culture in Old Regime France* (Oxford: Berg, 2004).

17 Jan de Vries, "The Industrial Revolution and the Industrious Revolution," *Journal of Economic History*, 54, 2 (June 1994): 249–70; and John Brewer and Roy Porter, eds., *Consumption and the World of Goods* (New York: Routledge, 1993).

18 A good introduction to this debate can be found in Tessie P. Liu, *The Weaver's Knot: The Contradictions of Class Struggle and Family Solidarity in Western France, 1750–1914* (Ithaca: Cornell University Press, 1994); Coffin, *The Politics of Women's Work*; and de Grazia, ed., *The Sex of Things*.

19 For an introduction to this debate, see Neil McKendrick, John Brewer, and J. H. Plumb, *The Birth of a Consumer Society: The Commercialization of English Society* (Bloomington: Indiana University Press, 1982); Rosalind H. Williams, *Dream Worlds: Mass Consumption in Late Nineteenth-Century France* (Berkeley: University of California Press, 1982); Chandra Mukerji, *From Graven Images: Patterns of Modern Materialism* (New York: Columbia University Press, 1983); Grant McCracken, *Culture and Consumption: New Approaches to the Symbolic Character of Consumer Goods and Activities* (Bloomington: Indiana University Press, 1990); and de Grazia, ed., *The Sex of Things*.

20 For a good introduction to this complex problem, see Samuel D. Kassow, James L. West, and Edith W. Clowes, "The Problem of the Middle in Late Imperial Russian History," in *Between Tsar and People: Educated Society and the Quest for Public Identity in Late Imperial Russia*, ed. Edith W. Clowes, Samuel D. Kassow, and James L. West (Princeton: Princeton University Press, 1991), 3–14.

21 Alexander Gerschenkron, "Economic Backwardness in Historical Perspective," *Economic Backwardness in Historical Perspective: A Book of Essays* (Cambridge, Mass.: Belknap Press, 1962): 5–30 for the classic statement concerning Russia's backwardness. An example of the prevalence of this view of Russian economic development can be found in David Mackenzie and Michael W. Curran, *A History of Russia and the Soviet Union*, third edition (Chicago: Dorsey Press, 1987), 453–59.

22 Richard S. Wortman, *Scenarios of Power: Myth and Ceremony in Russian Monarchy*, 2 vols. (Princeton: Princeton University Press,

1995 and 2000); Priscilla Roosevelt, *Life on the Russian Country Estate: A Social and Cultural History* (New Haven: Yale University Press, 1995); and Arcadius Kahan, *The Plow, the Hammer, and the Knout: An Economic History of Eighteenth-Century Russia* (Chicago: University of Chicago Press, 1985).

23 *PSZ*, no. 8301 (1740), 320–21; and no. 8680 (1742), 732–34. Catherine the Great ordered women at court to wear a special gown for all important occasions. *Russkii kostium, 1750–1830* (Moscow: Vserossiiskoe teatral'noe obshchestvo, 1960); and Wortman, *Scenarios of Power*, I: 136.

## I    THE EMPEROR'S NEW CLOTHES:
## THE CREATION OF A FASHION INDUSTRY

1 For a history of the Russian economy during this period, see Arcadius Kahan, *The Plow, the Hammer, and the Knout: An Economic History of Eighteenth-Century Russia* (Chicago: University of Chicago Press), 1985; and Richard Hellie, *The Economy and Material Culture of Russia, 1600–1725* (Chicago: University of Chicago Press, 1999).

2 Lawrence Langner, *The Importance of Wearing Clothes* (New York: Hastings House, 1959), 132. For a discussion of military uniforms, see Daniel Roche, *The Culture of Clothing: Dress and Fashion in the "Ancien Régime"*, trans. Jean Birrell (Cambridge: Cambridge University Press, 1994), 221–56; and Philip Mansel, "Monarchy, Uniform, and the Rise of the Frac, 1760–1830," *Past and Present*, 96 (August 1982): 103–32.

3 All branches of service had at least five or six different uniforms worn for separate and distinct occasions. There were uniforms for everyday wear, dress uniforms for special occasions, summer uniforms, and uniforms for traveling. Special government commissions issued frequent regulations concerning the wearing of uniforms. For example, the *Digest of Russian Laws* contained the regulations for civil servants. See A. A. Dobrovol'skii, ed., *Svod zakonov Rossiiskoi imperii*, 2nd edition (St. Petersburg: Zakonovedenie, 1913), III: 1741–60. The best introduction to the history of Russian uniforms for all branches of government is L. E. Shepelev, *Tituly, mundiry, ordena v Rossiiskoi imperii* (Leningrad: Nauka, 1988).

4 L. E. Shepelev, *Tituly, mundiry, ordena v Rossiiskoi imperii* (Leningrad: Nauka, 1988), 12–26.

5 Rossiiskii gosudarstvennyi istoricheskii arkhiv (RGIA), f. 469, op. 9, ch. 1, d. 5, ll. 1–4.

6 For a fascinating discussion of the Romanov dynasty's attempts to bring European ceremony and ritual to Russia, see Richard S. Wortman, *Scenarios of Power: Myth and Ceremony in Russian Monarchy*, 2 vols. (Princeton: Princeton University Press, 1995 and 2000).

7 E. V. Kireeva, *Istoriia kostiuma: Evropeiskii kostium ot antichnosti do XX veka* (Moscow: Prosveshchenie, 1976), 131.

8 For more on the impact of Peter the Great's dress decrees, see Raisa M. Kirsanova, *Russkii kostium i byt XVIII–XIX vekov* (Moscow: Slovo, 2002), 9–51.

9 A good introduction to this debate can be found in Jan de Vries,

"The Industrial Revolution and the Industrious Revolution," *The Journal of Economic History*, 54, 2 (June 1994): 249–70.

10  The most complete discussion of this phenomenon can be found in Beverly Lemire, *Fashion's Favorite: The Cotton Trade and the Consumer in Britain, 1660–1800* (Oxford: Oxford University Press, 1991).

11  Roche, *Culture of Clothing*; Alexander J. Warden, *The Linen Trade: Ancient and Modern* (London: Longman, Roberts & Green, 1864); and Lemire, *Fashion's Favorite*.

12  G. G. Gromov, "Odezhda," *Ocherki russkoi kul'tury XVII veka* (Moscow: Izdatel'stvo Moskovskogo universiteta, 1979), I: 202–18; and M. N. Levinson-Nechaeva, "Odezhda i tkani XVI–XVII vekov," *Gosudarstvennaia oruzhenaia palata Moskovskogo kremlia* (Moscow, 1954), 307–86.

13  *Opisanie pervoi publichnoi vystavki rossiiskikh manufakturnykh izdelii, byvshei v Sankt-Peterburge v 1829 goda* (St. Petersburg: Tipografiia ekspeditsii zagotovleniia Gosudarstvennykh bumag, 1829), 6. Catherine II's 1782 decree ordering all court dress to be made from Russian silk can be found in *PSZ*, series 1, vol. 21, no. 15,569.

14  For eighteenth-century developments in textiles, see Kahan, *Plow*, chapter 3; Mikhail I. Tugan-Baranovsky, *The Russian Factory in the Nineteenth Century*, trans. Arthur Levin and Claora S. Levin (Homewood: Richard D. Irwin, Inc., 1970), Part One.

15  *Otchet deiatel'nosti Ministerstva imperatorskogo dvora po prigotovleniiam i ustroistvu torzhestv sviashchennogo koronovaniia ikh imperatorskikh velichestv v 1896 godu* (St. Petersburg: Izdaniie koronatsionnoi kantseliarii, 1896), II: 163–65.

16  For an introduction to the history of textile production in Russia, see *The Industries of Russia: Manufactures and Trade*, trans. John Martin Crawford (St. Petersburg: n.p., 1893); G. Schulze-Gävernitz, *Krupnoe proizvodstvo v Rossii (Moskovsko-Vladimirskaia khlopchatobumazhnaia promyshlennost')*, trans. B. V. Avilov (Moscow: Izdanie magazina Knizhnoe Delo, 1899); K. A. Pazhitnov, *Ocherki istorii tekstil'noi promyshlennosti dorevoliutsionnoi Rossii*, 2 vols. (Moscow: Izdatel'stvo Akademii Nauk SSSR, 1955 and 1958); and Ralph Odell, *Cotton Goods in Russia*, Department of Commerce and Labor, Bureau of Manufacturers Special Series, no. 51 (Washington: Government Printing Office, 1912).

17  Odell, *Cotton Goods*, 7.

18  E. Chernov, "Nashi fabriki i zavody: Tsindel'," *Zhivopisnaia Rossiia*, 27 (8 July 1901): 366.

19  Olga Crisp, *Studies in the Russian Economy before 1914* (London: Macmillan, 1978), 32.

20  Ibid., 141–50; Kahan, *Plow*, 136–38; and V. A. Kovrigina, "Nemetskaia sloboda v Moskve kontsa XVII-nachala XVIII veka," *Voprosy istorii*, 6 (1997): 146.

21  Throughout this study, both sexes served as apprentices, journeymen, and masters. While the Russian language allows for the inclusion of men and women with distinct words, English does not. Unless otherwise specified, my use of these terms includes both sexes.

22  D. I. Fonvizin, *Brigadir / Nedorosl'* (Leningrad: Khudozhestvennaia Literatura, 1972), 78.

23  Vasilii A. Riazanov, *Vzgliad po khod portnogo masterstva v Rossii* (St. Petersburg: Gutenbergovaia tipografiia, 1847), 4–7.

24  "Avtobiografiia Platonovoi, Anny Fedorovny," Gosudarstvennyi Arkhiv Rossiiskoi Federatsii (GARF), f. 3986, op. 1, d. 1, ll. 8–9.

25  "Avtobiografiia Iusima, A. G.," GARF, f. 6862, op. 1, d. 32, l. 20.

26  "Gomel'skii soiuz Shveiprom v Podol'e," GARF, f. 6869, op. 1, d. 13, l. 17 ob.

27  N. Matveevskii, *Portnoi* (St. Petersburg: Tipografiia Karla Mettsinga, 1857), 13–15.

28  "Vospominaniia Pirogova," GARF, f. 6869, op. 1, d. 12, ll. 12–14.

29  Matveevskii, *Portnoi*, 1–3.

30  M. I. Pokrovskaia, "Peterburgskaia rabotnitsa," *Mir bozhii*, 12 (1900): 31.

31  Rabotnitsa, "Trud rabotnits-portnikh," *Vestnik portnykh*, 6–7 (2 January 1914): 8.

32  I. Eremeev, *Gorod S.-Peterburga s tochki zreniia meditsinskoi politsii* (St. Petersburg: Tip. M. D. Lomkovskogo, 1897), 70–72, 199–203.

33  Portnikha A. P., "V passazhe," *Listok soiuza rabochikh, portnykh, portnikh i skorniakov*, 8 (1906): 6. (*Listok*) Before the invention of electric irons, sewing workshops were always stifling because of the need to keep the irons hot. Stoves were stoked constantly so that the irons were ready at all times.

34  S. I. Gruzdev, *Trud i bor'ba shveinikov v Peterburge, 1905–1916: Istoricheskii ocherk* (Leningrad: Izdanie Leningradskogo oblastnogo soiuza rabochikh shveinoi promyshlennosti, 1929), 14–16.

35  Tovarishch portnikha no. 25, "K portnikham," *Listok*, 19 (1906), 6.

36  Gruzdev, *Trud*, 15.

37  Ibid., 10.

38  "Vospominaniia 'Uchenika' Poliakova," GARF, f. 6869, op. 1, d. 13, l. 102.

39  E. A. Oliunina, *Portnovskii promysel v Moskve i v derevniakh Moskovskoi i Riazanskoi gubernii* (Moscow: Tvo. tipografii A. I. Mamontova, 1914), 7–8.

40  Tovarishch, "Ot Ganri," *Listok*, 16 (1906): 6.

41  "Dvadtsatiletie Bakinskogo soiuza shveinikov," GARF, f. 6869, op. 1, d. 13, l. 104.

42  "Avtobiografiia Sokolinskogo Grigoriia Mikhailovicha," GARF, f. 6869, op. 1, d. 43, l. 75.

43  Claudia Kidwell, *Cutting a Fashionable Fit: Dressmakers' Drafting Systems in the United States* (Washington: Smithsonian Institution Press, 1978), 4.

44  Gruzdev, *Trud*, 5.

45  Matveevskii, *Portnoi*, 22–25.

46  For an introduction to the literature on Russian guilds, see K. A. Pazhitnov, *Problema remeslennykh tsekhov v zakonodatel'stve russkogo absoliutizma* (Moscow: Izdatel'stvo Akademii Nauk SSSR, 1952); F. Polianskii, *Gorodskoe remeslo i manufaktura v Rossii v XVIII v.* (Moscow, 1960); A. I. Kopanev, *Naselenie Peterburga v pervoi polovine XIX veka* (Leningrad: Izdatel'stvo Akademii Nauk SSSR, 1957); Victoria E. Bonnell, *Roots of Rebellion: Workers' Politics and Organizations in St. Petersburg and Moscow, 1900–1914* (Berkeley: University of California Press, 1983); and Reginald

E. Zelnik, *Labor and Society in Tsarist Russia: The Factory Workers of St. Petersburg, 1855–1870* (Stanford: Stanford University Press, 1971).

47 Eremeev, *Gorod S.-Peterburga*, 501–02.

48 Matveevskii, *Portnoi*, 34–50.

49 Ibid., 25–72.

50 Gruzdev, *Trud*, 5.

51 Tatiana Strizhenova, *Soviet Costume and Textiles, 1917–1945*, trans. Era Mozolkova (New York: Flammarion, 1991), 68–73.

52 Leo Tolstoy, *Anna Karenina*, trans. Constance Garnett (New York: Random House, 1965), 323.

53 Nikolai Gogol, "Shinel'," *N. Gogol', 1802–1852: Vechera na khutore bliz dikan' ki, Mirgorod, Povesti* (Moscow: Moskovskii rabochii, 1970), 529.

54 Ibid., 536.

55 Ibid., 528–36.

56 In the rest of the story, someone steals Akakii's new coat just a few days later, which causes him to die of despair.

57 Gruzdev, *Trud*, 5.

58 For examples, see the entry for Fr. Fredlikh in *Ves' Peterburg*, (1907), 1,338; and F. I. Il'gekit in *Ves' Peterburg* (1912), 1,535.

59 *Svod zakonov*, book III (1832), 70.

60 "Vedomost' Moskovskoi remeslennoi upravy," RGIA, f. 18, op. 2, d. 435, l. 3.

61 *Sanktpeterburg po perepisi 10 dekabria 1869 goda* (St. Petersburg: Tipografiia Maikova, 1875), III: 8–10, 42–45, 92–95, 196–99. The compilers of the census state clearly that all of their figures are approximate and do not reveal the exact number of workers in any of the trades.

62 The 1869 Petersburg census listed foreign garment workers by nationality and religion. See ibid., 144–47, 196–99.

63 Riazanov, *Vzgliad*, 2.

64 "Po prosheniiu portnogo mastera Eduarda Ditrikha s proektom ob otkrytii v Sankt-Peterburge zavedeniia: 'Remeslennoe spravochnoe mesto dlia masterov, podmaster'ev, rabotnikov i masterits vsiakogo roda,'" RGIA, f. 1287, op. 37, d. 727; and "Po proektu portnogo tsekha mastera Eduarda Diderikha ob uchrezhdenii v Sankt-Peterburga Spravochnoi Kontory dlia lits zanimaiushchikhsia proizvodstvom portnogo remesla," ibid., d. 1624.

65 "Ob otkrytii v Sankt-Peterburge voskresnye klassy," RGIA, f. 1287, op. 37, d. 1931; and N. Rubakin, "Voskresnyie shkoly," *Entsiklopedicheskii slovar'*, ed. F. A. Brokgauz and I. A. Efron (St. Petersburg: Tipo-Litografiia I. A. Efrona, 1892), VII: 255. For a history of the Sunday-school movement in Russia, see Zelnik, *Labor*, 173–99.

## 2   THE GENDERING OF SEWING IN RUSSIA

1 P. I. Glukhovskii, *Otchet general'nogo kommisara russkogo otdela Vsemirnoi Kolumbovskoi Vystavki v Chikago* (Petersburg: Tip. V. Kirshbauma, 1895). For a general history of the exhibition, see David F. Burg, *Chicago's White City of 1893* (Lexington: University Press of Kentucky, 1976).

2 *World's Columbian Exposition 1893 Chicago: Catalogue of the Russian Section* (St. Petersburg: Imperial Russian Commission, Ministry of Finance, 1893), 244–71.

3 Burg, *Chicago's White City*, 209. According to Burg, the exhibition marked the recognition of women's contributions to American society. A woman's congress was held at the Women's Building during the spring of 1893. See ibid., 239–49.

4 Jean H. Quataert, "The Shaping of Women's Work in Manufacturing: Guilds, Households, and the State in Central Europe, 1648–1870," *American Historical Review*, 90, 5 (1985): 1,124.

5 Anne Phillips and Barbara Taylor, "Sex and Skill: Notes Towards a Feminist Economics," *Feminist Review*, 6 (1980): 79.

6 Quoted in J. L. Black, "Educating Women in Eighteenth-Century Russia: Myths and Realities," *Canadian Slavonic Papers*, 20, 1 (March 1978): 23.

7 Bonnie G. Smith, *Changing Lives: Women in European History Since 1700* (Lexington: D. C. Heath and Co., 1989), 26–33 and 82–84.

8 Fénelon, *De L'Éducation des filles* (Paris: Librairie Hachette, 1920); and Jean-Jacques Rousseau, *La Nouvelle Héloïse: Julie, or the New Eloise*, Judith H. McDowell, trans. (University Park: Pennsylvania State University Press, 1968). For a discussion of how this transformation in women's social roles occurred in France, see Lieselotte Steinbrügge, *The Moral Sex: Woman's Nature in the French Enlightenment*, trans. Pamela E. Selwyn (New York: Oxford University Press, 1995).

9 An excellent discussion of domesticity can be found in Leonore Davidoff and Catherine Hall, *Family Fortunes: Men and Women of the English Middle Class, 1789–1850* (Chicago: University of Chicago Press, 1987).

10 Steinbrügge, in *Moral Sex*, 18, states that Fénelon's educational philosophy was particularly oriented toward household management. For a discussion of writers who influenced Catherine II's educational policies, see Richard Stites, *The Women's Liberation Movement in Russia: Feminism, Nihilism, and Bolshevism, 1860–1930*, revised edition (Princeton: Princeton University Press, 1991), 3; David L. Ransel, *Mothers of Misery: Child Abandonment in Russia* (Princeton: Princeton University Press, 1988), 31–38; J. L. Black, *Citizens for the Fatherland: Education, Educators, and Pedagogical Ideals in Eighteenth-Century Russia* (Boulder: East European Quarterly, 1979), 152–71; and Carol S. Nash, "Educating New Mothers: Women and the Enlightenment in Russia," *History of Education Quarterly* (Fall 1981): 301–16.

11 A comprehensive history of Smol'nyi can be found in N. P. Cherepnin, *Imperatorskoe vospitatel'noe obshchestvo blagorodnykh devits: Istoricheskii ocherk, 1764–1914*, 3 vols. (St. Petersburg: Gosudarstvennaia Tipografiia, 1914). For a discussion of the educational philosophies of Catherine the Great and Betskoi, see ibid., I: 26–43.

12 *PSZ*, 1st series, no. 12,154.

13 *PSZ*, 1st series, no. 12,323.

14 V. Ia. Stoiunin, "Obrazovanie russkoi zhenshchiny," *Pedagogicheskie sochineniia*, 2nd. edition (St. Petersburg: Tipografiia M. M. Stasiulevicha, 1903), 480.

15  Stites, *Women's Liberation Movement*, 3.

16  E. Likhacheva, *Materialy dlia istorii zhenskogo obrazovaniia v Rossii, 1796–1828* (St. Petersburg: Tipografiia M. M. Stasiulevicha, 1893), 186.

17  Richard Wortman discusses Maria Fedorovna's important influence on court ideology and ritual. See Richard Wortman, "The Russian Empress as Mother," *The Family in Imperial Russia: New Lines of Historical Research*, ed. David L. Ransel (Urbana: University of Illinois Press, 1978), 60–74. See also ibid., *Scenarios of Power*, 250–54; Likhacheva, *Materialy*, passim; and Barbara Alpern Engel, *Mothers and Daughters: Women of the Intelligentsia in Nineteenth-Century Russia* (New York: Cambridge University Press, 1983), 23–25. On Maria Fedorovna's love of the arts, see Cherepnin, *Imperatorskoe vospitatel'noe obshchestvo*, I: 471–81. Margaret Darrow argues that in France aristocratic women used domesticity to reassert their elite social status. See Margaret H. Darrow, "French Noblewomen and the New Domesticity, 1750–1850," *Feminist Studies*, 5, 1 (Spring 1979): 41–65.

18  Cherepnin, *Imperatorskoe vospitatel'noe obshchestvo*, I: 477.

19  This social distinction could also be found in housekeeping. While teachers instructed non-noble girls in cooking, washing, and accounting as part of the school curriculum, noble girls did not receive such classroom instruction. However, Maria Fedorovna instructed that each noble girl would periodically serve as a classroom monitor (*dezhurnaia*). Her duties included supervision of the kitchen, laundry, and general order in the school. Thus, non-noble girls were taught how to work and noble girls how to supervise. See "Vysochaishee povelenie Imperatritsy Marii Fedorovny Sovetu Vospitatel'nogo Obshchestva blagorodnykh devits otnositel'no obucheniia vospitannits domovodstva," in Cherepnin, *Imperatorskoe vospitatel'noe obshchestvo*, III: 238–40. Jean Quataert observed a similar phenomenon in German sewing schools for a later period. See Quataert, "The Shaping of Women's Work," 1,141.

20  Elena Rostopchina, "The Unfinished Sewing," *An Anthology of Russian Women's Writing, 1777–1992*, ed. Catriona Kelly (New York: Oxford University Press, 1994), 19–21.

21  Rozsika Parker, *The Subversive Stitch: Embroidery and the Making of the Feminine* (London: The Women's Press, 1984), 1–16. It is interesting to note that Nadezhda Durova describes her intense dislike of needlework. In her memoirs, sewing became a symbol of her hatred for the "woman's lot." See Nadezhda Durova, *The Cavalry Maiden: Journals of a Russian Officer in the Napoleonic Wars*, trans. Mary Fleming Zirin (Bloomington: Indiana University Press, 1989), passim.

22  Jennifer M. Jones, "'The Taste for Fashion, and Frivolity': Gender, Clothing and the Commercial Culture of the Old Regime" (Ph.D. diss., Princeton University, 1991), 271–87; and Parker, *The Subversive Stitch*, 5.

23  *PSZ*, 1st series, no. 3,708 and no. 3,980.

24  Vladimir Dal', *Tolkovyi slovar' zhivogo velikorusskogo iazyka* (St. Petersburg: Izdanie knigoprodavtsa-tipografa M. O. Vol'fa, 1882), 4: 112.

25  Stites, *Women's Liberation Movement*, 4–6.

26  Nikolai Gogol, *Dead Souls*, trans. David Magarshack (New York: Penguin Books, 1961), 36.

27  For a comprehensive history of Russian charity, see Adele Lindenmeyr, *Poverty Is Not a Vice: Charity, Society, and the State in Imperial Russia* (Princeton: Princeton University Press, 1996).

28  For a discussion of Maria Fedorovna's role as the head of Russian charity, see Ransel, *Mothers of Misery*, 70–76.

29  Joseph Bradley compares the foundling home with another welfare organization, the workhouse, which was also introduced into Russia by Catherine the Great. See Joseph Bradley, *Muzhik and Muscovite: Urbanization in Late Imperial Russia* (Berkeley: University of California Press, 1985), 267–69.

30  Overwhelmed by the large numbers of children who were brought to the foundling homes as a result of the open admissions policy adopted under Betskoi, Maria Fedorovna eventually changed the policy so that more children remained in the countryside. For a fuller discussion, see Ransel, *Mothers of Misery*, 31–83.

31  A list of these organizations can be found in Imperatorskoe Russkoe Tekhnicheskoe Obshchestvo (RTO), *Professional'nye zhenskie shkoly v Rossii i prepodavanie rukodeliia v obshcheobrazovatel'nykh uchebnykh zavedeniiakh*, ed. N. M. Korol'kov, 6–7 (St. Petersburg: Tipografiia Iu. N. Erlikh, 1890).

32  Ibid., 35 and 41.

33  E. S. Shumigorskii, *Imperatorskoe zhenskoe patrioticheskoe obshchestvo, 1812–1912: Istoricheskii ocherk* (St. Petersburg: Gosudarstvennaia tipografiia, 1912), 204.

34  "Patrioticheskoe obshchestvo," *Entsiklopedichskii slovar'*, ed. F. A. Brokgauz and I. A. Efron (St. Petersburg: Tipo-Litografiia I. A. Efrona, 1898), 23: 38. For a list of the members of the society, see A. F. Bardovskii, *Patrioticheskii institut* (St. Petersburg: Tipografiia T-ve E. Veierman, 1913), 230–32.

35  Stoiunin, "Obrazovanie russkoi zhenshchiny," 485.

36  A. Ia., "Zhenskoe obrazovanie," *Entsiklopedicheskii slovar'* ed. F. A. Brokgauz and I. A. Efron (St. Petersburg: Tipo-Litografiia I. A. Efrona, 1898), 22: 867–68.

37  Stites, *Women's Liberation Movement*, 37.

38  Ibid., 30–33.

39  Quoted in E. Likhacheva, "Nachalo zhenskikh gimnazii v Rossii," *Vestnik Evropy*, 3 (March 1897), 168.

40  Christine Ruane, *Gender, Class, and the Professionalization of Russian City Teachers, 1860–1914* (Pittsburgh: University of Pittsburgh Press, 1994), 29–31 and 78–79. The Mariinskaia schools were later changed to *gimnaziia*.

41  In 1853 the Empress Alexandra Fedorovna requested that the noble girls attending Smol'nyi Institute spend less time making lace and satin flowers and devote themselves to clothing production. Thus, even at Smol'nyi Institute the social dimension to sewing was beginning to breakdown. See Cherepnin, *Imperatorskoe vospitatel'noe obshchestvo*, II: 79.

42  Quoted in Likhacheva, "Nachalo zhenskikh gimnazii," 173–74.

43  For a fuller discussion of this issue, see Ruane, *Gender*.

44  Stites, *Women's Liberation Movement*, 35.

45  Maria Vernadskaia, "Zhenskii trud," *Sobranie sochinenii pokoinoi*

*Marii Nikolaevny Vernadskoi, urozhd. Shigaevoi* (St. Petersburg, 1862), 94.

46  Ibid., "Naznachenie zhenshchiny," 119.

47  Ibid., "Zhenskii trud," 102.

48  Ibid., 100 and 106–07.

49  Ibid., 105.

50  Ibid., 106.

51  Nikolai G. Chernyshevsky, *What Is to Be Done? Tales About New People*, trans. Benjamin R. Tucker (New York: Vintage Books, 1961), 18.

52  On Chernyshevskii, see Stites, *Women's Liberation Movement*, 118. On the family values of the utopian socialists, see Claire Goldberg Moses, "Saint-Simonian Men/Saint-Simonian Women: The Transformation of Feminist Thought in 1830s' France," *Journal of Modern History*, 54 (June 1982): 240–67.

53  Stites, *Women's Liberation Movement*, 118–21.

54  For a history of the sewing machine, see Grace Rogers Cooper, *History of the Sewing Machine* (Washington: Smithsonian Institution Press, 1968).

55  Ruth Brandon, *A Capitalist Romance: Singer and the Sewing Machine* (New York: J. B. Lippincott Company, 1977), 111–40; Ava Baron and Susan E. Klepp, "'If I Didn't Have My Sewing Machine . . .': Women and Sewing Machine Technology," *A Needle, A Bobbin, A Strike: Women Needleworkers in America*, ed. Joan M. Jensen and Sue Davidson (Philadelphia: Temple University Press, 1984): 30–45; and Fred V. Carstensen, *American Enterprise in Foreign Markets: Studies of Singer and International Harvester in Imperial Russia* (Chapel Hill: University of North Carolina Press, 1984), 28–38.

56  Ibid., 27.

57  M. Ia. Kittary, *Obozrenie sanktpeterburgskoi vystavki russkoi manufakturnoi promyshlennosti 1861 goda* (St. Petersburg: Tipografiia Lermantova i Komp., 1861), 323.

58  *Tovarishchestvo na paiakh Zh. Blok, Illiustrirovanyi preis-kurant shveinoi mashin vsekh sistem* (Moscow: Tov. A. A. Levenson, 1905), 3.

59  See Carstensen, *American Enterprise*; and Robert Bruce Davies, *Peacefully Working to Conquer the World: Singer Sewing Machines in Foreign Markets, 1854–1920* (New York: Arno Press, 1976), 243–333.

60  Carstensen, *American Enterprise*, 28–78.

61  *Katalog shveinym mashinam amerikanskim i nemetskim iz zavoda, ustroennogo po amerikanskoi sisteme, L. Bol'mana v Vene, glavnyi sklad dlia Iuzhnogo Rossii v Odesse, u Gustava Al'bertovicha Tsorina, na Aleksandrovskom prospekte, d. 9* (Odessa: Tip. L. Nitche, 1868), 5.

62  Ibid., 6.

63  Ibid., 8.

64  Joan Wallach Scott, "'L'Ouvrière! Mot impie, sordide . . .': Women Workers in the Discourse of French Political Economy, 1840–1860," *Gender and the Politics of History* (New York: Columbia University Press, 1988), 142.

65  George Siegel, "The Fallen Woman in Nineteenth-Century Russian Literature," *Harvard Slavic Studies*, 5 (1970): 102–03.

66  Anton Chekhov, "An Attack of Nerves," *The Portable Chekhov*, ed. Avrahm Yarmolinsky (New York: Penguin, 1977): 242–43. Emphasis added.

67  For a detailed account of these women migrants, see Barbara Alpern Engel, *Between the Fields and the City: Women, Work, and Family in Russia, 1861–1914* (New York: Cambridge University Press, 1994). See also Rose L. Glickman, *Russian Factory Women: Workplace and Society, 1880–1914* (Berkeley: University of California Press, 1984). For a discussion of working women in France, see Joan Wallach Scott, "'L'Ouvrière!'", 139–63.

68  For a fuller discussion of this, see Ben Eklof, *Russian Peasant Schools: Officialdom, Village Culture, and Popular Pedagogy, 1861–1914* (Berkeley: University of California Press, 1986).

69  For an account of some of the relief agencies, see Bradley, *Muzhik and Muscovite*, 249–357; and Adele Lindenmeyr, "A Russian Experiment in Voluntarism: The Municipal Guardianships of the Poor, 1894–1914," *Jahrbücher für Geschichte Osteuropas*, 30 (1982): 429–51.

70  The Russian Technical Society collected data on these schools and published this information in 1890. See RTO, *Professional'nye zhenskie shkoly*, 3–166.

71  M. Dukhovskoi, "Shveinaia masterskaia dlia zhenshchin," *Trudovaia pomoshch'*, 7 (September 1900): 188. *Trudovaia pomoshch'* contains numerous small articles about similar workshops and sewing schools.

72  Obshchestvo rasprostraneniia prakticheskikh znanii mezhdu obrazovannymi zhenshchinami, *Svedeniia o tseli i sostav Obshchestva, o ego shkolakh i uchrezhdeniiakh i o prieme uchenits* (Moscow: Tipo-litografiia A. V. Vasil'eva i Ko., 1900), 3.

73  Ibid., *Otchet za 1909–10 uchebnyi god* (Moscow: Tip. Tor. Doma M. V. Balgin Ko., 1911): 64–65.

74  M. G. Levitskii, *O zhenskom prikladnom i remeslennom obrazovanii* (St. Petersburg: Tipografiia S. Dobrodeeva, 1882), title page.

75  Phillips and Taylor, "Sex and Skill," 82–83.

*3*  THE RISE OF READY-TO-WEAR

1  For a discussion of the changes in the garment trades, see Judith G. Coffin, *The Politics of Women's Work: The Paris Garment Trades, 1750–1915* (Princeton: Princeton University Press, 1996); Beverly Lemire, *Dress, Culture, and Commerce: The English Clothing Trade before the Factory, 1660–1800* (London: St. Martin's Press, 1997); and James A. Schmiechen, *Sweated Industries and Sweated Labor: The London Clothing Trades, 1860–1914* (Urbana: University of Illinois Press, 1984).

2  Philippe Perrot, *Fashioning the Bourgeoisie: A History of Clothing in the Nineteenth Century*, trans. Richard Bienvenu (Princeton: Princeton University Press, 1994), 52–54.

3  N. Matveevskii, *Portnoi* (St. Petersburg: Tipografiia Karla Metinga, 1857), 75.

4  An advertisement for Madame Teodor's courses can be found in the 1904 Petersburg city directory. The advertisement lists two locations in Petersburg, one each in Moscow and Saratov. *Ves' Peterburg na 1904 g.* (St. Petersburg: A. S. Suvorin, 1904), 34. Vasilii A. Riazanov, *Vzgliad po khod portnogo masterstva v Rossii*

(St. Petersburg: Gutenbergovaia tipografiia, 1847); and Aleksandr I. Katun, *Portnoi: Pervyi Rossiiskii khudozhestvennyi al'bom-uchebnik shit'ia damskogo i muzhshkogo plat'ia* (St. Petersburg: Leshtukovskaia Parovaia Skoropechatnia P. O. Iablonskogo, 1907).

5   The best history of this fascinating topic is Claudia B. Kidwell, *Cutting a Fashionable Fit: Dressmakers' Drafting Systems in the United States* (Washington: Smithsonian Institution Press, 1979).

6   Schmiechen, *Sweated Industries*, 25.

7   E. A. Oliunina, *Portnovskii promysel v Moskve i v derevniakh Moskovskoi i Riazanskoi gubernii: Materialy k istorii domashnei promyshlennosti v Rossii* (Moscow: Tvo. tipografii A. I. Mamontova, 1914), 17–18.

8   "Kniga tarifov," *PSZ*, first series, XLV: 66–67.

9   Tariff statutes included *bel'ie* along with clothing. It is difficult to find an exact English translation for *bel'ie*. Throughout the imperial period, *bel'ie* included not just underwear but also men's shirts, nightclothes for both sexes, and women's camisoles, slips, and other garments worn under the dress, and thereby constituted an enormous sector of the clothing industry. The Russian term is similar to the French *linge*, meaning linen. In France, all of the goods that were originally made from unbleached linen in the early modern period were called lingerie. The Russian word *bel'ie*, meaning all clothing made from unbleached material, was then adopted to signify this category of clothing. See Vladimir Dal', *Tolkovyi slovar' zhivogo velikorusskogo iazyka* (Moscow: Russkii iazyk, 1981), I: 155.

10   "Kniga tarifov," 180–81.

11   For a history of Russian tariff policy, see Konstantin Lodyzhenskii, *Istoriia russkogo tamozhennogo tarifa* (St. Petersburg: Tipografiia V. S. Balasheva, 1886).

12   Ibid. As far as I have been able to determine, fashionable clothing here meant clothing purchased in dressmaking shops and fancy-goods stores. Everything else was subject to import duties. See also *Opisanie pervoi publichnoi vystavki rossiiskikh manufakturnykh izdelii, byvshei v Sankt-Peterburge v 1829 goda* (St. Petersburg: Tipografiia ekspeditsii zagotovleniia Gosudarstvennykh bumag, 1829), 12–13.

13   G. G. Peizen, "O torgovykh operatsiiakh Peterburgskogo porta s inostrannym gosudarstvami," *Sovremmenik* (May 1858): 138–56.

14   *Gosudarstvennaia vneshniaia torgovlia v raznykh ee vidakh za 1854 god, stat'i* 251, 361, 362.; *Gosudarstvennaia vneshiaia torgovlia . . . za 1857 god, stat'ia* 333. These government figures do not represent the total number of clothes that entered Russia during those years. Smuggling remained a constant problem throughout the century, so it must be assumed that these numbers were higher. Nevertheless, it is impossible to calculate how much higher. See D. Riazanov, "Kontrabanda gotovym plat'em," *Moskovskie vedomosti*, 76 (17 March 1882): 5, and 77 (18 March 1882): 4. For the government reply that denied Riazanov's accusations of smuggling, see "Otvet na stat'iu G. Riazanova," *Moskovskie vedomosti*, 101 (13 April 1882): 4.

15   For a discussion of these issues, see Peter Gatrell, *The Tsarist Economy, 1850–1917* (London: B. T. Batsford, 1986), 165–67; Theodore H. von Laue, *Sergei Witte and the Industrialization of*

*Russia* (New York: Athenum, 1969), 27–30. On the role of the textile manufacturers, see Muriel Joffe, "Regional Rivalry and Economic Nationalism: The Central Industrial Region Industrialists' Strategy for the Development of the Russian Economy, 1880–1914," *Russian History*, 11, 4 (1984): 398–421.

16   Oliunina, *Portnovskii promysel*, 17–18.

17   G. Petukhov, "Obzor proizvodstva gotovogo verkhnogo plat'ia," *Uspekhi russkoi promyshlennosti po obrazam ekspertnykh kommissii Nizhnegorodskoi vystavki* (St. Petersburg: Tip. V. Demakova, 1897), 137.

18   Ibid., 137–38.

19   The Austrian government also instituted a protectionist tariff in 1882. For a discussion of these complex issues, see Nicholas V. Riasanovsky, *A History of Russia*, 5th ed. (New York: Oxford University Press, 1993), 386–87; C. A. Macartney, *The Hapsburg Empire, 1790–1918* (New York: Macmillan, 1969), 534 and 616; and David F. Good, *The Economic Rise of the Habsburg Empire, 1750–1914* (Berkeley: University of California Press, 1984), esp. 226–28.

20   "Kozha, kozhanye tovary, bashmaki i raznye predmedy tualety (Otchet G. Eduarda Pollan fon Borkenau, fabrikanta v Briune)," *Russkii manufakturist*, 10 (15 June 1884): 355–56.

21   Oliunina, *Portnovskii promysel*, 66–67; and "Beloomut: Vospominania Ivana Tepiakova," GARF, f. 6869, op. 1, d. 11, l. 1.

22   Oliunina, *Portnovskii promysel*, 72.

23   Ibid., 90.

24   Ibid., 59. Oliunina gives 3,952 as the number for rural garment workers, but her figures did not include all the Moscow districts that participated in the garment trades. Therefore, the real number is higher than the one she gives.

25   Vserossiiskii natsional'nyi soiuz, Moskovskii otdel, *Germanskie i Avstriiskie firmy v Moskve na 1914 god* (Moscow: Russkaia pechatnia, 1915), 36.

26   T. S. Aleshina, "K istorii proizvodstva odezhdy v kontse XIX–nachale XX veka: Po materialam Gosudarstvennogo istoricheskogo muzeia," *Muzei*, 19 (1989): 93.

27   Oliunina, *Portnovskii promysel*, 66–67.

28   Ministerstvo Torgovli i Promyshlennosti, *Torgovlia i promyshlennost' Evropeiskoi Rossii po raionam*, 13 vols. (St. Petersburg: Tip. V. F. Kirshbauma, 1909–11).

29   *Doklad Vysochaishe uchrezhdennoi Kommissiia dlia izsledovaniia polozheniia sel'skogo khoziaistva i sel'skoi proizvoditel'nosti v Rossii* (St. Petersburg: Tipografiia tovarishchestva obshchestvennaia pol'za, 1873), I: 225–52.

30   Ibid., 243–44.

31   Ibid., 225.

32   Barbara Alpern Engel, *Between the Fields and the City: Women, Work, and Family in Russia, 1861–1914* (New York: Cambridge University Press, 1994), 34–63; and Judith Pallot, "Women's Domestic Industries in Moscow Province, 1880–1900," *Russia's Women: Accommodation, Resistance, Transformation*, ed. Barbara Evans Clements, Barbara Alpern Engel, and Christine D. Worobec (Berkeley: University of California Press, 1991): 163–84.

33   *Sbornik statisticheskikh svedenii po Moskovskoi gubernii*, t. VII, vyp.

II  *Zhenskie promysli*, comp. M. K. Gorbunova (Moscow: Tipografiia S.V. Gur'ianova, 1882).

34  Ibid., iv–v.

35  Ibid., 31.

36  Ibid., 144.

37  Ibid., ix.

38  Ibid., 152.

39  Wendy R. Salmond, "The Modernization of Folk Art in Russia: The Revival of the Kustar Art Industries, 1885–1914" (Ph. D. dissertation, University of Texas, 1989), 48–49.

40  Elena Polenova and Maria Iakunchikova are the best-known of these artists. See ibid., 48–90.

41  S. A. Davydova, "Ocherk kruzhevnoi promyshlennosti v Rossii," *Kustarnaia promyshlennost' Rossii: Zhenskie promysli* (St. Petersburg: Tipo-Litografiia Iakor', 1913), 9.

42  For one typical example, see Olga Semyonova Tian-Shanskaia, *Village Life in Late Tsarist Russia*, ed. David L. Ransel (Bloomington: Indiana University Press, 1993), 118–23.

43  N. Kablukov, "Obshcheekonomicheskoe znachenie zhenskikh kustarnykh promyslov i sposoby sodeistviia im," *Novoe slovo*, 5 (February 1896): 65–66. Emphasis in the original.

44  Rose L. Glickman, *Russian Factory Women: Workplace and Society, 1880–1914* (Berkeley: University of California Press, 1984), 80.

45  Ibid., 145–50.

46  Laws banning night work for women were common in Europe. See Bonnie Smith, *Changing Lives*, 290–91; and Judith Coffin, *Politics*, 125–29. The French law banning night work for women and adolescents was passed in 1892, seven years after the Russian law.

47  Christine Ruane, *Gender, Class, and the Professionalization of Russian City Teachers* (Pittsburgh: University of Pittsburgh Press, 1994), 104. While women's vocational education was discussed at the other two congresses, only at the 1889 Congress did it spark controversy.

48  "Vstupitel'naia rech predsedatelia Ia. T. Mikhailovskogo," *ZRTO*, 2 (February 1891): 2.

49  S. A. Davydova, "O prakticheskikh rukodel'nykh uchebnykh kursakh dlia podgotovki masterits i uchitel'nits po remeslam, prepodavaemym v zhenskikh professional'nykh shkolakh," *ZRTO*, 2 (February 1891): 40.

50  "Prenie po dokladu A. M. Kotomina," *ZRTO*, 4 (April 1891): 190.

51  Ekaterina N. Ianzhul, *Rukodelie kak predmet obucheniia v narodnoi shkole* (St. Petersburg: Tip. M. M. Stasiulevicha, 1890). She was also the wife of I. I. Ianzhul, a prominent political economist and member of the Russian Technical Society.

52  For information about Davydova and a partial list of her writings, see Salmond, "The Modernization of Folk Art," 51–52.

53  S. A. Davydova, "I prakticheskikh rukodel'nykh uchebnykh kursakh dlia podgotovki masterits i uchitel'nits po remeslam prepodavalemym v zhenskikh professional'nykh shkolakh," *ZRTO*, 2 (February 1891): 35–41.

54  "Prenie po dokladu S. A. Davydovoi," *ZRTO*, 2 (February 1891): 45.

55  "Prenie po voprosam, predlozhennym Biuro IV Otdeleniia S"ezda," *ZRTO*, 2 (February 1891): 53.

56  "Preniia po voprosam, predlozhennym Biuro IV Otdeleniia S"ezda," *ZRTO*, 2 (February 1891): 56.

57  It was customary at this Congress to attempt to resolve all differences of opinion before voting on resolutions. Indeed, most resolutions passed unanimously. The fact that this resolution did not suggests the acrimony of the debate.

58  V. S. Sudylkovskii, "Igol'no-shveinoe i vyshival'noe masterstva v shkole, kak predmet obucheniia i, posle shkoly, kak sredstvo k propitaniiu, na osnovanii fakticheskikh dannykh," *ZRTO*, 4 (April 1891): 152.

59  "Prenie po dokladu V. S. Sudylkovskogo," *ZRTO*, 4 (April 1891): 169–72.

60  N. A. Osokin, "Professional'noe napravlenie zhenskikh gimnazii i progimnazii," *ZRTO*, 4 (April 1891): 133–41.

61  For France, see Coffin, *Politics*, 229–50. For England, see Clementina Black, *Sweated Industry and the Minimum Wage* (London: Duckworth, 1907); and Schmiechen, *Sweated Industries*. For the history of sweated homework in the United States, see Eileen Boris, *Home to Work: Motherhood and the Politics of Industrial Homework in the United States* (New York: Cambridge University Press, 1994).

62  The only serious analysis of this situation can be found in Oliunina, *Portnovskii promysel*. Her work was not part of a larger government investigation. Published in 1914 on the eve of World War I, it did not spark the kind of campaign that Clementina Black's study did in England.

## 4  THE FASHION PRESS IN IMPERIAL RUSSIA

1  See Kirsten Hoganson, "Cosmopolitan Domesticity: Importing the American Dream, 1865–1920," *American Historical Review*, 107 (February 2002): 55–83; and Daniel L. Purdy, *The Tyranny of Luxury: Consumer Cosmopolitanism in the Age of Goethe* (Baltimore: Johns Hopkins University Press, 1998).

2  Daniel Roche, *The Culture of Clothing: Dress and Fashion in the "Ancien Régime,"* trans. Jean Birrell (Cambridge: Cambridge University Press, 1994), 474–75.

3  For an early example of this type of costume plate describing Russian dress, see I. Georgi, *Opisanie obitaiuskchikh v Rossiiskom gosudarstve narodov* (St. Petersburg, 1776–77).

4  For more on this, see Jennifer M. Jones, *Sexing La Mode: Gender, Fashion, and Commercial Culture in Old Regime France* (Oxford: Berg, 2004), 25–33; Roche, *Culture of Clothing*, 474–82; Vyvyan Holland, *Hand Coloured Fashion Plates, 1770–1899* (London: B. T. Batsford, Ltd., 1988), 31–53; and Madeleine Ginsburg, *An Introduction to Fashion Illustration* (London: Her Majesty's Stationery Office, 1980), 3–8.

5  For a discussion of these changes, see François Boucher, *20,000 Years of Fashion: The History of Costume and Personal Adornment* (New York: Harry N. Abrams, 1987), chapters 10 and 11; Aileen Ribeiro, *The Art of Dress: Fashion in England and France, 1750–1820* (New Haven: Yale University Press, 1995); and ibid.,

*Fashion in the French Revolution* (London: B. T. Batsford, Ltd., 1988).

6 Roche, *Culture of Clothing*, 480–94; Jones, *Sexing La Mode*; and Clare Haru Crowston, *Fabricating Women: The Seamstresses of Old Regime France, 1675–1791* (Durham: Duke University Press, 2001).

7 For an analysis of men's relationship to clothing, see Christopher Breward, *The Hidden Consumer: Masculinities, Fashion, and City Life, 1860–1914* (Manchester: Manchester University Press, 1999), esp. 1–21.

8 Gary Marker, *Publishing, Printing, and the Origins of Intellectual Life in Russia, 1700–1800* (Princeton: Princeton University Press, 1985), 184–211.

9 Ibid., "The Creation of Journals and the Profession of Letters in the Eighteenth Century," *Literary Journals in Imperial Russia*, 12; Nikolai Novikov, "Preduvedomlenie," *Modnoe ezhemesiachnoe izdanie ili Biblioteka dlia damskogo tualeta, chast'*, 1 (St. Petersburg: Tip. Veitbrekhsha i Shiora, 1779), no pagination. Frequently, *Modnoe ezhemesiachnoe izdanie* is credited as Russia's first fashion magazine. While its title does suggest a concern for fashion, in fact, the magazine contains no articles about dress, and the only fashion plates were models of hats. Instead, it was intended to provide light entertainment while dressing, which does not make it a true fashion magazine.

10 Catriona Kelly, *A History of Russian Women's Writing, 1820–1992* (Oxford: Clarendon Press, 1994), 19–78; and Gitta Hammarberg, "Flirting with Words: Domestic Albums, 1770–1840," *Russia Women Culture*, ed. Helena Goscilo and Beth Holmgren (Bloomington: Indiana University Press, 1996): 297–315.

11 For a discussion of Prussian censorship, see Mary Lee Townsend, *Forbidden Laughter: Popular Humor and the Limits of Repression in Nineteenth-Century Prussia* (Ann Arbor: University of Michigan Press, 1992), 171–91.

12 For a history of censorship in Russia, see Charles A. Ruud, *Fighting Words: Imperial Censorship and the Russian Press, 1804–1906* (Toronto: University of Toronto Press, 1982).

13 RGIA, f. 777, op. 1, d. 1015, ll. 1–2.

14 RGIA, f. 772, op. 1, d. 787, l. 2–2 ob. In 1839 Vissarion Belinskii chose the inauguration of *Vestnik parizhskikh mod* to criticize what he felt was Russians' excessive love of European finery. See Vissarion Belinskii, *Sochineniia* (Moscow: Tipografiia A. I. Mamontova, 1881), I: 480–83. For a discussion of the development of a female reading public, see Kelly, *Russian Women's Writing*, 19–78.

15 RGIA, f. 772, op. 1, d. 1024, l. 3; and ibid.., d. 1741, l. 1.

16 RGIA, f. 777, op. 1, d. 1408, ll. 6–10.

17 RGIA, f. 777, op. 1, d. 1629, ll. 1–6.

18 RGIA, f. 777, op. 2, d. 103, ll. 1–7.

19 "Chto takoe moda," *Novyi russkii bazar (NRB)*, 4 (1868): 38–40. This article chronicled the introduction of western dress into Russia, emphasizing the role of clothing in distinguishing the upper from the lower ranks of society.

20 RGIA, f. 777, op. 1, d. 1408, l. 24; and RGIA, f. 772, op. 1, d. 2070, l. 6.

21 RGIA, f. 777, op. 1, d. 1408, ll. 78–79.

22 RGIA, f. 777, op. 2, d. 80, ll. 1 and 5.

23 RGIA, f. 772, op. 1, d. 5753, l. 3.

24 For a fuller description of Mei and her magazine, see Carolyn Marks, "Providing Amusement for the Ladies: The Creation of the Russian Women's Magazine in the 1880s," in *An Improper Profession: Women, Gender, and Journalism in Late Imperial Russia*, ed. Barbara T. Norton and Jehanne Gheith (Chapel Hill: Duke University Press, 2001): 93–119.

25 RGIA, f. 772, op. 1, d. 5753, l. 26.

26 For a look at how one magazine attempted this, see Christine Ruane, "The Development of a Fashion Press in Imperial Russia: *Moda: Zhurnal dlia svetskikh liudei*," *An Improper Profession*, 74–92.

27 "Peterburgskie mody," *Vaza*, 7 (1856): 102.

28 "Modnyi svet," *Moda*, 1 (1 January 1852): 3.

29 Ibid., 3 (1 February 1852): 18–19.

30 RGIA, f. 777, op. 2, d. 1, ll. 2 ob. and 3.

31 An example can be found in *Moda*, 2 (1858): 45.

32 "Otvety na mnogochislennye pros'by," *Moda*, 1 (1 January 1857): 26.

33 RGIA, f. 777, op. 2, d. 88, l. 1.

34 "Zametka," *Moda*, 16 (15 August 1856): 136.

35 For more on Mei, see Marks, "Providing Amusement," 100–01.

36 For more on the role of women in journalism, see the essays in Norton and Gheith, *An Improper Profession*.

37 "Kostium russkii i obshcheevropeiskii," *Moda*, 14 (15 July 1856): 114.

38 Ibid., 115.

39 Ibid., 114.

40 For a further discussion, see Margaret Beetham, *A Magazine of Her Own? Domesticity and Desire in the Woman's Magazine, 1800–1914* (New York: Routledge, 1996).

41 RGIA, f. 776, op. 3, d. 450, ll. 1–5.

42 Ibid., ll. 10–12.

43 Ibid., ll. 13–28.

44 RGIA, f. 777, op. 2, d. 96, l. 12.

45 RGIA, f. 777, op. 2, d. 28, ll. 58–ob.

46 RGIA, f. 777, op. 4, d. 138, l. 4.

47 RGIA, f. 776, op. 3, d. 424, ll. 1–3.

48 RGIA, f. 776, op. 4, d. 98, l. 1.

49 RGIA, f. 776, op. 3, d. 424, ll. 54–55.

50 RGIA, f. 777, op. 2, d. 63, l. 2.

51 This German magazine had a total of thirteen foreign editions all across Europe. See Holland, *Hand Coloured*, 113.

52 RGIA, f. 777, op. 4, d. 138, l. 4.

53 "Ot izdatelia," *Vestnik mody (VM)*, 1 (1 January 1885): 1.

54 In 1895 Alovert changed the masthead to modern Russian lettering flanked by bouquets of flowers. Apparently, he felt the rather obvious nod to Russian patriotism was no longer necessary, although the magazine was still dedicated to "the Russian woman." See also Marks, "Providing Amusement," 108–09.

55 RGIA, f. 777, op. 4, d. 138, l. 4.

56 *Pamiati Germana Dmitrievicha Goppe, 1836–1885* (St. Petersburg: Tip. M. p. s., 1885), 1–2.

57 Marks, "Providing Amusement," 108; and "Sotrudniki *Vsemirnoi*

*illiustratsii* v techenii 10-ti let, 1869–1878," *Vsemirnaia illiustrat-siia*, 520 (16 December 1878), supplement.

58 Marks, "Providing Amusement," 108.

59 *Pamiati Goppe*, 2. Emphasis in the original.

60 These events in Russia mirrored similar trends in western Europe where a few publishing houses controlled the fashion press, thereby placing male publishers in charge of women's magazines. See Beetham, *Magazine*, 115–30.

61 *Pamiati Goppe*, 1.

62 Mark D. Steinberg, *Moral Communities: The Culture of Class Relations in the Russian Printing Industry, 1867–1907* (Berkeley: University of California Press, 1992), 77–78.

63 RGIA, f. 776, op. 4, d. 98, l. 4; and *Modnyi svet (MS)*, 4 (1868): 25.

64 RGIA, f. 776, op. 6, d. 284, l. 4; and Marks, "Providing Amusement," 108.

65 Claudia B. Kidwell, *Cutting a Fashionable Fit: Dressmakers' Drafting Systems in the United States* (Washington: Smithsonian Institution Press, 1979).

66 "Vnimanie nashikh chitatel'nits," *VM*, 4 (1885): 59.

67 "Ot redaktsii," *VM*, 34 (1898): 316.

68 For a history of advertising in Russia, see Sally West, "Constructing Consumer Culture: Advertising in Imperial Russia to 1914" (Ph.D. dissertation, University of Illinois, Urbana, 1995).

69 "Ob"iavleniia," *NRB*, 2 (1868): 22; and Marks, "Providing Amusement," 98.

70 "Ot redaktsii," *NRB*, 35 (1870): 281.

71 "!! Novoe izdanie !! dlia portnikh," *VM*, 40 (1893): 381.

72 RGIA, f. 776, op. 4, d. 98, ll. 124–24 ob.

73 RGIA, f. 776, op. 5, d. 9, ll. 1, 28, and 39.

74 *Muzhskie mody*, 11 (1875): 1.

75 "Ot redaktsii," *Muzhskie mody*, 1 (1878): 1.

76 For a discussion of American publishers' attempts to create a male counterpart to women's magazines, see Helen Damon-Moore, *Magazines for the Millions: Gender and Commerce in the Ladies' Home Journal and the Saturday Evening Post, 1880–1910* (Albany: State University of New York Press, 1994).

77 RGIA, f. 777, op. 4, d. 138, l. 4.

78 Marks, "Providing Amusement," 110–13.

79 "Znachenie risunka v knige," *Vsemirnaia illiustratsiia*, 520 (16 December 1878), supplement: 5.

80 Jeffrey Brooks, *When Russia Learned to Read: Literacy and Popular Literature, 1861–1917* (Princeton: Princeton University Press, 1985), 113.

81 The supplement underwent a name change in 1912 to *Latest Fashions (Noveishie mody)*.

82 Brooks, *When Russia Learned to Read*, 111–15.

83 S. K. Chaikovskii, "Sel'skie uchitelia o sel'skikh uchitel'nitsakh (Tri pis'ma v redaktsiiu)," *Russkii nachal'nyi uchitel'*, 5–6 (1883): 417–18.

84 RGIA, f. 777, op. 2, d. 63, l. 14. Six years later, Alovert advertised *VM* as "the most complete" and "the best" fashion magazine. "Ot izdatelia," *VM*, 49 (1886): 537.

85 RGIA, f. 776, op. 4, d. 98, l. 68; and Marks, "Providing Amusement," 109–10.

86 RGIA, f. 776, op. 8, d. 1208, ll. 1–6.

87 RGIA, f. 776, op. 8, d. 1748, ll. 3–5.

88 RGIA, f. 776, op. 3, d. 424, ll. 138–39 and l. 147. There is no indication in the archives as to why Mueller, the head of the Goppe publishing firm during those years, chose to cede control to Alovert.

89 Alovert apparently relinquished his rights to publish *Fashion World* during World War I. In 1916, P. A. Bogel'man is listed as publisher and editor of the magazine. Unfortunately, the censorship archives do not contain any information about this transfer.

90 For example, in 1879, *New Russian Bazaar* received permission to publish fashion plates without government approval. RGIA, f. 776, op. 3, d. 450, l. 157. There is no record in the censorship files of any magazine getting into trouble with the authorities over the content of fashion plates.

91 RGIA, f. 777, op. 2, d. 96, l. 19.

92 Ibid., l. 87.

93 Ibid., l. 89. I have chosen to illustrate this point with material from *New Russian Bazaar* because the censorship files contain brief descriptions of the offending stories. Nevertheless, the censors rejected stories from all the major magazines.

94 The censorship files do not contain the name of the author of this tale.

95 RGIA, f. 776, op. 3, d. 450, ll. 138–45.

96 RGIA, f. 776, op. 3, d. 424, l. 11.

97 RGIA, f. 776, op. 4, d. 98, ll. 53–54.

98 RGIA, f. 777, op. 2, d. 96, l. 83 and 105; and ibid., d. 63, l. 37.

99 RGIA, f. 776, op. 4, d. 98, l. 157 ob.

100 "Ot izdatelia," *VM*, 49 (1886): 537.

101 Ginsburg, *Introduction to Fashion Illustration*, 10–11.

102 RGIA, f. 776, op. 8, d. 284, l. 41.

103 Steinberg, *Moral Communities*, 7–12.

104 "Ot redaktsii," *Modnyi magazin*, 20 (1880): 232.

105 "Ot redaktsii," *VM*, 16 (1888): 177.

106 Ginsburg, *Introduction to Fashion Illustration*, 10; Holland, *Hand Coloured*, 102–05; "Ot redaktsii," *MS*, 32 (1870): 285; and "Ot redaktsii," *NRB*, 33 (1870): 260.

107 N. Alovert, "Ot izdatelia," *VM*, 13–14 (15 June 1917): 200.

108 "Ot kontory," *VM*, 21–22 (15 October 1917): 215.

109 "Ot kontory," *VM*, 23–24 (15 November 1917): 265.

110 "Ot redaktsii," *Muzhskie mody*, 1 (1878): 1.

111 Brooks, *When Russia Learned to Read*.

5 CLOTHES SHOPPING IN IMPERIAL RUSSIA

1 David Chaney, "The Department Store as a Cultural Form," *Theory, Culture, and Society*, 1, 3 (1983): 27.

2 E. I. Moiseenko, "Mastera-portnye 'nemetskogo plat'ia' v Rossii i ikh raboty," *Trudy Gosudarstvennogo Ermitazha*, 15 (1974): 141–51.

3 Robert Gohstand, "The Internal Geography of Trade in Moscow from the Mid-Nineteenth Century to the First World War" (Ph.D. dissertation, University of California, Berkeley,

1973), 116–17; and F. Tastevin, *Histoire de la Colonie Française de Moscou* (Paris: n.p., 1908).

4 Rossiiskii gosudarstvennyi arkhiv goroda Moskvy (RGIA g. Moskvy), f. 14, op. 2, d. 364, ll. 1–29. The two Russian names are Konstantin Popov and Praskovia Tret'iakova. The names can be found on l. 29.

5 Michael F. Hamm, *Kiev: A Portrait, 1800–1917* (Princeton: Princeton University Press, 1993), 32; and Patricia Herlihy, *Odessa: A History, 1794–1914* (Cambridge, Mass.: Harvard University Press, 1986), 263–65.

6 In the United States, stores that sold fabrics, trimmings, and other items were called dry-goods stores. In order to remain closer to the French and Russian meaning, I have chosen to translate the name of the store as a fashion store.

7 Philippe Perot, *Fashioning the Bourgeoisie: A History of Clothing in the Nineteenth Century*, trans. Richard Bienvenu (Princeton: Princeton University Press, 1994), 55.

8 Gohstand, "Internal Geography," 120; Emile Haumant, *La culture française en Russie (1700–1900)* (Paris: Librairie Hachette et Cie., 1910), 449–51; and Leonce Pingaud, *Les Français en Russie et les Russes en France* (Paris: Librairie Académique Didier, 1886), 74–79, 461–70.

9 Tastevin, *Histoire*, 64–65.

10 Ivan Pushkarev, *Opisanie Sanktpeterburga i uezdnykh gorodov S. Peterburgskoi gubernii* (St. Petersburg, 1841): III: 96–97; and "Modnyi svet," *Moda: Zhurnal dlia svetskikh liudei* 23 (1 December 1851): 177–79.

11 Ol'ga Polikarpova, "Progulki po Passazhu," *Rodina* (July 2000): 72.

12 T. S. Aleshina, "K proizvodstve odezhdy v kontse XIX-nachale XX veka: Po materialam Gosudarstvennogo Istoricheskogo muzeia," *Muzei* 10 (1989): 93.

13 Pushkarev, *Opisanie*, 16.

14 A. Kra-vskii, *Mozhno li v Moskve torgovat' chestno?: Sovremennye zametki* (Moscow: Tipografiia E. Lissner i Iu. Roman, 1886), 10.

15 "Delo o masterskoi damskikh nariadov," RGIA, f. 768, op. 3, d. 454, ll. 89 ob. and 94 ob.

16 Ibid., ll. 167–70.

17 Polikarpova, "Progulki," 72.

18 A. I. Kopanev, *Naselenie Peterburga v pervoi polovine XIX veka* (Leningrad: Izdatel'stvo Akademii Nauk SSSR, 1957), 140.

19 *Vidy vnutrennei torgovli i promyshlennosti v Sanktpeterburge* (St. Petersburg: Tip. Ed. Pratsa, 1868), 59–60.

20 I have compiled these figures from *Sanktpeterburg po perepisi 10 dekabria 1869 goda* (St. Petersburg: Tipografiia Maikova, 1875), III: 8–10 and 42–45.

21 Iu. Ianson, "Naselenie Peterburga i ego ekonomicheskii i sotsial'nyi sostav," *Vestnik Evropy* 10 (1875): 629–30.

22 *Petrograd po perepisi 15 dekabria 1910 goda* (St. Petersburg, 1911), II: 10 and 20.

23 I. Eremeev, *Gorod S.-Peterburga s tochki zreniia meditsinskoi politsii* (St. Petersburg: Tip. M. D. Lomkovskogo, 1897), 203–04.

24 This information is taken from an unpublished manuscript on the history of the Moscow garment trades. See "Istoriia prof. Soiuza shveinikov v Moskve i tsentral'no-

promyshlennoi oblasti do Fevral'skoi revoliutsii," GARF, f. 6869, op. 1, d. 35, ll. 8–9.

25 Joseph Bradley, *Muzhik and Muscovite: Urbanization in Late Imperial Russia* (Berkeley: University of California Press, 1985), 74.

26 Gohstand, "Internal Geography," 687–88.

27 Polikarpova, "Progulki," 71.

28 Gohstand, "Internal Geography," 687–88; Polikarpova, "Progulki," 71; and Irina Paltusova, *Commercial Advertisements and Packages in Russia, XIX–XX centuries* (Moscow: Gosudarstvennyi Istoricheskii Muzei, 1993), 5.

29 Quoted in Gohstand, "Internal Geography," 30.

30 For a fuller discussion, see Michael Miller, *The Bon Marché: Bourgeois Culture and the Department Store, 1869–1920* (Princeton: Princeton University Press, 1981). Pushkarev warned visitors to Petersburg to beware of sales at the *magaziny*. He claimed that they were just trying to get rid of inferior goods. See Pushkarev, *Opisanie*, III: 55.

31 Aleshina, "K proizvodstve," 93; and Pushkarev, *Opisanie*, III: 96–97.

32 D. A. Zasosov and V. I. Pyzin, *Iz zhizni Peterburga 1890–1910-kh godov: Zapiski ochevidtsev* (Leningrad: Lenizdat, 1991), 98. The store later became the DLT department store.

33 Gohstand, "Internal Geography," 213–16; Zasosov and Pyzin, *Iz zhizni*, 239–41 for a list of Petersburg markets; and Bradley, *Muzhik and Muscovite*, 84–86.

34 For a description of these markets in Moscow, see Ivan Belousov, *Ushedshaia Moskva: Zapiski po lichnym vospominaniiam s nachala 1870 godov* (Moscow: Moskovskoe tovarishchestvo pisatelei, 1927), esp. pp. 72–73.

35 N. Skavronskii, *Ocherki Moskvy* (Moscow: Moskovskii rabochii, 1993), 30–31. Emphasis in the original. Skavronskii was a pseudonym for Ushakov.

36 Belousov, *Ushedshaia Moskva*, 36; and Bradley, *Muzhik and Muscovite*, 64–65.

37 Skavronskii, *Ocherki*, 64.

38 A. Afanas'ev, "Cherty russkikh nravov XVIII stoletiia," *Russkii vestnik*, 11 (1857): 279.

39 For a good description of the Petersburg Gostinyi Dvor, see Fadei Bulgarin, "Gostinyi Dvor," *Ocherki russkikh nravov ili litsevaia storona i izpanka roda chelovecheskogo* (St. Petersburg: Tipografiia Eduarda Pratsa, 1843): 65–80.

40 Gohstand, "Internal Geography," passim; Bradley, *Muzhik and Muscovite*, 83–84. A lively description of this process can be found in A. B. Granville, *St. Petersburg* (London: Henry Colburn, 1829), II: 409–11.

41 I. A. Slonov, *Iz zhizni torgovoi Moskvy (Polveka nazad)* (Moscow: Tipografiia T-va Pechatnogo i Izdatelskogo Dela, 1914), 70.

42 Quoted in James H. Bater, *St. Petersburg: Industrialization and Change* (Montreal: McGill University Press, 1976), 116–18. See William Steveni, *Petrograd: Past and Present* (London: Grant Richards Ltd., 1915), 102–03. Bulgarin tells a similar story about haggling for tobacco. See Bulgarin, "Gostinyi Dvor," 76–77.

43 Gohstand, "Internal Geography," 28 and 29.

44 Quoted in A. Gudvan, *Ocherki po istorii dvizhenii sluzhashchikh*

*v Rossii* (Moscow: Izdanie TSK SSTS, 1925), 26. See also G. Vasilich, "Moskva 1850–1910 g.," *Moskva v ee proshlom i nastoiashchem*, X–XI (Moscow: Moskovskoe Kn-izdat.T-vo Obrazovanie, 1910): 9.

45 "Gostinyi Dvor i Passazh," *Moda: Zhurnal dlia svetskikh liudei*, 8 (1851): 61.

46 G.Vasilich, "Ulitsy i liudi sovremmenoi Moskvy," *Moskva v ee proshlom i nastoiashchem*, XII (Mosow: Moskovskoe Kn-izdat. T-vo Obrazovanie, 1912): 6. My attempts to find biographical information about Vasilich have been inconclusive. He or she wrote a number of popular histories about the Decembrists and the reign of Alexander I, in addition to the articles cited above. Beyond a list of publications, I have been unable to find anything more about the author. Indeed, it is quite possible that Vasilich may even have been a pseudonym, further obscuring the identity of the author. My thanks to the Slavic Reference Service at the University of Illinois in Urbana for providing me with this information.

47 "Vneshnyi vid Moskvy srediny XIX veka," *Moskva v ee proshlom i nastoiashchem*, X–XI (Moscow: Moskovskoe Kn-izdat.T-vo Obrazovanie, 1911): 49.

48 Vissarion Belinskii, "Peterburg i Moskva," *Filiologiia Peterburga*, ed. N. Nekrasov (St. Petersburg: Izdanie knigoprodavtsa A. Ivanova, 1845), 58.

49 Alla Povelikhina and Evgenii Kovtun, *Russkaia zhivopisnaia vyveska i khudozhniki avangarda* (Leningrad: Avrora, 1991), 23.

50 For a description of the changing Petersburg clothing styles, see Genrikh fon-Attengofer, *Mediko-topograficheskoe opisanie Sanktpeterburga* (St. Petersburg: Imp. Akademiia Nauk, 1820), 179–97. See also Belinskii, "Peterburg i Moskva," 80.

51 Polikarpova, "Progulki," 71.

52 I. T. Kokorev, *Ocherki Moskvy sorokovykh godov* (Moscow-Leningrad: Akademiia, 1932), 125–31.

53 Beverly Lemire, "Peddling Fashion: Salesmen, Pawnbrokers, Taylors, Thieves, and the Second-hand Clothes Trade in England, c. 1700–1800," *Textile History*, 22, 1 (1991): 76. See also Madeleine Ginsburg, "Rags to Riches: The Second-hand Clothes Trade 1700–1978," *Costume*, 14 (1980): 121–35.

54 For an excellent analysis of this phenomenon, see Joan Neuberger, *Hooliganism: Crime, Culture, and Power in St. Petersburg, 1900–1914* (Berkeley: University of California Press, 1993).

55 Vasilich, "Ulitsy," 7.

56 The play can be found in *Russian Satiric Comedy: Six Plays*, ed. and trans. Lawrence Senelick (New York: Performing Arts Journal Publications, 1983), 27–65.

57 *Opisanie pervoi publichnoi vystavki rossiiskoi manufakturnykh izdelii v Sankt-Peterburge 1829 goda* (St. Petersburg: Tipografiia ekspeditsii zagotovleniia Gosudarstvennykh bumag, 1829), 28 and 32–33.

58 Ministerstvo vnyutrennykh del, *Ekonomicheskoe sostoianie gorodskikh poselenii Evropeiskoi Rossii v 1861–1862 gg.* (St. Petersburg: Tipografiia K. Vul'fa, 1863), passim. The cities are: 1–5: Arkhangel'sk, Grodno, Kostroma, Novgorod, Ufa, Chernigov; 6–10: Viatka, Kaluga, Petrozavodsk, Perm, Riazan', Simbirsk, Simferopol', and Tver'; 11–15: Vladimir, Astrakhan', Vologda, and Vitebsk; 16–20: Kursk, Mogilev, and Kamenets-Podol'skii; 20–40: Kazan', Kovno, Orel, and Kherson.

59 Ibid., passim. The cities are: 1–10: Kishinev, Vologda, Ekaterinoslav, Kostroma, Minsk, Petrozavodsk, Ufa, Perm, Pskov, Riazan', Tambov; 11–20: Kazan', Kursk, Nizhnii Novgorod, Penza, Poltava, and Yaroslavl'; and 20 or more: Orel, Tula, and Khar'kov.

60 Fortunately for the historian, both the Russian National Library in Moscow and the Russian Public Library in St. Petersburg have a small collection of pre-revolutionary mail-order catalogues. These materials are the source upon which I have based my analysis.

61 For an example, see *Magazin i fabrika ofitserskikh veshchei N. Zhigunova Kommissionera Tul'skogo Oruzheinogo zavoda v Bol'shoi Sadovoi* (St. Petersburg: Tipografiia R. Golikhe, 1861).

62 RGIA g. Moskvy, f. 2009, op. 1, d. 23. Unfortunately, this was the only figure contained in the store's records that have survived.

63 *Illiustrirovannyi preis-kurant L'va Rubashkina v Łodzi* (Łodz: Elektrichesk. Tip. L. Gutshtadta, 1914), 1–2.

64 Muir i Merilees, *Sezon vesny 1899 goda* (Moscow: Tipo-litografiia Tva. I. N. Kushnerev i Ko., 1899), inside back cover.

65 Muir i Merilees, *Sezon oseni i zimy 1908–1909* (Moscow: Tipografiia Muira i Mereliza, 1908), back cover.

66 *Preis-Kurant magazina gotovogo muzhskogo, damskogo, i detskogo plat'ia F. N. Konkina, Moskva, Il'inka* (Moscow: Tipo-litografiia Tva. I. N. Kushnerev, 1893), 4.

67 Muir i Merilees, *Preis-Kuranty Muir i Mereliz, osen' i zima 1890–91* (Moscow: Tipo-litografiia Tva. I. N. Kushnerev i Ko., 1890).

68 *Preis-kurant vysochaishe utverzhdennogo akts. Obshch. Zhirardovskikh manufaktur Gille i Ditrikha* (Moscow: Tipo-litografiia Kushnereva, 1888), 3–4. For another example, see *Preis-kurant frantsuzskogo magazina* (St. Petersburg: Tip. Vilenchika, 1897).

69 *Preis-kurant (so stikhami) fabriki nepromokaemoi odezhdy t. g. M. Khaikevich i Ko. v Dvinske* (Griva-Zemgallen': Tip. T. M. Segala, 1896), 8–9.

70 M. i I. Mandl', *Preis-kurant, osen'-zima 1893* (Moscow: Tipo-litografiia Kushnerev, 1893), 1.

71 Ibid., 1; and *Muir i Mereliz* (Moscow: Tipo-litografiia T-va I. N. Kushnerev i Ko., 1888), vii.

72 Ibid., vi.

73 *M. i I. Mandl'* (Moscow: T-vo tipografii A. I. Mamontova, 1895), 1.

74 T. D. German Brakhman i Ko., *Preis-kurant gotovogo muzhskogo, damskogo i detskogo plat'ia i formy vsekh uchebnykh zavedenii* (Moscow: Tipo-litografiia O. I. Lashkevich, 1895), 48.

75 *Velichaishii Frantsuzskii Torgovyi Dom Voennogo i Statskogo Plat'ia Brat'ia Mori (Mori Freres)* (St. Petersburg: Tipo-litografiia M. Rozenoer, 1911), no pagination.

76 *Muir i Merilees* (Moscow: Tipo-litografiia T-va I. N. Kushnerev i Ko., 1888), vi–vii.

77 The instructions for returns were included in many catalogues. For example, see *Muir i Merilees, Sezon vesny 1899 goda* (Moscow: Tipo-litografiia Kushnereva, 1899), inside of back cover; M. i I. Mandl', *Preis-kurant osen'-zima 1893* (Moscow: Tipo-litografiia Kushnerev, 1893), 1.

78 *Muir i Merilees* (Moscow: Tipo-litografiia Kushnereva, 1893), 1.

79 Jeffrey Burds, *Peasant Dreams and Market Politics: Labor Migration and the Russian Village, 1861–1905* (Pittsburgh: University of Pittsburgh Press, 1998), 143–85; and Barbara Alpern Engel, *Between the Fields and the City: Women, Work, and Family in Russia* (New York: Cambridge University Press, 1994).

80 M. K. Gorbunova, *Sbornik statisticheskikh svedenii po Moskovskoi gubernii* (Moscow: Tipografiia S. V. Gur'ianova, 1882), vol. VII, *vyp*. IV, passim.

81 Anne Lincoln Fitzpatrick, *The Great Russian Fair: Nizhnii Novgorod, 1840–90* (Oxford: Macmillan, 1990), 56–61.

82 Those firms that participated in the fairs frequently mentioned this in their mail-order catalogues. For an example, see T. D. German Brakhman i Ko., *Preis-kurant gotovogo muzhskogo, damskogo i detskogo plat'ia i formy vsekh uchebnykh zavedenii* (Moscow: Tipo-litografiia O. I. Lashkevich, 1895), front cover.

83 "Formation of the Company and Organisation of the Business," RGIA g. Moskvy, f. 1292, op. 1, d. 104, ll. 2–3. Italics in the original.

84 "Spiski magazinov obshchestva," RGIA g. Moskvy, f. 1292, op. 1, d. 107, ll. 5–6.

85 Ibid., d. 26, l. 95.

86 "O proverke torgovykh i promyslykh zavedenii po Beloomutskogo volosti," RGIA g. Moskvy, f. 1943, op. 1, d. 150, l. 6.

87 RGIA g. Moskvy, f. 1943, op. 1, d. 104, ll. 4–5.

88 Ibid., l. 5.

89 "Pis'ma otd. Ekaterinoslav," ibid., d. 26, ll. 1–2.

90 Ibid., f. 1943, op. 1, d. 150, l. 31.

91 Ibid., ll. 3–4.

92 Ibid..

93 Ibid., d. 26, l. 105.

94 Ibid., d. 26, ll. 43, 252, and 253.

95 Ibid., d. 104, l. 6; and d. 16, ll. 55–86.

96 *Nastoiashchie shveinye mashiny Kompaniia Zinger v N'iu-Iorke na Brodve*, No. 149 (Moscow: Tip. V. Chicherina, 1895).

97 For an example, see Kompaniia Zinger, *Illiustrirovannyi preis-kurant chastei shveinykh mashin 9WI i 9WS (dlia semeinogo upotrebleniia)* (St. Petersburg: Kompaniia Zinger, 1909).

98 *K. G. Tsimmerman* (Sevastopol', no date), 1.

99 *General'nyi eksport shveinykh mashin: P. Krauzel'burg, Golta, Khersonskaia guberniia* (Tipografiia G. Eikisman, 1912), 3.

100 Fred V. Carstensen, *American Enterprise in Foreign Markets: Studies of Singer and International Harvester in Imperial Russia* (Chapel Hill: University of North Carolina Press, 1984), 91; and RGIA g. Moskvy, f. 1292, op. 1, d. 130, ll. 6–7, 37.

101 Ibid., ll. 8–9, 38.

102 It is interesting to note that Singer chose a man for its logo in Tunisia. The logo is reproduced in Judith G. Coffin, *The Politics of Women's Work: The Paris Garment Trades, 1750–1915* (Princeton: Princeton University Press, 1996), 93.

103 For a history of men's costume, see *Russkii kostium* (Moscow: Vserossiiskoe teatral'noe obshchestvo), vols. 1–5, passim; V. M. Glinka, *Russkii voennyi kostium, XVIII–nachala XX veka* (Leningrad: Khudozhnik RSFSR, 1988); and L. E. Shepelev, *Tituly, mundiry, ordena v Rossiiskoi imperii* (Leningrad: Nauka, 1991), passim.

104 Rachel Bowlby, *Just Looking: Consumer Culture in Dreiser, Gissing, and Zola* (New York: Methuen, 1985), 1–17.

105 Thorstein Veblen, *The Theory of the Leisure Class: An Economic Study of Institution* (London: Macmillan Company, 1899), 167–87.

106 "Modnyi svet," *Moda: Zhurnal dlia svetskikh liudei*, 23 (1 December 1851): 177–79.

107 For a history of the women's movement in Russia, see Richard Stites, *The Women's Liberation Movement: Feminism, Nihilism, and Bolshevism, 1860–1930* (Princeton: Princeton University Press, 1978).

108 For a discussion of the work's impact on Russian society, see Laura Engelstein, *The Keys to Happiness: Sex and the Search for Modernity in* Fin-de-Siècle *Russia* (Ithaca: Cornell University Press, 1992), 218–21.

109 L. N. Tolstoi, *Kreitserova Sonata, Pol'noe sobranie sochinenii*, vol. 27 (Moscow-Leningrad: Gosudarstvennoe izdatel'stvo khudozhestvennoi literatury, 1933), 22–23.

110 Ibid., 26.

111 Rose L. Glickman, *Russian Factory Women: Workplace and Society, 1880–1914* (Berkeley: University of California Press, 1984), chapter 3.

112 Iulii L. Elets, *Poval'noe bezumie (K sverzheniiu iga mod)* (St. Petersburg: Tipografiia Shtaba Voisk Gvardiia i Peterburgskogo Voennogo Okruga, 1914).

113 Ibid., 269–70.

114 Ibid., passim. This tendency to view men as the victims of their wives' scandalous spending was an essential part of "conspicuous consumption" and the gendered construction of shopping. See Stuart and Elizabeth Ewen, *Channels of Desire: Mass Images and the Shaping of American Consciousness* (New York: McGraw-Hill, 1982), 147–50.

115 Elets, *Poval'noe bezumie*, 91.

116 Gudvan, *Ocherki po istorii dvizheniia sluzhashchikh v Rossii*, 136–40. See also Laurie Bernstein, *Sonia's Daughters: Prostitutes and Their Regulation in Imperial Russia* (Berkeley: University of California Press, 1995).

117 Elets, *Poval'noe bezumie*, 144–49.

118 RGIA, f. 768, op. 3, d. 454, l. 169 ob. For a history of women actresses, see Catherine A. Schuler, *Women in Russian Theatre: The Actress in the Silver Age* (New York: Routledge, 1996); and Louise McReynolds, *Russia at Play: Leisure Activities at the End of the Tsarist Era* (Ithaca: Cornell University Press, 2003), 113–31.

119 Bowlby, *Just Looking*.

120 Émile Zola, *Au Bonheur des dames* (Paris: Bibliothèque Charpentier, 1910), passim.

121 For a fuller discussion, see Rosalind H. Williams, *Dream Worlds: Mass Consumption in Late Nineteenth-century France* (Berkeley: University of California Press, 1982).

122 Elizabeth Wilson, *The Sphinx in the City: Urban Life, the Control of Disorder, and Women* (Berkeley: University of California Press, 1991), 6. The emphasis is in the original.

123 Zola, *Au Bonheur des dames*, passim.

124 Williams, *Dream Worlds*, 14.

## 6  ADORNED IN DREAMS: CLOTHING AND NATIONAL IDENTITY

1   Elizabeth Wilson, *Adorned in Dreams: Fashion and Modernity* (London: Virago Press, 1987), 2.

2   For an introduction to the study of the self in Russian history, see the essays in Laura Engelstein and Stephanie Sandler, eds., *Self and Story in Russian History* (Ithaca: Cornell University Press, 2000).

3   P. K. Stepanov, *Istoriia russkoi odezhdy* (Petrograd: n. p., 1916), 3.

4   Hans Rogger, *National Consciousness in Eighteenth-Century Russia* (Cambridge, Mass.: Harvard University Press, 1960), esp. 1–7 and 45–84. The quote is on p. 68.

5   *Russkii kostium, 1750–1830* (Moscow: Vserossiiskoe teatral'noe obshchestvo, 1960), I: 13–14; and Richard S. Wortman, *Scenarios of Power: Myth and Ceremony in Russian Monarchy* (Princeton: Princeton University Press, 1995), I: 136.

6   Quoted in *Russkii kostium*, I: 12.

7   See Rogger, *National Consciousness*, 71, for a list of these "Russian" traits.

8   *Russkii kostium*, I: 12; Raisa M. Kirsanova, *Stsenicheskii kostium i teatral'naia publika v Rossii XIX veka* (Moscow: Artist. Rezhisser. Teatr, 1997), 313; and V. M. Glinka, *Russkii voennyi kostium, XVIII–nachala XX veka* (Leningrad: Khudozhnik RSFSR, 1988).

9   Richard Sennett, *The Fall of Public Man* (New York: W. W. Norton, 1992), 163–64.

10  Nicholas V. Riasanovsky, *Nicholas I and Official Nationality in Russia, 1825–1855* (Berkeley: University of California Press, 1959).

11  Wortman, *Scenarios of Power*, I: 333–62.

12  L. E. Shepelev, *Tituly, mundiry, ordena* (Leningrad: Nauka, 1991), 188.

13  Evgenia Kirichenko, *Russian Design and the Fine Arts, 1750–1917* (New York: Harry N. Abrams, 1991), 35–89. For more on the arts in this period, see Richard Stites, *Serfdom, Society, and the Arts in Imperial Russia: The Pleasure and the Power* (New Haven: Yale University Press, 2006).

14  Quoted in Nicholas V. Riasanovsky, *The Image of Peter the Great in Russian History and Thought* (New York: Oxford University Press, 1985), 99. For a discussion of Chaadaev, see ibid., 98–106; and Andrzej Walicki, *The Slavophile Controversy* (Notre Dame: University of Notre Dame Press, 1989), 83–117.

15  Alexander Herzen, *My Past and Thoughts*, trans. Constance Garnett and abridged by Dwight Macdonald (Berkeley: University of California Press, 1973), 301.

16  Daniel R. Brower, *Training the Nihilists: Education and Radicalism in Tsarist Russia* (Ithaca: Cornell University Press, 1975).

17  Barbara Alpern Engel, *Mothers and Daughters: Women of the Intelligentsia in Nineteenth-Century Russia* (New York: Cambridge University Press, 1983; and Kirsanova, *Stsenicheskii kostium*, 238–42).

18  A. V. Viskovatov, *Istoricheskoe opisanie odezhdy i vooruzheniia rossiiskikh voisk* (St. Petersburg, V Voennoi tip, 1842), I: 2; Johann Georgi and Ivan Glazunov, *Opisanie vsekh obitaiushchikh v rossiiskom gosudarstve narodov* (St. Petersburg: Izdvizheniem knigo-

prodavtsa Ivana Glazunova, 1799); and P. S. Pallas, Robert Johnston, and W. Miller, *Views of Eighteenth-Century Russia: Costumes, History, Customs* (New York: Portland House, 1990).

19  Nathanial Knight, "Science, Empire, and Nationality: Ethnography in the Russian Geographical Society, 1845–1855," *Imperial Russia: New Histories for the Empire*, ed. Jane Burbank and David Ransel (Bloomington: Indiana University Press, 1998): 108–41; and Joseph Bradley, "Subjects into Citizens: Societies, Civil Society, and Autocracy in Tsarist Russia," *American Historical Review* (October 2002): 1,094–123. For a history of the rise of archeology, see Brent E. Maner, "The Search for a Buried Nation: Prehistoric Archaeology in Central Europe, 1750–1945" (Ph. D. dissertation, University of Illinois, Urbana, 2001).

20  Knight, "Science, Empire, and Nationality," 125. These surveys can be found in the archive of the Russian Geographical Society in St. Petersburg.

21  See Kirichenko, *Russian Design*, 91–132, for a fuller discussion and examples of this interchange between art and scholarship.

22  "Instruktsii sobraniia predmetov dlia russkoi etnograficheskoi vystavki i russkogo muzeia, ustroivaemykh obshchestvom liubetelei estestvoznaniia," *Izvestiia Obshchestva liubitelei estestvoznaniia, antropologii i etnografii*, vol. 2, *Antropologicheskoe otdelenie* (Moscow: Tipografiia S. P. Arkhipova, 1865): iii.

23  For more on Stasov's role as a music critic and supporter of Russian nationalist music, see Vladimir Vasilevich Stasov, *Selected Essays on Music*, trans. Florence Jonas (New York: Frederick A. Praeger, 1968), 1–14; Richard Taruskin, *Musorgsky: Eight Essays and an Epilogue* (Princeton: Princeton University Press, 1993), 3–37.

24  Vladimir Stasov, *Russkii narodnyi ornament: Shit'ë, tkani, kruzheva* (St. Petersburg, 1872), iii.

25  The *kika* was a particular kind of woman's headdress. Ibid., x–xi.

26  Ibid., xvi–xvii.

27  Ibid., xix.

28  Yuri Olkhovsky, *Vladimir Stasov and Russian National Culture* (Ann Arbor: UMI Research Press, 1983), 123.

29  V. A. Prokhorov, *Materialy po istorii russkikh odezhd i obstanovki zhizni narodnoi* (St. Petersburg: Tipografiia Imperatorskoi Akademii Nauk, 1881): I: 1–5. Although Prokhorov worked on this book for decades, he died after only one volume was published. His son published two volumes posthumously. See "Prokhorov," *Entsiklopedicheskii slovar'* (St. Petersburg: Tipo-Litografiia I. A. Efrona, 1898): XXV: 579; and Stepanov, *Istoriia russkoi odezhdy*, 2.

30  Prokhorov accentuated the connection between Scythians and Slavs by hyphenating the words, *Skify-Slaviane*.

31  Prokhorov, *Materialy*, I: 11 and 14. A *plakhta* and a *ponëva* were aprons made from homespun material and embroidered with elaborate designs. See Raisa M. Kirsanova, *Kostium v russkoi khudozhestvennoi kul'ture 18-pervoi poloviny 20 vv.* (Moscow: Bol'shaia Rossiiskaia Entsiklopediia, 1995), 215 and 221–22. A *koftochka* was a woman's short jacket.

32  Prokhorov, *Materialy*, I: 69.

33  Wortman, *Scenarios of Power*, II: 235–305.

34  V. M. Glinka, *Russkii voennyi kostium, XVIII-nachala XX veka*

(Leningrad: Khudozhnik RSFSR, 1988), 86–89; and Pavel Shipov, *Russkaia voennaia odezhda* (St. Petersburg: Tipo-litografiia N. Evstrifeeva, 1901).

35  François Boucher has identified the caftan as one of five archetypes of clothing, originating in the East. See François Boucher, *20,000 Years of Fashion: The History of Costume and Personal Adornment* (New York: Abrams, 1987), 12.

36  Kirsanova, *Kostium*, 198–99; "Papakha," *Entsiklopedicheskii slovar'* (St. Petersburg: Tipo-Litografiia I. A. Efrona, 1897), XXII: 718.

37  V. P. Bezobrazov, ed., *Otchet o vserossiiskoi khudozhestvenno-promyshlennoi vystavki 1882 goda v Moskve* (St. Petersburg: Tipografiia V. Bezobrazova i Komp., 1884), 66.

38  For a discussion of opera in Russia before 1880, see Julie A. Buckler, *The Literary Lorgnette: Attending Opera in Imperial Russia* (Stanford: Stanford University Press, 2000), esp. 12–56.

39  Wendy Salmond, *Arts and Crafts in Late Imperial Russia: Reviving the Kustar Art Industries, 1870–1917* (New York: Cambridge University Press, 1996), passim; Alison Hilton, *Russian Folk Art* (Bloomington: Indiana University Press, 1995), 227–44; Kirichenko, *Russian Design*, 152–56; and Camilla Gray, *The Russian Experiment in Art, 1863–1922* (London: Thames and Hudson, 1976), 22–27.

40  For a wonderful analysis of this phenomenon, see Salmond, *Arts and Crafts*.

41  For a fuller discussion, see ibid., passim; and Kirichenko, *Russian Design*, chapter 4.

42  Richard Wortman, "Publicizing the Imperial Image in 1913," *Self and Story in Russian History*, 94–95.

43  Maslenitsa means "Butter Week". Members of the Russian Orthodox faith were not supposed to consume dairy products during Lent. The festivities marked the last chance to eat butter, cheese, and milk products until Easter Sunday. See Um., "Maslenitsa," *Entsiklopedicheskii slovar'* (St. Petersburg: Tipo-Litografiia I. A. Efrona, 1896): XVIII: 755–56.

44  A. M. Konechnyi, "Petersburgskie narodnye gulian'ia na maslenoi i paskhal'noi nedeliakh," *Peterburg i guberniia: Istoriko-etnograficheskie issledovaniia*, comp. and ed. N. V. Iukhneva (Leningrad: Nauka, 1989): 21–52. For an English translation, see A. M. Konechnyi, "Popular Carnivals During Mardi Gras and Easter Week in St. Petersburg," *Russian Studies in History*, vol. 35, no. 4 (Spring 1997): 52–91.

45  M. I. Pyliaev, *Staryi Peterburg*, 1889 reprint (Leningrad: Titul, 1990), 436–38.

46  Mark Ferro, *Nicholas II: The Last of the Tsars*, trans. Brian Pearce (New York: Oxford University Press, 1991), 35; and Wortman, *Scenarios of Power*, II: 378.

47  Nadine Wonlar-Larsky, *The Russia That I Loved* (London: The Women's Printing Society, 1937), 77–81. The author is Nadezhda Dmitrevna Nabokova, the daughter of Minister of Justice Dmitri Nabokov under Alexander II and Alexander III.

48  Charles Spencer, *Léon Bakst* (New York: St. Martin's Press, 1973), 32–35. The costume designs are on p. 41; and Irina Pruzhan, *Léon Bakst*, trans. Arthur Shkarovski-Raffé (New York: Penguin Books, 1987), 18.

49  "Spektakl' i bal v Ermitazhe," *Sankt-Peterburgskie vedomosti* (9 February 1903): 4.

50  I would like to thank Jack Kollman for helping me ascertain the beginning of Maslenitsa in 1903.

51  Alexis's second wife, Natalia Naryshkina, was the mother of Peter the Great.

52  "Kostiumirovannyi vecher u Ikh Velichestv," *Sankt-Peterburgskie vedomosti* (13 February 1903): 3.

53  The one exception was Nicholas II's mother who wore a lilac velvet gown embellished with fur and pearls. See "Kostiumirovannyi bal v Kontsertnom zale," *Sankt-Peterburgskie vedomosti* (15 February 1903): 3.

54  Ibid., 3–4.

55  "Kostiumirovannyi vecher u Ikh Velichestv," *Sankt-Peterburgskie vedomosti*, 3; and Wortman, *Scenarios of Power*, II: 377–78. The Voeikov quote is from Wortman.

56  *Al'bom kostiumirovovannogo bala v Zimnem Dvortse v fevrale 1903g.* (St. Petersburg, 1904); and Wortman, *Scenarios of Power*, II: 378. These photographs can be found in many recent books as well.

57  Wonlar-Larsky, *Russia*, 99–100.

58  Ibid., 101.

59  For more on Musorgsky and his debt to the European musical tradition, see Taruskin, *Musorgsky*.

60  Elizabeth Souritz, *Soviet Choreographers in the 1920s*, trans. Lynn Visson, ed. with additional trans. Sally Banes (Durham: Duke University Press, 1990), 22–23; and http://www.ballet.co.uk/contexts/la_bayadère.htm.

61  Wonlar-Larsky, *Russia*, 101.

62  Quoted in Salmond, *Arts and Crafts in Late Imperial Russia*, 133.

63  Alexandre Benois, *Reminiscences of the Russian Ballet*, trans. Mary Britnieva (London: Putnam, 1941), 153.

64  Ibid., 154.

65  For more on the *World of Art*, see Janet Kennedy, *The "Mir iskusstva" Group and Russian Art, 1898–1912* (New York: Garland, 1977); and John E. Bowlt, "Stage Design and the Ballets Russes," *The Journal of Decorative and Propaganda Arts* (Summer 1987): 28–30.

66  Lynn Garafola, *Diaghilev's Ballets Russes* (New York: Oxford University Press, 1989), chapter 1.

67  For more on Petipa, see Souritz, *Soviet Choreographers*, 21–24; and Vera Krasovskaya, *Marius Petipa and "The Sleeping Beauty,"* trans. Cynthia Reed (New York: Dance Perspectives, 1972).

68  Garafola, *Diaghilev's Ballets Russes*, 3–49.

69  Ibid., 47.

70  Michel Fokine, *Fokine: Memoirs of a Ballet Master*, trans. Vitale Fokine, ed. Anatole Chujoy (Boston: Little, Brown, and Company, 1961), 72.

71  Garafola, *Diaghilev's Ballets Russes*, 48–49.

72  Pruzhan, *Léon Bakst*, 18; and Spencer, *Léon Bakst*, 32–35.

73  Quoted in Mary Fanton Roberts, "The New Russian Stage, A Blaze of Color: What the Genius of Léon Bakst Has Done to Vivify Productions Which Combine Ballet, Music, and Drama," *Craftsman*, 29 (December 1915): 265.

74  Garafola, *Diaghilev's Ballets Russes*, 16–17.

75  For a brief discussion of the Oriental Museum's collection, see Yury A. Petrosyan, "St. Petersburg's Oriental Pearl," *The St. Petersburg Muraqqa'* (Milan: Leonardo Arte, 1996), 9–10.

76  Quoted in Roberts, "The New Russian Stage," 265.

77 Quoted in ibid.

78 Bowlt, "Stage Design and the Ballets Russes," 36. See also Michelle Potter, "Designed for Dance: The Costumes of Léon Bakst and the Art of Isadora Duncan," *Dance Chronicle*, 13, 2 (1990): 154–56.

79 Quoted in Pruzhan, *Léon Bakst*, 25.

80 Quoted in Garafola, *Diaghilev's Ballets Russes*, 46.

81 The classic introduction to a growing literature on European Orientalism is Edward W. Said, *Orientalism* (New York: Vintage Books, 1979).

82 Debora L. Silverman, *Art Nouveau in* Fin-de-Siècle *France: Politics, Psychology, and Style* (Berkeley: University of California Press, 1989), passim; and Nancy J. Troy, *Modernism and the Decorative Arts in France: Art Nouveau to Le Corbusier* (New Haven: Yale University Press, 1991), 8–21.

83 Quoted in Garafola, *Diaghilev's Ballets Russes*, 287.

84 Ibid., 273–99. The quotation is on p. 276.

85 Sally Banes, "*Firebird* and the Idea of Russianness," in *The Ballets Russes and Its World*, ed. Lynn Garafola and Nancy Van Norman Baer (New Haven: Yale University Press, 1999), 118.

86 Quoted in Peter Wollen, "Fashion/Orientalism/The Body," *New Formations*, 1 (1987), 21.

87 Modris Eksteins, *Rites of Spring: The Great War and the Birth of the Modern Age* (New York: Doubleday, 1989), 9–54, esp. 48.

88 Quoted in Wollen, "Fashion/Orientalism/The Body," 21.

89 Ibid., 18–20; and Christopher Breward, *The Hidden Consumer: Masculinities, Fashion, and City Life, 1860–1914* (New York: Manchester University Press, 1999), 240–61.

90 Farid Chenoune, *A History of Men's Fashion*, trans. Deke Dusinberre (Paris: Flammarion, 1993), 136.

91 Wollen, "Fashion/Orientalism/The Body," 5. Lazenby Liberty, the founder of the English Liberty store, coined the phrase "modernist body." See ibid., 26. Denis Roche, "Considerations on Leo Bakst's Art," *Inedited Works of Bakst* (New York: Brentano, 1927): 62–67.

92 Wollen, "Fashion/Orientalism/The Body," 31. For Poiret's description of his trip to Russia, see Paul Poiret, *King of Fashion: The Autobiography of Paul Poiret* (Philadelphia: J. B. Lippincott, 1931), 120–26; for his comments on Bakst and his influence, see pp. 182–83.

93 This Russian influence on French fashion continued into the 1920s and 1930s. Nadezhda Lamanova won the Grand Prize for her designs at the 1925 "Exposition internationale des arts décoratifs et industriels" in Paris. A new generation of Russia's avant-garde artists such as Alexandra Exter, Liubov Popova, and Sonia Terk Delaunay developed their own theories of color and line that influenced *haute couture*. After the 1917 Bolshevik Revolution many Russian women émigrés in Paris and elsewhere supported their now destitute families through their work in the fashion industry, keeping alive the Russian influence on *haute couture*. See Tatiana Strizhenova, *Soviet Costume and Textiles, 1917–1945* (Paris: Flammarion, 1991); Lidya Zaletova, et al., *Revolutionary Costume: Soviet Clothing and Textiles of the 1920s* (New York: Rizzoli, 1987); and Alexandre Vassiliev, *Beauty in Exile*, trans. Antonina W. Bouis and Anya Kucharev (New York: Harry N. Abrams, Inc., 2000).

94 Mica Nava, "The Cosmopolitanism of Commerce and the Allure of Difference: Selfridges, the Russian Ballet, and the Tango, 1911–1914," *International Journal of Cultural Studies*, 1, 2 (1998): 163–96.

95 Ibid., 187–89.

96 Ibid., 166. See also Ulf Hannerz, "Cosmopolitans and Locals in World Culture," *Theory, Culture, & Society*, 7, 2–3 (1990): 237–51.

## 7 ADORNED IN DREAMS: FASHION, LABOR, AND POLITICS

1 For more on this, see Mark D. Steinberg, *Moral Communities: The Culture of Class Relations in the Russian Printing Industry, 1867–1907* (Berkeley: University of California Press, 1992); and Victoria E. Bonnell, *Roots of Rebellion: Workers' Politics and Organizations in St. Petersburg and Moscow, 1900–1914* (Berkeley: University of California Press, 1983).

2 S. I. Gruzdev, *Trud i bor'ba shveinikov v Peterburge, 1905–1916* (Leningrad: Izdanie Leningradskogo oblastnogo soiuza rabochikh shveinoi promyshlennosti, 1929), 28; S. N. Prokopovich, *K rabochemu voprosu v Rossii* (St. Petersburg: Izdanie E. D. Kuskovoi, 1905), 48; and Reginald E. Zelnik, *Labor and Society in Tsarist Russia: The Factory Workers of St. Petersburg, 1855–1870* (Stanford: Stanford University Press, 1971), 340–41. This strike was identified as the first strike in the city of St. Petersburg. However, as Zelnik points out, this label ignores the labor unrest that had been brewing in that city since the 1850s.

3 *Birzhevye vedomosti* (*BV*), 26 May 1870.

4 For more on this, see Louise McReynolds, *The News Under Russia's Old Regime: The Development of a Mass-Circulation Press* (Princeton: Princeton University Press, 1991).

5 Zelnik, *Labor*, 340.

6 Bonnell, *Roots*, 5–6.

7 For some recent examples, see Bonnell, *Roots*, for a view of Russian developments, and for a history of Jewish workers, Ezra Mendelsohn, *Class Struggle in the Pale: The Formative Years of the Jewish Workers' Movement in Tsarist Russia* (New York: Cambridge University Press, 1970). It is not my purpose to criticize the work of these excellent historians, but rather to combine their insights into a new synthesis. Further work needs to be done in order to determine whether the intersection of Jewish and Russian developments in the garment trades was true for other occupations.

8 For more on this subject, see John Doyle Klier, *Russia Gathers Her Jews: The Origins of the "Jewish Question" in Russia, 1772–1825* (DeKalb: Northern Illinois University Press, 1986).

9 Mendelsohn, *Class Struggle*, 6; and Evreiskoe kolonizatsionnoe obshchestvo, *Sbornik materialov ob ekonomicheskom polozhenii evreev v Rossii* (St. Petersburg: Tipografiia Sever, 1904): I: 195 (*Sbornik*).

10 Quoted in Mendelsohn, *Class Struggle*, 14.

11 For conditions in the garment trades, see *Sbornik*, I: 265–68.

12 Ibid., 15. See also James A. Schmiechen, *Sweated Industries and Sweated Labor: The London Clothing Trades, 1860–1914* (Urbana:

University of Illinois Press, 1984) for a discussion of the impact of these Jewish immigrants on the garment trades in London; and Nancy L. Green, *Ready-To-Wear and Ready-To-Work: A Century of Industry and Immigrants in Paris and New York* (Durham: University of North Carolina Press, 1997).

13  For a concise discussion of Haskalah in Russia, see Steven J. Zipperstein, *The Jews of Odessa: A Cultural History, 1794–1881* (Stanford: Stanford University Press, 1986), 11–13.

14  For more on Jewish students and the universities, see Benjamin Nathans, *Beyond the Pale: The Jewish Encounter with Late Imperial Russia* (Berkeley: University of California Press, 2002), 201–307; Samuel Kassow, *Students, Professors, and the State in Tsarist Russia* (Berkeley: University of California Press, 1989); and Susan K. Morrissey, *Heralds of Revolution: Russian Students and the Mythologies of Radicalism* (New York: Oxford University Press, 1998).

15  Mendelsohn, *Class Struggle*, 45.

16  Ibid., 27–115; and Gosudarstvennyi arkhiv Rossiiskoi Federatsii (GARF), "Shveiniki v revoliutsionnom dvizhenii dvatsat' piat' let tomu nazad," f. 6869, op. 1, d. 32, l. 1.

17  J. L. H. Keep, *The Rise of Social Democracy in Russia* (Oxford: Clarendon Press, 1963), 40.

18  Mendelsohn, *Class Struggle*, 52–53; and Iu. Martov, *Razvitie krupnoi promyshlennosti i rabochee dvizhenie v Rossii* (Moscow: Kniga, 1923), 62.

19  "Iz istorii Soiuza portnykh Belorussii," GARF, f. 6869, op. 1, d. 11, ll. 6–7 ob; and M. Kolchinskii, "Iz istorii zarozhdeniia Soiuza shveinikov g. Kremenchuga," GARF, f. 6869, op. 1, d. 11, ll. 8–12.

20  Nahum A. Bukhbinder, "Evreiskoe rabochee dvizhenie v Gomele, 1890–1905 gg.: Iz neizdannym arkhivnym materialam," *Krasnaia letopis'*, 2–3 (1922): 38.

21  *Sbornik*, I: 267.

22  Bukhbinder, "Evreiskoe rabochee dvizhenie," 42–43; and Aron Groznyi, "Gomel'skii soiuz Shveiprom v Podol'e," GARF, f. 6869, op. 1, d. 13, l. 17.

23  Ibid.

24  Ibid.

25  "Iz istorii soiuza portnykh Belorussii," GARF, f. 6869, op. 1, d. 11, l. 7.

26  Bukhbinder, "Evreiskoe rabochee dvizhenie," 70.

27  Mendelsohn, *Class Struggle*, 49–53. According to Mendelsohn, a tsarist official in 1892 brought the law to the attention of the socialists, who used it quite successfully to agitate among artisans. The rule was republished in the Artisan Regulations.

28  Groznyi, "Gomel'skii soiuz," l. 17. A copy of an appeal to garment workers from the organizers of this strike can be found in Bukhbinder, "Evreiskoe rabochee dvizhenie," 90.

29  Groznyi, "Gomel'skii soiuz," l. 17.

30  Ibid., l. 17 ob.

31  Bukhbinder, "Evreiskoe rabochee dvizhenie," 68–70. For more on the 1903 Gomel pogrom, see Shlomo Lambroza, "The Pogroms of 1903–1906," and Hans Rogger, "Conclusion and Overview," in *Pogroms: Anti-Jewish Violence in Modern Russian History*, ed. John D. Klier and Shlomo Lambroza (New York: Cambridge University Press, 1992), 207–12 and 341–44. Both historians argue that the 1903 Gomel' pogrom marked an important turning point for Jews and the Russian government's attitude toward them. For more on the Gomel' pogrom, see Henry J. Tobias, *The Jewish Bund in Russia From Its Origins to 1905* (Stanford: Stanford University Press, 1972), 225–30.

32  On the importance of the strike activity in the Pale upon developments in the Russian heartland, see Yulii Martov, *Zapiski sotsial-demokrata* (Berlin: 1922; Cambridge: Oriental Research Partners, 1975); Keep, *Rise*, 39–49; Mendelsohn, *Class Struggle*, 45–62; and Bonnell, *Roots*, 131.

33  "Avtobiografiia Iusima, A. G.," GARF, f. 6869, op. 1, d. 32, ll. 14–20.

34  "Vypiski o sobraniiakh torgovykh sluzhashchikh g. Moskvy," GARF, f. 6875, op. 1, d. 30, l. 29 and 59; d. 70, ll. 4–5, 7–9, 14, 26–28, 58, 64, 69. For more on salesclerks, see A. Gudvan, *Ocherki po istorii dvizheniia sluzhashchikh v Rossii* (Moscow: Izdanie TSK SSTS, 1925); and Bonnell, *Roots*.

35  Abraham Ascher, *The Revolution of 1905: Russia in Disarray* (Stanford: Stanford University Press, 1988): I: 211.

36  Gruzdev, *Trud*, 29.

37  Ibid., 29–31.

38  "Vospominaniia A. Voronova," GARF, f. 6869, op. 1, d. 41, ll. 24–25.

39  See Bonnell, *Roots*, 457 and 462, for a list of the various unions that formed in Petersburg and Moscow in 1905. Although the evidence for other cities is very fragmentary, the same process occurred in the provinces as well.

40  Ibid., 470 and 478. For another example, see "Ustav Vilenskogo Prof. Obshchestvo rabochikh portniazhnogo dela," GARF, f. 6869, op. 1, d. 18, l. 2.

41  Bonnell, *Roots*, especially chapters 3 and 4.

42  "Vospominaniia Davidova," GARF, f. 6869, op. 1, d. 13, l. 93.

43  Tovarishch F. I. O. [F. I. Ozol], "Eshche o khoziaichikakh ili posrednikakh," *Listok*, 14 (1906): 4–5. Ozol was the editor and publisher of this periodical as well as a founder of the Petersburg union. This issue was raised again a year later in the same journal. B. Petrov, "O shtuchnikakh," *Listok*, 5–6 (1907): 6; and R, "Eshche o shtuchnikakh," *Listok*, 5–6 (1907): 7.

44  For the Moscow prohibition, see N. Shevkov, *Moskovskie shveiniki do fevral'skoi revoliutsii* (Moscow: Izd. M. G. S. P. S. trud i kniga, 1927), 7. See also "Ustav prof. soiuza portnykh i shapochnikov goroda Omska," GARF, f. 6869, op. 1, d. 18, l. 1.

45  Bonnell, *Roots*, 370. For more on this issue, see Rose L. Glickman, *Russian Factory Women: Workplace and Society, 1880–1914* (Berkeley: University of California Press, 1984), 196–208. According to Glickman, the one exception was the knitters' union. A group of Jewish knitters came to Petersburg in 1902 and set up an illegal union which nurtured female members.

46  To reconstruct these events I have used two unpublished sources and newspaper articles. The unpublished accounts are "Vospominaniia S. Kitavina po istorii prof. soiuza rabochikh po izgotovleniiu odezhdy Moskovskogo promyshlennnogo raiona," GARF, f. 6869, op. 1, d. 33; and Elizaveta Oliunina, "Shveiniki v rab. dvizhenii do 1917 g.," GARF, f. 6869, op. 1, d. 34.

47  Shevkov, *Moskovskie shveiniki*, 7.

48 Official accounts can be found in "S"ezd portnykh," *Tovarishch* (9 August 1906), 2; and Shevkov, *Moskovskie shveiniki*, 10–13.

49 "Professional'nye soiuzy i obshchestva," *Russkaia zemlia (RZ)* (25 August 1906), 3; and "Professional'nye soiuzy," *RZ* (31 August 1906), 3.

50 Ibid.; and "Rabochaia zhizn'," *RZ* (1 September 1906), 3.

51 "Professional'nye soiuzy," *RZ* (5 September 1906), 3; and "Rabochaia zhizn'," *RZ* (14 September 1906), 3. For a list of strike demands, see "Po masterskim: Ot Mandlia," *Listok*, 15 (1906): 11.

52 "Po masterskim: Ot Mandlia," *Listok*, 15 (1906): 10.

53 "Bor'ba u Mandlia," *Listok*, 8 (1906): 8.

54 The other demands were for a nine-hour workday from 8:30 am to 7:30 pm, with an hour lunch break and two half-hour tea breaks; the abolition of overtime and fines; sanitary improvements in the workshops; paid leaves of absence with a guarantee of employment at the end of the leave; no dismissal for participating in a strike; and no work on official holidays, including May Day. "Po masterskim: Ot Mandlia," *Listok*, 15 (1906): 10–11; GARF, f. 6869, op. 1, d. 33, ll. 87–88; and ibid., d. 34, ll. 113–14.

55 For similar developments among printers, another artisanal group, see Steinberg, *Moral Communities,* chapter 7.

56 Ivan Tepiakov, "Beloomut," GARF, f. 6869, op. 1, d. 11, ll. 1–2.

57 The head of the Mandl' Company in 1906 is only identified as Mandl' in the sources. Almost certainly it was Ludwig I. Mandl', who was in charge of the company during World War I.

58 GARF, f. 6869, op. 1, d. 33, ll. 88–89.

59 Ibid., l. 89.

60 GARF, f. 6869, op. 1, d. 11, l. 2; and d. 60, ll. 45–47.

61 "Professional'nye soiuzy," *RZ* (21 September 1906), 3; "Professional'nye soiuzy," *RZ* (22 September 1906), 3; and "Professional'nye soiuzy," *RZ* (1 October 1906), 3.

62 "Professional'nye soiuzy," *RZ* (1 October 1906), 3; GARF, f. 6869, op. 1, d. 33, ll. 90–93; and d. 34, l. 114. The proposed piece rates can be found in GARF, f. 6869, op. 1, d. 20, ll. 1–2.

63 For a report on the union meeting, see "Iz Moskvy," *Listok*, 17 (1906): 5–6.

64 "Po masterskim: Ot Mandlia," *Listok*, 15 (1906): 10.

65 GARF, f. 6869, op. 1, d. 34, l. 114.

66 "Professional'nye soiuzy," *RZ* (1 October 1906), 3.

67 "Razgrom magazinov," *RZ* (3 October 1906), 3.

68 GARF, f. 6869, op. 1, d. 33, ll. 96–97.

69 Bonnell, *Roots*, 287.

70 "Professional'nye soiuzy," *RZ* (10 October 1906), 3.

71 "Professional'nye soiuzy," *RZ* (17 October 1906), 3.

72 "Rabochaia zhizn'," *RZ* (17 October 1906), 3.

73 In her unpublished history, Oliunina argued in favor of an inclusive union while Kitavin opposed such a move. See GARF, f. 6869, op. 1, d. 34, l. 116; and ibid., d. 33, l. 109. Both of these documents written twenty years after the Moscow strike reveal the deep divisions within the union over this issue.

74 GARF, f. 6869, op. 1, d. 34, l. 116; and "Professional'nye soiuzy," *RZ* (22 September 1906), 3.

75 A two-month strike in Lodz resulted in an agreement to end sweating. The result was that home workers and sweaters lost their jobs. Shop owners simply did not have enough capital to set up enough workshops. See GARF, f. 6869, op. 1, d. 34, l. 267.

76 Shevkov, *Moskovskie shveiniki*, 14.

77 "Vospominaniia tov. M. Kuleshova," GARF, f. 6869, op. 1, d. 59, l. 60; and Shevkov, *Moskovskie shveiniki*, 14.

78 Gruzdev, *Trud*, 44–45. The regulations can be found in GARF, f. 6869, op. 1, d. 17, ll. 8–11.

79 Gruzdev, *Trud*, 36–38; and GARF, f. 6869, op. 1, d. 41, l. 50–50 ob.

80 Gruzdev, *Trud*, 38.

81 "Soiuz portnykh protiv zakazchikov," *BV* (11 February 1913): 3.

82 Gruzdev, *Trud*, 39; and GARF, f. 6869, op. 1, d. 59, l. 137 ob.

83 GARF, f. 6869, op. 1, d. 59, l. 138; and Gruzdev, *Trud*, 39. For more on collective bargaining, see Bonnell, *Roots*.

84 "Uzhasy damskikh masterskikh," *Peterburgskaia gazeta (PG)* (23 April 1913): 4; and ibid. (24 April 1913): 3.

85 "Uzhasy damskikh masterskikh," *PG* (24 April 1913): 3.

86 "Masteritsy modnykh masterskikh – nadeiutsia," *PG* (27 April 1913): 4.

87 Nikolai Breshko-Breshkovskii, "Belye negritianki modnykh masterskikh," *PG* (25 April 1913): 3.

88 For more on prostitution in Russia, see Laurie Bernstein, *Sonia's Daughters: Prostitutes and Their Regulation in Imperial Russia* (Berkeley: University of California Press, 1995), esp. 146–61.

89 "Vesti i slukhi," *BV* (25 April 1913): 2.

90 N. Sh-p, "Stolknovenie portnykh s khoziaevami," *Vechernee vremia* (26 April 1913), 3.

91 Vas. B., "Portnye bastuiut!," *PG* (27 April 1913), 3.

92 Gruzdev, *Trud*, 40.

93 B. Ianov, "Damy bez letnikh tualetov!," *PG* (29 April 1913): 2.

94 "Zabastovka portnykh prodolzhaetsia," *PG* (1 May 1913): 3.

95 "Den' pervogo maia," *BV* (2 May 1913): 2.

96 "800 portnykh-zabastovshchikov," *PG* (5 May 1913): 4; and Del'ta, "Nakanune likvidatsii port. zabastovki," *Peterburgskii listok* (5 May 1913): 3.

97 "Aresty i obyski," *BV* (7 May 1913): 2; and ibid. (9 May 1913): 4.

98 "Vesti i slukhi," *BV* (10 May 1913): 2.

99 "Vesti i slukhi," *BV* (14 May 1913): 4.

100 "K zabastovke portnykh," *PG* (14 May 1913): 5.

101 "Vesti i slukhi," *BV* (23 May 1913): 3; and GARF, f. 6869, op. 1, d. 59, l. 138 ob.

102 "Razgrom magazina na Nevskom prospekte," *PG* (28 May 1913): 5; and "Razkrytie krazhy v magazine 'Venskii Shik,'" *PG* (29 May 1913): 6.

103 GARF, f. 6869, op. 1, d. 59, l. 138 ob.; and Gruzdev, *Trud*, 40.

104 GARF, f. 6869, op. 1, d. 59, l. 138 ob.; and d. 34, l. 273.

105 Gruzdev, *Trud*, 41–42.

106 GARF, f. 6869, op. 1, d. 34, ll. 266–67; and Bonnell, *Roots*, 406.

## 8 THE WAR ON FASHION

1　For more on dress reform, see Elizabeth Wilson, *Adorned in Dreams: Fashion and Modernity* (London: Virago, 1987), 208–27; and Stella Mary Newton, *Health Art and Reason: Dress Reformers of the Nineteenth Century* (London: John Murray, 1974).

2　M. M. Volkova, *Krasota, gigiena i reforma zhenskoi odezhdy* (St. Petersburg: Tip. Doma Prizren. Maloletn. Bedn., 1899), 101–04.

3　Vrach, "Iz zhizni: Gigiena sovremennykh zhenskikh mod," *Zhenskii vestnik*, 1 (1905): 15–17. It is possible that the author of this article is Dr. Maria Pokrovskaia, editor of the magazine.

4　M. Novikova, "Zhenshchina i moda," *Zhenskoe delo*, 35–36 (10 October 1910): 9.

5　Hans Rogger, "Russia," *The European Right: A Historical Profile*, ed. Hans Rogger and Eugen Weber (Berkeley: University of California Press, 1965), 444.

6　N. P. Eroshkin, "Russkoe Sobranie," *Modern Encyclopedia of Russian and Soviet History* (Gulf Breeze: Academic International Press, 1983): XXXII: 231–32; and Hans Rogger, "The Formation of the Russian Right, 1900–1906," *California Slavic Studies*, III (1964): 69–71.

7　Quoted in V. Levitskii, "Pravye partii," in *Obshchestvennoe dvizhenie v Rossii v nachale XX v*, ed. L. Martov and others (St. Petersburg: Tipografiia T-va Obshchestvennaia pol'za, 1914): III: 357.

8　John Joseph Brock, Jr., "The Theory and Practice of the Union of Russian People, 1905–1907: A Case Study of 'Black Hundred' Politics" (Ph.D. dissertation, University of Michigan, 1972), 154–68; and Rogger, "Formation," 84–93.

9　Soiuz russkikh zhenshchin, *Ustav soiuza russkikh zhenshchin* (St. Petersburg: Tipografiia Rossiia, 1908), 1 and 3.

10　Ibid., 1–7.

11　Soiuz russkikh zhenshchin, *Otchet a deiatel'nosti sostoiashchego pod Avgusteishim Ee Velichestva Gosudaryni Imperatritsy Aleksandry Fedorovny pokrovitel'stvom Soiuza Russkikh Zhenshchin* (St. Petersburg: Tipo-Litografiia Spb. Tiur'my, 1912), 2.

12　Ibid., 6–8; and "V soiuze russkikh zhenshchin," *Peterburgskii listok* (9 May 1913): 13.

13　Ibid., 2–3.

14　Iulii L. Elets, *Poval'noe bezumie (K sverzheniiu iga mod)* (St. Petersburg: Tipografiia Shtaba Voisk Gvardii i Peterburgskogo Voennogo Okruga, 1914), i.

15　Ibid., 6.

16　Ibid., 17.

17　Ibid., 91.

18　Ibid., 301.

19　Ibid., 304.

20　E. Likhacheva, "Poval'noe bezumie," *Zhenskii vestnik*, 3 (1914): 76–79.

21　Al. Khlebnikova, "K voprosu o *Poval'nom bezumii* – zhenskikh modakh," *Zhenskii vestnik*, 4 (1914): 112–13. Apparently, Khlebnikova was actively involved in the dress reform movement in Russia. In an earlier article, she called for a boycott against fashion. See Al. Khlebnikova, "O reforme zhenskogo kostiuma (Otvet na anketu)," *Zhenskii vestnik*, 9 (1912): 184–85. Italics in the original.

22　Adov, *Bezumnoe povalie (Otvet na knigu g. Eletsa)* (St. Petersburg: Tipografiia A. Smolinskii, 1914), 4.

23　Ibid., 24.

24　Ibid., 13.

25　Ibid., 16–17.

26　Lev Bakst, "Moda," *PG* (20 February 1914): 3.

27　Lev Bakst, "Ob iskusstve segodniashniago dnia," *Stolitsa i usad'ba*, 8 (20 April 1914): 18.

28　Ibid., "Moda," 3.

29　Ibid., "Ob iskusstve," 18–19.

30　For a good summary of Russia's economic troubles during World War I, see Michael T. Florinsky, *The End of the Russian Empire* (New York: Collier Books, 1971), 32–53; and Peter Gatrell, *Russia's First World War: A Social and Economic History* (Harlow: Pearson, 2005).

31　Irma Laurent, "Vmesto mody," *Zhenskoe delo*, 15 (1 August 1914): 25. This name change lasted all of two issues, the column quickly reverting to its former title, "Moda."

32　Apparently a number of other goods entered Russia through Sweden, but this also caused more problems than it solved. See Florinsky, *The End of the Russian Empire*, 37.

33　N. Alovert, "Ot izdatelia," *VM*, 37 (1914): 73; and "Ot redaktsii," *Modnyi kur'er*, 11 (1915): 119.

34　*Damskii mir*, 8 (1915): 36.

35　"K nashim podpischitsam," *MS*, 12 (1914): 1–2.

36　N. A., "Bud'te berezhlivy!," *Modnyi kur'er*, 37 (1915): 330. Nikolai Alovert, the magazine's publisher, was probably the author of this piece.

37　GARF, f. 6869, op. 1, d. 35, l. 24.

38　Ibid., l. 25; GARF, f. 6869, op. 1, d. 34, ll. 321–22; Paul Gronsky and Nicholas Astrov, *The War and the Russian Government* (New Haven: Yale University Press, 1929), 254; and S. I. Gruzdev *Trud i bor'ba shveinikov v Peterburge, 1905–1916: Istoricheskii ocherk* (Leningrad: Izdanie Leningradskogo oblastnogo soiuza rabochikh shveinoi promyshlennosti, 1929), 98–99.

39　For more on this, see Robert B. McKean, *St. Petersburg Between the Revolutions: Workers and Revolutionaries, June 1907–February 1917* (New Haven: Yale University Press, 1990), 297–317.

40　The calls for women needleworkers were ubiquitous during World War I. Articles announcing the formation of workshops and distribution centers regularly appeared in the newspapers. All women's magazines carried these appeals as well. For a typical example, see *Damskii mir*, 8 (August 1915): 28.

41　P. V. Ol', *Foreign Capital in Russia*, trans. Geoffrey Jones and Grigori Gerenstain (New York: Garland, 1983).

42　For more on this, see Ruth Amende Roosa, *Russian Industrialists in an Era of Revolution: The Association of Trade and Industry, 1906–1917*, ed. Thomas C. Owen (Armonk: M. E. Sharpe, 1997); Thomas C. Owen, *Capitalism and Politics in Russia: A Social History of the Moscow Merchants, 1855–1905* (Cambridge: Cambridge University Press, 1981); and Alfred J. Rieber, *Merchants and Entrepreneurs in Imperial Russia* (Chapel Hill: University of North Carolina Press, 1982).

43 Roosa, *Russian Industrialists*, 115.

44 Quoted in ibid., 117.

45 Ibid., 135.

46 Moskovskoe Kupecheskoe Obshchestvo, *Doklad Kommissii po vyiasneniiu mer bor'by s germanskim and avstro-vengerskim vliianiem v oblasti torgovli i promyshlennosti* (Moscow: Tipografiia A. N. Ivanova, 1915).

47 Quoted in Roosa, *Russian Industrialists*, 112.

48 RGIA, f. 23, op. 28, d. 1312, ll. 2–3, 25.

49 The other Moscow uniform factory, the Karl Til' Company, apparently suffered a similar fate – its name was changed to "Postavshchik." Unfortunately, I have been unable to locate any documents to explain what happened. See Iurii Kir'ianov, " 'Maiskie besporiadki' 1915 g. v Moskve," *Voprosi istorii*, 12 (1994): 140; and GARF, f. 6869, op. 1, d. 35, l. 24.

50 Boris E. Nolde, *Russia in the Economic War* (New Haven: Yale University Press, 1928), 8–11.

51 Ibid., 13.

52 RGIA, f. 23, op. 28, d. 1312, ll. 15, 42, 45.

53 The article appeared in *Rech'* and can be found in ibid., l. 44. It is not clear from the few surviving documents that a Herman Mandl' was ever involved with the firm. Since Mandl' is a fairly common Austrian name, it is quite possible that this was just another inaccurate rumor about the company.

54 Vserossiiskii Natsional'nyi Soiuz, *Germanskie i Avstriiskie firmy v Moskve na 1914 god* (Moscow: Russkaia pechatnia, 1915); and Eric Lohr, *Nationalizing the Russian Empire: The Campaign Against Enemy Aliens During World War I* (Cambridge, Mass.: Harvard University Press, 2003), 27.

55 Nolde, *Russia*, 12–17.

56 Lohr, *Nationalizing*, 66–68.

57 Quoted in Nolde, *Russia*, 17.

58 "Provokatsiia obshchestva 1886 goda," *Russkoe slovo* (6 May 1915): 5; and Kniaz' Vsevolod N. Shakhovskoi, *Sic transit gloria mundi: Tak prokhodit mirskaia slava, 1893–1917 gg.* (Paris: n. p., 1952), 172–74.

59 "Bor'ba s nemetskim zasil'em," *Moskovskii listok* (7 May 1915): 3.

60 "Manifestatsii," *Russkoe slovo* (15 May 1915): 5.

61 Lohr, *Nationalizing*, 42–43.

62 Sergei Riabichenko, *Pogromy 1915 g.: Tri dnia iz zhizni neizvestnoi Moskvy* (Moscow: n. p., 2000), 5; and *Moskovskie vedomosti* (26 May 1915): 4.

63 *Moskovskie vedomosti* (27 May 1915): 4.

64 RGIA, f. 23, op. 28, d. 2713, 2682, and 2802.

65 Lohr, *Nationalizing*, 32–33.

66 Ibid., 34; and Riabichenko, *Pogromy*, 8–10.

67 Riabichenko, *Pogromy*, 22–23.

68 Ibid., 28.

69 Ibid., 19–20.

70 RGIA, f. 23, op. 28, d. 264, l. 4. According to archival documents, Filipp was a member of the second Moscow merchants' guild in 1915, despite his German name. See ibid., l. 112.

71 Vserossiiskii Natsional'nyi Soiuz, *Germanskie*, 5.

72 Lohr, *Nationalizing*, 35–37; and Riabichenko, *Pogromy*, 55.

73 Lohr, *Nationalizing*, 36.

74 RGIA, f. 23, op. 28, d. 1312, l. 12.

75 RGIA, f. 23, op. 28, d. 2860, l. 11.

76 GARF, f. 6869, op. 1, d. 60, l. 58; and RGIA, f. 23, op. 28, d. 1312, l. 43.

77 "Likvidatsiia T./D. M. i I. Mandl'," *Utro Rossii* (28 May 1915): 4; and "Iskliuchenie L. Mandlia iz tsekha," *Utro Rossii* (2 June 1915): 4.

78 RGIA, f. 23, op. 28, d. 3204, l. 11; and d. 1312, l. 12.

79 RGIA, f. 23, op. 28, d. 805, ll. 165–66 and 180.

80 RGIA, f. 23, op. 28, d. 805, l. 117 and l. 47. The Singer folders contain articles from *Novoe vremia*, *Za Rossiiu*, and other newspapers. For more on the image of the spider web in Russia, see Orlando Figes and Boris Kolonitskii, *Interpreting the Russian Revolution: The Languages and Symbols of 1917* (New Haven: Yale University Press, 1999), 169–71.

81 Vserossiiskii Natsional'nyi Soiuz, *Germanskie*, 73.

82 RGIA, f. 23, op. 28, d. 805, l. 43; and Robert Bruce Davies, *Peacefully Working to Conquer the World: Singer Sewing Machine in Foreign Markets, 1854–1920* (New York: Arno Press, 1976), 284.

83 For an excellent history of Kompaniia Zinger and Flohr's role, see Fred V. Carstensen, *American Enterprise in Foreign Markets: Studies of Singer and International Harvester in Russia* (Chapel Hill: University of North Carolina Press, 1984), 13–103.

84 RGIA, f. 23, op. 28, d. 805, ll. 164–65.

85 Ibid., l. 204.

86 Ibid., ll. 37–38.

87 Ibid., ll. 44 and 165.

88 The name of Russia's capital city, St. Petersburg, was changed in 1914 to Petrograd as part of the anti-German campaign. Petersburg was too Germanic-sounding for Russian patriots.

89 RGIA, f. 23, op. 28, d. 805, l. 71.

90 Ibid., l. 73.

91 Ibid., ll. 82–83, 89–90. The other sewing-machine companies in Russia were German. For an example of a company that the government liquidated because of the German connection, see RGIA, f. 23, op. 28, d. 1668. The company was called Popova and Company. It had been established in 1900 by a Moscow merchant woman, Elizaveta Popova, but by 1914 a number of Germans sat on the board of directors. As a result, this "German" company was forced to shut down.

92 Ibid., ll. 164–72. For a discussion of company policies and secrecy about its operations, see Davies, *Peacefully Working*, 280–84.

93 RGIA, f. 23, op. 28, d. 805, ll. 124–24 ob. and l. 97.

94 Ibid., ll. 251–53 ob.

95 Ibid., d. 806, ll. 26–27 ob. and 42–42 ob.

96 Davies, *Peacefully Working*, 305.

97 Paul P. Gronsky, *The War and the Russian Government* (New Haven: Yale University Press, 1929), 42.

98 Quoted in ibid., 29.

99 Florinsky, *The End*, 48.

100 Ibid., 32–54.

101 Ibid., 268.

102 Eugene M. Kayden, *The Cooperative Movement in Russia During*

*the War* (New Haven: Yale University Press, 1929), 72. See also Yanni Kotsonis, *Making Peasants Backward: Agricultural Cooperatives and the Agrarian Question in Russia, 1861–1914* (New York: St. Martin's Press, 1999).

103   For more on these riots, see Iu. I. Kir'ianov, "Massovye vystupleniia na pochve dorogovizny v Rossii (1914–fevral' 1917 g.)," *Otechestvennaia istoriia*, no. 3 (1993): 3–18; and Barbara Alpern Engel, "Not by Bread Alone: Subsistence Riots in Russia during World War I," *Journal of Modern History*, 69 (December 1997): 696–721.

104   For more on this, see S. O. Zagorskii, *State Control of Industry in Russia during the War* (New Haven: Yale University Press, 1928), 75–96.

105   Lars T. Lih, *Bread and Authority in Russia, 1914–1921* (Berkeley: University of California Press, 1990), 12; and Engel, "Not by Bread Alone," 714.

106   Nolde, *Russia*, 52–60.

107   RGIA, f. 32, op. 1, d. 586, ll. 1–8. For the published text, see *Stenograficheskie otchety*, 1 (4 May 1916): 1–8.

108   Between February and May of 1916, the major European powers banned the importation of luxury goods. Although the lists for each country differed, all banned "fashion goods." See RGIA, f. 32, op. 1, d. 586, ll. 164–68 for the French ban; ll. 171–74 ob. for the English embargo; ll. 175–83 ob. for the German response; and V. G., "Zapreshchenie vvoza predmetov roskoshi," *Promyshlennost' i torgovli*, 13 (26 March 1916): 374–75 for a report on the Austrian legislation.

109   RGIA, f. 32, op. 1, d. 586, ll. 92 and 93 ob.

110   Ibid., ll. 83–85 ob.

111   Ibid., l. 103.

112   V. G., "Zapreshchenie," 375–76.

113   "Reglamentatsiia mod," *BV*, no. 15,506 (18 April 1916), 3.

114   N. Shebuev, "Modoborchestvo," *Sol'ntse Rossii*, 329/23 (1916): 12–15.

115   Nolde, *Russia*, 158–59. Baron Nolde was also a member of the subcommittee and thus was intimately acquainted with Langevoi and his views.

116   RGIA, f. 32, op. 1, d. 586, ll. 9–29.

117   See "Khronika – V Sovete Ministrov," *Torgovo-Promyshlennaia Gazeta* (14 September 1916): 2; and "Ob ogranichenii vvoza v Rossiiu predmetov roskoshi," *Sobranie uzakonenii i rasporiazhenii pravitel'stva uzdavaemoe pri pravitel'stvuyushchem Senate*, 298 (28 October 1916) otd. 1, 2,358.

## EPILOGUE

1   N. Shebuev, "Modoborchestvo," *Sol'ntse Rossii*, 329/23 (May 1916), 13–14.

2   "Vecher mod," *PG* (15 May 1916): 9.

3   "Vecher mod," 9; and Shebuev, "Modoborchestvo," 14.

4   Ibid.; and N. A. [Nikolai Alovert], "Russkaia zhenskaia odezhda," *Modnyi kur'er*, 17 (1 August 1916): 265.

5   Shebuev, "Modoborchestvo," 13.

6   N. A., "Russkaia zhenskaia odezhda," 265.

7   For an introduction to this topic, see Tatiana Strizhenova, *Soviet Costume and Textiles, 1917–1945* (Paris: Flammarion, 1991); Lidya Zaletova, Fabio Ciofi degli Atti, Franco Panzini, and others, *Revolutionary Costume: Soviet Clothing and Textiles of the 1920s* (New York: Rizzoli, 1989); and Alexandre Vassiliev, *Beauty in Exile*, trans. Antonina W. Bouis and Anya Kucharev (New York: Harry N. Abrams, 2000).

# Index

ballet in Imperial Russia 166, 171–72
Ballets Russes 171–81, *173–75*
   Oriental ballets 176–77
balls 165–66
   Winter Costume Balls 164–70, *167–70*
barter process 128
Baskin, Ber 187
Bayer, Joseph: *Die Puppenfee* 166, 172
Beaton, Cecil 177
Belorussia: Jewish labor movement 185, 186–88
Benois, Alexander 171, 172, 177
Bestuzhev-Riumin, M. A. 90, 96
Betskoi, Ivan 45, 49
biological imperative of women 217
Blagoveshchenskaia, Ol'ga Aleksandrovna 103
Bloody Sunday (1905) 190
Bloomer, Amelia/"bloomers" 12, 94
Bogen, Adolf 226–27
Bolshevik Party 17, 241
Bonnell, Victoria 192
bourgeoisie
   and clothing 12
   late development 15
Bowlt, John 176
Breshko-Breshkovskii, Nikolai 204
British Empire and fashion 4
Brooks, Jeffrey 112
Brousy, Joséphine *60*
Bublikov, A. A. 232, 234
Bund (General Union of Jewish Workers in Russia and Poland)
   186, 187
"Byzantine" architecture 153
Byzantine origins of Russian dress 158–59

caftans 1, 159, 160
*Capital City and Country House* (magazine) 218–19
capitalism
   concern over domination of German capital 223–25, 230
   and consumption 14, 148
   peasants' embrace of 76–77
   and Russian fashion industry 14–16, 19–22
   sales of sewing machines 58–61
Catherine II (the Great), Empress of Russia 15, *45*, 49
   and education of women 44–45
   promotion of Russian dress 152–53, 160
   working hours ruling 187
censorship and fashion press 89–90
   Central Censorship Administration 90–91, 92–93, 94, 96, 99, 106,
     107–08, 108–10
Chaadaev, Petr: "Philosophical Letter" 153–54
Chaliapin, Fedor 166
charitable institutions: education of girls 49–53, 63, 120–21, 147, 214
Chebysheva, A. P. 212
Chekhov, Anton: "An Attack of Nerves" 62

Chernyshevskii, Nikolai 54
   *What Is to Be Done?* 56–58, 62
Chicago *see* World's Columbian Exposition
children as apprentices 26–27, *27, 29,* 183
"city clothes" 10, 67
   and emancipation of women 217
   of peasants and workers 74–75, *74, 76,* 77, *77, 79, 81,* 132, 138, 231,
     235
   as uniform of Soviet era 242
City of Lyon department store, Moscow 123–24
class *see* social status
clients *see* customer relations
clothing: definition and use of term 2, 4
collective bargaining and strikes 203, 206
Columbian Exposition, Chicago *see* World's Columbian Exposition
"commercial cosmopolitanism" 180–81
conservative movements 211–14
   *see also* right-wing movements
consumption
   and development of capitalism 14, 148
   development of consumerism 127–28, 149
     and fashion press 113
     and western style stores in Russia 128, 145–46
   gendering of shopping 115, 143–48
   peasants and provincial consumers 74–75, 138, 141, 143, 231–32
   in wartime
     and anti-German sentiment 227
     consumer riots 227, 231–32, 240
     shame of fashionable women 233–34
     unobtainability and ban on luxury goods 231–35
   *see also* luxury goods trade; ready-to-wear manufacturing; shops
     and shopping
cooperatives
   cooperative workshops (*artel'*) 201
   and wartime shortages 231
*Cornfield* (magazine) 106–07
cosmopolitan identity and clothing 4, 8, 98
   conservative rejection of 211–12
   and modernism 98, 180–81
Cossack uniform *78,* 160
"Cossacks" (English fashion) 4
costume
   definition and use of term 4
   ethnic costumes for Russian operas 164
   national costume 88, *213,* 214, 217, 238
     preserving "Russian" dress 8, 17
   Nicholas II's Winter Costume Balls *6,* 165–70, *167–70*
cotton cloth 23, 24, 139
court dress *47, 64, 150*
   Catherine the Great promotes Russian dress 152
   Nicholas I's reforms 153, 154
   Nicholas II's Winter Costume Balls *6,* 164–70, *167–70*
   Peter the Great's decrees 1, *3,* 21–22
court social calendar 165–66
crafts and women's work